THE SCOTTISH GARDENER

THE SCOTTISH FIELD SERIES No. 1

Victoria Park, Whiteinch, Glasgow

GEORGE M. STUART

The Scottish Gardener

HUTCHINSON OF LONDON

HUTCHINSON & CO. (*Publishers*) LTD
178-202 Great Portland Street, London, W.1

London Melbourne Sydney
Auckland Bombay Toronto
Johannesburg New York

★

First published 1963

*This book has been set in Baskerville type face. It has
been printed in Great Britain by George Outram & Co.
Ltd., in Perth, Scotland, on White Cartridge paper.*

Contents

1 GENERAL

Tools 12. Soil preparation 13. Manures and fertilisers 17. Lawns 21.

2 VEGETABLES

Rotation of crops 26. French gardening 29. Soil insects 32. Asparagus, corn cob and seakale, 35. Beans 38. Brussels sprouts 40. Cabbages 41. Cauliflower and broccoli 44. Cucumbers 47. Herbs 50. Leeks and celery 53. Marrows 56. Mushrooms 57. Onions 59. Peas 63. Potatoes 65. Rarer vegetables 68. Root vegetables 71. Salad crops 73. Tomatoes 75.

3 FRUIT

Planting trees 82. Greenfly 85. Cross-pollination 87. Budding 89. Fungoid diseases 92. Winter pruning 95. Storage 98. TOP FRUITS–Apples 100. Pears 104. Plums 107. SOFT FRUITS—Blackberries 110. Blackcurrants 113. Gooseberries 118. Raspberries 121. Strawberries: in the open garden 124; under glass 125; virus diseases 128. Vines 130.

4 FLOWERS AND DECORATIVE PLANTS

Spring-flowering greenhouse plants 136. The herbaceous border 139. Hardy annuals 142. Native lowland plants 146. Fragrant plants 148. African violets 151. Alpines 153. Anemones 156. Antirrhinums 159. Begonias 161. Bulbous plants 163. Cacti and other succulents 165. Campanulas 168. Carnations 171. Chrysanthemums 173. Clematis 175. Crocus 178. Dahlias 180. Delphiniums 182. Ferns 184. Gladioli 186. Lilies 189. Meadow rues 192. Phloxes 194. Primulas 196. Roses 198. Roses: species 202. Saxifrages 205. Sweet peas 207. Tulips 210. Wallflowers 212.

5

5 SHRUBS

Propagation by cuttings 216. Hedges 218. Dwarf shrubs 221. Wall shrubs 223. Peat-loving shrubs 226. Barberries 228. Conifers 230. Daphnes 233. Rock roses and sun roses 235. Magnolias 238. Rhododendrons 240.

6 THE ROCK GARDEN

Construction 246. Alpines 248. Arctic plants 250. Heaths 253.

MONTHLY CALENDAR 256.

INDEX 273.

Illustrations

The vegetable garden in spring   Facing page 16
Making the best use of land   16
Brussels sprouts, cauliflower and cabbage   17
Beans and peas   32
Marrows under cloches   33
Lettuces in a soil-warmed frame   33
Earthing-up celery   48
Ripening onions   48
Marrows, asparagus and radishes   49
Root vegetables   64
A well-shaped plum tree   65
Tomatoes in fruit   65
A vine in spring   65
Runner formation of strawberries and inter-row cultivation   80
Fruit tree planting   81
Cropping apples in the first year   96
Blackcurrant bush pruning   97
Big bud mite in blackcurrants and manuring   112
Giant-pouch calceolaria and saintpaulia   113
Cacti and succulents   128
Crocus, tulips and narcissus   129
Delphiniums, primulas and antirrhinums   144
Climber and floribunda roses   145
A hybrid tea rose and the rose beds in spring   160
Pelargoniums   161
Chrysanthemums   176
Preparing and planting shrub cuttings   177, 192
Division of plants   193
Magnolias   208

CONTENTS

	Facing page
Garrya elliptica, mock orange, lilac and flowering currant	209
Butterfly flower and double cherry	224
Shrubs combined with herbaceous plants	224
Planting a wall garden	225
Established wall gardens	240
Planting a rock garden with primulas	241
Planting heaths in the rock garden	256
Established rock gardens	256, 257

Line Drawings

	Page
Double and single digging	14 *and* 16
Soil insects	32
Tomato dry set and blossom end rot	78
Shield budding	91
Pruning	95
Apple tree forms and the 'cordon' system	101
Normal and reverted blackcurrant leaves	114
Blackcurrant and gooseberry or red currant bushes	115
Blackcurrant, gooseberry and red currant cuttings	115

ACKNOWLEDGEMENTS

For permission to reproduce illustrations of radishes, magnolias, mock orange, *Garrya elliptica,* lilac, flowering currant, butterfly flower, and double cherry, the publishers are indebted to Dobbie & Co., Edinburgh; and for illustrations of brussels sprouts, cauliflower, cabbage, dwarf French beans, runner beans, marrows, asparagus, beet, turnips, carrots, saintpaulia, mixed cacti and succulents, delphiniums, antirrhinum, and chrysanthemums (Dobie's Rainbow Mixture) to Samuel Dobie & Son, Chester.

8

Introduction

by

ROBERT L. SCARLETT, C.B.E.

Throughout the centuries Scottish gardeners have not only been noted for their practical achievements, but for their attractive and easily understood presentation of gardening techniques in written form. George Murrison Stuart was an outstanding example of these dual gifts. The son of a well-known gardener, he was born at King Edward, Aberdeenshire, in 1887, and received a good practical grounding at Cullen House and Murthly Castle gardens. He followed this with a course at the Royal Botanic Garden, Edinburgh, and then decided to embark on a teaching career. His first experience was in the west, but he very soon joined the staff of the Edinburgh and East of Scotland College of Agriculture, where he was to give the lifetime of service which made his name a household word in the Border counties.

Equally at home in almost any field of gardening, he made fruit growing a very personal interest and used his quick eye for possibilities to great effect. The tale is often told of how he spotted a completely clean strawberry plot in a farm garden when disease had reduced cultivation to a minimum: he induced the owner to extend and the results were spectacular. One of the first inspectors under the Seed Potato Inspection Scheme, he amassed a fine collection of varieties to help train students in correct identification, and his work in bringing modern scientific methods into use marks a turning point in the seed potato trade.

In 1941 he was appointed Senior Lecturer in Horticulture on the Edinburgh College staff, and fervently advocated increased home food production from allotments throughout the war, his services being recognised by the award of the M.B.E. in 1947. He served on all the principal Scottish horticultural committees, and excelled as much as a demonstrator as he does in his writings, of which it is pleasant to find so much preserved in the present volume. A pioneer, in that he was the first student in Scotland to gain the National

9

Diploma in Horticulture, he also achieved the rare distinction of being President of the Royal Caledonian Horticultural Society for three successive years, also winning the Society's Neill Prize.

With a deep understanding of both the difficulties and the advantages inherent in our Scottish climate, he demonstrated in his own garden how much could be done in a very modest space without creating a burden, and this book is his fitting memorial. Here the reader can study the methods Stuart recommended and benefit from the lifelong experience of one of Scotland's most able gardeners.

· I ·

General

Tools 12. Soil preparation 13. Manures and fertilisers 17. Lawns 21.

General

Tools

FEW PEOPLE trouble to look after their garden tools as they should. Gardeners who ill-treat their implements never enjoy working with them, for rusty tools are less efficient, since the soil clings to them, and have a short life.

Use a flat piece of stick, such as a wooden tally made in the form of a spatula, to remove soil and then rub over the tool with a piece of oily rag. If steel or iron tools are not in constant use, dip them for a few minutes in a solution of soda or powdered lime, and this will prevent rusting for a long time, even although they are exposed continually to a moist atmosphere. The motto in the tool shed should be 'a place for everything and everything in its place'. After cleaning and oiling, it is much better to hang tools up than to store them in a corner, for they will be less liable to rust, and the long wooden shafts of hoes and rakes will not warp so readily.

The handles of tools are usually made of ash, and when new should be smoothed down with a piece of emery paper to remove rough edges and rubbed with a rag dipped in linseed oil to protect against damp and prolong the life of the wood.

The spade is the most essential and most commonly used tool in the garden, in fact, most crops could be grown using this alone, and the British-made spade is considered the best in the world.

Next in importance is the digging fork which is necessary for stirring the soil and in many cases may be substituted for the spade. It is used for weeding, digging amongst plants and lifting crops.

The rake is used to break clods, remove stones and to level the surface before making a seed bed. Varying in size from 6-16 ins., it is usually of iron, but occasionally a wooden headed rake with tough, hard wood teeth can be used with advantage in light soils.

Hoes, which should have a steel blade welded to an iron neck, vary in size and form. There are some very fine modern designs to choose from. The draw hoe is used mainly for drawing drills, thinning and earthing-up crops, and for stirring the soil between the plant rows although the latter is more often done with a push or Dutch hoe, pushing the blade horizontally through the soil at about $\frac{1}{4}$-$\frac{1}{2}$ in. below the surface to leave the soil finely broken and even.

Besides the simpler tools mentioned, the modern gardener also has the advantage of motor-driven lawn mowers, electric hedge-cutters, new types of spraying equipment, and for the larger garden, when soil and weather conditions permit, motor-propelled rotary hoes which prepare the land for sowing and planting. Even plant labels have been affected for, although white-painted wooden labels still serve for temporary purposes, machines are available to punch the letters into long-lasting lead labels, ideal for permanent plants such as fruit trees, roses and shrubs.

Soil preparation

Although sandy soils are well drained, warm up fairly early in spring and are relatively easy to dig, they have disadvantages, for they tend to dry out quickly and, unless precautions are taken, the plants suffer. Furthermore, as a result of their naturally poor water-holding powers, when the plant nutritional material they contain becomes available for absorption, i.e. in a liquid state, it naturally drains away to a lower depth, and so often goes beyond the reach of plant roots. One thing we can do to improve such soils, and incidentally increase their moisture-holding capacity, is to dig in a good supply of decayed vegetable compost each year. Well-rotted farmyard manure is best because it provides not only decayed vegetable and animal matter but also a reasonably good supply of plant foods. To-day it is not easy to obtain, and we are compelled to use other things such as horticultural peat which, although not providing any nutritious elements, does increase the moisture-retaining properties of a sandy soil. Spread about a $1\frac{1}{2}$-in.-deep layer of such peat over the ground and fork it into the top foot of soil, supplementing it in advance of sowing and planting by adding fertilisers. As a rule more than one year's treatment on such lines is necessary.

Clay soils are generally regarded as heavy, wet, cold and late.

They certainly hold more moisture than sandy soils and this makes them heavy to dig. Water takes a long time to warm up, hence such soils are cold in early spring and in consequence we may be, and often are, forced to sow and plant later. They also tend to lack adequate supplies of air for the beneficial soil bacteria, etc., because the air spaces between the soil particles are often filled with water. The problem of excess moisture can be solved in some cases by draining with tile pipes but it is only very rarely that such a measure has to be adopted in private gardens. There are times, however, when a hard impervious layer of clayey material is found between soil and subsoil which may prevent surplus water draining away from the upper soil to lower levels.

We call such a layer a 'pan' or 'moorband'. When this is broken and destroyed by deep cultivation, i.e. double-digging, an improvement soon becomes apparent; the top soil is not so wet and usually the following crops are very much better. In addition, instead of digging or forking really well-rotted farmyard manure or compost into the top soil of clayey ground, less decayed more fibrous material is recommended. Horticultural peat is now used with excellent results

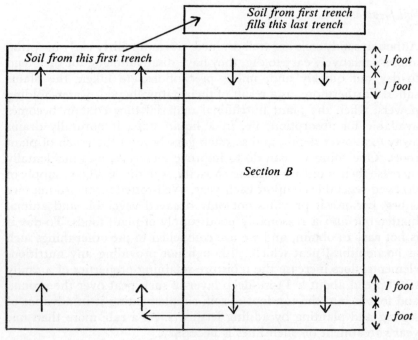

Single Digging

on clayey soils to 'open them up' and make them more friable. Ashes forked into some clayey soils show good results, for they open up the ground and improve it physically, but it must be emphasised that only furnace ashes or small clinker-like grit should be used, and on no account ashes from a household fire.

Before digging a piece of ground one spade deep, it is advisable to divide it lengthwise into two or more equal sections, each about 12 to 15 ft. broad—or less in small gardens. Set the garden line along the division and make a mark in the soil with a hoe or spade to act as a guide. Assuming we have two sections—for our purpose we can call the left hand one 'A' and the other 'B'—open a trench one foot deep and one foot wide along the top of section 'A' and place the soil thus removed near, but just outside, the top end of section 'B'. Dig section 'A' first; the soil from the second foot-width of ground is turned over into the trench from which the soil was removed, and so on until we reach the bottom end of that section. The last trench in 'A' section is filled in with soil at the bottom end of section 'B'—thus opening the first trench of 'B'. Dig section 'B' and fill in its last trench with the soil which was originally removed from the first trench of section 'A'.

Digging can be a backaching job, and the rule should be little and often. The temptation to put the spade in at an angle to make the task easier should be resisted because the spade will only be turning over about 5 or 6 ins. of soil instead of a full spade's depth.

Never dig or work the ground when it is frozen, wet or sticky— that tends to do more harm than good. Endeavour to get clayey ground dug over in autumn or early winter and don't waste time chopping each spadeful of soil into small pieces after it has been dug over—winter frosts will do that job, breaking it down admirably to produce a fine tilth for spring sowing and planting. Leave the digging of lighter, sandy soil until late winter but try to get it finished by mid-February at the latest, to permit the soil to become reasonably firm for March sowing and planting. If farmyard manure, vegetable refuse or peat is being dug in, spread it over the ground before digging but do not spread out more than can be dug in during one session.

A digging fork is often preferred to a spade, for the prongs can be pushed down to their full depth with little effort, and it helps to mix the best of the manure or vegetable compost with the top foot of soil where most of the beneficial bacteria are located.

Reference has been made to the necessity of double-digging, i.e. digging two spades deep, especially where a 'pan' or 'moorband' is present. There is no need to do it annually—once in four or five years should usually be enough, and sometimes its benefits outlast even this period. The ground to be double-dug should be divided as for single digging. We need a good spade, digging fork, shovel, two sticks each two feet long for measuring purposes, and a short garden line 15-20 ft. long to stretch across the section.

With one of the measuring sticks at each side of the section to be double-dug, mark off two feet from the top edge of section 'A' and stretch the short garden line across at the 2 ft. mark. Take all the soil out of this portion to a depth of one foot, and place it at the top end of section 'B' as in single digging. After the trench has been cleared of loose soil with a shovel, get down into it and turn over the subsoil in it with a fork to the depth of 1 ft., i.e. it is turned over and left *in situ*. There are cases where the 'pan' is so hard that a pickaxe has to be used to help with the initial breaking before the fork can be used efficiently. When the base of the trench has been thoroughly pulverised to a depth of 1 ft., use the measuring sticks and along the top of the soil mark off another 2-ft.-wide strip and place the short garden line in position to show where it finishes. The whole of the soil to the depth

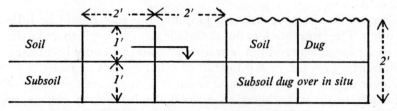

Sectional Drawing of Double Digging

of 1 ft. in this second 2-ft.-wide strip is dug over and placed in the first trench where the subsoil has been forked over. Again use the shovel to remove all the loose top soil left in the second trench. This systematic method is carried out until the whole of section 'A' has been double-dug. The last trench of section 'A' is filled in with soil removed from the first trench of section 'B'. When the whole of section 'B' has been double dug, its last trench is filled in with soil taken from the first trench opened in Section 'A'.

If well decayed farmyard manure or vegetable refuse compost is being incorporated with the soil during double digging, try to mix it with the top foot of soil as it is being turned over into the previous trench—don't bury it. Coarser material could, with advantage, be forked into the subsoil, as it is being turned over, to improve its physical condition.

16

The vegetable garden, as prepared in spring.

Making the best use of land: carrots are grown between the rows of lettuce.

Brussels sprouts, Hybrid Jade Cross.

Cauliflower, White Heart.

Cabbage, Dobie's Ballhead.

Double digging should always be done during autumn and winter to allow the soil to settle down again before spring sowing and planting.

So much for the initial preparation. As regards surface cultivation during the growing season, use the Dutch hoe frequently between the rows, not only to keep weeds under control, but also to produce a fine soil mulch on the surface of the ground. This helps to reduce the amount of moisture lost by evaporation when droughty conditions prevail, and allows air to enter the soil for the benefit of plant roots and beneficial soil bacteria.

Manures and Fertilisers

The soil may be regarded as a kind of larder from which a plant draws a variety of foods, and must be replenished in the same way. Failure to do so means ill-nourished plants and poor crops. Plants, like ourselves, require a variety of nutrients, a few of them in larger quantities than others, e.g. carbon, oxygen, hydrogen, nitrogen, phosphate, potash, calcium, iron, magnesia, manganese, sodium, chlorine and boron. They obtain carbon from the air; hydrogen from water, and oxygen from both air and water. All the other foods are obtained in liquid form, i.e. in a weak solution from the soil, which can only be absorbed through the fine hairs near the root-tips.

The soil generally contains plenty of iron, magnesia, manganese, sodium, chlorine, boron, etc.—often referred to as 'trace' elements, because only a very small quantity of each is needed by the plants—and the usual digging operations are sufficient to get enough of these into a liquid state. It is only occasionally that we have to make good a deficiency by direct application.

Relatively large quantities of nitrogen, phosphate and potash are required by cultivated plants, however, and unfortunately the soil does not as a rule contain adequate supplies, which means we have to add them ourselves to get good crops. Nitrogen promotes growth, i.e. the production of leaves, shoots and stems; phosphate encourages the development of a good rooting system, especially in young plants, and in older plants it is associated with flower, fruit, seed, tuber and bulb production. Potash helps a plant to produce carbohydrates—sugar and starch—and also assists in building up some resistance to diseases.

Nitrogen is particularly essential with crops such as lettuce, cabbages, savoys, etc., of which we use the leaves, and for producing strong, healthy young shoots of asparagus, and leaf stalks of celery

B

17

and rhubarb. But, if we are too lavish with manures and fertilisers containing a good percentage of nitrogen in our flower beds, then leaf, shoot and stem growth is apt to be developed at the expense of bloom. To develop larger flowers for exhibition, it is frequently recommended that the plants be fed with weak liquid manure when the flower buds begin to show. A flower is really formed of ordinary leaves which have been modified to perform a special job, e.g. to attract insects to bring pollen necessary for the fertilisation and production of seed; we must therefore wait until that special modification has taken place, that is, when flower buds begin to appear, before we begin this type of feeding. Liquid manure (made from a bag of animal excreta suspended in a tub of water) contains a lot of nitrogen, and therefore needs dilution. To apply the manure, we add one cupful of the concentrated solution from the tub to two gallons of water, very gradually increasing the strength in subsequent applications. Drought deprives the soil of water to dilute the necessary foods, and as a rule the plants do not make much headway until this lack is remedied.

In growing fruit, onions and potatoes, although phosphate plays a very important part, we must remember some nitrogen and potash is also needed. Such crops as carrots, beet, parsnips, turnips and potatoes have food stores of sugar or starch in the parts we eat—hence potash is an item of importance in their cultivation; but they also require some nitrogen and a little phosphate.

It is now known that the bulk of our garden plants like a slightly acid soil, even cabbages and cauliflowers and others of that family. Peas and beans like a soil which is on the border between acidity and alkalinity i.e. a neutral soil; pinks, carnations and Sweet Williams are in the same category. To apply lime to the soil as a routine measure, for example, every third or fourth year at 14 lb. per 30 sq. yds., could quite easily produce an unnecessarily alkaline or sweet soil, but all plants require a small quantity of lime or calcium as food, and lime has to be used where the soil has become too sour or acid.

Nitrogen, phosphate and potash are given in the form of either organic or inorganic manures which are usually referred to as fertilisers. The former are derived from what was originally living material, e.g. farmyard manure, poultry and pigeon manure, compost heap material, hoof and horn meal, bone meal, and the latter are of the mineral type, e.g. sulphate of potash, superphosphate, nitrate of soda, etc.

Organic manures not only add nitrogen, phosphate and potash to the soil, but also a lot of humus or organic matter which plays a very important part in improving its physical condition, hence their great value to the grower. The organic matter also provides a home for beneficial bacteria. Inorganic manures or fertilisers supply only plant foods and some of them, such as sulphate of ammonia and sulphate of potash, only one. They are sometimes called 'artificial' fertilisers but this is a complete misnomer.

Farmyard manure is especially valuable, for it not only provides a large amount of organic matter to improve and maintain the soil in a good physical condition, but also the three plant foods, nitrogen, phosphate and potash—though not in equal quantities. The amount of nitrogenous material is high, and there is a fair quantity of potash, but the amount of phosphate is comparatively low, since the animals retain much of this from their food to build up bone, muscle and milk. In view of this it may sometimes be advisable to make good the deficiency with a phosphatic fertiliser. As to quantity, dig in three average-sized barrowloads to every 30 sq. yds. of ground. Well-decayed manure is ideal for light sandy soils, but for the heavier clayey types manure which contains more straw and is less decayed is better, to open them up and improve their texture.

Poultry and pigeon manure is one of the richest in the organic class—it contains nitrogen, phosphate and potash in well-balanced quantities. Considering its richness, use half the amount recommended for farmyard manure. A good method is to mix a barrowload of decayed compost heap material, leaf mould or horticultural peat with a barrowload of poultry or pigeon manure and then apply it at the same rate as farmyard manure.

Well-decayed compost heap material will return to your soil what came out of it, i.e. plenty of humus, plus some nitrogen, phosphate and potash. After it has been dug into the soil a top dressing of a balanced fertiliser, such as Growmore, should be applied a week or two in advance of sowing or planting and hoed in. If possible dig in three to four barrowloads of compost heap material per 30 sq. yds.

Nitrogenous fertilisers contain the plant food nitrogen; common examples are sulphate of ammonia, nitrate of soda and nitro-chalk, each of which is relatively quick acting, though sulphate of ammonia is a bit slower than the other two. Do not apply them in autumn or winter, otherwise the nutritious material will be washed out through the soil and lost. For application before sowing or planting, I prefer to use sulphate of ammonia, but it should be given a week or two beforehand, at the rate of a pound and a half per 30 sq. yds., and hoed or raked into the ground. When used during the growing season, any of the three is suitable, but try to keep them off the plants and their foliage, sprinkling them carefully between the rows at one pound and a half per 30 sq. yds., and then hoeing the ground. I myself prefer to use a little at a time but often, i.e. half a pound of any one of them per 30 sq. yds. on each of three occasions, say, at three week intervals.

Soot, which should be stored in a dry place for a while before using is also a nitrogenous fertiliser, although not so rich in plant food as those mentioned previously. It also makes the soil darker and, in consequence, sun heat is more readily absorbed and retained. Give it a trial on ground where cabbages, etc., are to be grown, but apply it a week or so in advance of planting, at the rate of a bucketful per 30 sq. yds., and hoe it well in.

Dried blood is an organic nitrogenous fertiliser. It may be applied either before planting or during the growing season at the rate of 3-4 lb. per 30 sq. yds. and hoed in.

The four most commonly used phosphate fertilisers are basic slag, bone meal, steamed bone flour and superphosphate. Basic slag, an inorganic fertiliser, is a by-product from steel works, and also contains lime. It is slow-acting, the phosphate it contains taking rather a long time to become available in liquid form for absorption by the plant roots, therefore it must be applied in autumn or winter after digging, but it is good in clayey soils and should be given at the rate of 5 lb. per 30 sq. yds. Bone meal and steamed bone meal are two organic phosphatic fertilisers, but again they are both relatively slow in effect and have to be applied in autumn or winter, after digging, at the rate of 5 lb. per 30 sq. yds. Superphosphate is an inorganic fertiliser and is much quicker in action than the other three. It is usually applied at the rate of 3 lb. per 30 sq. yds., a little in advance of sowing or planting, and raked in. If an application is necessary during the growing season, between the rows of plants, take care to keep it off the foliage.

Potash is given in the form of Kainit, muriate of potash and sulphate of potash, the last-named being the one most commonly used today. Generally, soils of the clayey type are naturally richer in potash than sandy ones, which are often deficient. Potash does not wash out of the soil, so we may apply it any time, i.e. after autumn and winter digging; just before sowing or planting; during the growing season between the rows of plants; but in every case the normal rate of application is 2 lb. per 30 sq. yds.

Compound fertilisers, i.e. containing nitrogen, phosphate and potash, are sometimes required and may be mixed as follows:

Two parts by weight sulphate of ammonia
Three   ,,   ,,   superphosphate .
One   ,,   ,,   steamed bone flour
Two   ,,   ,,   sulphate of potash

This mixture is applied at the rate of 5 lb. per 30 sq. yds., and is quite good for supplementing peat or vegetable refuse from the compost heap when it is impossible to obtain farmyard manure. I have used it on many occasions with good results, but the tendency today is to save time, labour and often inconvenience, by buying one of the many prepared fertilisers. Many compound fertilisers, specially blended for green vegetables, tomatoes, potatoes, chrysanthemums, roses, lawns, pot plants, etc., are available.

Lime: hydrated lime, often called 'garden lime', is most often used by gardeners. As mentioned earlier, it contains the plant food calcium, but plants do not want a lot. To check if soil requires lime, collect in a clean pail about 20 trowelfuls of soil from different parts of the plot, mixing it thoroughly, and take enough to fill a 2-lb. brown-paper bag. Enclose a note of your name and address, repeating it on the outside, and send for testing to the Secretary of the Agricultural College serving your area: The Edinburgh and East of Scotland College of Agriculture, West Mains Road, Edinburgh 9; The West of Scotland College of Agriculture, 6 Blythswood Square, Glasgow, and for those in the northern area, the Macauley Institute of Soil Research, Aberdeen. It is advisable to ask not only for a lime test, but also for the phosphate and potash content of the soil sample.

Always remember that plants, like ourselves, require a balanced diet. If too much of one particular food is applied, the balance in the soil can be upset, and the best results are not achieved. For example, if too much lime is given, it can and often does create a potash deficiency in the soil to which the plants react, while an excess application of potash may create a magnesium deficiency.

Lawns

A good well-kept lawn enhances the appearance of a house and provides the ideal setting for flower beds and borders.

The ground should be reasonably good, and prepared by forking over the whole area thoroughly to a depth of about 10 ins. and removing all good-sized stones and weeds, especially those with fleshy roots, e.g. docks, dandelions, thistles, and couch grass stolons. If this is done during autumn and winter, the lawn seed may be sown during the following late spring, but if the preparatory work is done in the spring, then sowing should be postponed until later in the year. The main thing is to have the ground weed-free and with a good tilth before sowing. Although most agricultural grasses thrive when lime is given in reasonable quantities, lawn grasses do not appreciate it to the same extent—a slightly acid soil suits them. In the circumstances, after the initial digging has been completed, it is a good plan to spread a little horticultural peat and some specially prepared lawn fertiliser over the soil surface and fork it into the top 4 ins. of soil. This ensures that a supply of organic matter is present and a quantity of plant food is made available for the grass. Suitable fertilisers may be obtained already prepared from seedsmen and nurserymen, and should be applied as recommended on the package.

Despite all this preparation, it is more than likely that weed seeds will be present in the soil and those brought near the surface will soon germinate. Before doing any further work, wait until the first crop of weeds shows, then on a warm day, when the soil is dry, destroy them with a Dutch hoe. If the ground was very weedy before the initial digging began, this measure should be repeated.

The final preparation consists of first tramping the whole area while it is reasonably dry to firm the ground, then raking to produce a fine level surface tilth free from stones. If, through lack of experience, a level surface cannot be produced by raking, take a good-sized piece of straight board, and with someone holding the other end, draw the edge over the soil.

Always choose a windless day for sowing; the two grasses known as Chewing's Fescue *(Festuca fallax)* and Brown-top Agrostis *(Agrostis tenuis)* are generally used. Seedsmen sell lawn mixtures containing these two grasses which are used at the rate of 1 to 1½ oz. per square yard, but it is possible to buy them separately and I have often used them mixed together in the following proportions with good results:

> 3 parts by weight Chewing's Fescue
>
> 1 part   „   „   Brown-top Agrostis

Before sowing, weigh out an ounce or 1½ oz. of seed, whichever rate of sowing is to be used, and measure off a square yard of the lawn surface on which to scatter it, to give some indication of what an ounce or 1½ oz. of seed looks like on a square yard of ground. This acts as a guide when sowing the remainder of the lawn. A mixture containing some dwarf evergreen rye-grass would be more suitable for a lawn not intended mainly for ornamental purposes, but purely as a playground for children. After sowing, lightly rake in the seed—I usually rake it first north to south and then east to west.

The first cutting should be done when the young grass has grown about 2 ins., but before this is done go over the whole lawn and remove 'weed' grasses with an old dinner fork. These may be detected by their slightly taller and broader leaves, especially on lawns where varieties, such as Chewing's Fescue and Brown-top Agrostis, with very fine leaves have been sown. It is also advisable to remove other weeds. At the first cutting don't cut too short, although for subsequent cuttings the lawn-mower can be gradually lowered. If the mower is not fitted with a box, brush off the mowings and put them on the compost heap.

Established lawns should be fed annually. One can buy suitable top-dressing preparations from seedsmen and nurserymen for spring and autumn application, but use them at the rate specified on the package.

Moss on a lawn is due more often than not to poverty of the soil and, as moss is rarely seen in lawns where the grass grows well, the lawn grasses should be fed each year. If moss has become established a preparation may be bought from seedsmen to destroy it. About a fortnight after application, rake out and remove the dead moss, and where a fairly large bare patch has been left, sprinkle a little fine grass seed and cover with a thin layer of fine soil. Again, for weeds such as daisies, plantains, and dandelions, there are also special lawn weed preparations which may be used to eradicate them, but to remove the odd occasional offender put 3 drops, not more, of cigarette-lighter fuel on the growing point of each weed. Within a day or two they will have disappeared without trace. There are yet other preparations available in seedsmen's shops to destroy clover without damaging the grass. Worm casts often make a lawn look untidy, but Mowrah Meal applied at 6 oz. per square yard and well watered in, with a hose-pipe for preference, will in most cases bring the worms to the surface, when they must be removed by brushing.

Always remember that, since lawns are composed of growing plants they need to be fed, and that they will not appear at their most decorative unless attention is paid to detail, such as trimming the edges neatly with lawn edging shears.

Vegetables

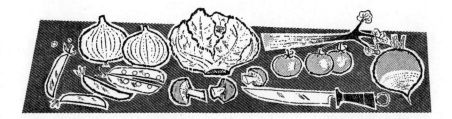

Rotation of crops 26. French gardening 29. Soil insects 32. Asparagus, corn cob, and seakale 35. Beans 38. Brussels sprouts 40. Cabbages 41. Cauliflower and broccoli 44. Cucumbers 47. Herbs 50. Leeks and celery 53. Marrows 56. Mushrooms 57. Onions 59. Peas 63. Potatoes 65. Rarer vegetables 68. Root vegetables 71. Salad crops 73. Tomatoes 75.

Vegetables

Rotation of Crops

WHEN ALLOCATING VEGETABLE crops to specific sections in the garden, attention must be paid to a system of rotation based on plant food requirements, and to the necessity of avoiding contamination with insect pests and fungoid organisms from plants which were previously grown there.

Some vegetables require a greater amount of certain manurial substances than others, and it is a good plan to follow a crop requiring a small quantity of a particular food with another requiring a larger amount.

The danger of growing the same kind of crop on the same piece of ground year after year is shown in the case of members of the cabbage family being attacked by the fungoid disease commonly known as 'finger-and-toe' or 'clubroot'. Any cabbage, savoy, cauliflower or Brussels sprouts grown there during the following year are likely to become infected as soon as they are planted and the crops will be most disappointing. Continual cropping of a specific area with the same type of vegetable also tends to make the plants lose vigour and become more susceptible to disease. In addition to helping combat disease a well arranged crop rotation is more economic since less manure is required. Crops such as peas and beans collect the plant food nitrogen from the air, through the agency of bacteria in their root nodules, later releasing it into the soil, thereby making it available for succeeding crops. Shallow-rooted vegetables should be alternated with deep-rooted ones since they draw their food from different levels of the soil.

The following table indicates the principles of a well-balanced crop-rotation scheme, the vegetable plot being divided into four sections:

Group A Crops requiring chiefly:	Group B Crops requiring chiefly:	Group C Crops requiring chiefly:	Group D Crops requiring all three plant foods in balanced proportions:
Phosphates & potash	Nitrogen & phosphates	Nitrogen & potash	Nitrogen, phosphates & potash
Potatoes, peas and beans	Cabbage, cauliflower, Brussels sprouts, broccoli, kale, savoys and swedes	Carrot, parsnip, beet and salsify	Onion, leek, shallot, celery, spinach

For Group A crops the ground should be dug and manured with organic material during the winter and phosphatic and potassic fertilisers applied, either shortly before, or soon after sowing or planting. Early potatoes should be lifted during July and early August, and in September—without further digging—the site planted with young cabbages which will heart next spring. The remainder of the plot should be dug deeply, farmyard manure being applied during the winter and the ground left fallow until planting begins in spring with green crops mentioned in Group B. The necessary fertilisers may be added prior to planting or as a top dressing during the growing season. In the third year, the plot should be well dug in preparation for root crops from Group C, the soil having been dressed ten days before with sulphate of potash at 2 lb. per 30 sq. yds., which should be hoed or raked into the surface, but no farmyard manure should be used for these crops. Later a little nitrogenous fertiliser, e.g. 1 lb. sulphate of ammonia per 30 sq. yds., may be applied carefully between the rows. Crops from Group D should be planted in the fourth year. A liberal application of farmyard manure must be dug into the soil well in advance of sowing or planting and a dressing of compound fertiliser hoed or raked into the surface a week or ten days before. Shallots do not need farmyard manure, but they may benefit from an application of a complete fertiliser such as Growmore, applied between the rows during the growing season.

During the fifth year crops recommended for Group A can again be grown on the plot, but in the former potato area, peas and beans should be grown and vice versa. In this way, no piece of ground will bear the same crop more than once in every four years and in some cases, e.g. potatoes, only once in eight years, and, if the ground is dug two spades deep for the deep-rooting crops such as onions, leeks and celery, it will be systematically double-dug every fourth

27

year. Other and less common vegetables fit into one or other of these groups, according to their manurial needs.

When the seed containing the embryo of a future plant plus a store of plant foods is sown under favourable conditions a chemical change takes place within its coat. The starch is converted into sugar, which is soluble in water, and with its store of proteins, which are nitrogenous, provides food during the early stages of germination. The plumule and radicle unfold and elongate rapidly and soon the plumule, seed leaves and shoot appear above the ground as a young seedling. The apex of the stem develops and forms leaves, and as the radicle or root uncurls and its tip is directed downwards, it forms root hairs and takes a firm hold of the soil from which it gets its future nourishment. Germination is now complete and the embryo has become a seedling. Sowing is very important and good quality seed should be used, taking care not to sow too thickly, since this results in the waste of seed and labour in thinning out. Seeds may be sown either directly in the open where they are to grow or in specially prepared seed beds, but favourable weather and soil conditions should be chosen. Never sow seed into wet, cold soil.

To prepare a seed bed apply one ounce superphosphate to each square yard, to assist the seedlings to form roots freely, and after some days the soil should be made as friable as possible by tramping and raking. Care should be taken to sow at the proper depths, placing small seeds near the surface and larger seeds proportionately deeper, since germinating seeds breathe in air, and if buried too deeply the plant will die. Sowing in flat-bottomed drills is better than broadcasting and after sowing and covering the seed *never* pat the soil with the spade. To sow small seeds directly from a slit in the packet means they will fall too thickly. Instead, take a pinch to rub between forefinger and thumb, so that they can be evenly and sparingly released along the drill. One or two strands of black thread stretched across the seed rows will scare birds, or cloches placed over the rows will not only protect the growing plants, but also hasten germination.

Thin out the seedlings as early as possible after germination. The distance to leave between them varies according to species, but aim at keeping the strongest and sturdiest and avoid overcrowding.

Young plants for transplanting, must be well watered before lifting to keep as much soil adhering to the roots as possible and avoid damage to the root hairs. Never pull them up by the stems before loosening the ground with a digging fork—again to avoid root damage.

The following seed table shows depths at which seed in medium soil should be sown and the approximate quantities per acre:

Kind of seed	Depth to sow	Amount of seed to sow approx. length of drills	Seed required to sow one acre	
Beans, broad	3½ ins.	1 pint per 50 ft. drill	3 to 4 bush.	Sow in open
Beans, French	2 to 3 ins.	1 pint per 80-100 ft. drill	2 to 3 bush.	,,
Beans, runner	2 to 3 ins.	1 pint per 80-100 ft. drill	2 bush.	,,
Beet	1¼ ins.	1 oz. per 50 ft. drill	18 to 20 lb.	,,
Borecole or Kale	¾ in.	¼ oz. or less will meet most requirements	1 to 2 lb.*	Sow in seed bed for transplanting
Broccoli	¾ in.	¼ oz. or less will meet most requirements	1 to 2 lb.*	,,
Brussels sprouts	¾ in.	¼ oz. or less will meet most requirements	1 to 2 lb.*	,,
Cabbage	¾ in.	¼ oz. or less will meet most requirements	1 to 2 lb.*	,,
Carrot	1 in.	1oz. per 100-150 ft. drill	6 to 8 lb.	Sow in open
Cauliflower	¾ in.	As for cabbage	2 to 3 lb.*	Sow in seed bed for transplanting
Celery	½ in.	Small packet will meet most requirements	3 oz.	Sow under glass
Leek	1 in.	Small packet will meet most requirements	3 lb.*	Sow in seed bed for transplanting
Leek	1 in.	1 oz. per 100-120 ft. drill	5 to 7 lb.	Sow in open
Lettuce	½ in.	1 oz. per 120 ft. drill	3 to 4 lb.*	Sow in seed bed for transplanting
Onion	1 in.	Small packet will meet most requirements	3 lb.*	,,
Onion	1 in.	1 oz. per 100-120 ft. drill	14 lb.	Sow in open
Parsley	1 in.	1 oz. per 80-100 ft. drill	8 lb.	,,
Parsnips	1¼ in.	1 oz. per 150-180 ft. drill	8 to 10 lb.	,,
Peas, early	2 to 3 ins.	1 pint per 50-60 ft. drill	4 to 5 bush.	,,
Peas, late	2 to 3 ins.	1 pint per 60-80 ft. drill	3 to 4 bush.	,,
Radish	1¼ in.	1 oz. per 60 ft. drill	30 lb.	,,
Spinach	2 ins.	1 oz. per 60 ft. drill	8 to 10 lb.	,,
Swede	1 in.	1 oz. per 150 ft. drill	7 lb.	,,
Turnip	1 in.	1 oz. per 150 ft. drill	5 to 7 lb.	,,

*In this case the amount of seed to produce plants for planting one acre.

French Gardening

Much interest is being taken in French Gardening, or what has come to be known as the intensive system of cultivation of early vegetables and salad crops in the private garden today. Considerable quantities of such early produce grown in frames in France and the Netherlands were formerly imported into this country, but conditions during the Second World War tended to create a demand for home-grown produce. Green vegetables are more attractive and appetising when used immediately after gathering and are rich in vitamins, mineral salts and roughage. The French gardener's year begins about the third week in August.

In French gardening Dutch lights are used, and consist of single sheets of glass, 58 ins. by 32 ins., pushed carefully into grooves from the base of the light framework and held in position by wooden stops. The lights are placed on a frame which can easily be made at home. The simplest frames are those made of 1½-in. deal planks, at least 15 ins. high at the back and 9 ins. at the front, in order to throw off rain and catch the sun. The corners should be strengthened by iron bands on the outside to prevent sagging and the woodwork should have an annual coat of white lead paint, preferably in the autumn before cropping commences. Never use creosote, as the fumes will have disastrous effects on the plants. To obtain maximum sunlight the range of single span frames should run from east to west on a well-protected site, such as the south side of a building, wall or hedge where the cold winds from the north will be broken.

For heating, fermenting horse manure, hot water or steam, or electricity may be used. The former should be collected during the summer and autumn, stacked and then mixed with spent hops, lawn mowings or hardwood tree leaves. It should be turned frequently, and, at the beginning of January, packed fairly deeply and tightly into the frames and covered by a 6-in. deep layer of soil. Hot water or steam-heated pipes laid about 6-8 ins. below the soil near the perimeter of the frame, are the most common method and have long been used to raise the temperature of the soil in French garden frames.

When making up the beds in the frames a fertile soil is necessary and preferably one which has been steam sterilised to destroy dormant weed seeds, after being mixed with the organic manures and fertilisers. Since French gardening involves mixed cropping, it is essential that the soil is fertile and well supplied with humus. When organic material is scarce, commercial fertilisers may be used in addition or as a substitute.

Apply a complete fertiliser at the rate of 1 oz. per sq. yd., mix well and work into the soil a week or so before seed sowing or planting. A smooth, thoroughly pulverised seed bed is very important as coarse lumpy soil is apt to lead to uneven sowing, with the result that germination is patchy and poor. Lime in the form of ground limestone improves the texture of certain soils, and aids in correcting undue soil acidity, but vegetables grow best in slightly acid soil, so lime should be used with discretion. The crops grown together in one frame on this system are usually lettuce, carrots and early turnips followed by cauliflower when most of the three other crops have been harvested.

The soil should be prepared and placed in the frames about the end of December or the beginning of January. Make it reasonably firm, rake it level and fine, and ensure that it is reasonably moist before sowing or planting. Carrot seed—Amsterdam Forcing or Early Nantes—is then sown broadcast (but by no means thickly) and lightly raked in, about the middle of the month. Immediately afterwards lettuce—compact varieties such as Gotté à Forcer or Green Frame—are transplanted 8 ins. apart each way among the carrot seed. The lettuces are raised from seed sown at the beginning of the previous October in a cold frame and when large enough to handle are pricked out as seedlings, 2 ins. apart each way in another cold frame. In the centre of each square formed by four lettuce plants sow two or three early turnip seeds of the Demi-longue à Forcer variety, and cover with a little soil.

The lights are now placed in position and no water will be necessary till the end of March. No ventilation is required but when there is danger of night frost, cover the glass with grass straw mats or sacking.

In spring when most of the lettuce has been cut, remove the glass sashes or frame lights to give open-air treatment and water the carrots and turnips. When the bulk of the carrots and turnips have been harvested, Early London or Snowball cauliflowers may be planted, 5 under each light. The young plants for this purpose will have raised from seed sown in the previous autumn and carefully wintered in frames, or under more congenial conditions from spring-sown seed. After transplantation full ventilation and plentiful watering should be given, and an occasional application of nitro-genous fertilisers if necessary. The first heads are usually ready for cutting about June. When the last of the cauliflowers has been cut the frames can be used to grow such crops as self-blanching celery, marrows and French beans.

In recent years various types of continuous cloche have been used to bring crops to quick maturity without using artificial heat. These consist of a ridge of glass sheets held together by special wires, placed over rows of plants. The low barn type is very popular and there are several different makes on the market. Spring crops grown in this way include lettuce, beet, carrot, onion, peas, French and runner beans and turnips but undoubtedly the most popular is lettuce. Peas can be sown during January or early February in single rows, the seed placed 3 ins. apart alongside two rows of lettuce seedlings. No staking is necessary and the cloches can be removed during April and placed over other vegetable crops. Carrots also yield satisfactory results, but seed should be sown in rows.

Soil Insects

Insects that spend their larval life in the soil are often particular enemies of the gardener, since it is during this stage that they damage the roots and underground stems of growing crops. Soil grubs are not always conspicuous, and it is only when the plants begin to wilt and die that their presence is suspected and remedial measures can be applied. The soil affords them natural protection from the parasites and birds which prey upon them and from adverse weather conditions, such as drought in summer and frost during winter. The following are the most important and common pests:

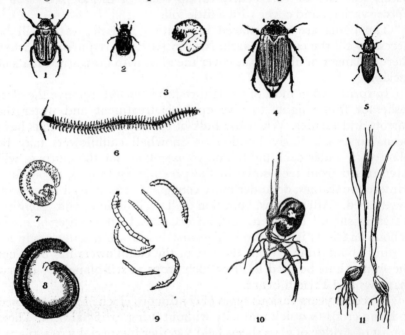

1. Summer chafer; 2. Garden chafer; 3. Grub of cockchafer; 4. Cockchafer;
5. Adult click-beetle; 6. Centipede; 7. Spotted millipede; 8. Black millipede;
9. Wireworm; 10. Bean attacked by millipede; 11. An attacked barley plant.

Wireworms—the larvae of at least three species of the beetle, *Agriotes*, commonly known as 'skip jack' or 'click beetle'—are general feeders and most destructive. They attack roots and sometimes the stems of carrots, lettuce, potatoes, tomatoes, and a host of cultivated plants, and are especially fond of carnations.

The beetles deposit their eggs from May to July, beneath the soil surface among grass and other herbage, and when the tiny larvae are hatched they feed on the nearby roots, living near the surface in

Dwarf french beans, Dobie's Greenfeast.

Runner beans, Dobie's Yardstick.

Peas, pods full and inviting.

Marrows under cloches in May.

A soil-warmed frame: Cheshunt 5B lettuces in April.

warm weather and descending more deeply in cold weather, especially in winter. The wireworm takes about three years to mature and, when fully grown, averages about 1 in. in length, has a yellowish body composed of numerous segments with three pairs of legs near the head, which is hard and horny and furnished with powerful jaws. Whizzed naphthalene forked into the soil will help to drive them away, and constant cultivation between the rows of crops with a digging fork or hoe will expose them to birds. Aldrin dust may be applied to the soil well in advance of sowing or planting and raked into the surface, but tramp the ground afterwards to firm it; later, hoe regularly.

Wireworms are readily attracted by bait—germinating wheat or oat grains are most effective—which should be prepared some three weeks in advance of sowing or planting. Wheat or oats are sown in rows 3 ft. apart and 2-3 ins. deep and the larvae will gather round the bait in the next few days. When the seedlings are about 6 ins. high, they should be dug up and the larvae destroyed while feeding on the roots. Trapping the wireworms by means of pieces of potato, carrot or mangel buried about 1 in. below the surface of the soil is another method of controlling the pest. Place a wooden skewer into each piece of bait so that they may be found more easily, examine the traps daily and destroy any wireworms.

Ground or carabid beetle larvae (*Carabidae*) resemble those of the wireworm in shape and size, but are a dull brown or black with a lighter under-surface. They are very active, with strong biting jaws, and have two whiskers on the top of their tails. This family feeds on various other grubs in the soil and is, therefore, regarded as a gardener's friend.

Leather-jackets are the grubs of 'daddy-long-legs' or 'crane-fly' (*Tipula oleracea*). The adult insects are quite harmless, but the grubs are the most destructive that infest our garden soils, since they cut the tap-roots of many plants and are particularly fond of grasses on lawns and bowling greens.

From June to September, the female crane flies lay about three hundred eggs in the soil, near the roots of plants and amongst grass, and in about two weeks the young larvae appear and feed on the roots of plants through autumn and winter. They are worm-like, legless maggots, cylindrical in shape and of an earthy-brown colour with a hard head, furnished with jaws. They pupate in midsummer, emerging as winged adults in the autumn.

To bring up the grubs to the surface of lawns so that they can be destroyed, water with D.D.T., or dust with D.D.T. powder or

c

33

mowrah meal at the rate of 4 ozs. per sq. yd. and follow it immediately with a copious watering. If bricks, boards, tiles or even pieces of turf are laid down as traps near where leather-jacket grubs are suspected among vegetables and examined each morning, many will be found underneath and can be destroyed. Other preventive and remedial measures are those used in the case of wireworms.

Millipedes—sometimes known as 'thousand feet' because they have two pairs of legs to each body segment—are smallish, rather sluggish in habit and, when disturbed, coil themselves up like a watch spring. Their hard bodies resemble these of the leather jacket larvae and there are many different species, the two most troublesome being *Julus* (*Blanjulus*) *Pulchellus*, the spotted or snake millipede, which is slender, about 1 in. long when fully grown, and has a yellowish-crimson spotted body; and *Polydesmus complanatus* which is flatter with a lilac-tinted body. Eggs are laid in early spring and summer in little nests in the soil, hatching out in 10-14 days.

Millipedes are sometimes introduced into the garden in leaf mould and other organic matter, living and dead, and are usually found in clusters attacking seeds and destroying seed leaves of young seedlings. They gnaw the roots of a great variety of plants, eat into bulbs, tubers, corms, strawberry crowns and fruits and even attack young strawberry roots. They can be trapped by burying pieces of potato or carrot. Aldrin dust applied to the soil in small quantities will help to get rid of these pests. Vegetable compound fertilisers which contain aldrin are now available. Dusting the soil with whizzed naphthalene at the rate of 3 oz. per sq. yd. and dug in when the ground is vacant acts as a repellent, and thorough drainage of the land and an application of lime are also beneficial.

Centipedes (*Geophilus*) are allied to the millipedes but are easily distinguished from them by their brighter brown colour and longer legs, one pair to each body segment instead of two. They are very active and run away when disturbed which also helps to distinguish them from millipedes, but they are friends of the gardener as they are carnivorous and feed on small slugs and snails and on small immature insects.

The cockchafer grub or May bug (*Melolontha vulgaris*), of which there are several species, the largest being the true cockchafer, is the most alarming of all the plant pests found in the soil in the larval stage. The larvae are large, flat and bloated-looking with a pearly white skin, a bright, light brown head and a purplish tail and they lie in a C-shaped curve. Birds relish them.

Adult cockchafers are on the wing in the evenings during May and June. The female lays her eggs about 3 ins. beneath surface of the ground and after four to six weeks the larvae appear and live up to four years in the soil. For the first year they do little harm, but during the second, third and fourth seasons they feed on all kinds of roots including those of herbaceous plants, vegetables, trees and shrubs. As they increase in size the damage is more marked and, collectively, they do a lot of damage. The white, soft pupae pass the winter in an earthen cell until the adults emerge in May. Aldrin dust applied to the soil surface helps to control them.

Other chafer beetles similar to the large cockchafer are the garden and rose chafers, but these pupate within the year. They are doubly troublesome, as the adults, as well as the grubs, feed on the plants. The rose chafer beetles feed on leaves of roses and disfigure the plants, and the garden chafer beetles attack the leaves of apple trees and the young fruit. To control the adults when feeding on the fruit trees and rose bushes, dust or spray the plants with D.D.T.

Root aphis (*Pemphigus auriculae*) frequently occur on the roots of primulas and auriculas and cause serious injury to the plants. They are white or pale yellowish and are covered with white 'meal' or 'wool'. They produce live young which feed by piercing the roots and removing the sap. The simplest control measure is to wash the roots with a solution of nicotine added to soapy water.

A comparatively new soil pest insecticide is aldrin dust. It does not taint vegetables, providing at least three weeks are allowed to elapse between application and the gathering of the crop. Fertilisers are also available which contain aldrin, therefore, they provide nutrients for the plants plus an insect control.

Asparagus, Corn Cob, and Seakale

The edible asparagus (*Asparagus officinalis*) is one of our oldest vegetables and has been in cultivation in our gardens for over 300 years. Its restricted culture is largely due to ignorance of its requirements and it is considered by many an expensive luxury, but in fact, no vegetable will give such a good return for so little trouble. Once established, a bed has been known to yield good crops for over fifty years.

It is a hardy perennial and consists of a cluster of fleshy roots connected by the stem, where a quantity of buds are formed and from which shoots grow annually. When young and tender these shoots are delicious if cooked and served with butter. Uncooked and chopped into small pieces, they also make a valuable addition to the salad bowl and have the flavour of fresh green peas.

There are male and female plants, and when grown from seed approximately equal numbers of each are produced. Experiment has shown that male plants give a 50 per cent heavier yield, but unfortunately the sexes cannot be determined until flowering during the third or fourth year of cropping, the season normally being from the end of April until the end of June.

The plants thrive in a variety of soils but are most successful in a medium loam, provided it is well drained and free from acidity. Double dig the ground, working a liberal quantity of decayed farmyard manure into the upper layer of soil. In gardens make the asparagus beds 4½ ft. wide, and fork and rake a dressing of 4 lb. of bone meal per 30 sq. yds. into the surface. Just before planting, rake in a dressing of 2 lb. of sulphate of potash per 30 sq. yds. and a dusting of ground lime. Early in April make the surface fine and mark off the bed, allowing three rows, 18 ins. apart and 9 ins. from each side. Carefully lift with a fork the one-year-old seedlings or 'maidens', sown in a specially selected site the previous spring, and grade them —discarding all thin and wiry plants as these would be of little use for cropping, but do not allow the roots to become dry between lifting and replanting. Set them 6-7 ins. apart in channels made with the spade and plant very firmly, covering the crowns with three to four inches of soil. In the following April remove every alternate plant, using these to fill blank spaces previously marked with sticks or to form another bed or row. The plants should ultimately be 12-14 ins. apart. Asparagus is grown chiefly by the wide-bed system, although many gardeners prefer to grow their crops in single rows, allowing 3 ft. between rows.

In autumn, the plants should be cut to the ground and, in late winter or early spring, given a surface application of farmyard manure, to help retain moisture at the roots during the growing season. A dressing of 3 oz. per sq. yd. of a complete fertiliser, such as Growmore, in the spring, plus a single dressing of 1 oz. per sq. yd. of sulphate of ammonia after the crop is finished, will stimulate new growth and strengthen the crowns for the next season. The after-treatment consists in keeping the beds clean and removing withered shoots in the autumn. Old beds can be improved by an annual application of basic slag at the rate of 4 lb. per 30 sq. yds.

Cutting—always done with a special asparagus knife—must begin only in the third year, and should be light, only half that of a normal season, on the first occasion. In following years there will be a rapid increase in supplies.

Varieties commonly grown are Connover's Colossal, an English variety; early and late Argenteuil are French, and Mary Washington, an American variety, is said to resist rust and produce a high percentage of first grade shoots.

Corn cob, sweet corn or Indian maize (*Zea mais*), a native of America where it is extensively grown for use as a vegetable, should be gathered and cooked entire when young and tender. It thrives in a high temperature with plenty of sunshine during the growing season and the best crops are produced on deep, warm soils rich in farmyard manure and treated with a compound fertiliser containing plenty of phosphates.

Sow in pots or boxes, under glass, in late March or early April, later putting the seedlings into 3 in. pots and when hardened-off, transplanting them 18 ins. apart in the open ground in early June in rows 2½ ft. apart. As the plants bear both male and female inflorescences, the latter being wind pollinated, they may be planted in blocks rather than single lines, allowing 18 ins. between the plants each way, and cloches or Dutch lights may be used to protect them until established. Since they are shallow-rooters, careful cultivation with the hoe and watering in dry weather are essential.

Cropping should begin about the middle of August with early varieties. The grain must not be allowed to harden before cutting and often experience is necessary in deciding exactly when the grain falls within the 'milk' stage. The heads should either be twisted off or cut off with a knife. Prepare cobs by removing the husk, put into boiling water with a little salt and cook for ten to twelve minutes. The more rapidly the plants are grown the less time will be required for cooking. If cooked too long, the skins of the grain become brown and tough.

Varieties suitable for Scottish conditions are limited. Golden Bantam is a dwarf variety of good cropping qualities and of excellent flavour. John Innes Hybrids raised from seed mature early and give a good yield. They are not themselves a strain but first crosses between two strains, and seedsmen now remake the crosses each year to maintain supplies. Golden Market is an early variety, golden in colour and of excellent flavour.

Seakale (*Crambe maritima*), as indicated both by its botanical and popular names, flourishes near the sea coast. Indigenous to Britain, it is a hardy perennial plant of some importance as a high-class vegetable, especially when forced, and is very tender when the shoots and leaf stalks are properly blanched.

Propagation is by means of 'thongs'—pieces of roots removed

from the plants after they are lifted for forcing in October-November. Before storing in sand until planting, the 6 in. thongs should be prepared by cutting the growing end nearest the crown (which will produce buds giving rise to new plants) straight across, and the thinner, rooting end, slantwise.

Roots that are to be forced in two years from planting should be grown in deeply worked and heavily manured ground, plenty of farmyard manure being dug in well in advance and a dressing of superphosphate applied ten days before planting. The manuring encourages rapid growth and the formation of strong crowns, suitable for forcing. Plant the prepared 'thong' roots during April, either by using a dibble or placing them upright in a trench made with a spade and covering the tops with about 1 in. of soil. An application of nitrate of soda at the rate of 1 oz. per sq. yd. during the growing season will stimulate growth. Prune away surplus shoots from each crown during the first year and allow only one shoot to grow so as to form a good crown. Flower stems, if they appear, should be cut off. Protect from sharp frost by using partly decayed leaves or peat moss if the roots are to be left in the open during the winter.

Seakale crowns for forcing are lifted in October-November, trimmed and stored in sand until required. To force the plants, the roots should be placed in deep sand-filled boxes or flower pots, plunged under the greenhouse staging and covered with inverted flower pots or any other device to keep out the light.

Those to be forced in the open can be blanched by placing large boxes or seakale pots over the crowns and then covering these with any fermenting material, such as a mixture of leaves and straw. A bed of seakale, properly made and well manured will last and crop heavily for many years, in fact, like good wine, it is improved by age.

Beans

There are three types of beans cultivated in gardens—the broad bean, which is regarded as being a native of Persia, French and runner beans, both reputed to be of Indian origin.

All pod-bearing crops have the advantage over other vegetable plants in that they are able to utilise free nitrogen from the atmosphere as a source of food, through the bacteria in the nodules on their roots, whereas other plants depend upon supplies available in the soil. This plant food promotes growth, i.e. the production of leaves, shoots and stems.

Before sowing beans or peas the application of farmyard manure is usually unnecessary since the soil will have been liberally manured for the onions and leeks preceding them in the crop-rotation scheme, but, if organic matter or humus is lacking, it is advisable to incorporate some decayed vegetable compost with the soil during digging operations to improve the texture and moisture-retaining properties. The ground should be thoroughly dug during the autumn or winter, and a week or two before sowing apply and rake into the surface 3 lb. of superphosphate and 2 lb. of sulphate of potash to every 30 sq. yds.

Broad beans deserve to be more popular in Scotland. Make the first sowing about the end of February or early in March when soil and weather conditions are favourable, and for continuous supplies sow at monthly intervals up to the end of May. First, rake the soil surface to make it level and produce a reasonably fine tilth, then sow a double row in a drill 3 ins. deep and 6-8 ins. wide, the two rows being 5 ins. apart and the seeds 8 ins. distant from each other along the row. Fill in the drills with soil, but (before the final layer of soil is replaced), firm it lightly with the head of the rake. A mere dusting with lime after sowing is often beneficial. The distance between adjacent drills, should not be less than 2 ft. or more than $2\frac{1}{2}$ ft.

The pea and bean weevil is a serious danger to young plants when they begin to develop their first main leaves, since the adult insects will devour the leaves and shoots of seedlings and eat notches in the edges of the more mature plants' leaves, while the larvae may destroy the roots. Unfortunately, birds are often blamed for the damage to foliage, since the weevils are the same colour as the soil and remain concealed under its particles during the day, feeding mainly at night, and are difficult to detect. Try scraping a little earth away from the affected plants and wait for the weevils to move in search of a fresh hiding place. They will at first feign death on being disturbed, but patience will be rewarded. Control is either by spraying the seedlings with a weak solution of liquid derris or dusting them with derris powder, in the late evening or early morning. Hoe at frequent intervals during the growing season.

Blackfly often attacks broad beans near the growing point, soon after flowering is completed and, to safeguard the crop, it is a good plan to leave two leaves above the last cluster of flowers and remove the growing point of each plant immediately flowering is finished.

After harvesting, cut the bean stalks or haulm off at soil level and leave the roots in the ground to decay because the nodules on them contain a good supply of nitrogen, of use to following crops, i.e. early autumn-planted cabbages for cutting in spring.

39

With regard to varieties, try one of the Longpod kinds—usually catalogued under such names as Prolific, Champion, or Exhibition—the Green or White Windsor kinds are also good.

Dwarf French beans appear to be gaining popularity in Scotland. Start sowing about mid-April and continue until mid-June making the drills 2-3 ins. deep and sowing one row in each drill; allow 12 ins. between the seeds and 2 ft. between drills.

Hoeing during the growing season keeps down weeds and helps to maintain moisture in the soil, although during dry weather it may be necessary to give the plants a good watering. Never allow the pods to become too old before using them, otherwise there will be a marked deterioration in their quality. Fortunately, dwarf French beans are not troubled to any great extent by pests and diseases. The varieties Canadian Wonder and The Prince are popular.

Runner beans, or scarlet runners as they are sometimes called, are not so extensively grown in Scotland as in England, but will flourish in any good garden soil and, as with other bean crops, if they follow onions or leeks there should be no need to add more dung.

Do not sow until all danger of frost is past, otherwise the young seedlings may suffer damage. Generally, the end of May or early June is safe enough. Draw two drills each 2-3 ins. deep and about 12 ins. apart and place the seeds 9 ins. apart in each drill—the two drills combined are often referred to as a row. Poles or stakes, about 5 ft. high and meeting at the top in an inverted V, should be placed in position early for the plants to climb or tall wire netting, or pea netting—well supported—may be used.

Give the plants a light, misty spray with water every evening on dry days during the flowering period since this helps the pods to set. Harvest before the pods become too old. Prizewinner, Scarlet Emperor and Exhibition are good varieties.

Brussels Sprouts

Brussels sprouts should be sown thinly during late March or April, when soil and weather conditions are favourable, in drills about ½ in. deep and 9 ins. apart in either a cold frame or a well-prepared seed-bed outdoors. As they are members of the cabbage family and susceptible to club-root, or finger-and-toe disease, precautions should be taken by dusting a little 4% calomel dust, along each drill before sowing.

The young plants will be ready for transplanting in late May or June, 2½-3 ft. apart each way, and will provide crops for late autumn, winter and spring. When sprouts are required earlier, for late summer and early autumn use, sow thinly during early August, and after wintering in the seed-bed, the young plants may be planted out next spring.

Brussels sprouts follow last year's potato, pea or bean crops in the rotation scheme, and, since they are gross feeders, must have a soil well-enriched with decayed farmyard manure, or decomposed vegetable refuse, incorporated during thorough preparation well in advance of planting. Apply four good barrowloads to every 30 sq. yds. of ground, and a week or two before planting, add 3 lb. super-phosphate and 1½ lb. sulphate of potash per 30 sq. yds.

Tramp the ground firmly and rake it to produce a reasonably fine tilth and level surface, then draw drills about 2 ins. deep and 6-8 ins. wide, and plant along the centre of each by using a dibble or trowel—see notes in the section on cabbages—and dust each hole with a little 4% calomel dust before planting.

As Brussels sprouts are often planted 3 ft. apart between the rows, a catch crop can be grown. A row of radishes or lettuce, for example, will be harvested before the foliage of the sprouts spreads over the ground they occupy.

Hoe frequently between the rows during the growing season. Some growers remove a number of the lower main leaves of the plants whilst they are still green to increase the yield, but such plants do not give such good results as those left to grow naturally, though it is not a bad plan to remove the large leaves once they have turned yellow or brown.

Cabbage caterpillars frequently attack the plants, but are easily controlled by a derris liquid spray, which is non-poisonous to human beings. This should be used in accordance with the recommendations on the container, and a cupful of milk should be added as a 'spreader' to every two gallons of diluted spray.

Exhibition is a good, hardy, fine-flavoured variety which does well under Scottish conditions. Rous Lench produces hard, solid, dark-green sprouts and Dalkeith is a reliable hardy variety with large firm sprouts—both the latter find favour amongst Scottish growers.

Cabbages

Fresh, green vegetables are of great importance in our diet, and the cabbage is one of the most popular. Unfortunately, many amateur gardeners do not always get the best results because the plants

41

become infected with club-root or finger-and-toe disease, which so distorts the root system that it fails to function properly. Any infection from this disease contaminates the soil and it would be asking for trouble to plant any of the cabbage family in the same ground during the next few years without due precautions being taken. It is a good plan to use 4% calomel dust—in the seed drills prior to sowing, and in the dibble holes when planting—for all members of the family.

To obtain continuous supplies over as long a season as possible, sow the cabbage seed thinly in drills, about ½ in. deep and 9 ins. apart in a well-prepared seed bed. The popular Scottish variety McEwan's Early or Flower of Spring should be sown about mid-July, ready for planting-out in September at 12-in. intervals in rows 15 ins. apart. This will provide a crop for cutting in early spring. A good succession will be obtained if some of the plants which were on the small side for the first planting, are lifted when they are a bit larger and planted a little later.

Both these plantings fit into the crop rotation scheme if they are made in ground from which early or second early potatoes have been lifted, and provided the site was reasonably well prepared and manured for the potato crop, and club-foot control precautions taken, as mentioned above the young plants should grow quite well. Trample the soil, for all members of the cabbage family like it reasonably firm, and then rake it lightly to produce a fairly level surface. Alternatively, the young plants may be grown on ground previously occupied by a crop of peas or beans. After the old pea or bean haulms have been removed, don't dig the ground but rake it to loosen the top inch or two and leave the surface level, or a row of cabbages may be planted directly on the site of a pea or bean row.

Set the garden line where the row is to be, draw a drill about 6-8 ins. wide and 2 ins. deep with a draw hoe and plant in the centre. The sides of the drill provide a little protection for the young plants, and during subsequent surface cultivation the drill gradually becomes filled in and makes earthing-up less necessary.

Give the seed bed a good watering a few hours before the young plants are carefully lifted to preserve a good rooting system. It is a common practice to place the plants in holes made with a dibble, but the amateur is better advised to use a trowel, keeping the back of the trowel next to the garden line and pulling the soil outwards. If a dibble hole is too shallow it does not permit good planting, and if it is too deep, an air pocket may be left below the roots when the hole is filled in. That is where the trowel scores, though it takes longer to do the job, it does make a hole wide enough to enable us to see that the roots are resting on the base of the hole. Whichever method is used make the hole large enough for the roots to be allowed down to their fullest extent and the plant covered up to its lowest leaves, and always plant firmly, ensuring that the soil is pressed back into the hole close to the plant.

The next sowing, again an early variety, should be made about the end of August, but the young plants are left in the seed bed all winter and planted out in spring when soil and weather conditions are favourable. Plant in drills, as previously recommended, but this time make them 18 ins. apart and allow 15 ins. between the plants. These will give a summer crop.

Sow a main crop variety about the end of March for planting out in May and June to provide a crop for cutting during late summer and autumn. Plant the young cabbages 18 ins. apart in 2-in. deep drills, 2 ft. apart. Try Golden Acre, and that old favourite Winningstadt; a very good late, hardy variety is January King.

Red cabbage is not grown to any great extent in Scottish gardens, but it is a useful vegetable for pickling in autumn. Sow in March and cultivate the plants as though they were main-crop green cabbages; a few plants will meet most household requirements.

In the case of young plants which have been overwintered in the seed bed for planting out in spring, and also for the main crop sown in spring to be planted out in May and June, it is advisable to prepare the ground, i.e. last year's potato, pea or bean site, during the winter. This is done by forking or digging it to a good spade's depth and enriching it with an application of farmyard manure or decomposed refuse from the compost heap. After digging, apply a phosphatic fertiliser by scattering 4-5 lb. bone meal over every 30 sq. yds. of ground—this is slow-acting, hence its application during winter. Another method is to apply 3 lbs. superphosphate, a quick acting fertiliser, per 30 sq. yds. a week or two before planting, but in every case, apply in addition 1-1½ lb. sulphate of potash to every 30 sq. yds. in advance of planting. It was once the custom to apply lime to all ground intended for cabbage, cauliflower, etc., because it was regarded as a good precautionary measure against club root disease. This was a good idea when the soil was sour or acid, for the more acid the soil was the more it favoured club root disease, but when too much lime was applied it resulted in the soil becoming too alkaline. These crops give the best results when it is just slightly on the acid side, and now that we have the preparation known as 4% calomel dust as a control measure against club root, lime does not require to be applied with the sole intention of controlling this disease.

All these additions of farmyard manure and fertilisers recommended for the spring, and May and June plantings, may seem unnecessary when those planted in September did not receive them, but the former had the advantage of soil enriched with nitrogen by earlier pea and bean crops. If autumn plantings are given additional dressings of manures and fertilisers containing nitrogen, which promotes growth, the plants may develop a 'soft' growth which would undermine their hardiness to withstand severe wintry conditions.

Prior to planting cabbages in spring, and May and June, on ground which was well dug and manured in winter, make the ground firm by tramping, but not when it is too wet, and rake the surface to produce a reasonably fine tilth. Afterwards draw drills about 2 ins. deep and plant in the same way as autumn-planted plants. During summer, Dutch hoe frequently.

If necessary a little nitrogenous stimulant in the form of 1 lb. of sulphate of ammonia per 30 sq. yds. of ground, hoed or raked in, between the rows, will induce growth, unless the stunting is caused by disease or drought. Avoid the crystals of sulphate of ammonia being deposited on the leaves when applying it, since it will 'burn' or plasmolyse them.

Caterpillars frequently cause a lot of damage. The remedy is to spray the plants with non-poisonous derris liquid, diluted according to directions on the container, adding a cupful of milk to every 2-2½ gallons of dilute spray to act as a 'spreader' or 'wetter'.

Cabbage-root fly maggots can also cause considerable damage and to avoid loss of crop by these pests use one of the preparations sold for this purpose—they usually contain 4% calomel dust.

Although certain varieties of cabbage have been mentioned here, there are of course many others and to add to the interest in gardening try something new each year, either for autumn or spring sowing.

Cauliflower and Broccoli

Cauliflower and broccoli (which is a hardy type of cauliflower), are the most delicate of all the Brassica tribe of vegetables. The flower-buds form a close, firm, white head or curd, rich in vitamin C and mineral salts. Dr. Johnson said, 'Of all the flowers in the garden I like the cauliflower'. Until the French Revolution, quantities of English cauliflowers were sent regularly to Holland and the Low Countries, and even France depended on Britain for seed, but now we cannot keep up with the demands for the home market.

Cauliflower and broccoli are raised from seed sown either in a specially prepared seed bed in the open, or under glass in a frame or seed box, a light loam is ideal with 1 oz. superphosphate and 2 oz. powdered lime per sq. yd. worked into the soil surface some ten days in advance. With carefully selected varieties, and the aid of Dutch lights, cloches and the ordinary garden frame, practically all-year-round production can be achieved. The varieties are very numerous and are divided into four main groups according to their types and the different times of sowing and planting—autumn sowings to produce heads for cutting in May and June; winter and early spring sowings to produce heads for cutting in July and August; late spring sowings to produce heads for cutting in September to November, according to the weather; late spring sowings of broccoli to produce heads for cutting from January till June.

Some of the early summer cauliflower varieties are All the Year Round, Snowball, Cambridge Early No. 5 and Early London. Sow thinly in frames at the end of September or early October. After germination the seedlings should be pricked out into other frames, where they are kept all winter, or potted up into very small pots. During mild weather the lights may be taken off to allow free ventilation and watering, which must be done with the utmost care to avoid mildew and damping off. Transfer the plants at the beginning of April to a sheltered border that has previously been prepared and manured with farmyard manure. Plant firmly 18 ins. apart each way in shallow drills, using a trowel so that the roots are not unduly disturbed, and provide shelter with light twigs or cloches over them.

Very early cauliflower can be obtained by placing five plants under each Dutch light, but remove the glass when the weather is favourable after the plants become established. During spells of dry weather cauliflowers are apt to form premature heads known as 'buttons', a condition that renders the crop useless and watering is therefore very important. Soot water or a weak solution of sulphate of ammonia as a nitrogenous stimulant will give the heads a bright fresh colour and make the leaves dark green.

By sowing thinly in frames towards the end of March, cauliflower can be grown ready to cut in July and August. The plants should be hardened off by removing the frame lights about ten days before they are transplanted outdoors in early May.

To produce a late summer and autumn crop, sow in an open seed bed during April, and transfer the plants to their growing quarters in early June, but manure the land well ahead of planting as these cauliflowers require good treatment.

A good late August and early September variety is Early Autumn Giant; and for late autumn cutting Veitch's Autumn Giant. They develop good heads with white curds. An excellent hardy variety for Northern areas is Walcheren which may be regarded as in the broccoli class, it stands well in all weathers and develops compact, white heads. Plenty of space is necessary for these varieties to develop, therefore, allow 28 to 30 ins. between the rows and 24 ins. between plants. It is advisable to mix soil and water to form a 'puddle' and dip the roots in this before planting. Plant very firmly and afterwards water in. Examine the crop at intervals when the heads are maturing and break one or two leaves over the curds to prevent discoloration, and as an added protection against frost.

Cauliflower can be grown under glass in a tomato house, provided the correct treatment and the right varieties, such as All the Year Round or Early London, are chosen. Broadcast the seed thinly, in early September in a cold frame, water in, place the lights on the frames and cover with mats until germination. The mats can then be removed, the frame freely ventilated, and the seedlings pricked out 3 ins. apart each way in another frame.

Prepare the soil in the greenhouse by adding farmyard manure, a little hoof and horn meal, some superphosphate and sulphate of potash, forking this well into the top 4 ins. of soil. Set out the young plants when they are large enough 2 ft. apart each way; afterwards thoroughly water them in. Keep the temperature about 48° F./9° C., rising by sun heat to 60° F./16° C., and as they grow, give plenty of water and ventilate freely during mild weather. Damp down the house and plants on bright days. The crop will mature in April when good heads can be cut.

The numerous varieties of broccoli tend to perplex the gardener, and some are not very hardy under Scottish weather conditions. Four or five are sufficient if they are well chosen, and arranged to ensure a succession of crops. A suggested order is—Snow's Winter White, a very old but most useful variety, producing lovely heads in January and February; Leamington, another old variety, is one of the most hardy for March cutting. St. George and Royal Oak are two excellent varieties for cutting during April and May and, lastly, one of the latest varieties to mature is Clucas's June, which often produces splendid heads of the finest quality well into June. The three last-named are hardy, very distinct and should be grown in every garden.

The French Roscoff types will not withstand the varying weather conditions, therefore, it is rather risky to plant them in Scotland.

Sow the main broccoli crop in April, but it is wise to make another sowing as late as the first week in May. As soon as the plants are large enough to handle, set them out, preferably in ground where peas have been grown. Any time during June or early July will do, but after mid-July it is too late even for late maturing varieties. The less loose the soil, the more sturdy growth will be and the plants have a better chance of withstanding severe winter weather. The plants should be placed at intervals of $2\frac{1}{4}$ ft. in rows $2\frac{1}{2}$ ft. apart, the soil packed firmly round each. Water freely during dry weather.

Over-feeding of broccoli with nitrogenous fertilisers during the summer months may result in excessive damage to the sappy plants by frost during the ensuing winter. Potash manure applied before planting produces a better type of growth and more attractive heads.

The white and purple kinds of sprouting broccoli—the latter being the more hardy—are very distinct from the white single-headed sorts. They are most useful and prolific, and from a small number of plants large quantities of small heads can be cut from early spring until the plants break into bloom. The cultivation of these is the same as for the single-headed type. To enable broccoli to produce good heads, plant them on ground which has been well treated with decayed farmyard manure, plus an application of 2 lb. of sulphate of potash per 30 sq. yds. hoed in about a week before planting. This, supplemented by good cultivation, generally gives good results.

As a precaution against club root disease attacking cauliflower and broccoli plants, treat the seed drills and dust the dibble holes with 4% calomel dust as recommended for cabbages and Brussels sprouts.

Cucumbers

Cucumbers belong to the same family as vegetable marrows and melons and are supposed to have originated in Asia and Africa. Nowadays they may be grown outdoors during summer—the more favourable the weather, the better the results—and credit must be given to plant-breeders who have produced suitable varieties for the purpose. Heated glasshouses and frames are commonly used, the former in particular for the earliest crops.

For early cucumbers sow between January and March, the latter month being the most suitable for most gardeners, who may otherwise find it difficult to provide accommodation for them with so many demands on greenhouse space. The temperature must be about 70-75° F./21-24° C., and it is best to sow one seed in each 3 in. pot, using a compost of damp peat and fibrous loam, which will not dry out readily or become too wet. Too much moisture will lead to deterioration of the seed before germination, and although a reasonable amount is necessary, try to eliminate the necessity to water the pots between seed-sowing and germination.

To assist germination it is a good plan to put some fine, damp horticultural peat in a propagating frame or box set on the greenhouse staging, and plunge the seed pots in it up to their rims since this helps to keep the seed compost in an ideal condition. Cover the pots with a sheet of glass and a piece of paper to keep the compost sufficiently damp until the seeds germinate, when this should be removed. Keep the young plants close to the glass, as they need light, and water frequently. Cucumbers produce long slender trailing shoots, and can be prepared for subsequent training and support by staking each young plant early with a small bamboo cane.

In due course the plants are transplanted into their fruiting quarters, mounds of compost approximately 18 ins. high—one to each plant. These are made of good old turfy loam, which is better still if it contains plenty of fibre, to which some old decayed farmyard manure has been added. Do not riddle the compost, rather leave it on the rough and lumpy side. Each mound is built up on a reasonably-sized solid base placed relatively near the glass on the greenhouse staging. If more than one plant is to be grown, the mounds must be 3 to 4 ft. apart. Where there is no staging and the glass at the side of the house begins only a little above the inside soil level it is often more convenient to build a continuous ridge of compost on top of the greenhouse soil relatively near the glass. Alternatively, grow the plants in large pots set on staging—this usually meets the amateur growers' requirements best of all.

To support the cucumber stems, have wires about a foot apart stretched the full length of the greenhouse under the roof and about a foot from the glass. Another method is to train the leading shoot of each plant, allowing no side growths, to the lowest wire, usually relatively near; after that side shoots or laterals should be allowed to develop on each side of the leading shoot to produce fruit. As soon as the main or leading shoot reaches the top of the training wires, or other support, nip off its growing point, to induce the production of more fruit-bearing lateral shoots. When each lateral is about $1\frac{1}{2}$-2 ft. in length, its growing point is also removed.

Throughout the growing season maintain a night temperature of

Using cardboard tubes to earth
up celery for show purposes.

The ripening of onions is
assisted by bending over their
necks.

Marrows, Little Gem

Asparagus.

Radishes, Cherry Belle

not less than 60° F./16° C. with a day temperature of between 70-75° F./21-24° C. and on no account let the plants suffer from drought. Keep a warm, damp atmosphere by lightly spraying the walls and paths every morning and evening with tepid water. Unfortunately, these conditions may not suit all other plants which may be growing in the greenhouse, but in any case it is better to stop damping down when the cucumber flowers appear. It is a good plan to help pollination for early crops by tying a dry rabbit's tail to a bamboo cane and touching the male flowers, which have stamens and pollen, and then touching the female blooms which have a pistil but no stamens; pollination is necessary to induce the formation of fruit. As a rule hand-pollination is not required for later crops.

Cucumbers can also be grown in a frame where heat is provided by fermenting farmyard manure, i.e. a hot-bed, but it is now almost impossible to obtain a sufficient quantity. Make the hot-bed in the open with fresh moist stable manure to a depth of 3 ft., tramping it down firmly during the operation, and place a light wooden garden frame on top.

When the temperature of the hot-bed has dropped to about 75° F./24° C., place a mound of fibrous turfy loam, to which some old decayed manure has been added, in the centre of each frame light. Allow the mound to warm up and put a young cucumber plant on it. Ventilation is often necessary on hot days, to prevent the temperature rising beyond 75° F./24° C. To make the young plants produce the necessary lateral growth for fruit production, remove the growing point of each one after about three to five leaves have been formed. When about four lateral growths have developed they must be spaced evenly over the area covered by each frame light, i.e. one to each corner. After each of these laterals has produced about five leaves, their growing points are in turn removed to produce fruiting laterals. To prevent overcrowding, the old system of removing the growing point of a lateral when it has begun to develop a fruit is still a good one, but pinch it off to leave at least one or two leaves beyond the young fruit. Attend carefully to the watering of cucumbers growing in a frame, syringing lightly with tepid water about 5 p.m. (summer time) every afternoon on sunny days and then closing the frame to bottle-up some of the sun heat.

If no artificial heat is available, plant in a cold frame, again using fibrous turfy loam enriched with old dung, but not until about early June when all risk of frost has passed. Pinch out the growing points as previously recommended and utilise the sun's heat by closing the frame in the late afternoon to increase the temperature.

Ridge or outdoor cucumbers may also be grown, but are not very common in Scotland. Sow in 3-in. pots about late April in a heated greenhouse, and after the plants have been carefully hardened off, plant them outdoors in early June, when there is little risk of frost. Place them either on small mounds of compost made of turfy loam enriched with well-decayed farmyard manure, or dig some old farmyard manure into the open ground site and then make it into a mound or ridge. For most amateurs one or two plants outdoors are sufficient. To encourage the production of fruiting laterals, pinch out the growing point of each young plant after it has made about five or six leaves. Train the laterals outwards at equal distances apart, and prevent their being disturbed by securing them to the soil with pieces of bent wire or hooked sticks. As a mound of soil dries out more readily than flat ground, make sure the plants do not suffer from drought.

Unfortunately cucumbers are susceptible to a number of diseases. Fruit rot attacks the tip of the young fruits, causing a soft rot, and the affected fruits should be removed and burnt. Collar rot attacks the stem at soil level, causing wilting and death: all affected plants must be destroyed. Of the many varieties Telegraph is still a general favourite, especially for heated greenhouses, and Conqueror is worth a trial in a heated or cold frame: those suitable for outdoor cultivation usually have the word Ridge in their names, e.g. King of the Ridge, Ridge King, etc.

Herbs

Herbs are the distinct group of annual, biennial and perennial plants used either medicinally or for flavouring and garnishing in the kitchen. One school of thought here staunchly advocates plain unseasoned fare, but on the Continent they are wiser and realise that the use of herbs does not necessarily mean high flavouring. Most are mild and simply add piquancy to a meal. Those most often grown are parsley, mint, sage, thyme and marjoram—all easy to raise and an asset to any garden—but there are a number of others well worth cultivating.

The herb 'garden' may be a small bed with a south or south-west exposure, well drained and thoroughly trenched in the first place with plenty of leaf mould and wood ash from the garden bonfire added. A top-dressing of leaf mould or old potting compost every spring will keep the soil surface cool and encourage surface root action.

It is an advantage to arrange the annuals together at one end, the perennials at the other, and the biennials in the middle—replanting the perennials in fresh ground every three or four years.

Herbs are propagated by seed, cuttings and division, and the beginner may rapidly establish a border with the help of friends.

Hardy annuals are sown in open ground in April and early May, but the seed of half-hardy needs to be raised under glass, the seedlings pricked-off into boxes and later, when hardened off, planted outdoors towards the end of May. Biennials and perennials are grown with more difficulty from seed and, when only a few plants are wanted, it is better to buy from a nursery.

Cuttings of thyme, sage and other shrubby plants may be taken either in spring, or in August and September, and rooted in a cold frame. Perennials are best divided in the spring.

Balm (*Melissa officinalis*) is a fragrant plant, of which the leaves are used for making balm tea or wine. Propagated annually from cuttings either in the autumn or spring, it thrives in a fairly heavy soil and spreads quickly.

Bush Basil (*Ocymum minimum*) and Sweet Basil (*O. basilicum*), are deliciously scented half hardy annuals, giving a flavour rather like cloves. As both are rather tender, they should be sown in boxes in heat, pricked out, then hardened off and replanted outdoors towards the end of May 9 ins. apart and 1 ft. between the rows. The full-grown plants are pulled up, tied into bunches, and hung up to dry for winter use.

Caraway (*Carum carui*) is a biennial cultivated for the sake of its seeds, used in flavouring and confectionery. It can be grown as a root crop, but this is seldom done, although the leaves are occasionally eaten in salads. Sow during May, in drills 10-12 ins. apart, thin the seedlings to 8-in. intervals, and harvest the seed when it ripens the following autumn.

Chervil (*Anthriscus cerefolium*) is an annual resembling parsley in its growth. Pinches of seed should be sown from April onwards to August, the last sowing standing through the winter. The leaves can be used for salad flavouring and garnishing when only a few inches high.

Fennel (*Foeniculum vulgare*) is a tall handsome perennial with very fine foliage and goes well with fish. It can either be grown from seed, or increased by annual division of the plants. The flowers should not be allowed to develop unless seed is required.

The pot marjoram (*Origanum onites*) is useful for soup flavouring. Sow in spring and transplant the seedlings 1 ft. apart each way when they are large enough to handle. When the shoots are cut, they are tied into small bundles and dried for winter use. The sweet marjoram (*Origanum majorana*) is also a fragrant herb and its best when treated as an annual, for it cannot survive our winter climate. Sow in spring in shallow drills made 1 ft. apart and thin out the seedlings to about 8 ins.

There are several varieties of mint (*Mentha viridis*), but the narrow-leaved kind is easily the most popular. It can be propagated either by division or cuttings in the spring and will last for years in the same bed, being in fact almost impossible to eradicate once the roots have become established. A top dressing of leaf mould, before growth begins in spring, will encourage succulent shoots, and when the growing season is ended in autumn, small bunches should be hung up and dried for winter use. Fresh mint can be obtained easily in winter by placing a few roots in a box in heat to force growth.

Parsley (*Carum petroselinum*) is one of the most generally grown herbs, three types being known. Most popular is the green curled and long stemmed. Sow during April and again in July, choosing a rich deep soil, since it is deep-rooting. A few plants lifted in September and placed in a cold frame will be particularly useful during long spells of frosty weather. Parsley makes an attractive edging to garden paths.

The green-leaved purslane (*Portulaca oleracea*) is used both for cooking purposes and in salads, and it is also an admirable substitute for spinach. Sow in spring and thin out the seedlings to 8 ins. apart. Purslane is an annual, and a native of S. America and the W. Indies.

Rue (*Ruta graveolens*) is used for garnishing, but it must be used sparingly for the leaves have a strong odour. Propagate by cuttings and division of the roots.

Savory has two forms, the annual Summer Savory (*Satureja hortensis*) and the perennial Winter Savory (*S. montana*). The former is raised from spring-sown seed, set in shallow drills and the plants thinned out to 12 ins. apart, and the latter may either be raised in the same way or by cuttings. The aromatic leaves of both are used in soup and for flavouring peas and beans.

Sage (*Salvia officinalis*) is a fragrant shrub propagated by cuttings rooted in a cold frame, which should be planted out in spring about 2 ft. apart, the bushes being renewed every third or fourth year. It is widely used for flavouring and in stuffings.

Tarragon (*Artemisia dracunculus*) is a perennial used in salads and soups. Roots are planted in rows during April 2 ft. apart each way, and leaves for winter use are gathered and dried during the summer.

The common thyme (*Thymus vulgaris*) and the lemon thyme (*T. citriodorus*) both thrive in warm, well-drained sandy loam. Propagate by lifting and dividing old plants and setting out the pieces in rows 1 ft. apart. The leafy shoots are pulled up in late summer, and bunched and dried for winter use. The plants are very attractive to bees.

Leeks and Celery

The leek is essentially a Scottish winter and spring vegetable, though careful cultivation can make it available ten months of the year, since the hardier kinds can be left in the ground without damage, however severe the weather. It is an essential ingredient for Scotch broth, and is one of the few vegetables that cannot be grown too large, whether for exhibition or home use.

There are four main types, and a number of named varieties which are probably selections. London Flag is an early type—from which Walton Mammoth is probably a selection—and is fairly tall, with a thick stem and broad leaf. The Lyon has a fairly long stem with narrow leaves. Prizetaker, a variety of this type is not very frost resistant. Musselburgh is the most widely grown variety of leek, for centuries of selection have produced strains to withstand the severest weather, and it is also accepted as one of the best, producing heavy crops with thick stems and fairly stiff leaves. Midlothian and East Lothian are the counties where the most approved strains of this variety are grown for seed, but the Pot-leek or Northumbrian Leek, of which Finney's Tynedale is a selected strain, comes from the north of England, and is a short, very thick-stemmed plant which should not exhibit more than 5 ins. of blanched stem.

Leeks do not suffer appreciably from insect pests or fungoid diseases, and are easily grown, given deeply cultivated well-manured land. Usually a transplanted crop, they are now often sown thinly in the open and matured on the spot to save time and labour. The seed should be drilled in rows, 15 ins. apart.

Early sowings should be made under glass during January and early February in a specially prepared seed-bed, or boxes, if only a few plants are required. Sowing for the maincrop in the open should be done from early March onwards in a seedbed enriched with well-decayed manure; the shallow drills should be 10 ins. apart. Instead of reserving ground specially for leeks, save space by setting out the seedlings gradually as the ground used the previous autumn for planting early cabbages becomes cleared in spring.

When the cabbages have been removed dig in some old well decayed farmyard manure or vegetable compost and apply dressings of 1½ lb. each of sulphate of ammonia and superphosphate per 30 sq. yds. Firm the soil, then draw drills 15 ins. apart and 4 ins. deep, making holes 6-8 ins. apart with a dibber, and place a single plant in each. To facilitate planting, trim both root and leaves slightly on lifting them from the seed-bed, and set them in the holes up to the base of the green leaves. Leave the holes open and water in.

Exhibition leeks need a long growing period, and must be blanched to a greater extent than those grown for general use. Sow in the first week of January in a seedbox containing a rich compost of 2 parts light turfy loam, 1 part granulated peat, 1 part decayed stable manure and some coarse sand. Transfer the seedlings to small pots when large enough to handle and when these become well-filled with roots move the plants to 5-in. pots using a slightly richer compost. Pot fairly deeply and press the soil lightly around the roots. Harden them off in a cold frame at the end of March, when they will be fairly large and stout, and transfer them to permanent quarters at the end of April. Well in advance of planting outdoors, prepare a trench 18 ins. wide and about 1 ft. deep, digging a 4-in. layer of well-decayed farmyard manure into the bottom, then scattering on top 1 oz. per sq. yd. of a complete fertiliser, e.g. National Growmore, and forking it in. Plant the leeks 1 ft. apart each way, and afterwards give a good watering.

As they begin to grow it is necessary to begin to blanch the plants by tying a collar of brown paper loosely round the stems to exclude light, keeping it in position by a small cane placed each side. Water well and once a week use a solution of 1 oz. of a complete fertiliser in 1 gallon of water. As the plants grow taller, add further paper collars to increase the height of the blanched area; place a small quantity of soil close to the paper to hold it in position.

To avoid bruising the leaves and stems when lifting and preparing plants for exhibition, first remove some of the surrounding soil with a spade. Then, having tied the green leaves—once just above the blanched stem, once in the centre, and once near the tips—to prevent splitting, lift carefully. Remove the surface soil and dirt with cold water and a soft sponge, then wash thoroughly a second time before taking off the outer layer of leaves, and finally rinse in clear, cold water and cover with paper to exclude light. Good exhibition leeks should be pearly white, 15-18 ins. in length, and of a good thickness.

Exhibition leeks may be grown without making a trench. Prepare the ground as already recommended and, having made a drill 6-8 ins. wide and 2 ins. deep with a draw-hoe, plant one row. When growth begins, place a short brown-paper collar round the base of each plant as previously, but instead of adding further ones, as growth continues, remove the first collar and substitute a stout cardboard tube 15 ins. long and about 3 ins. in diameter, held firm against the wind by a stake on either side. This makes a blanched stem about 15-17 ins. in length. Prizewinners have been produced by this method many times. Some growers have found 15-in. long field drainpipes a handy alternative to cardboard tubes. Walton Mammoth is a good variety for exhibition but Northumberland Long Blanch, is the general favourite, though unfortunately it does not withstand our Scottish winter successfully.

Celery is indigenous to Great Britain and grows luxuriantly in watery ditches. In its wild state it is unpalatable but the cultivated form is a useful vegetable both cooked and uncooked.

There are three cultivated types—white, pink or red, and self-blanching. Excellent varieties of the white type are Giant White, and Dobbie's Invincible White. Of the many pink or red kinds superb Pink and Major Clark's Solid Red are large solid-hearted varieties of good flavour. The self-blanching celery, Golden Self-blanching, is the variety generally grown, although it sometimes goes under the name of Paris Golden Self-blanching.

Celery is raised from seed sown from the middle of February onwards in a slightly heated glasshouse or frame, the seedlings being pricked out into a cold frame or under Dutch lights. The soil should be sterilised to prevent infection from blight after germination, and young plants are later transplanted into well-prepared trenches, 15 ins. wide and about 9 ins. deep, the bottom being well broken up and heavily manured with farmyard dung. Place two rows 10 ins. apart in each trench, water frequently, and, as celery is a gross feeder, an abundance of liquid manure must be applied. To obtain perfect plants for exhibition purposes the stems must be blanched or etiolated. First examine the plants and remove any side shoots growing from the base, then tie the leaves loosely together, placing stiff brown paper around each plant and fastening it with two strands of raffia, adding sufficient soil to keep the paper in position and to exclude light. In about a fortnight, add another band of paper, taking care not to cover the heart or the specimens will not be perfect in shape. A third band of paper later, which must not be tied too tightly, will usually be sufficient thoroughly to blanch the stems.

Celery can also be blanched by slipping a field-drain pipe over each plant when nearly full grown, packing some wood-wool around the top of each pipe to keep out the light, and adding sufficient soil round the pipes to keep them in position. For general purposes blanching may be done by simply earthing up the plants gradually with the soil removed to make the trench.

Self-blanching celery requires no earthing up, but if it is grown in frames, the sides of these give some additional blanching. Seed should be sown under glass in March, and the plants pricked out into boxes. After hardening off the plants must be planted out closely and will need no further blanching. Since this type is easily damaged by frost, try to use it by the end of October.

Marrows

Marrows are habitually thought of as vegetables but they are actually fruits since they contain seeds. There are two types—the trailing and the bush.

The former are usually grown on a good-sized, cube-shaped heap of decaying or decayed vegetable refuse in an odd out-of-the-way corner of the garden, but can be quite decorative. Although good results can be obtained without any special preparation, it is better to plant the young marrow in a compost of good old loam, with plenty of fibre and an admixture of decayed farmyard manure, placed in a good-sized hole in the top centre of the heap. After harvest at the season's end, the whole heap of vegetable refuse will be in a grand condition for digging into the kitchen garden ground to maintain or improve its fertility.

Bush marrows are usually grown in rows in the open garden and planted about 3½ ft. apart in the rows, but generally one row, or even a couple of plants, will meet amateur requirements. Ground enriched with decayed vegetable refuse is beneficial, therefore dig some into the ground along with some old farmyard manure, well in advance of planting.

Sow during April, preferably in a heated greenhouse, placing the seeds separately in 3-in. plant pots containing a good compost, and gradually hardening them off before planting outdoors when all danger of frost has passed. In Scotland this is generally in early June.

Vegetable marrows do not like droughts, so that an adequate, but not excessive, supply of moisture must be available. The young shoots should not be allowed to become overcrowded—spread them out and, if necessary, remove one or two.

Many people like to use vegetable marrows when they are young and relatively small; but others prefer them when they are a bit older and larger. Large marrows are required for show purposes, therefore it may be to the grower's advantage to leave one or two to become really well-developed for exhibition at the local horticultural show. Fortunately, pests and diseases are not common on vegetable marrows. The trailing varieties are usually catalogued as Long Green or Long White, and the bush types as Bush Green or Bush White.

Mushrooms

The cultivation of the edible mushroom (*Agaricus campestris* or *Psalliota campestria*) has long been a special feature of commercial horticulture, although it is not extensively grown by the amateur gardener in Scotland. Cultivated mushrooms are varieties of the wild species, and the two most commonly grown are the white and the brown, the former being most favoured by the public. They can be grown successfully in old pits, tunnels and beneath railway arches and out-of-doors during the summer months, but by using properly constructed, well ventilated, steam-heated sheds so that a constant temperature can be maintained, a good crop is assured throughout the year.

To overcome lack of floor space, construct beds on shelves placed at least 2 ft. above each other or use boxes placed on racks. Beds can also be made in a greenhouse, either under the staging or, if preferred, along the centre of the house. Frames may be used, although summer culture under glass is not recommended, as difficulty may be experienced in maintaining suitable atmospheric conditions.

The most important aspect of mushroom cultivation is the preparation of the medium through which the spawn must grow, since mushrooms, like other fungi thrive on nitrogen. Stable manure containing a good quantity of wheat straw is a good source, provided it has been subject to fermentation, a process which must not proceed too far, otherwise the nitrogen is given off as ammonia. Mixed cow and horse dung is usually too wet and stodgy and excludes oxygen when made into beds, but a friable compost containing fresh horse manure and a large proportion of fermenting wheat straw maintains an open texture and allows plenty of air to enter.

Thoroughly wet a quantity of wheat straw to break down the carbohydrate-forming cell membrane of the straw, add stable manure and allow to remain in a high heap for about a week. Test the degree of fermentation by thrusting in a long stick, and when this becomes

57

well-warmed, turn the heap, placing the outer portions in the centre and applying a few cans of water (using a fine rose to distribute it thoroughly) if there are signs of dryness during the process. Shake out all lumps to avoid greasiness, and rebuild the heap to about 5 ft. as compactly as possible. It will soon heat up again and may even reach a temperature of 140° F./60° C. After this the manure will have lost some of its rankness, needing to be turned only every third or fourth day, and put together in a smaller compass. Watch for signs of burning which produces a grey colour and excessive dryness and, if necessary, apply more water.

As soon as the heap becomes cooler, and the whole has been sweetened, the manure is ready for making into beds. It should be hot and steaming without any disagreeable smell of ammonia and of a uniform dark brown colour and if the straw, when twisted, is easily broken into relatively short pieces and the compost is sufficiently moist to bind together, it is ready to be made into beds.

Beds may be made at any time of the year, 8-10 ins. deep on the floor, on shelves, or in boxes. If the compost has its correct moisture content it may be put together and beaten down, first by treading and then by ramming with a wooden mallet until the surface is made level. It will then settle down another two inches. The heat will again rise in a few days, but will not become dangerously hot, and then fall, to about 75° F./24° C. The maximum temperature of a mushroom house should be 65° F./18° C., but the most suitable temperature is from 55°-60° F./13°-16° C. Very little artificial heat is necessary, and much more harm is done by the use of too much fire heat than by too little. Spawning the beds should be done when the temperature is 70°-75° F./21°-24° C. at 3 ins. below the surface.

To ascertain that the beds are the correct temperature for spawning use a soil-bed thermometer. Cartons or bottles of pure culture mushroom spawn should be bought instead of the old-fashioned cake type, and used dry or semi-dry. Break up the contents into pieces about the size of a walnut and insert in the bed about 2 ins. below the surface and 8 ins. apart in staggered formation, covering each piece with a handful of the compost. Firm over the whole surface with a flat board and do nothing more until after three weeks by which time the white thread-like mycelia or 'roots' of the spawn will be seen to have 'run' throughout the surface of the compost in the entire beds or boxes. A coating of about 1-1½ ins. of a loamy soil, which has been made alkaline by the addition of hydrated lime, should be placed on the surface, neatly patted down and the whole watered with tepid water through a fine rose watering can.

Soil from beneath the turf of a grass field is usually good for this purpose. The beds should be examined daily and if found to be dry on the surface given a gentle watering, but overwatering must be avoided for this is the greatest source of trouble and the cause of many good beds being ruined. The paths and walls must be damped down daily to maintain a uniform moist atmosphere.

Three or four weeks after casing with soil, the tiny pin-headed mushrooms will appear and will grow rapidly. Collect them before they become too large and flat. Always gather the crop carefully by twisting the mushrooms out of the beds, taking them out cleanly and never cutting them with a knife. After the crop has been removed the holes should be filled in with some of the soil used for casing, the beds watered with tepid water and the house fumigated with a good insecticide. In another few days more mushrooms will appear and cropping should continue for three to four months. The spent manure, when removed from the mushroom house, may be used in a potting mixture or dug into the vegetable garden. Well-grown mushrooms should be dome-shaped, medium in size, with flesh-pink gills. The stems should be solid and free from maggot marks.

Occasionally, a fungus disease known as fusarium appears in the casing soil, where the spores produce a very fine thread-like mycelium which competes with that of the mushroom spawn rendering it unable to produce a good crop. It is difficult to eradicate but steam sterilisation of the casing soil before use will cut out the risk of contamination, because the spores are destroyed at a temperature of 160° F./71° C.

Sciarid flies are the most dreaded insect pest. Eggs are laid around the growing mushrooms, in the compost, and the larvae hatch out in less than a week and tunnel their way through the stalks into the young mushroom caps, where they feed for about three weeks and in about another week transform into the adults.

Another pest, the phorid fly, gains access to mushroom beds by flying in through open doors and ventilators. Its larvae feed on the growing spawn in the compost and on the young mushrooms, travelling up the stems in much the same way as the sciarids, although the attack is seldom as serious. Should either pest cause trouble it is advisable to consult the local Horticulture Advisory Officer regarding control measures.

Onions

Onions, in one form or another, are relished by almost everyone and enormous quantities are imported annually from Egypt, Spain and Brittany. For home growers, many excellent varieties are on the market and most seedsmen have their own special selections and strains.

The most suitable soil is undoubtedly a deep loam enriched with farmyard manure or garden compost dug in during the autumn or early winter, but onions also do well on the heavier types of soil provided they are well prepared before sowing or planting. They require a long season of growth and, as they are very deep rooting plants, the land ought to be double dug, the surface being left rough and lumpy so that the frost may penetrate and pulverise it thoroughly.

In spring, during dry weather, well in advance of planting, fork in a dressing of poultry or pigeon manure and soot, breaking up the soil lumps to a depth of 6 ins. and, when fairly dry, tramp to make firm. Prepare the bed by raking to produce a fine tilth and ten days or so before sowing or planting, apply a complete fertiliser, such as National Growmore, consisting of equal parts of nitrogen, phosphoric acid and potassium at the rate of 3 lb. to 30 sq. yds. The surface should then be hoed to incorporate the fertiliser and destroy any weed seeds which may have germinated after raking.

Onions may be sown at least four times in the year—early out-of-doors at the end of February or early March, when soil and weather conditions are favourable, in August out-of-doors, in January under glass and outdoors in June to produce onion sets.

To secure early crops it is advisable to sow early in the open and, only fresh seed should be used since it loses its viability rather quickly. Under the Seeds Act a declaration as to germination is supplied on the packet with all purchases.

The end of February or early March, provided soil and weather permit, is a good time to sow in the open. Sow in shallow drills 12 ins. apart so that the seed is covered with a layer of soil half an inch in depth. Thinning-out the seedlings is usually necessary; to 3 ins. apart at first and later to 6-9 ins. according to the variety; use the thinnings for salads. When not sufficiently spaced, onion bulbs make room for themselves by pushing their neighbours aside, and properly matured plants will produce approximately 1 lb. to every foot run of the row. Certain varieties may be sown during the second week of August for producing bulbs which ripen in early summer. Since the young plants are overwintered out-of-doors, and must be transplanted to a well-prepared piece of ground in spring, a rich seedbed is unnecessary.

60

For exhibition purposes or the production of a heavy crop of good keeping bulbs for winter and spring use, onions must be raised under glass for planting outdoors later. Sowing is done during early January in well-drained seed boxes, the top soil being separated from the potsherds at the base by a layer of good fibrous loam. The night temperature of the house need not exceed 55° F./13° C. The recommended compost is two parts good fibrous loam, one part well decayed leaf mould or peat, one part stable manure, supplemented with sand to keep the mixture open, and to each bushel of the mixture add 1½ oz. of superphosphate and ¾ oz. of ground limestone. The mixture, which should be quite firm, should reach to within half an inch of the box top. Sow thinly, cover with some fine soil, press down firmly, and water in. When the seedlings are large enough to handle, use a small dibber to prick them out 2 ins. apart each way into other boxes, using the same compost but adding ¼ lb. of John Innes base manure and ¾ oz. ground limestone to each bushel. Grow the seedlings near the glass to get plenty of light and syringe frequently. After they have become well established, remove to a cold frame, giving plenty of air when the weather is favourable, to harden off the plants before their final transplanting during the first week in May. After a good watering, use a garden trowel to lift them, avoiding breakage of the roots, and plant out at 9 ins. intervals in rows 12 to 15 ins. apart in a bed already well prepared and marked off.

Each hole should be deep enough to take the young plant's roots straight down to their fullest extent, and the base of each stem should be one inch below the surface. Press the soil firmly about the roots, water if the weather is dry, and syringe overhead morning and evening until they become established. If there are no facilities for sowing under glass January-raised plants may be had from a nurseryman.

Where onion fly maggot has been troublesome on onions produced from young plants, it may be advisable to grow from sets, which are not usually attacked by this pest to the same extent. To produce these at home sow thickly on a poor soil and in a partly shaded situation during June, so that in the autumn the young bulbs or sets will be about the size of small marbles. They should then be lifted and dried and preserved during the winter. In spring, plant the sets at intervals of 4-6 ins. in rows 12-15 ins. apart in well-prepared ground. By this method, good bulbs are often grown, but as a rule they are smaller than those produced by transplanting young plants in spring. Nowadays most seedsmen and nurserymen are able to supply amateur gardeners with sets of the Stuttgarter Riesen variety which produces a flattish type of onion and, because of heat treatment for about 14 weeks in winter is also much less likely to 'bolt' or run to seed than home-produced onion-sets. While the plants are growing they ought to be fed with a compound fertiliser, such as National Growmore, applied at the rate of 3 lb. to 30 sq. yds. about the middle of June and afterwards hoed into the soil surface.

Occasionally maggots make their appearance on the plants and in a very short time will seriously damage the whole crop, but there are two methods of control. One is to dust the seed with 4% calomel dust before sowing or, alternatively, to dust the open drills before sowing. A second dusting may be necessary when the seedlings are about 2 ins. high.

The subsequent general cultivation consists mainly in keeping down weeds by regularly hoeing the surface, taking care not to damage the young bulbs. Autumn-sown onions which have been transplanted will be ready for lifting early in August, and spring-sown ones in September.

In a good season the bulbs will ripen naturally, nevertheless it is a good plan to bend the foliage, but not break it, just above the bulb, a week or two before lifting and the yellowing of the foliage will indicate when they are ready for harvesting. In unfavourable seasons, when heavy rains keep the plants growing into the autumn, they can be helped by lifting the bulbs slightly with a digging fork to rupture the roots and stop the water supply. In about ten days the bulbs can be pulled up and laid on a wire trellis or tied into bunches and suspended on pea trainers. Afterwards dry off the bulbs thoroughly in a glasshouse until the outer scale leaves are quite brittle, when they can be re-tied and suspended from the roof of an outhouse.

Salad onions, or syboes, can usually be had by sowing Silver-Skinned Bunching or White Lisbon fairly thinly in July, and leaving them in the seed bed for pulling green from the following April to June. No thinning is necessary; just fork up and pull as required.

Onions for pickling—The Queen and Silver-skinned Pickling are typical varieties—should be sown broadcast very thickly during April, as it is not desired to produce large bulbs, and the land rolled to press the seed into a firm bed. Cultivation consists entirely in keeping down weeds.

For spring sowing and as a general crop James's Long-keeping is still popular and is one of the very best keepers. The old Ailsa Craig and Kelsae varieties are popular for exhibition. The latter is a good keeper, and is oval or pear-shaped with straw-brown outer skin and white flesh.

Peas

The pea, whether eaten in a fresh green or ripe dried state, is very nutritious and although it is generally admitted that varieties are perhaps too numerous, new ones are eagerly sought after, even when they may not be very distinct from some already known. Seedsmen generally classify peas according to their season of maturing, first early, second early, maincrop and late maincrop, but even so they mention those which have round seeds. To have early peas, ready for picking in June, it is better to sow round-seeded varieties. They are generally hardier than those which have wrinkled seeds. The crop is usually ready for picking roughly fifteen weeks from time of sowing in spring. Meteor and Kelvedon Viscount are round-seeded early dwarf varieties; Little Marvel, Kelvedon Wonder, Laxton's Progress and Peter Pan are hardy and prolific dwarf wrinkle-seeded varieties, 18-30 ins. high. Second early and maincrop varieties are Admiral Beatty, Kelvedon Monarch, Onward and Senator, which reach 30-42 ins. The late varieties, Lord Chancellor and Gladstone grow to about 3-4 ft. in height. Always buy seed of good stock, even if it is more expensive.

A rich, friable loam which is neither acid or alkaline is best for the pea family and if the soil does not contain sufficient calcareous matter to make it so, it should be added in the form of ground lime or chalk. The ground should be well drained and the surface left crumbly, so that rain water can pass freely through it. Sow the seed in ground that has been well manured for a previous crop, e.g. after a crop of leeks or onions, but if the ground lacks humus, some well-rotted manure or decayed vegetable refuse from the compost heap, dug in well in advance of sowing, will help to retain moisture at the roots. Sulphate of potash at the rate of 2 lb. and superphosphate at the rate of 3 lb. to 30 yds. should be mixed with the top layer of soil, some ten days before sowing. Nitrogenous fertilisers are unnecessary, especially when the soil is in good heart, since peas and all pod-bearing crops have the power, through the bacteria in the nodules on their roots, to take up free atmospheric nitrogen and turn it into nitrogenous compounds on which the plants feed, and this, in addition to the nitrogen obtained from the soil, is more than ample for their needs. For early crops, seed can sometimes be sown in

January but is generally better to start sowing about mid February and continue at intervals for successional crops until the first week in June. The first few sowings should be dwarf early varieties, followed by taller second-early and maincrop varieties, while for the last sowings, a good plan is to use dwarf varieties once again. The distance between the rows of peas should be equal to the height of the variety, i.e. 2 ft. between rows for a pea variety 2 ft. high and 4 ft. between rows for a variety 4 ft. high. The best direction for the rows is north and south. When mice are troublesome, coat the seeds before sowing with a little red-lead, or set traps in the neighbourhood.

Before sowing, rake the ground level, set the garden line, and take out a flat-bottomed drill about 6-8 ins. broad and 2 ins. deep with a broad draw-hoe or spade. Avoid thick sowing and consequent over-crowding. For early sowing, one pint of seed will serve for a row about 50-60 ft. long, and for maincrop and late varieties the same quantity may be allowed for 80 ft. After sowing, the soil must be returned over the peas and lightly firmed down with the back of the rake held in a vertical position. A light surface sprinkling of ground lime afterwards will prevent birds digging out the seeds. In late spring, when the soil is dry, it is a good plan to soak the seeds for about 12 hours before sowing. This sets up a chemical change and hastens germination. When the plants are well-developed, mulching with lawn mowings or spent hops is valuable and, along with good preparation of the land prior to sowing, should render watering unnecessary even in the driest weather. When a row of peas is sown, mark off the distance to the next row to be sown two weeks or so later.

Branch stakes can be put in position to support the growing plants when they are only a few inches high, and placed along both sides of the rows in such a way that an open space is retained at the top between the rows of stakes. Alternatively, use 4 in. mesh wire netting, or cord netting, 30-36 ins. wide stretched along the rows and held in position by 1½-in. sq. posts driven into the ground 2 yds. apart along each side of the rows. When peas are well up and staked, they need no further attention, other than an occasional hoeing to conserve moisture and keep down weeds. Gathering the crop should be done carefully, and as soon as it is fit for use.

It is essential that pests and diseases be carefully diagnosed and gardeners are advised, when in doubt, to consult horticultural officers of the College of Agriculture. Look out for pea and bean weevil (see Beans).

Pea thrips in some seasons cause considerable damage to crops

Beet, Housewives' Choice.

Turnips, Dobie's Model White.

Carrots, Tip Top.

A well-shaped 11-year old Victoria plum—the rule with plums is to leave well alone as far as pruning is concerned.

Tomatoes: a really fine truss.

A vine in spring: two shoots grow from each joint, but the weaker one should be pinched out.

by feeding on the growing shoots, foliage, blossom and developing pods. In severe attacks, the leaves and pods show a mottled, silvery appearance and the latter are often distorted and fail to form seeds. D.D.T. insecticide and derris dust will give satisfactory control if applied before flowering. Recently an insecticide called Hexyl was used with excellent results on a row of the exhibition variety Achievement, which grows to 5-6 ft., and the long pods carried 9-10 peas per pod. After early spraying when thrips were seen on a few growing points of the plants at the same time as the appearance of the first flower buds, no pods had a mottled or silvery appearance and no live thrips were found.

Pea mildew is common, more especially when the plants are in a sheltered position, but it only becomes severe at the end of the season on late varieties, and spraying with lime sulphur or liver of sulphur will help to keep it in check.

Potatoes

The potato is perhaps more generally grown than any other vegetable and it is rare to find even the smallest garden without at least one or two rows. Unfortunately potatoes are susceptible to a number of virus diseases which reduce the crop, and it is, therefore, important never to save one's own seed unless every plant is free from infection. Using a certified stock ensures healthy plants and a good crop of sound tubers.

It is an offence to plant non-immune varieties of second early and maincrop kinds in gardens whatever the area, owing to the danger of wart disease, although first early varieties may be planted under a general licence provided the area is not scheduled. Wart disease causes a reduction in yield and, if an outbreak does occur, notification is compulsory under the provisions of the Destructive Insect and Pests Act of the Department of Agriculture for Scotland.

Potatoes are divided into first early, second early, early maincrop and late maincrop varieties according to the time they are ready to harvest. As an early variety, it is best to plant a few rows of Di Vernon (immune to wart disease) for, if sprouted and planted out early in March in a sheltered sunny border, they can be lifted in about ten weeks time, provided weather conditions favour their growth. The habit is dwarf, the tubers flat, kidney-shaped, with purple markings around the eyes, and the quality is excellent. It is also a good variety for exhibition purposes. Duke of York (non-immune) is another good early variety and has thick, kidney-shaped, yellow-fleshed tubers. Many still grow this under its synonym Midlothian Early. Arran Pilot (immune) one of the many Arran varieties raised and introduced by the late Donald McKelvie, Lamlash, is long and oval with white skin and flesh, and is fairly dwarf and spreading. It is a good cropper but its cooking quality is only fair. Home Guard (immune) is another good early variety with white, oval tubers. Catriona is a good variety to follow the earlies. It is immune and has a tuber which resembles Di Vernon in shape and colour. Dunbar Rover (immune), is a second early, producing oval-shaped tubers with white skin and flesh, and is a tall upright grower fairly resistant to blight, as well as a good keeping variety of excellent flavour. An early maincrop potato still popular is Kerr's Pink (immune), a Banffshire variety, with round, pink tubers and a lovely white texture when cooked. Another good variety with tubers very like Kerr's Pink is Redskin (immune). Golden Wonder (immune) produces shapely kidney tubers, but it is not a particularly heavy cropper unless sprouted before planting and grown on heavily manured ground. In Scotland it is regarded as *the* potato for quality, and the tubers will keep in store until the following summer, and are very resistant to common scab. Finally, Dunbar Standard (immune) is one of the latest varieties to mature, with oval tubers, white skin and flesh, and has excellent cropping and cooking qualities.

This selection does not by any means exhaust the number of good varieties, and seedsmen's catalogues give abundant evidence of others which might be considered just as good.

Potatoes are frequently referred to as 'roots', but for a botanical point of view, they are really swollen underground stems, correctly called tubers. Preferably plant whole tubers, but should they be cut each piece must have one or two buds, or eyes, which grow from the axil of small scale-like leaves.

Success in potato culture depends greatly on the treatment of tubers to be used for seed. Every grower is familiar with the practice of setting up seed tubers for sprouting during January or early February. It is advisable to set up the tubers of early as well as late varieties so that they will produce short, stocky sprouts. Place the tubers or sets closely together eye-end uppermost, in shallow trays on a greenhouse shelf where it is light and sufficiently warm to exclude frost. Air and light harden the sprouts—the first produced are usually the strongest—and induce strong vigorous green shoots on the tubers which will not easily break off. By doing this the grower can afford to wait a week or two for suitable weather conditions before planting them out in the garden.

The potato is a sunloving plant and appreciates well-aerated soil so that no care or trouble should be spared in providing this. Deep, warm, well-drained friable soil, such as the lighter loams which contain a fair amount of organic matter, are most suited to this crop, and the ground must be thoroughly worked to a good depth by digging and applying farmyard manure or compost in the autumn. When farmyard manure is used, chemical fertilisers are not so essential but it is often more profitable to use a moderate dressing of a specially prepared potato fertiliser, which contains a fair proportion of potash (necessary for starch development) in addition to the dung.

One stone of seed, or sets, is needed for approximately 90 ft. of a row and the usual time to plant is between the end of March and early April. Potatoes should be grown in ridges and for early and second early varieties, allow 24 ins. between the rows and 12 ins. between the sets. Early and late maincrops require 27 ins. between the rows with the sets placed 12-15 ins. apart, according to variety. One method of planting is to mark off the ground in lines across the break, making holes 4-5 ins. deep with a trowel at regular intervals along the rows and placing one tuber in each hole. By returning and working parallel to the first row, the soil from the second row of holes can be used to fill those in the previous row and cover the potatoes.

A better method is to set the line for the respective rows and open a drill 4-5 ins. deep for each one with a spade or draw hoe, the potatoes being planted in the base of the drill at the proper distances and then covered with soil to leave a reasonably level surface. Always place the tubers on their sides with the sprouts pointing along the drill. When the shoots of the early planted varieties appear above ground the gardener should be constantly on the watch, as they are very tender and at the least sign of frost a little soil should be drawn over them.

As the season advances and the rows are distinctly seen, Dutch hoe the ground to destroy weeds. When the haulm is 6-8 ins. high, the ground between the rows should be well forked to loosen the soil, and the plants earthed-up to form ridges, taking care not to injure or expose the young tubers.

The early varieties are normally lifted for use whilst the shaws or haulms are still green. Crops required for storing are lifted when the haulm turns brown and the tuber skins are set and firm, but make sure every tuber is removed as those left may cause trouble as ground keepers the following year. When the tubers are dry, they should be stored in clamps or pits 3 ft. wide in an open, dry position, on the soil surface. Pile them up on the base of the clamp in a long ridge-shaped heap covering them first with a six-inch layer of dry straw, and then 6-8 ins. of soil, smoothing the surface with the back of a spade. As the soil is removed from the ground adjacent to the pit or clamp, a trench is formed at its base which drains off water and keeps the tubers dry. Shafts with wisps of straw should be left in the soil covering the apex of the clamp to provide ventilation and to prevent over-heating.

When land is too frequently cropped with potatoes it becomes 'potato sick' and the ground is unable to carry a full crop to maturity. If poorly developed, yellowish, dwarf plants are observed during the growing season lift one or two very carefully with a digging fork, examine the roots and if yellow, red or brown pin-head-sized balls are found on them in quantity then potato-root eelworm is the cause. The balls are the eelworm cysts, i.e. the dead females, and they contain a vast number of eggs. These cysts remain in the ground for at least three years, often longer, and will survive wet, drought, and frost. If potatoes are planted there again during the next three or four years the eggs in the cysts will hatch and the young eelworms invade the roots which consequently become unable to absorb sufficient food material from the soil and the plant's growth and tuber development suffer considerably. It is advisable not to put eelworm infested potato plant roots on the compost heap, and since tomatoes are very susceptible to eelworm, never take soil from potato ground for tomato-growing, unless it has been steam sterilised.

Potato scab is a fungoid disease which causes small 'scab-like' or 'wart-like' pustules on the skin of the tubers and spoils their appearance. Sometimes relatively slight, the trouble can be severe. The disease develops more readily when the soil contains sufficient lime to make it alkaline—potatoes like a slight acidity. To prevent its occurrence, never plant sets or seed tubers showing signs of infection. It is also a good plan to open continuous drills when planting and place an inch-deep layer of horticultural peat along the bottom of each. Plant the sets on the peat and cover them with another dressing of peat before filling the drill with soil.

Rarer Vegetables

The vegetable garden usually has space for some of the rarer kinds of vegetable, but it should not be forgotten that they need the same generous treatment and cultivation as the rest. The following are a suggested selection:

Chicory (*Cichorium intybus*) is a hardy perennial chiefly used as a salad plant, but the leaves may also be used as cattle fodder. The young leaves are green and rather bitter, but blanching in due course corrects this. The large fleshy roots are sometimes dried and roasted, and mixed with coffee.

To allow the tap roots to grow down perpendicularly, the ground must be double dug and well pulverised before the seed is sown in April and May in rows 15 ins. apart. The seedlings should be thinned out to 8 ins. between each, and towards the end of November the plants should be carefully lifted and heeled in at the foot of a north wall or stored in boxes. Roots begin to sprout soon after the plants are put into store and, about three weeks before they are needed for the table, a number should be placed in a deep box of soil with another close-fitting box inverted over them to exclude light and thereby blanch the leaves. The box should then be placed either on or under a greenhouse staging, and the plants watered from time to time to keep them growing.

Chinese artichoke (*Stachys tuberifera*) is a welcome winter vegetable. The small spiral tubers should be about 3 ins. long and almost an inch thick at their widest part. They need well drained and moderately rich soil, and should be planted during March at 12-in. intervals in rows 1½ ft. apart. They grow to about 18 ins. and their many shoots should be thinned out, allowing only the stronger ones to develop. Since they love moisture, they should be watered occasionally with weak liquid manure if the soil is dry and light. The white tubers are very brittle, and when they are lifted no small pieces of root must be allowed to remain in the soil, as they will otherwise give trouble as 'ground keepers' the next year. They are best boiled for about twenty minutes, then fried in deep fat until brown and served with grated cheese.

The chive (*Allium schoenoprasum*) is a hardy perennial and its leaves are used in soups and salads instead of young onions. Chives will grow in almost any soil, and are propagated by a division of crowns in spring or autumn, when they should be planted out in small groups. The oftener the leaves are cut the more tender the growth. In the autumn a few crowns should be lifted, potted and placed in the greenhouse to give a salad supply during the winter.

Endive (*Cichorium endivia*) is a hardy annual useful as a substitute for lettuce. The Green Curled is for summer and autumn use, and Green Batavian for a late autumn and winter supply. To ensure a succession over a long period, sow the former in late May and the latter in July and early August.

Prepare the ground by digging in plenty of decayed farmyard manure, then draw drills 12 ins. apart, and sow thinly, later thinning the seedlings to 12-in. intervals. Water liberally in dry weather. Early sowings should be blanched by the leaves being bunched together and then loosely tied. Plants from August sowings should be lifted and replanted during October in a cold frame, and will provide blanched hearts over a long period. Ventilate freely and shade a few of the plants at a time by placing a piece of sacking over them.

Garlic (*Allium sativum*) is useful in soups and stews. It succeeds in a warm, light but rich soil and is propagated by separating the cloves of the bulbs and planting them out at 6-in. intervals in rows 1 ft. apart in March, covering them with 2 ins. of soil. As the leaves yellow in autumn, the plants should be taken up, dried, tied into bundles and hung in an airy place.

Kohl Rabi (*Brassica oleracea Caulo-rapa*) has a flavour which is between that of the turnip and the cabbage, in fact the top part of the stem looks like a turnip. It is very hardy and resists drought.

Sow in drills 15 ins. apart in April and May, and thin out the young plants to 8-in. intervals when they are 1 in. high. An occasional soaking with water will make the crop more tender, and it should be harvested when the turnip-like swellings reach the size of a cricket ball, since if left until maturity they are inclined to toughen and coarsen. Keep the stems well above the soil during cultivation and hoe frequently. For general purposes Early White is the best early variety: Early Purple is rather more coarse and fibry. The leaves are used in the same way as spinach, and the roots, a good source of vitamin C, can be grated in salads or thinly sliced as a cucumber substitute.

Sugar Peas or Mange-tout (*Pisum sativum saccharatum*) are eaten pods and seeds together, in the same way as French beans. They are easily grown, but need a deeply dug soil well enriched at the top with plenty of humus. Decayed organic matter may be used instead of farmyard manure, provided that it is supplemented with fertilisers which supply phosphate and potash rather than nitrogen, since like the others of the pea family, sugar peas manufacture their own supplies of the latter.

First sowings are made in February and successional ones at intervals up to the end of May. Scatter the seed thinly in a 2-3-in. deep drill, cover with soil and make firm. In width the drill should be about the breadth of a spade, but the distance between the rows must not be less than the height of the plant. Twiggy branches of appropriate height should be inserted in the soil on each side of the row to provide support.

Root Vegetables

Root vegetables are a product of the summer season, yet are easily preserved for use during winter. Tap-rooted beet, carrot, parsnip and salsify are usually long and tapering, but turnip, swede, celeriac and globe beet mature, more or less, on the surface.

Sow root crops on a site well manured the previous year, but never on freshly dunged ground, since this will encourage the production of forked and coarse specimens. A compound fertiliser such as National Growmore, containing equal quantities of nitrogen, phosphoric acid and potassium, should be applied 2-4 oz. per sq. yd. at frequent intervals during the early stages of growth.

Beet are either round or long-rooted. The original Egyptian turnip-rooted variety was of coarse texture, but the Detroit Globe type produces globular roots growing very near the surface and easily visible, and the flesh of a good strain should have a deep blood-red hue. Sown at the end of April, they will mature during July. A few varieties have tapering roots about 12 ins. long and deep crimson, although Dobbie's Purple has a deep purple colour. Bell's Non-bleeding has deep red foliage and a broad-shouldered, gradually tapering root. To produce beet for winter use and storing, sow very thinly during early May in drills ¾ in. deep and 15 ins. apart and thin out the seedlings to about 8 ins. between each as soon as they are large enough to handle. Store the roots during the winter in a frost-proof shed among dry sand or peat, or pitted outdoors like potatoes.

Fresh carrots can be obtained during the greater part of the year. Amsterdam Forcing and Early Market can be sown in a hot bed in a frame during January for pulling during May and June, and successional sowings of an early variety such as Early Horn or Early Nantes may be sown out-of-doors in a warm border. If the soil is unfavourable, i.e. of the heavy type, and clean long roots of varieties such as James's Scarlet Intermediate or St. Valery are desired, then it is well worth while to make deep and reasonably wide-topped holes with a crowbar filling them firmly with fine soil to which fine, builder's sand has been added. Sow two or three seeds on top of each hole, cover them with about a ½ in. of fine soil, and thin out to one seedling per hole. The main crop of an intermediate variety should be sown in drills 12 ins. apart and ½ in. deep in March and

71

April to give a succession. The plants need thinning to 4-6 ins. apart, as they remain in the ground for a long season and require ample room to develop.

Carrots are susceptible to the attacks of the carrot fly maggot (*Psila rosae*). The female fly lays eggs around the tiny plants and the maggots hatch out and eat into the small roots. Frequent applications of lawn mowings between the rows throughout the growing season are occasionally an effective preventive, but the best control measure against this pest, and one both simple and cheap, is to treat the seed with carrot seed dressing before sowing. Carrots may be stored in the same way as beet.

The two most commonly grown varieties of parsnip are the Student and Hollow Crown. It is quite usual to see parsnip roots of extraordinary length at exhibitions, measuring as much as 36 ins. from crown to tip, handsomely tapered and of a light yellow colour. These are grown under special cultural conditions, in prepared holes as for carrots. Unfortunately, it is now rare to find many gardens in which parsnips are grown, except for exhibition purposes. Some people find the flesh too sweet, but if fresh roots are scraped, partly cooked and then roasted in deep fat, they are as delicious as they are nourishing. It is usual to make one sowing early in March when soil and weather conditions are favourable. The seeds should be sown in drills about 1 in. deep in rows 15 ins. apart. Thin the seedlings when they are large enough to handle, allowing 9 ins. between the plants in the rows. The roots should be left in the ground and lifted as required, those still remaining in early spring may then be lifted and stored in dry sand or peat, to maintain an extended supply.

Salsify is a hardy biennial, which was probably introduced from the Mediterranean area. The white-fleshed root, when scraped and soaked in a little vinegar, cooked in fat and served with parsley sauce, makes an appetising dish. Plants are easily raised from seed sown out of doors in drills 15 ins. apart, and about 1 in. deep, in a rich soil not recently manured. Seedlings should be thinned out to 8 ins. apart, and the roots kept in the ground all winter and lifted as required.

The garden turnip is soft, sweet and pleasantly flavoured, and a supply over a long period can be had by growing a number of varieties and by making small sowings at three-weekly intervals throughout the spring and summer. Early Milan or Snowball may be sown outdoors in early April in drills ¾ in. deep drawn 15 ins. apart and, to obtain quicker growth, can be covered with cloches. Thin the seedlings to about 5 ins. apart. Sowings of Golden Ball or

Orange Jelly, in rows 15 ins. apart, will ensure an autumn supply. Seedlings are thinned out from 6 to 8 ins. apart in the rows.

The swede turnip, which is much hardier than the white and yellow garden turnips, is especially useful during the winter and spring months. Sow early in May in drills 22 ins. apart, on rich, well worked soil and thin out to 9 to 10 ins. between each. To protect the crop in winter, the roots may be lifted and pitted like potatoes or soil may be drawn around the roots in December.

To give some stimulus to young turnips and swedes, a dressing of a complete fertiliser, hoed in between the rows greatly assists growth and helps the plants to develop roots rapidly.

Celeriac is a form of celery but has a swollen root like a turnip, though by no means so handsome in appearance, at the base of the leaf stems. The tuber-like roots are excellent when cooked, washed, sliced and mixed with salads, or used to flavour soup and gravy. Sow in March in a shallow pan or box, place in heat, and when the seedlings are about 3 ins. high, prick off into a cold frame, and, when hardened off, plant out into a warm border at 12-in. intervals in rows 2 ft. apart. Water liberally, giving occasional applications of liquid manure, and keep down the weeds. After roots are fully grown store them for winter use.

Salad Crops

Fresh vegetable salads are popular all the year round, but are in greatest demand during spring and summer. They are not only most refreshing, but supply many vitamins often otherwise lacking in present day menus. The man with the small garden is too apt, if he introduces salad crops, to be content to grow only a few lettuces, yet many other choice plants take up little space and need very little attention if the correct varieties are chosen and the soil is properly prepared.

Vegetables grown for salads should be tender, need not be large and, owing to their quick growth, every part of the plant may be utilised, so that there is practically no waste. They include lettuce, endive, onions, radish, sorrel, celery, mustard and cress.

Lettuce, the main salad ingredient, is fortunately easily grown, but to obtain crisp, succulent-hearted plants, a rich soil is essential. Make small sowings of suitable varieties at intervals in a cold frame during early spring, and out-of-doors during late spring and summer.

Plants raised in a frame may be transferred to the open border when large enough to handle, and those raised out-of-doors thinned out to about 4 ins. apart when they have made their second leaves. When the plants have advanced in growth—to five or six leaves—they should be thinned-out again, this time to 8-10 ins. apart, and a number of these second thinnings may be lifted carefully and transplanted 8-10 ins. between each, in rows 12-15 ins. apart, in a well prepared bed. Lettuce may also be grown as a catch crop between rows of tall peas which may be separated by 5-6 ft.

Soil moisture is important in the cultivation of lettuce, since if it is insufficient the plants fail to heart, or may be so checked in growth that they 'bolt' or flower prematurely and run to seed. The retention of moisture can be greatly improved by applying decayed farmyard manure to the soil well in advance of sowing or planting, and by Dutch hoeing to form a soil mulch. In addition, a supplementary dressing of a compound fertiliser, such as Growmore, or a mixture of 1½ lb. of sulphate of ammonia, 3 lb. of superphosphate and 2 lb. of sulphate of potash to 30 sq. yds., is advisable. Apply ten days before sowing or transplanting, and hoe or rake it into the soil surface.

The most satisfactory summer and autumn varieties of lettuce are All the Year Round, a medium green, large plant, which forms a firm heart of good flavour; Webb's Wonderful, with large dark green foliage, curled at the margins, makes a large, firm, globular heart; Trocadero Improved, medium to large with medium green leaves, a firm heart and slightly yellow in colour; Favourite, a fairly large, compact plant with light green puckered foliage, has a crisp heart; Continuity is of excellent quality, although not a popular commercial variety on account of the colour of the leaves, which are brown or purple-tinted.

Endive is another useful salad plant and, to produce a continuous supply, sow during June to early August in a warm border in shallow drills 12 ins. apart, thinning out the seedlings to the same distance in the rows. Water frequently and blanch the leaves by covering a few plants at a time with empty inverted flower pots, one to each plant.

Good varieties are Green-curled, small and delicate with moss-like foliage; and the Round-leaved Batavian, one of the most prolific. Plants lifted with their roots intact and placed in a cold frame will keep in good condition for many weeks.

Radishes grow slowly in poor soil, becoming almost indigestible, and for the best quality the soil must be moderately rich and deeply dug. They need a shady, cool part of the garden, and if sown every ten days or so throughout the spring and summer months, and kept well supplied with water, little trouble will be found in keeping up a

74

supply. Sow thinly, either broadcast or in shallow drills, as good roots cannot be produced when the plants are overcrowded. There are many excellent kinds. French Breakfast, a round-rooted type with red and white tips, and Sparkler, an olive-shape-rooted variety, red with white tips, are splendid. For winter use the Black Spanish, though tending to be coarse in flavour, is sometimes grown. After sowing in July, take up the roots in autumn and store in sand.

Mustard and cress add piquancy to any salad. For the greater part of the year, they usually give better results for the amateur grower if sown in boxes and placed in a greenhouse or a frame. To have the cress ready for use at the same time as the mustard, it must be sown three days earlier. During summer mustard and cress may be grown outdoors in a sheltered place. Aim at quick, free growth and sow frequently, thickly and broadcast every few days through the season, on very fine and level soil. Do not cover the seed with soil, but simply water it in and press it down on the soil surface with a piece of board, so that the seedlings come up free from grit.

If a good strain of sorrel is grown, propagation may be done readily by division of the crowns. The round-leaved and the broad-leaved French are fine types for general culture. In spring divide a small portion of the plants. Under these conditions a vigorous growth is maintained and by halving young plants much finer leaves are procured. Sorrel can also be grown by sowing in the spring in rows 12 ins. apart, thinning out the seedlings 6 ins. between each. Much valued on the Continent, this plant will give a constant supply of tender leaves throughout the year if it is given cold frame protection.

Green onions—judiciously used—are most useful and important for the salad bowl. In Brittany, the peasants almost live on them and attribute their good health to eating them uncooked, but seasoned with salt and pepper and a dash of vinegar.

Prepare the ground by digging and manuring in the spring, sow during July in rows 1 ft. apart and encourage quick free growth. Silver Skinned Bunching and White Lisbon are good varieties for the purpose and should be ready for use during the early spring and summer of the following year.

Celery (see Leeks and Celery) is a fairly hardy plant which occupies a high rank as a salad plant.

Tomatoes

Over three hundred years ago four varieties of tomato, or 'Love Apples' as they were more frequently known, were introduced from

South America, but though long grown ornamentally, the fruit did not become important as a food crop until this century.

Although the commercial grower sows tomatoes in late November and December to produce crops from May onwards, the amateur with a heated greenhouse will be well advised to delay until February, time enough to have fruit throughout the summer and autumn. If only a cool greenhouse is available buy young plants in May.

Sow in a light, sandy compost such as that recommended by the John Innes Institution—two parts, by bulk, of sterilised medium loam, one part granulated peat and one coarse river sand, adding to each bushel of the mixture $1\frac{1}{2}$ oz. of superphosphate and $\frac{3}{4}$ oz. of ground limestone or chalk. Fill a clean and well-drained seed box or pan with compost to within 1 in. of the rim, pressing it down moderately firm and water with tepid water through a fine rose. The seeds may be sown very thinly broadcast or placed singly about $1\frac{1}{2}$ ins. apart each way and then covered with fine, sifted soil, using a pane of glass and a sheet of paper over each seed box or pan to retain moisture and exclude light. Do not keep the temperature too low— try to maintain a night temperature of 55-60° F./13-16° C. When the seedlings appear, remove the paper and glass covers, and place the pans near the glass where they will get plenty of light. Before they become overcrowded, they should be transferred singly to 3-in. pots, containing a compost of seven parts, by bulk, of sterilised medium loam, three parts granulated peat, and two parts coarse river sand. To each bushel of the mixture add $1\frac{1}{2}$ oz. hoof and horn meal, $1\frac{1}{2}$ oz. superphosphate, $\frac{3}{4}$ oz. sulphate of potash, and $\frac{3}{4}$ oz. ground limestone or chalk. Water carefully, give plenty of light, and when the pots are filled with roots, set the plants in their fruiting quarters in the specially prepared and sterilised greenhouse soil or in 5-in. pots, as an intermediate repotting, using the same compost as before, but a little rougher in texture. When the first flower truss appears the plants must be transferred to their fruiting quarters, having sterilised the greenhouse soil well in advance. Ready sterilised soil, or special tomato composts containing this in combination with appropriate fertilisers, can be purchased. In any case never use soil in which potatoes have been grown since it may contain potato root eelworm, which is also a menace to tomatoes.

Water the young plants on the day before planting out, and, if they are to be grown in the greenhouse, ensure that the soil has a temperature of 57° F./14° C., and keep the house closed for a day or two afterwards. They should be set 18-20 ins. apart each way and individually supported by a short stake; later a string is tied loosely

first to the base of each plant and then to an overhead wire for training. Tying the plant to the string at intervals is generally only
necessary when fruit trusses have developed.

If there are no facilities for growing the plants in the greenhouse
soil, then pot them into 10-12 in. pots with a compost of sterilised
soil, rotted farmyard manure, and John Innes fertiliser base, and
place them on the greenhouse staging. Put a little of this prepared
compost over the usual plant-pot drainage system of crocks, then
cover the young plant's ball of roots with it, but leaving room for
subsequent top-dressings of the same mixture as the plant develops.
Again staking or other support is necessary. The same compost may
also be used in bottomless 9-in. whalehide pots, placed at appropriate
distances apart on an asbestos sheet, slightly tilted at one end to
facilitate drainage and covered by a 3-in. layer of furnace ashes, the
latter being no larger than $\frac{1}{4}$ in. Water both the compost and the
ashes, especially in the early stages.

Whichever method of cultivation is adopted, each plant should
be confined to a single stem by pinching out the young side growths
since fruit trusses are not, as generally supposed, produced in the
leaf axils but between leaves on the main stem. When they almost
reach the top of the greenhouse remove the main growing point, and
never allow them to suffer from lack of water. If an excessive amount
of foliage is produced, remove a few of the terminal leaflets near the
base to admit the sun's rays, but remember that the leaves are the
breathing organs of the plant and they also manufacture its food—
the heavier the crop of fruit, the greater the quantity of foliage
necessary. Give plenty of air during the height of the day in summer
and water early in the day. To assist the fruit to set and to avoid
'dry-set' lightly spray the plants overhead when in flower with tepid
water every morning between ten and noon, to produce a humid
atmosphere. Setting can also be helped by hand-pollination of the
flowers with a camel hair brush or a rabbit's tail tied to a short stick.
Failure to set fruit is generally due to the house atmosphere being too
dry during the day, although a damp, stagnant atmosphere during
the night may encourage disease on the leaves, therefore a little
ventilation at the top of the house should be allowed if the outside
temperature is not too cold.

When the plants produce small rootlets on or near the soil surface
it is important to top-dress them, and, provided that the soil is moist,
nothing gives better results than an application of decomposed
farmyard manure 2 ins. deep. Ensure that the house is well ventilated
day and night for at least a week afterwards, otherwise the ammonia

given off from the manure may scorch the foliage. Chemical general fertilisers such as National Growmore may be applied at frequent intervals as a top-dressing at 1 oz. per sq. yd. and will help to swell and colour the fruit. Plants growing in 10-in. pots require top dressings at frequent intervals with the same compost in which they are growing.

All fully swollen green fruits produced towards the end of September, will ripen and colour beautifully if removed from the plants, wrapped in cotton-wool and placed in a warm cupboard.

Ailsa Craig, Moneymaker, and Market King are excellent varieties, and Potentate, a short-jointed variety which crops well, and Vetomold are resistant to the leaf mould disease. The best yellow varieties, which for flavour are equal to the red, are probably Golden Perfection and Golden Sunbeam.

Physiological disorders of tomatoes are 'blossom-end rot', 'blotchy ripening', 'green-backs' and 'dry-set' of fruit. Blossom-end rot, which shows as a brownish depression at the end of the tomato

The results of tomato dry-set and blossom-end rot.

fruit furthest from the stalk, is usually due to the plants being too dry at the root. Blotchy-ripening and green-backs are usually the result of erratic feeding, and to keep the carbohydrates balanced in the plants, extra dressings of sulphate of potash should be given in dull weather, and of nitrogen (in the form of sulphate of ammonia) in bright weather, both at the rate of 1 oz. per sq. yd. of greenhouse border soil surface.

Dry-set is usually due to too dry an atmosphere during flowering, which prevents the pollen doing its job efficiently and causes small poorly developed fruits to appear on the trusses. Should a truss carry some normal-sized tomatoes along with very small undeveloped specimens, dry-set is the cause. The various root-rots or toe-rots are generally the result of growing the plants in unsterilised soil. The foliage fungus disease, *Cladosporium fulvum* is usually encouraged by insufficient ventilation. Spotted wilt virus disease, causing dark coloured concentric rings and mottling of the leaves, may be harboured on some ornamental flowering plants, such as schizanthus, growing in the vicinity of the tomatoes. The indiscriminate mixing of different kinds of flowering plants and other crops in the same greenhouse as tomatoes should be avoided.

In flower in May, showing the rapid formation of runners.

STRAWBERRIES

Inter-row cultivation the modern way.

Cutting away torn roots with sloping cut

PLANTING A FRUIT TREE

Spreading the roots before filling in.

A new use for nylon stockings.

·3·

Fruit

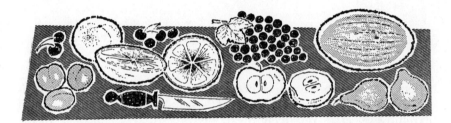

Planting trees 82. Greenfly 85. Cross-pollination 87. Budding 89. Fungoid diseases 92. Winter pruning 95. Storage 98. TOP FRUITS —Apples 100. Pears 104. Plums 107. SOFT FRUITS—Blackberries 110. Blackcurrants 113. Gooseberries 118. Raspberries 121. Strawberries: in the open garden 124; under glass 125; virus diseases 128. Vines 130.

F

·3·

Fruit

Planting Trees

SUCH GREAT PROGRESS has been made in the technique of fruit-growing that the modern orchard is usually composed entirely of carefully selected, relatively dwarf pyramidal trees and those of the bush type, propagated on selected root stocks and pruned so that they may fruit when fairly young.

These developments are of special interest to the amateur gardener, as well as to the commercial grower, since they mean that the owner of a moderate-sized plot need not be deterred by considerations of space from planting at least a few specimens of his favourite kinds. Not only will they bear more richly and heavily than their full-sized predecessors, but in many cases he can count on eating his own fruit in the first year after planting.

An orchard site should have an open aspect facing south or a little to the west of south, with the rows running approximately north and south, so that they receive the sun's rays directly about noon, when the maximum heat and light is obtained. It is nearly always necessary to have shelter, especially on the side of the prevailing winds, and if this is not provided by the natural contour of the ground, trees which are not likely to harbour fruit tree pests and diseases should be planted to form a shelter belt. Such trees, however, should be a reasonable distance from the orchard, so that they do not interfere with the natural healthy development of the fruit trees. Though a lot depends upon the site, locality and other environmental factors, it is an advantage if the wind break also prevents the early morning sun shining directly on the fruit trees when they are in flower, for should the blossom have been subject to overnight frost, a quick thaw next morning will do more harm than a slow one. In small private gardens there is not enough space to permit planting a wind-break, but full advantage should be taken of any available shelter. The myrobalan or cherry plum, *Prunus cerasifera,* makes a good tall wind-break hedge when planted no wider than 9 ins., apart and cut down to within 6 ins., of the ground after planting. It should be switched and cut to an acute angle like an inverted V at the apex each spring when, by reducing the young growths annually to about 1-1½ ft., a hedge 7 ft. high can be grown in five or six years in a moderately heavy soil. A wind break of trees or a hedge will break the force of the wind and thereby provide a good shelter belt, whereas a wall tends to force the wind up over its top to descend with increased force on any fruit trees or bushes planted, at a distance equivalent to approximately three times its own height, on the further side.

The worst site to choose for fruit growing is one on low-lying ground, formed into a pocket by surrounding higher levels, since cold air drains down from the heights, collects in the pocket, and in consequence the trees are more likely to suffer from frost in the spring and autumn. On the other hand, if the site is slightly lower on one side it allows the cold air to drain away to a lower level and thus the trees are protected. Where the site is known to be susceptible to frost, establish the fruit garden at its highest point. Boundaries of trellis, or even tall galvanised wire netting, will break the direct force of the wind, and provide some shelter in spring when pollenising insects are are at work.

For hardy fruit trees the best all-round soil is one with a little clay in it, for example a clayey loam overlying an open subsoil, which usually has good natural drainage. Stagnant water round the roots renders the trees more liable to apple canker and frost damage, and is also a contributory factor in low fruit yields.

Double-digging is the best method of breaking up the ground if the area is small, but do this well in advance of planting. Turf should be skimmed off and inverted over the lower spade depth of soil, after it has been dug and chopped up with the spade, before the top spit of soil is turned over on top. A few weeks afterwards, test the soil for lime, and if it is deficient apply at the appropriate rate, raking it into the surface. To get the best results bear in mind when planting that surface root action is an important factor in fruit production.

In a small area relatively dwarf pyramidal trees are most useful and can be planted at 6-ft. intervals in rows 8 ft. apart. Provided the foundation framework has been established by the nurserymen, fan-trained and single cordon trees are quite easy to handle, whether trained against walls or on wires. Dwarf bush apple trees are also suitable for small gardens and may be planted 10-12 ft. apart each way.

Fruit trees and bushes may be planted at any time from November to the end of March, provided the weather is open and the soil friable. Make a circular hole, somewhat larger in diameter than the spread of the roots, and deep enough to leave the part where the tree was budded or grafted about an inch above the soil level after planting is completed. A wooden stake, which has been treated under pressure with a good wood preservative, should be driven into the centre of the hole as a support. Trim off any damaged roots with a sharp knife or a pair of secateurs and, if the roots are dry, stand the young tree in a bucket of water for an hour or so before planting. It should then be placed on the lee-side of the stake, the roots being carefully spread out in their respective layers on all sides and covered with some of the finer soil, which should be well worked in amongst the root fibres. Ensure that all the roots are covered before tramping the soil to make it firm. Finally, fill up the hole with the rest of the soil, but do not tramp the top inch or two. Farmyard manure should not be added to the soil during planting operations, but in early spring, a forkful or two placed on the surface round the tree will act as a mulch to conserve moisture and provide nutritious elements. Nowadays there is no necessity to place a flat stone beneath the tree during planting because modern root stocks do not as a rule produce the type of tap-root which was formerly common. When fastening the tree to its support, use a thick cord or belt laced round the tree, and cross the ligature to act as a pad between the trunk or stem of the tree and the stake, before tying it at the back of the stake.

Young nursery trees are sent out with about 2 ft. of the previous summer's lateral growths on each main shoot, and if these are left unpruned weak growth results in the first season, and a number of buds on the lower part of each one will fail to grow and eventually disappear, leaving long lanky growths practically devoid of fruit spurs. Cut off about two-thirds of each of the previous season's 'leader' growths immediately above an outward pointing bud, and shorten any lateral, which is not required to form a leader to develop eventually into a main branch, to about 2 ins. Do this about a month after planting, and if it is followed by regular normal pruning, the tree will become well-shaped and develop fruiting spurs during its earliest years.

Use the hoe in spring, and frequently during the growing season

84

round the newly planted trees, since this not only benefits the plant roots by aerating the soil, but curbs the growth of weeds.

Greenfly

Scarcely a plant escapes the ravages of greenfly *(Aphis)*, and fruit trees and bushes are often badly damaged. Young shoots and leaves may be covered with them, and the nutritive juices so depleted that the affected parts are crippled or even the whole plant killed. Adults have six legs, a small broad, rotund body, long thin antennae, and a 'beak' for piercing the plant surface and sucking the sap. This rapidly passes through their bodies and is excreted in a semi-digested form as rich sugary drops, which are thrown off with the help of their hind legs. During dry weather, infested shoots become 'varnished' with their secretions, and the leaves of forest trees often show this to a marked degree.

The greenfly found on fruit trees in spring will have been hatched from the black, shiny eggs laid on the bark the previous autumn. They reach maturity in about ten days and bring forth living young, parthogenetically, but the last generation of each season is of both sexes and usually winged, though in some species the males are wingless. Eggs are then laid which are unharmed by the frosts of the ensuing winter.

There are numerous species, most having a complicated life history involving migration from the primary hosts to secondary ones, which may be weeds, herbaceous plants, shrubs and so on. Some cause leaves and shoots to curl; some distort the shoots and stems; some give rise to galls and tumours on the shoots and bark; some pass part of their life cycle on the roots and the rest on the upper part of the plant; and some transmit virus diseases from one plant to another.

Several species occur on apple trees, crippling their growth and reducing the crop. One, the permanent green apple aphis *(Aphis pomi)*, lays eggs, clustered thickly together on the young shoots and spurs, which hatch at bud-break but do little damage until June when they become abundant on the young growths, causing them to become stunted and malformed and often to die back from the tips. The rosy apple aphis *(Anuraphis roseus)* lays her small, shiny, black eggs singly, mainly on the sheltered side of spurs. The rosy aphis is slightly larger than the green apple aphis, and can be distinguished by its purplish colour and mealy appearance. The young aphides puncture the bark and leaves with their suckers, causing the leaves to curl backwards, thus forming shelter for themselves. They continue to increase their

85

numbers by producing live young on the leaves and shoots until early July when the winged forms appear to fly on to plantains *(Plantago)* where they reproduce for the rest of the season. In October, migrant forms return to the apple trees and produce egg-laying females, which in turn are joined by winged males and, after mating, eggs which survive the winter are laid on the young wood, around the base of the buds.

The leaf-curling plum aphis *(Aphis pruni)* is exceedingly destructive, since multiplication takes place by the million and the insects close up the pores of leaves by their tenacious excretions and the mealy exudations from their bodies. The leaves roll up, and under this cover the insects are protected from the weather. The damaged fruits remain small and deformed or drop to the ground.

The blackcurrant aphis *(Capitophorus ribes)* attacks the undersides of leaves from May onwards, invading the younger leaves and growing points, causing lumpy growths on the leaves or convex red or brown blisters on their upper surfaces, so creating hollows where the insects shelter in large numbers. In July and August the adults forsake the bushes and breed on dead nettle plants till the autumn, when they return to lay their eggs on the young wood of the black currants.

The leaf-curling currant aphis *(Amphorophora cosmopolitana)* feeds on both red and blackcurrant leaves, causing the young terminal leaves to curl. They migrate to the sow thistle in June, and return to their original host plant in October.

The gooseberry aphis *(Aphis grossulariae)* is deep green or greyish in colour, and occurs in colonies during May and June on the young growing shoots, sucking their sap and causing them to become stunted and malformed. Migration takes place in the summer, but they return in the autumn to lay eggs which hatch the following May.

Control of all these pests is by winter spraying with tar-oil-distillate washes to prevent the over-wintering eggs from hatching, but this must be done while the bushes are still dormant—not later than mid-February. These washes must not be used during frosty or wet weather, and the makers' instructions must be followed carefully.

If winter spraying has not been carried out, a derris or nicotine-soft-soap spray should be applied when the pests are actually feeding. The most suitable formula for the latter is ¾ (fluid) oz. of nicotine, 1 lb. of soft soap and 10 gallons of water. Dissolve the soap in a little hot water, then make up to 10 gallons and add the nicotine. Never use a nicotine spray immediately before picking the fruit.

Woolly aphis *(Eriosoma lanigerum)* or American blight, as it is often called, said to have been introduced from America in 1787, is an exceedingly common pest on apple trees. Its presence is easily detected during the growing season by the waxy white wool-like areas which develop on the bark, and under which the insects are found. On the shoots and branches it produces gall-like swellings, readily seen in winter, which often split and provide an opening through which apple canker spores may invade the tree.

The following year new growths, caused partly by the aphides and partly by the natural attempts of the trees to repair the damage, form round the gall-like swollen tissue, and shelter new broods in the crannies. Much can be done to control this pest by careful pruning in winter and an application of a tar-oil-distillate winter wash in November. When the cotton-wool-like colonies are noted during summer, paint them with methylated spirits, using a camel hair water-colour paint brush, and taking care not to put too much spirit on the bark of the tree. If, however, the tree is severely affected with woolly aphis, it is often more economical to uproot and burn it.

The strawberry aphis *(Capitophorus fragariae)* frequently causes severe malformation of the leaves and flower stems and general stunting, resulting in loss of crop and valuable plants: it is also a carrier of the dreaded yellow-edge virus disease. The adult insect, pale green with large legs, feeds on the young leaves and sucks the sap, multiplying at a tremendous rate. To make certain that plants are free from insects before planting, dip them in a strong solution of nicotine, soft-soap and water. Should the pest make its appearance on the plants while growing, spray them with a liquid derris wash or dust with derris powder, when the flower buds can be detected, and again fourteen days later.

Cross-pollination

The cross-pollination of fruit trees is of great importance to the grower.

The middle of the flower is generally occupied by the pistil and below it is a thick part, the ovary, containing female cells called ovules in one or more carpels, which will only develop into seeds after being fertilised with pollen. Ripened pollen grains, male organs, produced by the stamens or anthers do not stick together but escape from the opened anthers in the form of powder, and the stigma, the outgrowth at the top of the pistil, is often specially adapted for the reception and attachment of grains floating in the air. When these fall on the stigma they must develop a tube to carry the active male organs down through the style, the short tapering portion joining the ovary and the stigma, to the ovary. Seeds are the enlarged fertilised ovules with the developed plant embryos inside.

Male and female organs are sometimes produced in separate flowers, or even on separate plants, as in the old strawberry variety Tardive de Leopold, where the flowers are pistillate, i.e. female. The stamens and stigma, produced in one flower, generally ripen about the same time so that cross-pollination, although usually unnecessary to get fruit, often produces a larger crop. Where male and female organs produced in the same flower are self-sterile, fertilisation with pollen from another variety of the family is necessary. Nature is very generous. A single apple blossom may produce from 70,000 to 100,000 pollen grains and one honey bee may carry 50,000 to 70,000 pollen grains on its body, whereas only ten grains are necessary for complete fertilisation.

In the majority of economic plants, pollination is effected by means of insects, and the important part they play in the pollination of fruit trees, except mulberries, filberts, hazel nuts and walnuts, has been long recognised. The usefulness of hive bees cannot be disputed: other insect agents are bumble bees, wild bees, hover flies, wasps, midges, etc.

Experiments, both in America and at Wisley, have shown that the apple, pear and plum are not adapted for wind pollination, and neither are currants and gooseberries, for the pollen grains are sticky and adhere to form masses. The only method of transference is, therefore, through the agency of insects. Wind does, however, have some effect on pollination: moist winds aid the growth of the pollen tube and high winds remove the petals, so making the flowers less attractive (as has been proved at Wisley) to bumble bees, although hive bees still visit petal-less bloom.

Darwin's work proved that cross-pollination produces more and better seed. Some varieties of apples, pears and plums are self-sterile —known as triploids—and cannot set fruit with their own pollen, e.g. Bramley's Seedling, a good-keeping late culinary variety of apple which is grown on a very large scale. Triploid pollen is also useless on any other variety. Among the self-fertile varieties (diploids) of apples are Early Victoria, an early cooker; Lane's Prince Albert, a late cooker; and Ellison's Orange, a dessert for autumn use, but even these yield larger crops when cross-pollinated than when self-pollinated.

To obtain a crop from a triploid variety of apple, for example, plant two diploid varieties relatively near it which flower at the same time as the triploid tree. Both diploids will pollinate and fertilise the triploid, enabling it to give a good crop; and the diploids will also pollinate each other, with good results, but the sterile pollen of the triploid variety is of no use to itself or the diploid varieties. The three self-fertile varieties named above all flower at the same time as the self-sterile Bramley's Seedling, and will, therefore, help to produce a good crop.

There are also self-sterile and self-fertile varieties of pears. As with apples, if a self-sterile kind is planted, it is advisable to have two self-fertile varieties reasonably near it for cross-pollination purposes, but all must flower at the same time. The varieties Conference, William's Bon Chretien, and Clapp's Favourite are self-fertile, whereas Beurre d'Amanlis and Jargonelle are self-sterile.

Amongst plums, Jefferson's Gage, Coe's Golden Drop, Kirke's Blue and Pond's Seedling are self-sterile, whereas Victoria, Czar, Pershore, Oullin's Golden Gage and Gisborne's Prolific are self-fertile and useful for pollinating other varieties.

In commercial orchards cross-pollination is of paramount importance, and for every ten trees planted one should be a suitable self-fertile pollinator for the other nine, which are usually of one variety.

To get the best results from apple, pear and plum trees, and to obtain information regarding which varieties are of service to others, consult the local County Horticultural Advisory Officer.

Modern varieties of strawberries, raspberries, gooseberries and blackcurrants are self-fertile, therefore it is unnecessary to plant pollinators to bring about cross-fertilisation. In fact, nowadays large acreages planted with one variety only will yield a very good crop.

Budding

Many trees, shrubs, etc., cannot be propagated true to type by sowing seed. If ripe pips from an apple or pear are sown, the resulting trees will in each case be a heterogeneous collection of types. In these circumstances it is necessary to propagate particular varieties by vegetative means. Neither apples nor pears will root from cuttings but may be budded or grafted on to the bit of stem just above the rooting system of another closely related tree. For example, an apple variety can be grafted or budded on to either a young wild crab apple or a young Paradise apple. Once the buds of the graft, or the single bud inserted during the budding operation, commence growth these and these only are allowed to continue to develop: all growths from the rootstock, as the 'foster parent' is known, are removed.

A graft consists of a piece of a shoot, i.e. a lateral produced during

89

the previous summer and taken from the variety to be propagated. This is reduced to about 4 ins. and the graft to the other tree is made in spring when the latter shows signs of growth. Budding is usually done in July and the most popular form is known as shield budding, so named because of the appearance of the prepared bud with its shield of bark before it is inserted in the rootstock. Plants propagated in this way also grow much more vigorously than they would on their own roots. The technique is fascinating once it is mastered, and it is both invaluable and interesting to be able to propagate one's own apples, pears, and plums, not to speak of roses and other ornamental plants.

It is essential to secure the best buds and to operate with speed and care. Plants will only form a permanent union when budded or grafted on to members of the same botanical family, and when buds, or grafts of one variety unite well with rootstocks of another, they are said to be compatible.

In the case of apples, many varieties can be successfully budded on to the broad-leaved English Paradise rootstock. The kind of root-stock chosen influences the size of the resulting trees. For example, if the James Grieve dessert apple is budded on to the broad-leaved English Paradise (often known as Malling No. 1) it grows into a much taller tree than it does when budded on to a Jaune de Metz Paradise rootstock. Quince stocks are propagated by stooling, in the same way as Paradise stocks, and are used for propagating pears.

The parent rootstocks of apples, pears and plums should be planted out for stooling purposes in nursery rows during the dormant season, then cut back to 18 ins. from the ground, and allowed to grow for one season. The next winter, cut them back to an inch above ground level and when the young shoots which result are a few inches high, draw soil round the base of the parent plants which are then called stools to encourage development of roots. Further earthing up should be done to promote more root production as the shoots grow during the summer.

In November remove the soil around the stools, cut off rooted shoots carefully and plant them out in nursery rows for subsequent buddings. Leave the parent stools exposed until further shoots are produced, when earthing up must be repeated. A well managed bed will continue to produce for many years, especially if farmyard manure is added and there is good cultivation between the stools.

In summer, when the bark of the rootstocks previously planted out in nursery rows for subsequent budding readily lifts from the wood, make a T-shaped cut through it with a budding knife about 6 ins.

above ground level, then gently lift the bark on each side of the vertical cut with the back of the knife.

Collect the young shoots from which buds are to be taken from the healthy parents to be propagated, and immediately reduce the leaves to prevent loss of water by transpiration. They will keep in good condition for some days if they are stood in an inch of water, covered with a damp cloth and put in a cool place. They will also travel safely in cardboard boxes, if packed with sphagnum moss and wrapped in damp paper, with an outer layer of wax paper.

For actual budding select a shoot and remove the buds, starting at the apex. The two or three top buds are seldom used because their small size makes them difficult to handle. The knife blade should be inserted about ½ inch below the bud and a cut made upwards, underneath and beyond it. The bud is then pulled off, along with the short bit of leafstalk near it, towards the top of the shoot and the wood beneath and behind its 'eye' removed with a sharp jerk. If the stock has plenty of sap, there is no harm in leaving a small portion of wood under the bark of the bud when it is removed, but the actual eye beneath the bark of the bud must naturally be intact or union will not take place when the bud is inserted into the rootstock.

Insert the bud, with its bit of leaf stalk attached, into the T-shaped cut already made in the bark of the rootstock, and push it down to fit

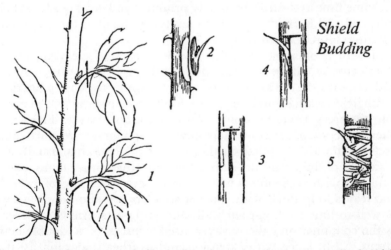

Shield Budding

1. Shoot selected for the removal of buds. Bars show where leaves are cut off.   2. Shield bud prepared.   3. Rootstock prepared with T-shape cut.   4. Bud fitted into incision.
5. Bud secured in place.

neatly underneath, cutting away the protruding portion of the bud bark which shows above the horizontal arms of the T-cut. The bud should then be tied firmly with moist raffia, or special rubber bands prepared and used for budding purposes. When the bit of leaf stalk falls off when touched, it is a sure sign that the bud has taken, i.e. it has formed a living union with the rootstock.

In the majority of species and varieties of plants budded, the inserted buds remain dormant and generally do not produce growth until the following spring when the rootstock is cut back to about 4 ins. above them. The 4-in. stump serves as a temporary stake to which the young shoot developing from the inserted bud is tied, but it is cut away at the end of the growing season. Wind damage to the young shoot should then be prevented by tying it to a bamboo cane, inserted in the soil, for support.

Fungoid Diseases

The old adage 'prevention is better than cure' is especially true of the fruit garden and growers must keep a sharp look-out for any sign of disease, particularly if there has been trouble in the previous season, so that measures can be taken before any appreciable damage is done.

The principles of clean cultivation must be strictly followed. Hawthorn hedges and rosaceous shrubs on waste land near a fruit plantation may 'carry over' fruit tree diseases, and should be sprayed at the same time as the fruit trees, any prunings and dead branches being collected and burned rather than left lying about on the ground as a potential source of infection.

Doubt is often expressed as to the efficacy of spraying, but the chief cause of failure is in the mode of doing it, e.g. using a sprayer with poor pressure, a faulty nozzle, or containing the wrong fungicide. A fungicide wash should form a perfect mist-like spray and penetrate into the trees, covering every inch of bark and leaves. The various pneumatic knapsack containers now on the market are particularly useful. They are strapped on the back of the operator, usually hold 3 gallons of fluid, and develop a fine, effective spray: many can be obtained with angle-joints which enable the underside of branches and leaves to be dealt with. Bucket sprayers are also handy, serving as well to lime-wash garden walls and outhouses. Any bucket serves as the container and the sprayer itself consists of a double-action pump, a 2-ft. lance with extension and overhead adaptor, 10 ft. of rubber hose and a strainer. They are easy to operate and light to carry.

Diseases causing scabbing and cracking on apple and pear fruits are undoubtedly the most widespread, but fortunately are not difficult to control. The fungus which attacks the apple is a different species from that which attacks the pear, although the damage is identical except that the cracks are often more pronounced on the latter. The fungi hibernate on the wood of the trees and appear on the leaves as round dark, sooty-like patches early in the summer. From there, spores are carried by wind and other agencies to the young shoots and fruits where they quickly germinate and form mycelium growths which show as dark brown patches on the leaves, and the fruits develop brown scab-like areas, sometimes with cracks. Soon after, thousands of spores are liberated from the infected portions and pass back on to the wood of the young shoots, causing blister-like patches as if gnawed by insects. Prevention is by thoroughly spraying each tree four times with lime-sulphur, so that the spores are killed immediately they alight. The first should be given when the green flower buds can be seen in the rosette of young leaves, at the strength of 1 pint of lime-sulphur in 39 pints of water; the second, at the same strength, when the pink petals show on the flower buds but no flowers are open, since otherwise damage might result. The third is given at petal fall and the fourth three to four weeks after petal fall, the strength for both applications being reduced to 1 pint of lime-sulphur in 99 pints of water. To use the solution at greater strength than that recommended by the manufacturers may scorch the foliage and cause the fruit to drop. A cupful of milk added to every two and a half gallons of diluted lime-sulphur spray, acts as a 'wetter', helping to ensure that the leaves and any fungoid growth is thoroughly wetted, and also as a 'spreader' ensuring more even distribution.

Sulphur-shy apple varieties must not be sprayed with lime-sulphur after blossoming.—Stirling Castle, Lane's Prince Albert, Beauty of Bath, Cox's Orange Pippin, Newton Wonder, Rival, and some of the newer varieties are in this category and liable to leaf scorch and fruit drop.

Scab infection on pears is difficult to control by the use of lime-sulphur but the trees can be safely sprayed with Bordeaux Mixture or any of the colloidal copper preparations and any of these fungicides can be used quite satisfactorily either before or after blossom. The variety Conference is highly resistant to scab, but Clapp's Favourite, Doyenne du Comice and Fertility are among the most susceptible.

Apple mildew is caused by a superficial fungus which appears during the summer as a white powdery mould on the young shoots, leaves and fruit spurs, and later causes stunting of the shoots and a tendency to leaf curl. It winters on the wood which assumes a greyish appearance, and the resting spores are readily spread to neighbouring

93

trees by air currents. As the buds expand in spring the fungal threads develop. Occasional spraying with a weak solution of lime-sulphur during early summer, and careful cutting out and burning of affected shoots and spurs as they appear is an effective check. Varieties susceptible to the disease are Allington, Bismarck, Early Victoria, Ecklinville Seedling, Golden Spire and Lord Grosvenor.

A disease causing blossom wilt on apples and pears makes its appearance when the trees are coming into flower. The dead flowers and leaves do not fall off but cling to the spurs, and the fungus growths continue down the flower stalks and infect the fruit spurs which develop a cankered appearance. If this occurs remove the affected spurs and burn immediately.

Brown rot of apples, often noticed just before the fruits are ready for picking, causes soft, brown, rotten patches. Fruits showing these symptoms must be discarded at once and never stored.

Brown rot and blossom wilt of plums and cherries, although very similar, will not, however, attack apples and pears, and vice versa. As before, blossom wilt causes damage to the flowers and canker-like growths on the fruiting spurs. The pustules resulting from brown rot on affected plum and cherry fruits may be grey or buff and the mycelium enters the fruits, causing them to be hard and mummified. To prevent the spread of infection cut out all withered flower trusses, remove all 'mummified' fruits—otherwise thousands of spores will be liberated in spring—and cut out all dead and canker-like infected spurs whenever they are seen. As a preventive measure spray the trees during February with a caustic-soda wash—1 lb. caustic soda and 1 lb. soft-soap in 10 gallons of water.

Silver leaf disease (*Stereum purpureum*) produces a silvery sheen on the leaves of plum, cherry, and many other kinds of stone fruit trees and bushes by creating an air space just below the upper surface of each leaf. It can only cause infection through wounds and since fructifications of the fungus occur only on dead wood, the latter should be removed and burnt in early summer, as is compulsorily laid down in the Ministry of Agriculture Silver Leaf Order of 1923. It is important when cutting out dead shoots to cut back into healthy wood, for all wood that is stained brown will contain the fungus mycelium, and to paint the cut surfaces with white lead paint—Stockholm tar is not satisfactory.

Canker disease, commonly associated with poor drainage, heavy rainfall and high nitrogen content in the soil, may be found on apple trees near fruit spurs, or on branches and the tree trunk. The affected areas are discoloured, more or less oval-shaped, sunken and fringed with a ridge of disintegrating tissue which flakes off irregularly and in severe cases the infected area may often encircle the branch or trunk, causing the death of shoots and branches above it. The fungus bears small whitish pustules which produce in spring and autumn bright red or crimson spores that can survive winter conditions. All diseased shoots, spurs and branches should be cut out and burned, and the wound painted with white lead. The aerating of badly drained land and proper manuring will help reduce the danger of canker.

Winter Pruning

A full understanding of winter pruning involves a knowledge of the conformation of fruiting trees and of the special terminology. The main stem or trunk does not merely support the entire framework of the tree and serve as its central axis, but is the channel for food supplies drawn by the roots from the soil which eventually reach the leaves. A number of main branches of varying length spring from it,

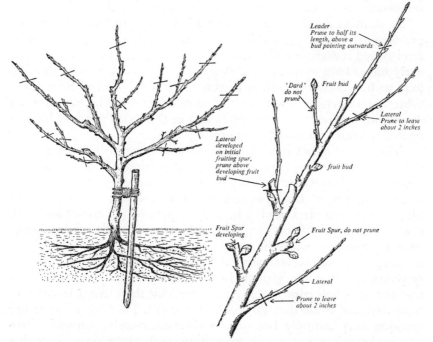

Left, planting and subsequent pruning of a three-year-old apple tree and (right) pruning the branch of an established apple tree.

and generally sub-divide at an early stage, the number of sub-branches increasing progressively according to the type of tree. Leaders are young terminal shoots produced during the preceding season to extend each main branch, and lateral shoots are those developed from the sides of the main branches, which may either be used to extend the tree 'framework' or be cut back to form fruiting spurs.

Young buds or 'eyes' are formed in leaf axils, i.e. where the leaf stalk joins the shoot or stem, and these may eventually develop into either growth shoots or buds which produce flowers. In many apple varieties such buds may be seen after leaf-fall in various stages of development. The terminal bud is usually the largest on a one-year-old shoot, i.e. a lateral or leader, the others decreasing in size from the tip down to the base, where frequently only small horizontal scars can be seen at first glance. The latter are the marks left by the fallen leaf stalks, but when these are examined carefully very small buds will be found just above each of them. Next year these buds may become quite conical and grow either into young shoots or flowers. Young shoots may be produced on old portions of a tree, developing from dormant buds when the upper or younger portion has been removed.

A 'dard' is a short lateral about 3 ins. long produced during the previous growing season, which has a rounded flower bud at the apex. Every dard is therefore a potential fruit producer. Fruit spurs in their early stages tend to resemble cavalrymen's spurs and usually develop four or five blossom buds, with rosettes of small leaves. Sometimes these spurs develop others in their turn, which may be too crowded or extend too far from the branch, and in this case they may have to be thinned out or reduced in length.

The balance between fruit production and vegetative growth depends on the ratio between the upper portion of the tree and its root system. Too severe pruning annually may cause excessive growth at the expense of fruit production, and excessive manuring with nitrogenous manures and fertilisers, especially if combined with severe pruning, will do the same. On the other hand, minimum pruning together with the application of potassic and phosphatic manures, may induce excessive fruit production. There will be little or no young vegetative growth, i.e. short leaders and very few laterals and the trees will consequently set more fruit than they can carry to maturity, and those they do will be too small. Therefore, if trees are growing very strongly but not fruiting sufficiently, withold nitrogenous manures but apply potassium and phosphates, reducing pruning to a minimum. In some cases bark-ringing may be advisable to induce fruiting. If crops are too heavy, nitrogenous manure should be applied, especially to culinary varieties, and vegetative growth

FIRST YEAR CROPPING
Dwarf Pyramid apple tree at the Scottish
Horticultural Institute, Invergowrie.

After summer pruning.

The fruit is encouraged to form adjacent to
the main stem.

Before pruning.

BLACKCURRANTS

After pruning.

should be induced by thinning out fruit spurs and severely cutting back the leaders. Skilful pruning can promote and stimulate vegetative growth when required; build the framework of a tree; modify the form of a tree; enable it to produce good crops of fruit; aid the formation of fruit buds; improve the quality and quantity of fruit and encourage regular cropping; facilitate the cultivation and harvesting of the crop; and remove dead wood and surplus branches to allow light into the centre.

In the first year fruit is less important than the proper formation of the tree's 'head', branch extension and development being controlled to produce the foundation of a well-shaped tree. After the tree is established and a good head developed, winter pruning consists of cutting off about one third of each main branch leader which developed during summer. Cutting should be done immediately above a good bud, which points outwards in the direction subsequent growth is required, and in this way the number of main branches is increased. As the tree extends in width the space between the upper portions of branches increases, and when there is room for a new young branch, a suitably placed lateral may be treated and pruned as a leader to encourage it to develop. Lateral shoots are usually pruned by shortening to about 1 to 1½ ins. to form a spur, and to a similar length if they have been produced at the base of a spur when other spurs are already present. The less winter pruning a young tree receives, the more quickly it will come into bearing.

If the crop has been good, and a fair amount of wood growth has been made during the summer, this balance should be maintained. With apples, the extension shoots should be shortened and the lateral shoots spurred back to form more fruit buds. If the crop has been abnormally heavy, however, and little or no growth has been made, all spurs showing numerous fruit buds should be drastically shortened. In cases where trees have produced few flowers and have made a large number of strong shoots, then the less one prunes the better, but if spring growth continues even without pruning, then it may be necessary to bark-ring the trees.

Pruning should be varied according to the type of apple and pear being grown. Some, such as Allington Pippin, Irish Peach and Worcester Pearmain, are 'tip-bearers' and carry their fruit buds at the end of the shorter lateral shoots especially in early years. In general, leave these fruiting laterals (somewhat longer than dards) if there is room for them. Other varieties such as Lane's Prince Albert and James Grieve are 'self-spurrers' carrying most of their fruit buds on naturally formed spurs, and these are much easier to prune, provided that

G   97

the leaders are not cut back too severely during the early stages when the trees are coming into bearing.

Plum trees need little pruning, since they bear most of their fruit on two-year-old shoots, and as much young wood as possible should be left so long as overcrowding is avoided. In plum trees growing against walls, most of the young growths in the centre and lower parts are often removed to secure a tidy appearance and, since only the young growths on the perimeter of the tree are left and fastened to the wall, these trees produce the bulk of their crop near the branch extremities with little or no crop in or near the centre.

Be cautious in pruning very old and neglected apple and pear trees. Cut out all dead wood and remove some of the branches close to their point of origin if there are signs of overcrowding, but spread the work over two or three winters, otherwise growth may be induced at the expense of fruit.

Storage

For apples and pears, successful storage depends not only on the place but also on the condition of the fruit and its being harvested at the proper time. It has been my experience that in districts where the rainfall is normally low—averaging 26-30 ins. annually—apples always mature and keep better than in districts where it exceeds 40 ins. Providing the fruits have not suffered any check in their development and finish, have been gathered at the correct time and stored properly, the late maturing varieties can be kept in perfect condition for many months. It is difficult, however, to fix a time for gathering apples and pears since much depends upon the variety, the root-stock on which it is worked, the soil type and weather conditions during the growing season.

Many growers are tempted to gather their fruits too early, especially when a few begin to drop prematurely as a result of other factors such as wind. A simple test to make sure the fruit is ready is to lift one or two to a horizontal position in the palm of the hand and if, with the slightest of pressure, they easily part from their spurs, the crop is fit for gathering: no twisting or pulling should be necessary. Alternatively, cut open an apple and if the pips are brownish, the fruit may be harvested. Highly coloured fruits at the top of a tree are usually ready for pulling first, and it is advisable to go over each tree two or three times, picking only those that are ready. Immature fruits do not ripen properly after gathering, while those left too long on the trees may become mealy when stored.

A few early dessert apples, such as Beauty of Bath, Gladstone, and Laxton's Advance tend to drop their fruits before they are fully ripe. This can be checked to a certain extent by wetting the fruit stalks with a pre-harvest hormone liquid about two to three weeks before normal harvesting time. It is, however, unnecessary to treat late maturing dessert varieties.

Fruits which ripen during August should be harvested just before they are absolutely ripe, for then they are better in flavour and quality, but late-maturing varieties should be left on the trees as long as possible so that they may improve in flavour and increase in weight. It is better to lose a few fruits through falling than to gather late-keeping varieties too soon, for they are liable to shrivel and lose their flavour when stored.

Damaged fruits, whether caused by bird pecks, insect injuries, fungus attacks or bruising, should be kept entirely apart from the sound and used as soon as possible. Take great care in handling, remembering that the stalk is part of the fruit and should not be removed. The receptacles used for picking, especially thin-skinned varieties such as Lane's Prince Albert and Stirling Castle, should have adequate padding, such as a lining of wood-wool or crumpled paper, to prevent bruises. When harvesting from high trees, a picking bag is handy and can be made out of clean sacking and webbing to form an apron with two pockets, thus leaving both hands free. Fruit must not be gathered and stored when wet.

All fruits are living things, in that they absorb oxygen and give off carbon-dioxide. By keeping the proportions of those two gases at a known concentration, and the fruit store at a low temperature, ripening can be slowed down to about half the speed it would normally take in air at a higher temperature.

Apples and pears can be stored in various places. The ideal conditions for keeping apples during the winter months are a slightly moist atmosphere, partial darkness and a cool steady temperature of about 35-38° F./2-3° C. but the best store-room is one with a thatched roof and sides, situated on the north side of a high wall or building, because the fluctuation of the internal temperature is less than in tiled or slated sheds.

Perfect conditions of storing are, however, not always available. When apples and pears have to be kept in the house, a cellar is the best place and the attic the worst, for it is usually too dry and draughty. Apples are liable to shrivel if kept in a room that is too dry and warm, and in such conditions the fruit should be wrapped in oil-proof paper before being placed in boxes. Another satisfactory method is to place a layer of moderately damp sphagnum moss on the shelves and in the boxes, placing the fruits on the moss, but not covering them. The damp moss in the dry air of the store, acts as a thermic regulator, by producing an evaporation which automatically keeps the air cool. Sphagnum moss lives for some time in the dark, retaining its chlorophyll action, thus it also serves to regenerate and purify the atmosphere by the absorption of emitted gasses and odours, and by this method James Grieve apples, a September-October variety, have been kept in perfect condition until Christmas.

In the storing of pears, more care is required than for apples. The temperature should be higher—from 40-45° F./4-7° C., and the atmosphere drier. The early summer pears, Doyenne d'Eté (a delicious little pear) and the old Jargonelle, should be eaten as soon as they are removed from trees; August—ripe pears are gathered just before fully mature and finished off in the fruit room; and the late maturing varieties picked when the fruits part freely from their spurs and then stored. Badly harvested pears become mealy or decay near the centre.

Dessert pears improve in flavour if brought into a warmer temperature, nearing 60° F. or 15° C., for a week or two to ripen. If allowed to mature fully in a low temperature they become tough and of poor flavour, instead of becoming buttery.

It is sometimes difficult to know when a pear is ripe for eating but this is indicated by giving a gentle press with the thumb quite near the stalk end where the fruit ripens first; similar pressure applied to any other part would soon cause decay to set in.

TOP FRUITS

Apples

Although the cost at the outset may be heavy, no form of fruit growing gives such quick returns and such a high grade as the 'cordon' system of trained trees, the comparison with the bush, pyramid and standard forms being very favourable. With cordons, the framework to which they are trained is provided by horizontal wires and bamboo canes placed at an angle so that the trees may be allowed to crop almost at once. A single cordon is a single-stemmed tree where all the lateral shoots are periodically shortened to encourage the formation of fruiting spurs; double, treble and quadruple cordons have two, three and four stems respectively. Not only is this type of trained tree fascinating to grow, given regular attention and properly pruned, but where space is limited, one can grow many more varieties.

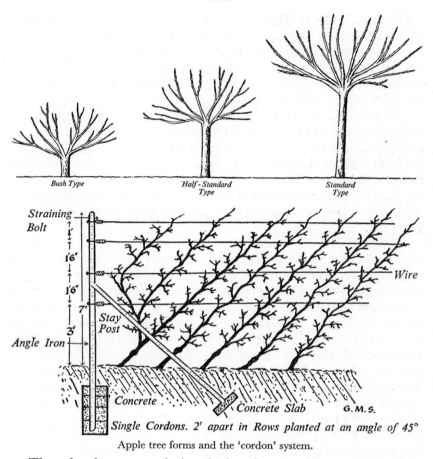

Bush Type   'Half - Standard   Standard
            Type   Type

Single Cordons. 2' apart in Rows planted at an angle of 45°

Apple tree forms and the 'cordon' system.

There has been a revolution during the past thirty years in root-stocks used for cordon apples, and the credit goes to the East Malling Research Station, the John Innes Institution and the general nursery trade. Trees are propagated by budding or grafting the scion variety on to a rootstock raised vegetatively, either by layering or stooling, and when ordering, the most suitable rootstocks for cordon type training must be carefully chosen.

Paradise Type IX (Jaune de Metz) rootstock is the weakest grower and poorest rooter of all, although long-lived under high cultural conditions. Trees worked, i.e. grafted or budded, on this root-stock, are relatively quick cropping, but it is not suitable when trees are to be grown on poor gravelly soil. It is, however, ideal for cordon apples on fairly strong land, although the trees need careful support as the roots are very brittle.

101

Paradise Type II (Doucin) is much used by commercial growers. Trees worked on this type crop early, although not so early as on Jaune de Metz, and it is excellent, especially on poor soils, and considered ideal for dwarf bush and pyramid trees. Unfortunately, some varieties grown on this rootstock are inclined to scorch, especially Laxton's Superb and Stirling Castle.

Paradise Type I (Broad-leaved English Paradise) is suitable for making good cordons and bush type trees of weak-growing varieties of apples, and is the best stock for heavy soils.

Fruit trees can be planted at any time during their dormancy between October and March, but early planting is preferable provided the weather is favourable and the soil in working condition, and it is ideal to plant them when they are not more than two or three years old.

Cordons planted against fences and walls need the support of wires and bamboo canes, though this can be more easily arranged if metal tags or 'vine eyes' are inserted in the wall. If more than one row is being planted in the open, allow 4 ft. between the rows and 2 ft. between the trees for single cordons and 3 ft. for double. After the ground is properly prepared, fix the supporting posts and wires. A post will be needed at each end and intermediate posts at 12 ft. intervals, 7 ft. above the ground, to carry four strands of galvanised wire set at 3 ft., 4½ ft., 6 ft. and 7 ft. respectively above ground level. To stand the strain of the taut wires over the years, the posts must be very firmly fixed, and those at the ends need strengthening by the addition of a strut on the inside, nearest the trees. Larch posts impregnated with a preservative and the parts below the ground soaked in a copper sulphate solution (1 lb. per gallon of water) are best, but old railway rails, or angle iron serve excellently when bedded in concrete.

When planting cordons at an angle of 45°, bamboo canes, 7 ft. long, should be fastened to the training wires between the posts with fine galvanised wire, and each tree tied to a bamboo cane with string. By planting cordons obliquely, the flow of sap in the trees is slowed down, enabling every lateral bud to develop fruiting spurs and ensuring a longer length of fruiting wood. To reduce shade to a minimum, it is advisable to run the rows from north to south, and incline the individual trees towards the south.

To prune, all lateral shoots should be cut back to about 4 or 5 ins. from each main stem during August. The second summer, cut back all side growth from these cut-back laterals to about 4 ins. above the previous year's cut. By then fruit buds should have formed on all pruned laterals, which will then become fruiting spurs, but if this has not happened, it may be necessary to bend and tie down the shoots at a sharp angle, without breaking them, and merely tip them during the winter. The extension shoot of each oblique cordon is left unpruned until it reaches the top wire. Later, unfasten the trees and the bamboo canes and lower them by about 5° during winter, and repeat this if necessary. Be careful when manuring not to give too much nitrogen, which may strengthen and induce growth at the expense of fruit. This element is best given in the form of a spring mulch, using farmyard manure or some slow-acting organic material such as spent hops or decayed vegetable compost whose bulk will add sufficient humus to the soil. Too much potash may do more harm than good, but it is most likely to be needed on light soils, where it might be better to apply a little annually in the form of sulphate of potash.

Good varieties of dessert apples for cordon training are Beauty of Bath, at its best in August; Christmas Pearmain, November-January; Egremont Russet, October-December; Ellison's Orange, September-November; James Grieve, September-October; Laxton's Advance, August; Laxton's Fortune, September-October; Laxton's Superb, November-February; Lord Lambourne, October-November; Merton Prolific, November-February; and Sunset, October-January.

The bush type of apple is also suitable for the private garden. Select the required varieties and ask the nurseryman for two to three-year-old Bush apple trees on a Paradise root-stock which will produce a reasonably sized dwarf apple tree. When planting allow a distance of 10-12 ft. each way between the trees, and make the hole wide enough to take the roots out to their fullest extent and deep enough to leave the part where it was grafted or budded an inch or so above soil level when planting is complete. Before planting drive a short but reasonably stout stake in the centre of the hole, remove any injured pieces of root from the tree with a pair of sharp secateurs, and plant the tree close up to the stake. Spread the roots out carefully and cover all the respective layers with soil before tramping to ensure firm planting. Fill in the remaining soil and tramp it, but leave the last inch or two loose on the surface. Carefully tie the tree to the stake, the top of which should not be among the branches. Do not apply farmyard manure during planting, but spread a forkful or two well out from the tree's main stem in early spring, just as growth begins, to keep the soil from drying out. Do initial pruning after planting while the trees are dormant.

If an apple is not making many young growths, i.e. laterals, or very short leaders, or if the foliage looks pale green during summer, it indicates that some nitrogenous feeding is necessary. In spring, apply a few forkfuls of well rotted farmyard manure and spread it out from the tree trunk to the main branch extremities.

There are also times when a lot of long laterals are produced and very little fruit. This can be rectified by what is known as bark-ringing which is done in May when the bark lifts easily from the wood. With a sharp knife remove a ¼-in.-wide strip of bark from half way round the tree trunk about 6-9 ins. above soil level, then remove another ¼ in. wide strip 4 ins. above that already removed, but from the other side of the trunk, then cover each wound with a piece of plastic tape as protection. The ends of each cut must not overlap.

Another method of checking exuberant young lateral growth is to use a fairly strong pliable, but not too thick, piece of wire twisted tightly round the trunk a few inches above soil level in May. Remove the wire strangle immediately the desired result has been achieved.

About every third year give a dressing of bone meal in autumn at the rate of 4-5 lb. per 30 sq. yds. and hoe it in. Spread it out to the full extremity of the tree's width. Bone-meal provides the tree with the phosphate which plays an important part in fruit production.

If during summer, the leaf margins turn brown and wither, it shows that the tree is suffering from a deficiency in potash and 2 lb. sulphate of potash per 30 sq. yds. of ground covered by the tree should be applied. Resist the temptation to exceed this, otherwise a magnesium deficiency may be induced.

Apple scab is a disease which often spoils the appearance of fruit. Control is by a fungicide such as lime sulphur, spersul or orthocide (which contains captan), but some apple varieties are sulphur-shy, and in these cases lime sulphur must be used with care.

Although Cox's Orange Pippin is regarded by many as the best English dessert apple, it does not give good results in Scotland where James Grieve, Ellison's Orange, Charles Ross, and Laxton's Fortune are popular. Good cooking varieties are Early Victoria, Grenadier, Lane's Prince Albert and Bramley's Seedling.

In larger private gardens, where more space is available, it is, of course, possible to plant half-standard and standard type trees. They are treated similarly to the bush type apple, and in the long run a much larger yield of fruit may be expected.

Pears

Good pears are luscious fruits characterised by a saccharine aromatic juice and a soft pearly liquid pulp, melting in the mouth. Some are slightly acid, and taste of musk; other flavours distinguished in some varieties are those of almond and honey. One French author described the flavour of the pear as that of the perfume of the rose. Most of the finest pears are of Continental origin, for the growers of France and the Netherlands have paid more attention to the raising of new kinds than those of Britain, but the names have undergone a popular corruption so that Beurré becomes Bury, and Bon-Chrétien turns into Bon-Crushing. The most ancient pear orchard in Scotland is at the old Abbey garden at Lindores, Fife, on the south bank of the River Tay, where the soil is said to be one of the most suitable—fine strong black loam that reaches a good depth.

The following varieties, in order of ripening, are those likely to prove satisfactory in the average Scottish garden. Laxton's Superb, is a hardy and prolific cropper. Ready in August, the fairly large, yellow fruit, if gathered before it is fully ripe, is full of rich juice with a brisk but slightly acid flavour. It is suitable to grow as a bush, and is partially self-fertile. The prolific Clapp's Favourite, ripe in August, is fairly large and yellow with bright pink flush on the side exposed to the sun. It is a good dessert variety and a general favourite for market purposes, but the fruit should be pulled just before it ripens as it does not keep. The tree does well as a cordon or bush and is a late flowering variety, mainly self-fertile.

Souvenir de Congrès, ripe in September, is a large, handsome yellow fruit with pink cheeks. It is very hardy and can be grown as a cordon, bush or espalier, but is rarely self-fertile. Dr. Jules Guyot, September, has a large, oval, yellow fruit with slight flush on side exposed to the sun. A hardy and prolific cropper with delicious flavour, it should be picked before it ripens as it does not keep in store more than a few days. It can be grown and trained as a cordon or bush and is self-fertile. Marguerite Marillat, September-October, has a large uneven-shaped fruit golden-yellow tinged red. The fruits should be pulled before they are ripe. This makes a fine bush tree, hardy and prolific. It flowers early and is self-fertile. Fertility, September-October, is a small to medium round yellow fruit of fair flavour, hardy and prolific. Suitable to train as a cordon and bush, it is unfortunately highly susceptible to pear scab, but should be in every collection as it is a good pollinator for other varieties, although self-sterile.

Louise Bonne of Jersey (Louise Bonne d'Avranches), October, has a small to medium sized conical yellowish-green fruit of excellent flavour, which must be pulled before it is ripe. A heavy cropper, this tree is suitable as a cordon or espalier against a wall, and is partially self-fertile and highly recommended for garden culture. Pitmaston Duchess, October-November is a very large long golden yellow, russetted pear of fair quality for dessert but excellent when cooked. Gather end of September for use during October and November. The tree is a rather shy cropper in some districts, partially self-fertile, and should be grown as a double cordon or bush. Conference, October-November, is a medium-sized russet-green fruit which should be picked in late September and stored till November. When properly ripened it is a delicious and aromatic flavoured pear, very resistant to pear scab. Recommended for all types of training, the tree is self-fertile and an excellent pollinator to mix with other mid-season flowering self-fertile varieties. Doyenne du Comice, November, a medium sized oval golden russet fruit, is the ideal pear with perfect flavour and aroma. A late flowering partially self-fertile variety, the tree does best against a south wall trained as a cordon and espalier. It is very susceptible to pear scab and the fruit should be pulled in October and stored for a few weeks before use. Glou Morceau ripens in December and is a large conical light green to greenish-yellow fruit, fading as it ripens in store to a pale gold, with juicy white flesh of excellent flavour. The slow ripening is valuable and the firm but melting flesh comes little short of Doyenne du Comice. This excellent self-sterile fruit will keep in good condition for over two months, and should be stored in October until December and January. Joséphine de Malines is a small smooth greenish fruit with russet around the stem, which will keep till March and may be given first place among the winter pears, particularly for market, where it is popular. The flesh is of a rose-yellow colour and has a tinge of rose perfume in its rich flavour. It is self-sterile.

Many pear varieties do not set fruit readily from their own pollen, and must be cross-pollinated from the diploid or self-fertile varieties which all collections should include. Always ensure that two self-fertile varieties are planted in the neighbourhood of a self-sterile variety, and that they all flower at the same period. Poor crops from free flowering trees are often attributed to frost damage, whereas this may be only a contributory factor, inefficient pollination being the true cause. If there is a deficiency of fruiting spurs and blossom, on the other hand, this condition may be helped by phosphatic fertilisers.

Since pears bloom earlier than apples, and the blossom is exposed to lower temperatures, they should be planted in the most sheltered position or against a south or south-west wall. A hot dry summer improves the flavour of the fruit and gives a firmer texture, although a high temperature does not hasten ripening, as it does with apples and plums, but tends to delay it.

Harvested in the green state, and properly stored, pears increase in sweetness as the fruit softens, but very few varieties keep for long even in very favourable circumstances. Unlike apples, they entirely lose their flavour in a moist atmosphere, and need a dry warm room or slightly heated chamber. If no artificial heat is available, they may be stored in drawers in the house.

When planting, care must be taken to ensure that the point of union of root-stock and scion, i.e. where the tree was grafted or budded, is kept above ground level and will always remain so, since if the trees are planted so that the union is below ground level, roots may grow from the scion or graft and the trees cease to remain dwarf and perhaps stop bearing fruit.

Pear trees should be well fed. A dressing of farmyard manure, or well-decayed vegetable compost, in the early summer will assist root formation and 1 oz. sulphate of potash and 2 oz. steamed bone flour per sq. yd. in spring, with a dressing of a compound fertiliser after the fruit is set, will help develop a good crop.

Plums

Plum trees give springtime its character of luxuriant blossom. The beauty of the autumn too, is largely in weighted branches of purple, blue, green, orange and golden yellow fruits. Their seed is produced in the form of a kernel enclosed in a hard, stony shell, the stone being embedded in a mass of edible pulp. The best varieties produce a delicious dessert fruit, which is formed within the cup of the flower, above the green calyx.

The bullace *(Prunus insititia)* is taller and the leaves are more downy than the plum and is regarded by some botanists as the origin of all the plums. It has a few thorns and the fruit, which is more oval in shape, is black or yellow and slightly acrid.

Plums are produced on short natural spurs at the ends and along the sides of the bearing shoots of from one to three years growth. The new fruiting branches are, therefore, two years old before the spurs come into bearing. A good supply of young shoots should be encouraged and allowed to grow every year, provided that the tree does not become overcrowded. In general, after the framework of the young trees is built up, very little pruning is necessary. Later, only young well-placed shoots should be allowed to expand into full growth, and dead wood, long cross-placed and irregular shoots must be removed to avoid overcrowding. Normally pruning should be done during early autumn or late spring, but when good-sized branches have to be removed do it in summer when the wounds heal quickly and are not susceptible to infection by the silver-leaf fungus.

Trees are propagated by budding during July and early August on to rootstocks raised vegetatively or from seed. Varieties budded on to myrobolan B, which does not produce suckers, give strong, vigorous and regularly cropping trees. The common plum root-stock has a slightly dwarfing effect on certain varieties, but unfortunately, it is not compatible with all. Soft-wooded plums, such as Victoria and most of the gages, however, succeed on this root-stock. The Yellow Pershore Plum is sometimes used as a rootstock for other varieties, but it is rather difficult to propagate in quantity.

Growers should plant 'maidens' or 'two-year-old' bush or half-standard trees. The fan-trained tree, to be planted against a wall, may be three years old when bought from a nurseryman but will require careful handling, and must not suffer from lack of moisture during the first year. Choice varieties as fan-trained trees are almost always planted against walls with an east, south-east or south-west aspect, which suit them better than a purely southern. Espalier and single cordon training are not recommended for plums. When plum trees are grown as trained specimens against a wall young shoots— the potential fruit-bearers—which stand out from the breast of the tree are, unfortunately, often removed in the interests of tidiness, so that most of the fruit is produced on the tree's perimeter. Large regular crops in open ground are best obtained from bush and half-standard trained trees. Planting plums in the vegetable garden, if there is insufficient space, may lead to damage of the fibrous roots near the surface during winter digging, and the manuring necessary for vegetables may not always meet the requirements of the fruit trees. Damage by frost during flowering is less likely when the trees are on high ground, but protection must be given from strong winds.

The plum prefers a moderately moist but fairly rich, sandy loam, with a fair amount of calcareous material, and flourishes in districts with an average annual rainfall of some 40 ins., such as the Clyde valley, the home of Scottish plums, whereas dessert apples do best when it does not exceed 26 ins. In *Manuring for Fruit* Dr. Griffiths says that a ton of plum fruits extract 13·7 lb. of mineral matter from the soil, so that the trees require a plentiful supply of organic nitrogen in the form of hoof and horn meal, shoddy or meat meal applied during late winter to produce a regular supply of annual shoot-growths and to give size to the fruits. In addition, regular supplies of farmyard manure and liberal applications of inorganic fertiliser should be given as top dressing in the spring, depending upon the nature of the soil and the vigour of growth.

For shallow soils, in addition to farmyard manure, mixtures of superphosphate, four parts, sulphate of potash, two parts, and sulphate of ammonia, two parts, applied at the rate of 2 oz. per sq. yd. are necessary. These fertilisers supply phosphoric acid, potassium and nitrogen in an easily assimilated form so that the cells and tissues are built up and perfect shoots, leaves, flowers and fruits produced. It is advisable to have the soil tested and if lime is lacking it should be added—though not in excess of the recommended quantity—as a top dressing in autumn, otherwise the trees will not give their best results.

Root-prune plum trees about three years after planting and again four year later. In autumn dig a trench 18 ins. deep round the tree, commencing about 4 ft. from the base of the trunk, and cut off all roots outside this, in addition to the strong tap root beneath the tree. Refill the trench with the removed soil and then manure the ground within the area where the roots have been severed.

When ordering, it is advisable to indicate not only the variety desired but also the specific rootstock on which it had been worked, so that it may suit the purpose for which the trees are intended to be trained.

The following are good dessert plums for walls: Coe's Golden Drop, which ripens in late September, is medium to large, oval, golden yellow spotted red, has a delicious flavour and is self-sterile but pollinated by the variety President. Denniston's Superb Gage, ready at the end of August, is round, medium-sized, yellowish-green fruit, with an excellent flavour, a hardy and prolific cropper, self-fertile. Golden Transparent Gage, which ripens in October, large, round, golden-yellow dotted with red, has a delicious flavour and is self-fertile. Jefferson's Gage, ready in September, is oval, large, golden-yellow and sweet, and is early flowering but self-sterile, and can be cross-pollinated with Victoria. Kirke's Blue, ripening in September, is dark blue-purple, sweet, a strong grower, may be grown in the open and is self-sterile, and pollinated by Golden Transparent Gage. Oullin's Golden Gage, ready in August, has medium to large, roundish-oval, golden yellow fruits, and is self-fertile.

Good culinary plums for the open include: Czar, ripening in August and early September, which has medium-sized, roundish-oval, purple-black fruits, is a prolific cropper, and self-fertile. Early Laxton, ready July, is a small, oval plum, yellow flushed red, early flowering and partially self-fertile, and is excellent for bottling and jam. Gisborne's Prolific, ripening in late August and early September, is medium size, roundish-oval, yellow, spotted red, self-fertile, makes a strong tree and is ripe before Victoria. Monarch, ready late September, is very large, round, purple, has a good flavour, and is an early flowerer and self-fertile, but a rather uncertain cropper. Pond's Seedling, ripening late September, is large, longish oval, deep red, and has excellent flavour and is fit for dessert, it is self-sterile but cross-pollinated with Czar. President, ready in October, is large, oval, deep-purple, self-sterile but cross-pollinated with Coe's Golden Drop, and an uncertain cropper. River's Early Prolific, ripens in August, small to medium deep purple, good for cooking and jam, is an early bloomer, partially self-fertile, and cross-pollinated by Monarch. Victoria, ripening in September, large oval, pinkish red, most popular variety for dessert and for jam, self-fertile, suitable for a wall or in the open ground, but is unfortunately susceptible to bacterial canker and silver-leaf fungus. Warwickshire Drooper, (Magnum Bonum), ready in September, medium sized, roundish oval, greenish-yellow dotted red, very hardy, makes a drooping tree, is self-sterile, and cross-pollinates with River's Early Prolific and Early Laxton, is a good canning and bottling variety.

SOFT FRUITS

Blackberries

Although all blackberries are brambles, many brambles do not produce blackberries. The fruiting blackberry *(Rubus fruticosus)* grows in great profusion in many parts of Scotland, in hedgerows, open woodland and old quarries. At its best in autumn, when all other small fruits are practically over, it deserves much attention as a garden fruit, for it yields very heavy crops which can not only be used with apples and elderberries in jam and tarts, but be bottled and canned for winter use.

Except in the case of Himalayan Giant, which bears fruit on canes two or even three years old, fruits are borne in small clusters on lateral shoots produced on wood grown the previous year. Propagation is by layering done in late July and early August. Dig shallow holes near the parent plants and in each heel a young growing shoot. Tip in firmly by bending them until they are nearly perpendicular. Each will continue to grow underground and become short-jointed and swollen, soon sending out adventitious roots. A bud breaks at the base of each shoot which grows upwards and in a short time appears above the ground to become a new 'tip-rooted' plant. The rooted tips do best if left in the ground until February, when they can be planted out into nursery rows to grow on for one year, but great care must be taken in lifting them because the new roots are brittle and easily broken. Bramble and hybrid berries may also be propagated from suckers dug up from around the base of established plants.

Planting can be carried out any time from October until March, provided the weather is open and the soil is in good condition for working, leaving about 10-12 ft. between the plants and 6 ft. between the rows, according to the variety. After planting, cut down the previous year's growth almost to ground level to encourage the development of strong canes the following summer. The majority of cultivated brambles and hybrid berries make very strong prickly canes which are awkward to handle and strong leather gauntlet gloves should be worn.

Train canes by the 'rope method' to facilitate picking. Stretch three strands of No. 10 gauge galvanised wire between upright posts 2, 3 and 5 ft. above ground level, tying the fruiting canes to the top two wires in the autumn. The following year, as new canes are being produced, they should be tied loosely together and fixed along the bottom wire. After fruiting, remove the old fruiting canes and spread out the new ones on the top two wires. The bramble requires fairly heavy manuring so that farmyard manure, poultry manure or decayed vegetable refuse should be forked into the soil during the winter, supplemented in early spring by 2 oz. sulphate of potash and 2 oz. steamed bone flour to each sq. yd.

Good varieties include Ashton Cross, a prolific bearer selected by the Long Ashton Research Station, bearing a deep black, large and evenly shaped fruit which ripens early. The plants make vigorous growth and should be set 6-8 ft. apart, but the canes are not so thorny and thick as most of the cultivated brambles. Himalayan Giant is a very strong-growing heavy cropper, and considered to be the best market variety. John Innes is also a very heavy cropper with excellent flavour and very few seeds, and since it is more bushy than most varieties, it can therefore, be planted 6-8 ft. apart.

Merton Thornless is entirely without prickles and the large excellently flavoured fruit is in season from late August until the end of September. The Parsley-leaved Bramble (*Rubus laciniatus*) has an ornamental value, and is a self-fertile variety, considered the best flavoured and one of the best for stewing. The flowers are white and

111

the fruits produced in handsome sprays, brilliant glossy black, large and ornamental. The plants are suitable for trailing over a pergola provided it is not too near a path, as the canes are very formidably armed with spines.

One of the best hybrid berries is the Boysenberry, raised by crossing a blackberry with a raspberry and a loganberry. The fine-flavoured fruit is very large, a dark wine colour, borne on long spurs, and less seedy than most of the other hybrids. The plants are exceedingly hardy, and being very deep rooters, resist drought. Japanese Wineberry *(Rubus phoenicolasius)* is a beautiful plant which should be given a place in every garden. The pleasantly acid fruit, borne in clusters in great profusion, is bright orange turning to crimson when fully ripe, and both the foliage and canes are very ornamental.Growth is strong and the red colour of the canes in winter makes this an attractive plant.

The Loganberry is said to be a true hybrid between the red raspberry and the blackberry and was raised by Judge Logan of California. It is very hardy and an abundant cropper with very large berries, dark red in colour, exceedingly juicy with a brisk acid flavour, and delicious when made into jam. The fruit ripens in July and continues until the end of September. The plants are moderately strong growing and should be planted about 6 ft. apart and trained fanwise to wires in the same way as the raspberry. Several interesting loganberry seedlings may be grown in gardens. The Newberry,for example, is a loganberry type which was introduced by Whiterigg and Page of Chislehurst and is said to be a cross between a loganberry and the Superlative raspberry. It is a strong growing shrub, six feet high, with long racemes laden with fruit.

The Lowberry is a handsome plant in early summer with practically thornless shoots, and white flowers about 1 in. across. It is a splendid dessert fruit, large, juicy, jet-black and borne in clusters similar to the loganberry, but less acid and excellent when stewed or made into jam. A moderately strong growing kind it succeeds in rather poor soils and should be spaced 6-8 ft. apart.

The Phenomenal Berry was introduced in 1900 or 1901 by Luther Burbank, the famous Californian plant breeder. He described it as 'hybrid between a raspberry and a blackberry, larger than the largest berry known hitherto'. The most delicious of all the hybrid berries for canning, it is bright red crimson raspberry colour, is exceedingly juicy and ripens a few days earlier than the loganberry, so extending the full fruiting season. It is very productive and of very strong and hardy growth.

A mulch of manure is applied.

BLACKCURRANTS

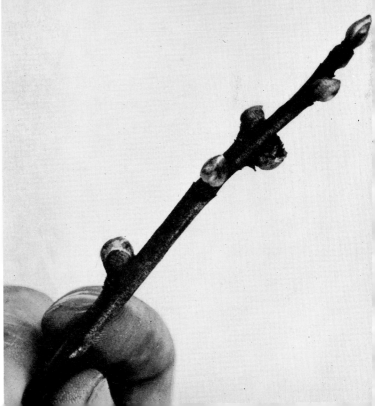

Note the round swollen appearance which indicates an attack of Big Bud: the mites live under the bud scales.

Giant pouch cal-
ceolaria, not easy
to grow but
beautiful in spring

Saintpaulia, Blue
fairy tale.

The Worcesterberry, a North American species of the genus *Ribes*, is closely allied to the gooseberry. Ripening late and hanging on the bushes till September, the fruits grow in profusion in small clusters on spurs, and are reddish-purple. It is propagated by cuttings, and the bushes should be planted 5 ft. apart and spur pruned like gooseberries.

Blackcurrants

Provided the most suitable varieties are grown, the climate of Scotland is not unfavourable to reasonably good crops of blackcurrants, but the yield will not be quite so high as in parts of England. Shelter from wind storms in spring when the bushes are in flower is of vital importance, and frost pockets should be avoided because frost during the flowering period can reduce yields and make some varieties not worth growing.

The common practice of planting vegetable crops among young bushes should not be adopted because it can interfere with the blackcurrant spraying programme. It is also generally better to grow them in open ground rather than train them against a wall, and partial shade and damp soil are not unfavourable.

Propagation is by cuttings, which must be from healthy bushes only, and growers can nowadays be sure when they buy two and three-year-old plants that they are free from disease, since it is an offence in Scotland to sell them unless they have been certified by the Department of Agriculture for Scotland, or the Ministry of Agriculture and Fisheries, during the previous growing season, as being true to type and free from 'reversion' (often called nettle leaf-disease), and big bud mite. Always ask for the relevant certificate number to be quoted on the bill, label or invoice.

Reversion is the most serious virus disease, and may cause part or even the whole bush, to be fruitless. When the leaves have fewer than five main veins or fewer than five veins on each side of the central main vein, and the serrations or notches on their edges are larger and fewer in number than on a normal leaf, then they have reverted and the bush should be uprooted and immediately burnt to avoid the disease spreading.

Big bud mite reduces fruit yield in proportion to the number of buds infested. Normal buds are narrow and pointed, but those affected with big bud mite are large and round and easily detected during winter and early spring, and if only a few are in evidence should be removed by hand picking and burned immediately. If the

H

113

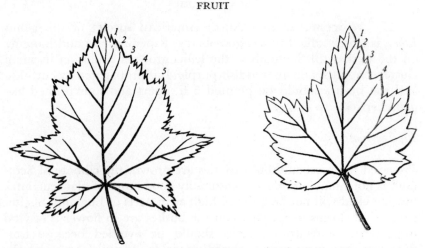

Normal and reverted blackcurrant leaves : *left,* normal leaf with five side veins on each side of the central main vein and a large number of small serrations on the leaf edge ; *right,* reverted leaf with less than five side veins and few but large serrations.

bush is very badly infested uproot it and burn it at once. Supplement the hand picking by an annual spraying in spring when the first formed leaves are about the size of a florin, using a mixture of half a pint of lime-sulphur in 19½ gallons of water, adding a cup of milk to act as 'spreader'. It is a good plan to spray with lime-sulphur every spring as a preventive measure, whether big bud is found or not.

During January, or before the middle of February, spray thoroughly with a tar-oil distillate winter wash to control aphis. Another serious and widespread foliage disease in some districts is rust fungus. This infects the five-needle pine and the spores are then carried by the wind to currant bushes, causing early defoliage in the autumn, and so weakening the plants for the following year. Spraying the bushes after the fruit is pulled with either lime-sulphur, at the same strength as for big bud mite, or Bordeaux mixture, made to the formula 4 lb. copper sulphate, 6 lb. hydrated lime, 100 gallons of water, will help to control this disease.

Stock can be increased by taking cuttings of soft or hard wood, the latter being the principal method used for propagation. The cuttings, made from young shoots produced during summer, are taken in autumn or early winter for immediate planting out of doors and, the earlier they are taken, the more readily they root. They should be about 8-9 ins. long when prepared, and the base cut straight below the bottom bud, but the terminal bud may either be removed from, or left on the shoot. A shoot 18 ins. long will make two, if cut in half above a bud. Plant in a 6-in.-deep drill placing them about 4 ins. apart, so that the top bud is not more than 2-3 ins. above the soil surface and, if more than one row is put in, allow 1½ ft. between the rows. Leaf mould makes an excellent top dressing for the cuttings.

Soft-wood cuttings about 3 ins. long—the cut being made just below the point at which a leaf stalk joins the stem—should be placed 6 ins. apart in a cold frame during May or early June and well-watered in. The frame lights should then be closed and shaded, the shading being gradually reduced and eventually discarded as

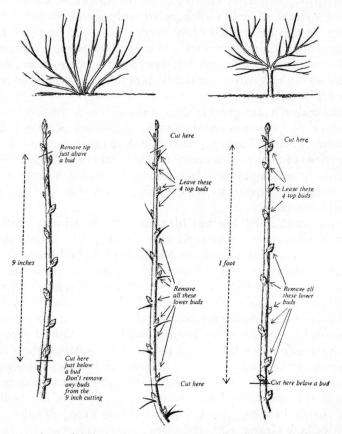

Blackcurrant and gooseberry or red currant bushes : In the blackcurrant bush on the *left above* all the main branches ideally develop from or below soil-level, this is why all buds are left on the cuttings. For gooseberries or red currants (*right*) it is much better to have a few inches of clean stem, this is why the buds are removed from the lower part of each cutting.

Below : In the drawing below is shown (*left to right*) the preparation of blackcurrant, gooseberry and red currant cuttings.

115

roots develop. When there is plenty of root growth, the plants should be hardened off gradually, then planted out of doors in nursery rows and cut back in order to encourage the development of basal buds. In the autumn of their second or third year they may be removed to their final fruiting quarters in well-manured land. The space between the plants depends upon the area available, but 6 ft. each way is a recognised standard, although a variety making a small bush, such as Baldwin, is frequently planted 5 ft. apart each way. Planting should be an inch or two deeper than in the nursery rows. In the spring following cut back all the shoots to about 2-3 ins. above soil level. A soil mulch, preferably well-decayed farmyard manure, should be applied early every spring and frequent hoeings will maintain a loose soil surface and keep down weeds. Alternatively, give a dressing of compound fertiliser, such as Growmore, and hoe it in, following this with a good mulch of decayed vegetable compost or horticultural peat.

Blackcurrants are gross feeders and much experimental work has been done on potted specimens at Long Ashton Research Station and other centres, proving that blackcurrants respond to heavy applications of farmyard manure and a balanced fertiliser. Nitrogen and potash are important, but phosphate is not a serious factor. Lime does not appear to be necessary, although it must not be withheld completely.

Prune established fruiting blackcurrants in winter, cutting old branches which have produced only short young shoots down to about 2 ins. Leave the branches which have a good number of long ones, since these produce the crop, but avoid overcrowding.

Over a period of years, the research and experimental stations have tested practically every variety, including some from Canada and the Continent. Some are now classified into four main groups.

Group I, represented by French Black, is a red-bud group—the buds are pinkish in winter, pointed, and the scales tightly packed. The bushes have many branches and the fruit trusses are short with medium-size berries of an acid flavour ripening in mid-season. Other names in this group, and now considered synonyms, are Seabrook's Black, Lee's Prolific, Black Naples, Mite Free, Mammoth and Ogden's Black Grape.

Group II, represented by Boskoop Giant, is another red-bud group but the buds are a slightly darker shade than those of Group I, and tend to be broad and blunt. The bushes make strong shoots which are of a spreading habit, and the blossom trusses are usually long and borne singly. The berries are rather sweet and easy to pick. This group includes Dutch Black, Prince of Wales, Black Bunch, Tony Black and Hoogendyke's Seedling.

Group III, the Goliath, is a green-bud group. The buds are closer together, pointed, conical and light in colour and the bushes erect. The foliage is relatively small and light in colour and there are many blossom trusses. The berries are fairly large, sweet and ripen mid-season. Victoria, Edina, Monarch, Bangup, Coronation, Nigger and Invincible Giant Prolific are synonyms of Goliath.

Group IV, Baldwin, is another green-bud group. The buds are long, rather large, conical and pointed. The bushes smallish and have small regular shaped leaves. Growth commences early but the berries ripen late, and have a tough skin and an acid flavour. The principal varieties are Baldwin, Daniel's September Black, Carter's Champion, Black Champion, Hill-top Baldwin.

Unclassified varieties include Cotswold Cross, raised and introduced by Long Ashton Research Station. The bush, a vigorous grower with large tough-skinned berries, resembles the Baldwin Group in habit of growth. Wellington XXX is also a vigorous grower with a spreading habit. The long bunches are produced in clusters, and the berries have a tough skin. Westwick Choice is another variety with dormant shoots of light brown. The bush is large and flattish and the bunches are long, with moderate-sized, tough-skinned berries. Others are Amos Black, Blacksmith, Davidson's Eight, Mendip Cross, Raven, Tinker, Westwick Triumph, Laxton's Giant, Laxton's Grape and Silvergieter's Black.

The following varieties gave the best results in four areas of Scotland during a cropping trial, conducted by the Scottish Fruit Trials Committee of the Scottish Agricultural Improvement Council, which lasted from six to seven years. In the West of Scotland: early varieties—Mendip Cross, Laxton's Grape and Silvergieter's Black; mid-season varieties—Cotswold Cross and Goliath; late varieties— Daniel's September and Baldwin.

In the North of Scotland; early varieties—Mendip Cross and Laxton's Grape; mid-season varieties—Blacksmith and Cotswold Cross; late varieties—Baldwin and Daniel's September Black.

In the Lothians: early varieties—Boskoop Giant and Laxton's Grape; mid-season varieties—Seabrook's Black and Raven; late varieties—Amos Black and Baldwin.

In the Dundee area: early varieties—Mendip Cross and Laxton's Grape; mid-season varieties—Cotswold Cross and Raven; late varieties—Baldwin and Amos Black.

The mid-season varieties Wellington XXX and Westwick

Choice generally did not show up well in the trials since they are very susceptible to frost damage during the flowering season, and gave relatively poor yields.

Gooseberries

The gooseberry (*Ribes grossularia*), a native of southern Europe and western Asia, is found in Britain growing wild in open woods and in hedgerows and regarded as a 'garden escape'. It is hardy, although the blossoms and leaves are sensitive to frost damage, deciduous and much-branched and its many prickles come singly or in pairs, occasionally in threes. The leaves are small and hairy on both sides and the flowers small, with greenish-yellow calyxes, produced in clusters of one to three in the leaf axils.

The gooseberry not only grows and bears well, but acquires its full richness of flavour better in the comparatively cool climate of Scotland and the north of England than in the warmer south. Large-scale cultivation is therefore common to Cheshire, Lancashire, Yorkshire and all Scotland. Many of the varieties are large and coarse but are very useful for culinary purposes, for the gooseberry, although not the first outdoor fruit to ripen, is the earliest fit for use.

The two-hundred-and-fifty varieties of gooseberry, have been classified into four main groups according to skin colour and the following are most popular:

The white skin group includes Careless, a bush of drooping habit. The berries are large, roundish, pale green or white, of good quality and flavour, useful both for pulling green or as dessert. It is a popular market variety as the berries become a fair size early in the season. Another member is White Lion, a strong grower of spreading habit, and a heavy cropper with fairly good flavour. It is a popular commercial variety for picking green and as dessert, and the berries are large, oblong, and slightly hairy.

In the green skin group is Howard's Lancer or Lancer, a very old variety introduced in 1831, which is popular for culinary and desert purposes. The berries are medium-sized, greenish-white, oval with thin transparent skin, of excellent flavour and late to mature. Another is Keepsake; with large, oval berries, suitable for dessert or cooking which can be picked early.

Gooseberries in the red skin group include Dan's Mistake, a strong upright grower, with round-oval berries, suitable for dessert and a fine exhibition variety. Lancashire Lad, a fairly upright bush has berries of dark claret red, oval and hairy. It is a mid-season, good cropping variety, valuable for dessert and culinary purposes. May Duke, a very upright grower, has fruit of a fair size, dark-red and roundish-oblong, which is one of the earliest for gathering green, and makes jam of excellent flavour. Warrington is a strong grower of pendulous habit with medium-size roundish-oval, bright red, hairy fruit of good flavour. It is a popular mid-season variety for dessert and preserving. Whinham's Industry, a large roundish bush, is a popular mid-season variety for picking green as well as for dessert. The berries are moderately large, oval, dark red, hairy and sweet.

The yellow skin group includes Cousen's Seedling, a bush of spreading habit. A good late maturing yellow, largely grown for dessert, it is slightly hairy with a fair flavour. Early Sulphur (Golden Ball, Golden Bull and Moss's Seedling are synonyms) grows erect, and has medium sized, roundish to oblong fruit, hairy and of fairly good flavour. It is very early and an abundant bearer. Langley Gage is of upright habit. The berries are smooth, medium in size, round-oval pale green tinged with yellow and have an excellent flavour. Leader is a small, bush variety but has large, roundish-oval berries greenish yellow in colour and of excellent flavour. It is a favourite late dessert variety. Leveller is a bush of spreading slightly pendulous habit with excellent flavoured berries, oval, yellowish-green, with almost smooth skin. This variety requires heavy manuring and high cultivation to produce the best quality fruit.

Propagation is usually by cuttings from young fruiting bushes taken in late autumn or early winter. Select well ripened young growths, about 12 or more inches long, cutting them transversely at the base very close to and beneath a bud, and then remove an inch or two from the tip of the cutting—cut just above a bud. Remove the basal buds, so that only four or five are left at the top. The bushes will then grow on a 'leg' and no suckers will form from below soil level. Retain all the prickles since these help to hold the shoots in the soil until rooted.

Cuttings will root out of doors in most soils, but a light sandy compost is best. Make a furrow about 6 ins. deep, with a spade, and insert the shoots 4-6 ins. apart in the rows, tramping the ground very firm. As cuttings have a tendency to lift and become loose, especially after frost, refirm the soil from time to time.

Roots may develop at any point on the cutting below ground, but the best are those at the base. At the end of the first season, the yearlings should be lifted, their upper roots cut off, and the young plants replanted about a foot apart each way and left for another season before setting out in permanent fruiting quarters.

The gooseberry will succeed in any good garden soil that contains a high percentage of humus, is open and fairly rich in potassium but, although the best-flavoured fruit is grown in an open situation, the bushes must be sheltered from high winds to prevent the damage to the young shoots. Plant them 5-6 ft. apart each way during the dormant season, between leaf fall and bud burst in the spring. Where space is limited, they may be trained against a trellis or wall as single, double or triple-cordons. Two-year-old bushes, carefully planted, will produce fruit the second year and continue bearing for many years if kept free from disease.

Fruit is borne on one-year-old shoots and on spurs, and pruning may be adapted either to quality or quantity. For really large fruit, all the laterals must be shortened to about 2 ins. during the winter months to form 'fruiting spurs', and the leaders cut back for extension purposes to an outward-pointed bud from one-half to two-thirds of their length, according to the vigour of the variety. Varieties of drooping habit should be cut to an inward and upward-pointed bud.

When the fruit is to be picked green for culinary purposes, quantity is the chief consideration, and pruning may, in due course, mean cutting out whole branches to keep the bushes sufficiently open and to stimulate strong new shoots. Very little spur pruning of the lateral shoots is necessary unless the bush centres are over-crowded, when a few of the strongest may be cut out to admit light and air. Summer pruning of 'spur bearing' bushes consists of cutting back the new lateral shoots to within 5-6 ins. of their base during July or early August, following this during the dormant season by winter pruning. The 'leaders' must not be summer pruned.

To prevent birds, especially the house sparrow, the tits and bullfinches, picking out the buds in winter, during frosty weather, thread the bushes with black cotton, or cover them by old fish-netting adequately supported above the bushes.

Lack of potash causes 'leaf scorch', the leaves becoming brown at the edge, and if this is noted it can be cured by applying sulphate of potash at the rate of 1-2 oz. per sq. yd. during winter, after pruning. Do not exceed this rate of application on any one occasion, but be prepared to repeat the treatment in successive years.

Every second or third year, give the soil a dressing of one of the organic manures such as farmyard manure, stable manure, decayed vegetable compost or one of the meat meals, which help to retain essential moisture in the soil.

One of the worst pests is the gooseberry sawfly, which lays its eggs in rows along the leaf veins. In a few days the caterpillars hatch out, and, starting at the edges, eat the whole of the leaves, so that unless they are controlled the bushes may be defoliated. Very often the initial stages of a caterpillar attack are found near the base of the bush, and it is necessary to keep a look-out for it if counter-measures are to be undertaken with success, especially since there may be two or three generations in one season. Control is easy by spraying or dusting the foliage with derris, which is non-poisonous.

Raspberries

The raspberry is a popular fruit in private gardens and allotments, and is usually well grown. It is propagated by freely-produced offsets or subterranean stems, commonly known as young canes. It is often better to establish nursery beds specially to supply planting stock than to draw too lavishly on fruiting plantations, and this also allows the grower to keep his stock healthy, since diseased plants can be ruthlessly rogued out.

The site for a plantation should be carefully chosen, avoiding low-lying or windy positions, since the former are likely to be frost pockets and wind does much damage to flower trusses and foliage. I have known of a plantation which had been in full bearing for thirty-five years, but a more usual period is ten to fifteen. Good drainage is essential, both on the surface and beneath, and the best soil is a deep sandy loam rich in humus. To avoid diseased plants order certified stock grown in nursery stool beds; a list of growers whose stocks were certified during the previous summer may be obtained from the Secretary, Department of Agriculture for Scotland, St. Andrew's House, Edinburgh, 1.

Plant any time from October to March, but since the easily damaged fibrous roots will only allow surface cultivation subsequently, take special care in thoroughly preparing the land a few weeks prior to planting by digging in a dressing of farmyard manure, 3 cwt. to each 30 sq. yds., to help conserve moisture at the roots. Plant at 2 ft. intervals in rows 5 ft. apart. Open the holes with a spade, set the plants slightly deeper than they were in the nursery rows, cover the roots with soil and tramp it down firmly. It is important not to damage the basal buds.

In the following spring, before growth commences, cut back the canes to a height of 9-12 ins. to encourage growth, and hoe between the rows just sufficiently deep to keep weeds under control. Normally, only about eight young canes are required for fruiting from each plant, or 'stool' as it is often called, therefore, during the early summer of subsequent years cut out surplus canes of those varieties producing large numbers of young shoots. Cut out, remove and burn all old fruited canes on established plantations as soon as the crop is finished, since this admits light and air and enables the young canes to mature before winter.

During the dormant season the young canes which have been retained must be supported to reduce wind damage, and this can be cheaply done with two lengths of 13-gauge galvanised wire stretched between wooden posts, the top wire being 4 ft. from the ground and the bottom about 2 ft. The young canes, usually six to eight per plant or 'stool', are then laced or tied fanwise to the wires with fillis string. Alternatively, use two wires at the 2-ft. level, and place the young canes between them and only lace or tie them to the top wire. In late spring the young canes may be tipped about 1 ft. above the top wire.

Raspberries need abundant moisture, especially during May and June, and this means that they respond a dressing of bulky organic matter, such as farmyard manure, which, in addition to supplying essential plant food elements, increases the water holding capacity of the soil, or, if this is not available use decayed vegetable compost. Whichever is used it is best applied as a surface mulch in spring. Before the manure or compost is applied 1½ lb. sulphate of potash and 3 lb. superphosphate to each 90 ft. of a row should be given yearly and lightly hoed in.

It is also advisable to give a dressing of nitro-chalk early in April to stimulate the young shoots and assist the fruiting canes in old plantations to produce laterals of sufficient growth before they come into flower. During the growing season suppress weeds by surface cultivation. The fruit ripens quickly and picking is best done in the early morning, at least every second day. After the fruited canes have been cut out and the new canes laced or tied to the supports, the ground between the rows should be dug over with a fork to the depth of 4 ins., taking care not to damage the young fibrous roots.

There are many varieties but the incidence of mosaic virus disease largely determines the best. The older ones—for example, Superlative, the Antwerps, Hornet and Baumforth's 'A' and 'B'— were at one time the leading varieties, but they have been superseded and are seldom seen to-day. Growers in Lanarkshire still favour Burnett Holm Seedling, a heavy cropping variety well suited for dessert purposes, with large, bright red fruit. The canes are very strong and abundant. Oddly enough it has never given favourable results when planted and grown in other Scottish counties. St.

Walfried, a Dutch variety once popular, is now rarely if ever, seen since the incidence of virus disease in it undermined its commercial and garden value. Norfolk Giant, a heavy-cropping late variety, produces bright red berries, firm, conical and somewhat acid in flavour. The canes are erect and strong, often attaining 7 ft.

Lloyd George, introduced in 1919, superseded earlier commercial varieties and heat-treated virus-free stocks have been planted commercially during recent years with good results. The fruit ripens early, is conical, firm, dark red and fairly sweet and the average-height canes are brownish white.

Malling Promise, one of the first to be introduced into commerce from East Malling Research Station, still finds favour with many commercial growers and private gardeners. It is a heavy cropper, ripening early and producing large, conical firm berries, bright red in colour with good flavour and excellent for canning. The plant is vigorous with abundant erect canes. Malling Enterprise (formerly known as Seedling 'E'), a mid-season variety which carries its fruit over a long period, has a large bright red fruit, roundish and firm. Though not one of the heaviest croppers, it is still popular because of its flavour. The canes are strong and vigorous but somewhat sparse.

Malling Jewel, formerly known as Seedling 'J', grows large to very large firm, conical fruit, bright red in colour becoming darker when fully ripe, and is a heavy cropper. It is sweet with a good flavour, ripens mid-season, and is good for canning. It produces fewer young canes than most, but has done exceedingly well in many parts of Scotland where it has now become one of the most widely grown both in field and garden.

Trials carried out on Malling Exploit, Malling Promise, Lloyd George, Malling Jewel, Malling Enterprise and Norfolk Giant, by the Fruit Trials Committee of the Scottish Agricultural Improvement Council at four stations in Scotland between 1952 and 1959 produced some interesting results. The highest average annual yields in West Scotland were produced by Lloyd George and Malling Jewel; in North Scotland, by Malling Jewel and Lloyd George; in the Lothians by Lloyd George and Malling Promise and in the Dundee area by Malling Promise and Malling Jewel.

Since no more than 8 young canes per stool are required and the excess must be cut and carried away, it is obvious that a variety producing an adequate but not excessive number is economically advantageous. Malling Jewel, a good cropper, appears to owe its increased commercial popularity to this characteristic.

Strawberries : in the Open Garden

In general, soil which is not too heavy or wet and grows reasonably good vegetable crops is suitable for strawberries, but frost pockets should be avoided. If possible plant on higher ground, which allows cold air to drain to lower levels so that there will be less danger of frost damage during the flowering period.

Strawberry plants may be planted in March and April, when soil and weather conditions are favourable, but flowers produced during the first summer should be removed, since the rooting system will not be sufficiently well developed to produce a worth-while crop. If they are planted in August and September, however, secondary roots develop soon afterwards and get a grip of the ground before frosty weather begins, so that the plants can produce both fruit and runners the following year. October or November is rather late for planting, since there is no time for the formation of new roots and frost may lift the young plants out of the soil.

Strawberries best follow an early vegetable crop, especially potatoes lifted in July and August, since the ground will have been previously prepared for these by being dug to a depth of 10-12 ins. and a reasonably good application of decayed farmyard manure, or well rotted vegetable refuse-heap compost worked in, supplemented by a suitable fertiliser. Further soil working given during the lifting of the potatoes incorporates the humus still more thoroughly with the soil and generally eliminates weeds. This means that it is only necessary to tramp the ground fairly firm and rake the surface to a fine and level tilth before planting the strawberries.

It is usual to set the plants at 18-in. intervals in drills 2 ft. apart, drawn with a draw hoe 1-1½ ins. deep, and 6-8 ins. wide, but if cultivation is mechanised or strong-growing varieties such as Cambridge Vigour or Talisman are being used in a rich fertile soil, the distance between rows must be 2½-3 ft. according to circumstances. Make holes with a trowel, deep enough to take the roots straight down to their fullest extent and to bring the crowns level with the base of the drill, so giving the young plants shelter. After frosty spells it may be necessary to refirm the plants in the ground, especially if they have been recently planted, by tramping along the sides of the drill, when soil and weather conditions are favourable. If planting has to be done in spring, the routine is the same, except that the ground must be manured well in advance and the fertiliser applied and worked into the soil a few days beforehand. Whenever planting is done, always keep down weeds by frequent shallow surface cultivation with a Dutch hoe, and move the soil towards the plants rather than away from them.

When the young green fruits can easily be seen, spread wheat or oat straw between the rows and close to the plants to prevent rain splashing them with soil, and especially in gardens keep off birds by nets supported on posts and ropes some distance above the plants until fruiting is over. Young runners will have by then developed and some of these should be left on the outer rows ready for the planting of a new bed in August and September. Since the straw covering tends to retard root development in the runners needed for this purpose, it is a good idea to set a few plants say, a dozen, elsewhere in the garden in August or September. These should not be allowed to fruit, but their runners should be trained from each four plants into the square of which they form the corners.

Runners on the inner rows of the main bed, together with all well-developed and older foliage, should be cut away soon after the fruit has been harvested. This may seem ruthless, but it leads to good crops the next year, as commercial growers well know. The refuse should be placed on the compost heap with the used straw.

Fruiting plantations need potash and phosphate fertilisers each autumn or early winter, e.g. a dressing of 2 lb. sulphate of potash and 5 lb. steamed bone flour to each 30 sq. yds. When growth begins in spring hoe in short and well-decayed farmyard manure or decayed compost heap refuse between the rows.

It is best to plant a new bed each year next to that planted the preceding one, uprooting the respective plantings after they have produced three crops—some growers uproot after the second.

The popular modern varieties are Cambridge Favourite, the most widely grown; Talisman, a vigorous grower, and Red Gauntlet. The older Royal Sovereign—once a very popular variety and considered the best flavoured though not the best cropper—is now rarely seen, in addition Huxley Giant, Auchincruive Climax, Sir Joseph Paxton, Scarlet Queen, etc., have now practically disappeared.

Strawberries : under Glass

The first ripe strawberries are always highly appreciated and in order to produce fruits for Easter many gardeners force plants in a greenhouse. There used then to be a gap until the ripening of the earliest outdoor variety but today, by using glass in various forms and without much artificial heat, fresh strawberries can be had from April until the beginning of August.

Set aside a small piece of ground and towards the end of August plant out specially selected runners to ensure a supply of maidens for potting up the following June and July. The runners should be set out in squares, 3 ft. apart each way. First dip the plants in a soft-soap-nicotine solution to make certain they are free from greenfly and other insect pests, then plant firmly in well-prepared ground, using a trowel, and making certain the crowns are just at surface level. If the crown is buried too deeply, the plant is liable to rot, and if the soil is not firm enough frosts lift them out of the ground.

Royal Sovereign was, undoubtedly, the best quality variety for this method, since it would grow in a wide range of soils, but its decline in present day popularity is associated with its susceptibility to virus diseases which spoil results. If a certified stock of this variety can be obtained give it a trial. Early Cambridge is another good variety for this purpose, but its flavour is not so good as that of Royal Sovereign, although both ripen at the same time. Again a certified stock is recommended.

Plants grown in the beds for runner production should be de-blossomed during May to prevent fruiting. Towards the end of June, fill some 3-in. flower pots with a good fibrous loam, packed firmly, and then plunge them to the rims in groups inside each square. The runners should then be placed singly on top of the pots and held in position, by pegs made from bracken fronds or bent wires, until roots form. The plants must be watered during dry weather, as drought is fatal to young plants while rooting.

The layering of the young runners is done in batches as and when they are produced by the mother plants. They usually root in from three to four weeks, and when the small pots are full of roots the connection with the parent plant should be severed. Those to be fruited in the greenhouse should be firmly potted up into 6-in. flower pots, using a good loam, a little decayed stable manure and some hoof and horn meal. A fairly large space at the top of each pot should be left for water. Stand them on a bed of very small furnace clinkers in full sun, syringing them daily during dry weather, and in September, move them to a cold frame, plunging them up to the rims in furnace ashes to prevent the pots being broken by frost. Practically no water will be necessary while the plants are in the frame. The plants that are to be fruited under Dutch lights and cloches need not be potted, but should be planted out into their permanent quarters.

The earliest well-developed plants selected for pot culture should be placed on shelves about 3 ft. from the roof glass of the

126

house in January, and small batches should be brought in regularly to keep up a supply of fruit from April onwards until those in the Dutch frames are ready. No heat is necessary at first, for at this stage it encourages foliage at the expense of flower trusses, but the temperature of the house should be regulated by careful ventilation, being kept low at night but rising to 55° F./13° C. on sunny days. Syringe the plants daily during sunny periods, water, but never allow the soil to get too wet or mildew may appear. The first batch of plants will produce flower trusses in March. Pollinate the flowers about midday, using a rabbit's tail. After the petals have fallen thin out the fruit, which will then have 'set', to 10 or 12 per plant. Maintain a moist atmosphere in the house and feed with a good general liquid fertiliser once a week until the fruits begin to colour. Feeding should then stop and the atmosphere be kept drier and cooler. When they are sufficiently grown, turn the fruit trusses to the sunny side of the shelf and support them with thin birch twigs. With careful management the fruit should be fully ripe in about four weeks from the time of petal fall.

For cultivation under Dutch lights and cloches, thoroughly prepare the ground where the strawberries are to be grown for fruiting, at least a month before setting them out, by digging in about one barrowload of well-decayed farmyard manure to every six square yards of the top spit of soil. Then, just before planting, apply 2 oz. per sq. yd. of hoof and horn meal and work it into the surface of the soil, which should then be firmed and marked off in rows.

Plant the pot-raised runners firmly—a single line of frames will allow three rows of plants 18 ins. apart each way, running east and west—water if the weather is dry, and they should be well established by the autumn. Then, in early February, after the soil surface between the plants has been lightly hoed, set the frames in place over them, and place the lights on the frames. To supplement existing food supplies a complete fertiliser, such as National Growmore, may be hoed in, 3 oz. per sq. yd., but no other treatment is needed until flowering except careful ventilation and watering. A close atmosphere encourages soft leaf-growth and mildew.

During flowering in April and May, open the lights freely by day to ensure insect pollination. After petal fall, remove the lights and place a clean layer of straw over the ground, working a little underneath the foliage, to keep the fruit from soiling. Then, water the bed thoroughly and replace the lights.

Maintain a fairly warm atmosphere as the fruit develops, giving very little ventilation, and very lightly spray the foliage morning and evening during sunny weather to keep it clean and help the swelling of the fruit. When the latter begins to colour, stop spraying, admit more air, and close the frames only on very cold nights. The lights may be removed when the fruit is ripening, birds being kept at bay by a herring net suspended on a wire stretched above the centre of the frames, although a few lights may be kept on part of the frame to hasten ripening, if the glass is sprayed with a weak solution of lime water to prevent the sun scalding the fruit.

For cloche work use the low barn type, 22 × 24 ins., set close together to make a continuous row and the ends closed with sheets of glass or boards. Two rows of plants may be spaced alternately on the site where the cloches will be set out in spring, although some growers allow only one. During flowering every fourth cloche should be lifted and placed on top of its neighbour in the daytime, to ensure pollination, and replaced at night. After flowering, remove the cloches, put straw round each plant, give a good soaking and replace. When the fruit begins to colour, remove one cloche in ten, and space the rest to allow about 4 ins. between each for ventilation. To prevent scorching it may be necessary to lime-spray the glass lightly, as with frames.

A good variety for growing under cloches is Cambridge Favourite provided a certified stock is used.

Strawberries : Virus Diseases

In recent years many plant diseases have been traced to the action of a virus. Control is difficult, since the troubles are so complex, and it is best to rogue out and burn affected plants. Aphides (greenfly) are mainly responsible for the spread of such diseases, e.g. the peach aphis *Myzus persicae*, and in the case of strawberries *Capitophorus fragariae*. A virus is picked up by the aphides as they feed on an infected plant and as these insects pass from plant to plant it is then injected later into a healthy one where the infection multiplies and is carried through the plant system by cell sap, thus affecting its growth and usually producing readily recognisable symptoms.

Important in Scotland are yellow edge and crinkle, to which many strawberry varieties are susceptible and which may both infect the same plant. The chief symptom of the former is a yellowing round the leaf margins in August and September, the plants themselves being often smaller and flatter than normal. Crinkle occurs in June and July and may be either mild, resulting in small chlorotic or

128

Notocactus tabularis.

CACTI

Mixed cactus and succulent plants.

Mammillaria elongata.

Crocus.

BULBS

Tulips (*Fosteriana*).

Double narcissus.

yellow spots which may increase in size with the growth of the leaf, but not necessarily preventing a reasonably good crop; or severe, when the spots increase, the leaves are crinkled to distortion and the crop is considerably reduced. Plants affected by either disease should be removed and burnt immediately.

The production of green-petalled flowers indicates green petal virus infection, and the plants should be uprooted and burnt at once. For no apparent reason its incidence varies from year to year. The Scottish Horticultural Research Institute at Invergowrie, near Dundee, has discovered another 'killer' virus affecting both strawberries and raspberries. Sometimes infected strawberry plants are killed and patches devoid of plants may be noticed in plantations. Whenever dwarf, flattish strawberry plants develop, see if the young leaflets are very small with yellowish, blister-like patches. This may mean they are affected by a 'soil-borne' virus, and all affected plants must be removed and burnt. It is a good plan to send one or two plants showing such symptoms to the Agricultural College serving your area—Aberdeen, Edinburgh or Glasgow—or to the Research Institute itself—to test and verify the presence of the infection.

Some varieties are sensitive and exhibit obvious symptoms of virus infection, but others may 'carry' the infection while still appearing healthy. These 'carriers', however, develop severe symptoms when infected by another virus from a neighbouring variety.

The Department of Agriculture for Scotland's Strawberry Inspection and Certification Scheme is an invaluable safeguard for the grower. When a stock is submitted for inspection, the Department's Inspectors examine it two or three times during the growing season and award a certificate (Special Stock-runner, Stock-runner or Standard) to the grower if a specified standard of purity and health is attained.

The Special Stock-runner certificate is reserved for approved virus-tested stocks or their progeny, propagated on the 'square block' system and grown not less than 100 yds. from all other strawberry plants, excluding parent stock. The stock must be pure and 100 per cent free from discernible virus and red-core infection, 99·95 per cent free from discernible eelworm and tarsonemid mite, and reasonably free from other pests and diseases. The plants are de-blossomed to prevent fruiting.

The Stock-runner certificate is granted to stock grown on the same system at a distance of 50 yds. from other than parent or sister stock. It must be 99·95 per cent pure, 100 per cent free from soil-borne virus and red core, 99·5 per cent free from any other discernible virus infection or from obvious eelworm and tarsonemid mite, and reasonably free from other pests and diseases.

The Standard certificate goes to stock grown in a fruiting plantation not more than two years old and which is 99·5 per cent pure; 100 per cent free from red-core and any soil-borne virus; 98 per cent free from other viruses, eelworm and tarsonemid mite, and reasonably free from other pests and diseases. No stock grown on ground known to have produced red-core infected plants or runners is ever certified.

Propagation beds should be frequently examined during the growing season and sprayed at least twice to prevent and control aphis—the first time towards the end of May, just before the migration period, and the second in June when the winged generation has finished flying.

Vines

The vine (*Vitis vinifera*) is said to be a native of the Caucasus, but it now grows wild in many parts of southern Europe where it was probably first introduced by the Romans. Although plants with pleasing decorative foliage can easily be grown in Scotland, to produce well ripened fruit it is necessary to supplement the warmth of the sun by artificial heat under glass.

The largest vine in the world grows at the Forth Vineyards, Kippen, Stirlingshire and belongs to Duncan S. Buchanan, whose father planted it in 1891. It is of the Gros Colman variety and yields well over 2,000 bunches annually. Almost equally famous is the Auchmore Vine at Kinnell, Killin, Perthshire which belongs to Mrs. McNab of McNab, and is a Black Hamburgh planted in 1832 by Robert Gardiner. The oldest Black Hamburgh vine in existence was planted at Hampton Court in 1768, from a cutting obtained from Valentine's Estate, Ilford, Essex, and the house has been enlarged from time to time as it has grown. The feeding roots of these famous vines go out far beyond the house.

There are numerous varieties of European grapes, but the available choice was formerly limited because of concentration on growing for exhibition, for which appearance was the primary consideration and flavour only secondary but today flavour is given a place of supreme importance. Among the best for cultivation under glass is Black Hamburgh, one of the finer all-round varieties, which produces large broad-shouldered bunches of round-oval, blue-black berries, with richly juicy, deliciously flavoured flesh. It does as well in a small greenhouse as in a large vinery. Buckland Sweetwater is an English seedling with juicy, very richly flavoured berries of pale yellow-green in large bunches. It is a fairly early grape and cannot be adapted for late work. Gros Colman or Cros Colmar grows big bunches of very large oval berries with thick black skins, and is popular as a late market variety where its appearance is the first consideration. Lady Downe's has bunches which are inclined to be oblong in shape, and the thickish black skins of the berries have a thin bloom when fully ripe. At maturity they are richly flavoured, but are otherwise acid. This is a useful variety for a late supply of fruit. Muscat of Alexandria has long tapering bunches of large, oval fruits, which are pale amber in colour with a strong delicious musk flavour. It is one of the very best varieties ever introduced to Scotland, and there are a number of very slightly differentiated sub-varieties. Among these the Tynningham Muscat is said to be a slight improvement, but needs a higher temperature to ripen, and Royal Muscadine, otherwise known as Golden Chasselas, has medium-sized tapering bunches with sweet juicy berries savouring of musk, which are white at first but assume an amber tint on maturity. The latter is one of the most useful varieties for the amateur, since it does well in a cool greenhouse, crops abundantly and the fruit keeps in good condition for a considerable time.

Propagation is by cuttings, layering or grafting. Cuttings with single eyes or buds are better than those with three or four and should be taken from firm well-ripened wood. Plant them in January, singly in small pots filled with a rich fibrous loam and a little sand, then plunge them into fibre and give them bottom heat of 70-75° F./ 21-23° C. After rooting pot them on into 4-in., and later 7-in. pots, so that by next autumn, strong well-rooted plants with ripe wood will be ready for planting out in the vinery border.

Layering should be done as soon as the leaves fall and when bottom heat is not available. Use a 9-in. pot, sunk 2 ins. below the soil level and three-quarters filled with good fibrous loam. Twist the shoot until it splits, then layer it into the pot and shorten to two eyes or buds which will soon grow into shoots, of which the weaker should later be cut out.

Grafting is easy and should be done when both the rootstock and scion are dormant, since bleeding will ensue if the wood is cut when sap is rising. Select the scions at pruning time and insert them in moist soil or sand. Cut back the root-stock or branch to where the scion is to be inserted, and in the first year the new shoot should grow between 10 and 20 ft. It is then cut back while dormant to about 3 ft. above the union.

The vinery border should be about 3 ft. deep and well drained to prevent stagnant water chilling the roots, therefore broken bricks should be laid in the bottom with a slope towards the drains. A good rich compost should be made of turfy loam mixed with some lime rubble, woodash and bone meal. This should be turned several times before being wheeled in to fill the border and planting may be done at any time during the dormant season. Cut back the 'rods', or main stems, to about 2 ft. in winter to prevent bleeding. Remove the plants from their pots and soak the roots in water before planting, carefully disentangling them and spreading them out in all directions when placing them in the hole. Then put the compost among and over the roots and firm the soil around the plants. During the first year, the strongest shoots should be allowed to grow unchecked so that the wood and buds ripen properly before winter, then by the end of January cut back to well-ripened wood. It is best not to fruit a vine until it is three years old.

The vine fruits on young wood of the current season's growth, so when shoots develop from the main stem they should be pruned back while dormant to one or two eyes, then the young lateral shoots should be carefully brought forward as they begin to grow and bent gradually into a horizontal position—a little at a time in order not to break them—and tied to the training wire. If two lateral shoots develop from a 'spur' after pruning, tie each to the nearest training wire, but later, when rudimentary bunches of grapes appear, retain only the stronger and remove the weaker. The rudiments of each bunch appear on the young shoots after the fourth leaf, and the shoots should then be pinched to two leaves beyond each bunch. This causes the growth of sub-laterals which should be stopped above their first leaf. As soon as the berries are set remove all surplus centre ones, using a pair of thin, long-bladed, sharp scissors to cut the stalks—this prevents overcrowding and allows each berry to swell unhindered. The bunch should form an inverted cone, of which the stalk is the axis, but where the main stalk sub-divides to form shoulders, the latter should be retained and tied up to the supporting wires. Never touch the actual berries with scissors or fingers when thinning, otherwise they may be blemished and decay. If a berry has to be slightly lifted, so that it can be cut off, then use a narrow piece of wood in which a v-shaped cut has been made at one end.

The quality of the grape depends on uniformly progressive growth of the foliage, and air, heat and moisture should be regulated to this end. Never ventilate to lower the temperature of the house, but simply to prevent it from rising too high, and always ventilate first from the top and later from the side. Vine borders must be kept moist, therefore it is advisable to water the border well before growth starts in spring, again when the berries are set and begin to swell; and frequently afterwards whenever the soil feels or looks dry. After harvesting, it may be necessary to soak the border thoroughly and syringe the foliage well with warm water to ward off red spider.

The vinery or greenhouse temperature should be about 50° F./ 10° C. at night, rising to 55° F./12° C. by day, when the rods start into growth, and should be increased by 5° F./3° C. as soon as the bunches can be distinguished, rising slightly every week thereafter until the bunches are in flower, when the temperature should be 70° F./21° C. at night. Reduce the temperature as soon as the berries begin to colour and increase ventilation both by day and night. While the vines are growing, the foliage must be syringed daily and the house kept damped down, but the house atmosphere must be kept much drier during flowering and when the fruit is colouring. At least one month after colouring should be allowed before harvesting, to develop the sweetness and richness of flavour of the fruit, otherwise the berries will be slightly acid and the skin tough.

·4·

Flowers and Decorative Plants

Spring-flowering greenhouse plants 136. The herbaceous border 139. Hardy annuals 142. Native lowland plants 146. Fragrant plants 148. African violets 151. Alpines 153. Anemones 156. Antirrhinums 159. Begonias 161. Bulbous plants 163. Cacti and other succulents 165. Campanulas 168. Carnations 171. Chrysanthemums 173. Clematis 175. Crocus 178. Dahlias 180. Delphiniums 182. Ferns 184. Gladioli 186. Lilies 189. Meadow rues 192. Phloxes 194. Primulas 196. Roses 198. Rose species 202. Saxifrages 205. Sweet peas 207. Tulip species 210. Wallflowers 212.

·4·

Flowers and Decorative Plants

Spring flowering Greenhouse Plants

THE REAL difficulty the gardener faces here is one of choice. Personal preference will play its part, and some take pride in growing successfully just those very plants which the circumstances of soil and position make least likely to flourish, but it is usually better to go with nature than against it. Keep an eye on other gardens in your neighbourhood, and the wild plants growing on any nearby open spaces, to see the types which make themselves at home most easily. And don't think solely in terms of rectangular flower-beds and borders, but exploit the opportunity for the unusual, whether in siting your greenhouse or placing a fern.

The first essential in growing plants in pots to be brought into the house when flowering, or for greenhouse decoration, is that they should be well drained. This means placing a large potsherd over the drainage hole of the pot, with the hollow side downwards, then smaller ones over and around it with some charcoal chips above, and the whole topped with rough fibre or peat to prevent soil seeping downwards and causing blockage.

Soil for potting purposes, best of all the top spit of turfy soil from a grassfield, should be stacked grass side down ten to twelve months before it is required to permit it to mellow. A good loam is generally darkish, containing plenty of fibre, and the final compost should be kept open by the addition of granulated or horticultural peat, chiefly composed of decayed sphagnum moss. It also needs an admixture of leaf-mould, consisting of partly decomposed hard-wood tree leaves collected in autumn (kept slightly moist and turned frequently to hasten decay) and either brown or white gritty river sand. When repotting plants the compost should be well-mixed and semi-moist, and the pots thoroughly clean inside and out. Firm the soil with the fingers so that no cavities are left between it and the pot, and finish off with a level surface.

The following may be grown for greenhouse decoration. Primulas, a genus comprising many lovely gems, are mainly hardy, but a few are half hardy Chinese species and varieties which are invaluable under glass. They like a soil compost consisting of about two parts of good turfy loam, one part of well-decomposed manure, one part good leaf mould or granulated peat, with a liberal addition of coarse sand. Particularly useful are the perennial *Primula obconica*, and the annual *P. malacoides*, which should be sown in early May in a well drained seed pan filled with porous soil. Keep the pan well shaded and near the glass, but not too warm, and when the seedlings appear in about three weeks time, prick them out into other pans 2 ins. apart each way, transferring them again when well established into 3-in. pots and finally into 5-in. On each occasion add a little decayed manure to the compost, and give free ventilation and shade from direct sunlight; water carefully otherwise damping off may result. Some of the choice strains of *P. obconica gigantea* are Red Chief and Wyaston Wonder and of *P. malacoides* Pink Sensation and Mauve Queen, which like other varieties of *malacoides* are nearly hardy and should be regarded as such—protection from frost is all they need.

Another species of Chinese primula is *sinensis*, which besides being available in crimson, blush, salmon, cerise and scarlet, also has double forms and giant-flowered hybrids which grow much taller than the ordinary form. There is also great variety in the foliage of this primula, which in some strains is fleshy with a downy surface and sinuated edges, and many of the hybrid flowers are as much as 2½ ins. across.

Sow seed in May and June on a light loamy soil, sprinkling it evenly on a somewhat rough surface, then press down, cover with paper and place in heat. After germination about three weeks later, remove the pans to a shady place and discard the paper. As soon as they can be handled, transfer the plants to 3-in. pots and gradually subject them to cooler treatment in a frame close to the glass. In September take them into the greenhouse again and repot them into 5-in. pots to flower.

Calceolarias or slipperworts belong to the Scrophulariaceae family and are divided into two sections the herbaceous, often called the greenhouse calceolaria, and the shrubby type, often used as a bedding plant outdoors, but both are very useful for spring display in the greenhouse. The former should be sown thinly in May or June in well-drained small pans containing a rough turfy loam with a fine surface of sifted soil and sand. Water with a fine rose, remembering that the seed is like snuff and should be pressed into the compost although no covering with soil is necessary. Place the pans in a cool greenhouse or frame, always keeping them protected from bright sunshine by a sheet of newspaper, and when the seedlings are large enough to handle, prick them out into pans, which should again be placed in a shaded frame. Later set them singly into small pots, and when roots fill them transfer to larger ones, and place in a cool greenhouse. During February or March repot into still larger pots containing a compost of 3 parts turfy loam, 2 parts leaf-mould or granulated peat, a little well decayed manure and some sharp sand. Avoid excessive heat which will develop plants of poor colour with deformed flowers, and grow in a cool greenhouse. Greenfly is the worst enemy, but fumigation with nicotine will keep this under control.

Two of the best shrubby kinds are *C. Clibranii*, about 3 ft. high and covered with bright shining yellow pouches an inch across, and the rich orange red *C. Banksii*, named after a curator of the Botanic Gardens, Glasgow. Both are raised from 2½-in. cuttings taken during June and July and inserted into small pots or pans containing a sandy well drained loam. They should be set 2 ins. apart and then placed under a hand light in the greenhouse which should be kept closed for a week or so until they root, when they should be given plenty of air. They will now make vigorous growth and will be ready for transferring to 4-in. pots at the beginning of August. These shrubby varieties do best in a somewhat heavy soil and must be kept cool and shaded. When they begin to grow in spring, they should be encouraged to branch by taking out the growing point of each shoot. Before they become pot bound they should again be transferred, this time into 7-in. pots, containing a good fibrous loam, with a 4-in. pot full of bone meal and some wood ash added to each bushel. As they begin to branch, they should be staked with thin, split bamboo canes, which will help also to display their natural growth.

Schizanthus, also known as butterfly flower or the poor man's orchid, is sown in July and again in August, in order to prolong the flowering period during April and May. Keep the plants as cool as possible at all times, and in potting them on from the seedling stage use a loamy mixture with a little decayed manure, and for the final potting, set them firmly in 8 in. pots. Pinch out the leading shoots when the plants are small, but do not repeat the process; simply stake them as they grow to keep them shapely. Dr. Badger's large-flowered hybrids are the best strain and bear pansy-shaped blooms, which have very large overlapping petals with a slight tendency towards doubling, and an endless variety of colours. As soon as the pots are full of roots, give a little soot water every week and, before flowering, feed occasionally with a little compound fertiliser.

The cinerarias form a most important group of easily-cultivated greenhouse plants, particularly useful from January to April. The flowers are fairly large and vary in colour from the most brilliant scarlet to very delicate blue and pink. There are three types, the tall growing *C. stellata,* with heads of star-like flowers; the dwarf, large-flowered *C. grandiflora*; and the semi-tall *C. intermedia.* They should be treated in the same way as herbaceous calceolarias and succeed best when grown in a cold frame, even in cold weather, provided frost is excluded. Take the plants into the cool greenhouse during September. They are fast rooting, and should never be allowed to suffer from lack of room, since this produces poor trusses of bloom.

The Herbaceous Border

Ideally the herbaceous border should be 10-15 ft. wide and at least a 100 ft. long. The background may be evergreen shrubs, an evergreen hedge, roses trained on trellis work or rustic poles, or walls clothed with flowering shrubs.

The border should be exposed to the full sun during most of the day and sheltered from the north and east by trees or tall shrubs, placed far enough away for their roots not to compete with those of the herbaceous plants.

In planting, the height, colour, habit, aspect, time and duration of flowering must be considered. Graduate the plants easily from back to front, avoiding rigid lines, and occasionally placing a taller plant nearer the front to give an undulating effect. Certain kinds may be planted in groups of three to five, but avoid frequent repetition.

Although most herbaceous plants need lifting and replanting occasionally, such as asters (Michaelmas daisies) and heleniums, the peonies, hellebores and phloxes do not like root disturbance.

The arrangement of the border requires a good deal of knowledge of the plants themselves to judge the space to allot to them. Some kinds look better when grown in a border by themselves, for example Michaelmas daisies; lupins and delphiniums also look well in separate beds as well as in the border.

Generally speaking, the majority of the vigorous growing perennials may be planted at any time after growth is nearly completed in the autumn, or in spring just before they commence to grow. Strong-growing sorts such as delphiniums, lupins, asters and phloxes can be moved at any time after they are cut down in autumn. When planting try to arrange that there will be some bloom in the border at all times from spring to autumn, and fill in any gaps with annuals and biennials grown close to the early flowering perennials before they go out of bloom.

Bulbs, such as tulips and daffodils, are best planted in small clumps near the back and centre early in the autumn so that plenty of time is allowed for them to make roots, and so ensure a good show of bloom in the spring and early summer before the other plants are too high. This placing also means that their dying foliage is hidden.

Near the front introduce groups of small plants with bold foliage, such as *Pulmonaria officinalis*, *Dicentra spectabilis*, alpine poppies, dwarf irises, dwarf campanulas, pinks, pansies and violas for the extreme edge, with groups of iberis and broad-leaved saxifrages, funkias, dwarf oenotheras and oriental poppies immediately behind.

Edges and edging plants should not be planted to show a hard, straight line, so that a ribbon edge of violas or catmint is inadvisable. The plants used should be perennial, the flowering period prolonged and in keeping with the arrangement of the grouping in the borders. Frequently the border runs alongside a gravel path, so that stones can be placed irregularly and a few dwarf plants such as dwarf achilleas, aubrietias, *Arabis albida*, var. *flore pleno*, *Thymus coccineus* and *Veronica rupestris*, can be introduced at intervals to break up the line.

The general management of the herbaceous border is not complex. Flower spikes of vigorous growing sorts, such as delphiniums, phloxes and asters are improved if some of their stems are thinned out early in the season; sometimes a second bloom is thereby induced. Train and stake with care, remembering that the tying up of the plants to one stake is objectionable unless the plant has only a single spike and the stake is camouflaged by the foliage. A circular piece of sheep netting placed about 2 ft. from the ground above each plant requiring support, and secured at the sides by appropriate sized stakes, permits the plants to grow through the interstices and makes staking almost invisible, especially when it is painted green, and will last for many years. Another method is to place two, or preferably, three, stakes around each plant, and to tie them with one or more pieces of string, according to height, avoiding bunching.

140

Always be prompt to remove decaying flower spikes and seed pods throughout the growing season.

Some of the more suitable showy kinds, arranged alphabetically under their botanical names include:

Achillea (Milfoil or Yarrow): the best kinds are *millifolium, roseum* or Cerise Queen 2½ to 3 ft.; and *ptarmica*, the Pearl pure white, 2 ft. high.

Alstroemeria (Peruvian Lily): the *chilensis* hybrids have many lovely shades of crimson, orange, rose, buff and yellow, grow about 2 ft. high and are invaluable as cut flowers.

Anchusa (Alkanet), mostly perennial, of which *italica* variety Dropmore, 3 ft., is a rich gentian blue and Opal, 3 to 5 ft., has pale blue flowers.

Aquilegia (Columbine), a charming group of hardy perennials which comprise a wide range of bright pleasing colours, and vary from 2-3 ft. The long-spurred hybrids are the most popular.

Aster (Michaelmas Daisy): there are all kinds and colours ranging in height from 1 to 6 ft., Gay Border Supreme and Little Boy Blue are lovely border varieties, but there are many others.

Astilbe (Goat's Beard): *Davidii*, rosy crimson, *Moerheimii* pure white and Vesuvius, pink.

Bocconia (Plume Poppy): these poppies usually have glaucous leaves, and terminate in plumes of blossoms of a creamy tint, *cordata* is the most common one grown.

Delphinium (Larkspur): the perennial ones are best of all the blue flowered border plants and last throughout the summer. They vary in height from 3 to 8 ft. Some choice varieties are Blue Gown, Lady Eleanor, Hudson Dell, D. B. Crane, and Belladona var. Wendy, a single flowered, brilliant deep cobalt-blue with white eye.

Geranium (Cranes-bill): *armenum* has purplish crimson flowers in July-August and grows about 2 ft. high.

Gypsophila (Chalk Plant): *paniculata,* single and Bristol Fairy, the double flowered variety are fine for cutting; Rosy Veil, flowers pale pink deepening to bright rose.

Helenium (Sneeze Wort), flowers late summer and autumn, Moerheim Beauty is rich crimson, Riverton Gem brilliant red and gold, and Riverton Beauty, pale yellow.

Lupinus (Lupin), the perennial varieties of *polyphyllus* occur in every imaginable shade and colour, and the Russell varieties are very attractive.

Lychnis (Campion), of which *chalcedonica*, the Jerusalem Cross, with scarlet flowers is very useful.

Phlox paniculata, syn. *decussata* (Herbaceous Phlox) shows a wide range of colour of which Daily Sketch, pale salmon pink; Zeppelin, white with crimson eye and Karl Foerster, bright orange red are outstanding.

Pyrethrum, both single and double varieties are suitable, and the long stems render the blooms popular for cutting: Dr. Borsch, single salmon red; James Kelway, crimson; Eileen May Robinson, salmon pink and Mont Blanc, pure white, double.

Rudbeckia (Cone Flower) of which *speciosa,* rich orange yellow with black disc, is a gem for border and for cutting.

Salvia (Sage), *superba* also known as *virgata nemorosa* is a handsome plant, producing masses of purple flowers in autumn.

Scabiosa (Pincushion Flower): hybrids from *S. caucasica,* such as Clive Greaves, Constancy, and *Goldingensis,* are attractive mauve and blue flowers, excellent for cutting.

Sidalcea (Greek Mallow) are easy to grow: Sussex Beauty, satiny pink and Interlaken, silvery rose of large size, are two of the best.

Thalictrum (Meadow Rue) *dipterocarpum flore pleno,* sometimes known as Hewitt's Double, has rich reddish-violet flowers.

Veratrum (False Hellebore), *nigrum* being the most popular, 3 ft. The large plated leaves and vigorous inflorescence makes it a most decorative border plant, but unfortunately it has poisonous properties. A plant which resents disturbance at the root.

Verbascum (Mullein), of which Gainsborough is a magnificent variety with soft yellow flowers.

Hardy Annuals

Hardy annuals will produce a wealth of bloom at a low cost and are so simple to grow that if good seed is planted in reasonably fertile soil, the seedlings properly thinned and given plenty of sun, even the beginner may be successful.

Dig the soil to a depth of about 12 ins., adding a liberal amount of humus, preferably leaf mould or a little decayed farmyard manure well in advance of planting, and rake in a compound fertiliser at the rate of 1 oz. per sq. yd. ten days before sowing. During the growing season Dutch hoe frequently between the rows to conserve moisture and prevent the surface soil from caking.

As hardy annuals need unrestricted sunlight from early morning until late afternoon, allow plenty of space. Buy the highest grade of seed and sow sparingly, thinning out the seedlings carefully when they show their first true leaves; sometimes the thinnings may be planted in other parts of the garden. The seed packet will usually give full details as to distances between drills and rows, and between thinned seedlings, but the latter is especially important as, if thinning is not done properly, the plants will produce only weak shoots and inferior blooms with a short flowering season. To produce bushy plants with more flowers, pinch out the growing point to induce the production of side shoots, but if quality is preferred to quantity, 'disbud' by removing the side shoots from the main growths leaving only a terminal bud on each.

Some plants need tying and staking to prevent drooping, but don't tie too tightly, or the stems will not develop properly. When picking flowers for the house, cut just above the junction of a leaf stalk with the main stem so that a second, or even third, crop may follow.

The annual Tickseed (*Calliopsis*, sometimes called *Coreopsis*), although differing from the perennial types in colour and habit of growth, has numerous clear yellow to deep maroon, flowers and is very suitable for town gardens and for cutting.

Cornflowers (*Centaurea Cyanus*) are taller if sown in September, than if sown in spring, and will then flower early the following June and continue throughout the summer. Thin the seedlings to one foot apart, to ensure the maximum quantity of bloom. The popular double blues and pinks are ideal for cutting and last a long time in water. Giant Sweet Sultan (*C. imperialis*) has a heavy scent, and the giant strains, varying from 1½-2 ft. in height, are excellent for cutting. This species can also be sown in autumn, preferably in a soil containing plenty of lime.

A beautiful hardy annual growing to about 2 ft. high is *Clarkia elegans*, which may be obtained as separate varieties, e.g., Glorious, crimson-scarlet; May Blossom, carmine rose; Orange King; Purple King; and Salmon Queen.

Larkspur (*Delphinium Ajacis*), among the most graceful of hardy annual border plants, is excellent for cutting and although it lacks scent the colour of the blooms make up for this. Thin the plants to one foot apart as they branch freely.

The Chinese or Indian Pink (*Dianthus Heddewigii*) is a very sweet-smelling annual, and the variety Gaiety has very deep fringed petals and looks well in small bowls.

The Californian Poppy (*Eschscholtzia californica*) is one of the easiest annuals to grow from seed sown outdoors. As slugs are particularly fond of the young seedlings, it is better to sow a few seeds in 3-in. pots, placing them in a cold frame until germination.

143

They can then be planted out in a sunny position without the root disturbance they dislike, and should be thinned to single plants, allowing them room to branch freely once they are established.

Godetias descend from *Godetia amoena*, var. *rubicunda* (syn. *Oenothera amoena*), and the varieties have a wide range in colour and may be either single or double, those which grow 2-3 ft. high being best for cutting.

As a background for other flowers, or by themselves, the white feathery sprays of *Gypsophila elegans grandiflora* are very attractive.

The Sunflower (*Helianthus*) should be sown outside in April, in a rich deep soil, as it is a gross feeder, in a sunny position and thinned out to 15 ins. apart to give ample space for blooming. It produces flowers from July to October which are very effective in large vases.

Rose or Tree Mallow (*Lavatera*), especially the variety Sutton's Loveliness which flowers from the end of August throughout September, is extremely showy when grown in a large bed and given ample room, but should be sown where it is to bloom as disturbance is resented. It grows 3 ft. or more high and the 15-18 ins. long flower stems look very attractive if arranged with their own foliage.

Love-in-a-mist or Fennel-flower (*Nigella damascena*), a delicate blue flower surrounded by a green mossy involucre and graceful foliage, will produce a second crop of flowers toward the end of August, continuing throughout September, if the plants are cut down to within two or three inches of the ground after the first flowering. New shoots will appear in about two weeks and the plants should then be given a light application of a compound fetiliser which is watered in.

Shirley Poppies (*Papaver Rhoeas*), sown thinly out of doors in early April, will bloom until late autumn. The seedlings cannot be transplanted as they have long tap roots, but thin them to about 9 ins. apart and support them with short bushy twigs. To keep them fresh in water, pick during the evening or early morning before they are completely open and plunge the stalk ends into almost boiling water.

The Marigold, often called the Scotch Marigold (*Calendula officinalis*), and the varieties Orange King and Lemon Queen are useful, the double forms being most effective. Seedlings grow rapidly and bloom profusely during the summer and autumn, but as soon as the flowers begin to fade, cut them off to encourage the production of new ones.

Parent of many annual varieties, *Coreopsis bicolor* is fairly tall, sometimes reaching 3 ft. high, with brown and yellow flowers produced on long wiry stems, and is ideal for house decoration:

Delphiniums, Pacific Giants.

imula sonchifolia.

HERBACEOUS
PLANTS

Antirrhinum, Dobie's Tetraploid.

A climber, Cocktail.

ROSES

A fine floribunda, Orangeade.

C. tinctoria and the two varieties Yellow Beauty and Crimson King, are useful border plants. Although really a perennial, *C. grandifllora*, will flower the same season if sown early in March, grows to about 2½ ft. high and produces large golden-yellow flowers.

The Californian *Limnanthes Douglasii*, a very showy, dwarf spreading annual of the geranium family, forms yellow tufts before its white blossoms in spring and early summer and is a useful edging plant for borders. It is often grown by beekeepers for its pollen in spring, and self-sown seedlings soon become established.

Night-scented Stock (*Matthiola bicornis*), producing flowers that are delightfully scented in the evening, should be sown where it is to bloom as it does not readily transplant.

Nasturtium (*Tropaeolum*), one of the most free flowering plants, whether trailer or dwarf, should be sown in the open in late spring in poor soil. The Tom Thumb section is the result of a sport from *T. majus*. The yellow-flowered Canary Creeper, *T. peregrinum,* is sometimes called *T. canariense,* although its native habitat is Peru and Mexico.

The following are some rather more unusual hardy annuals:

The Paint-brush Flower (*Emilia flammea,* syn. *Cacalia coccinea*), a showy tassel-like plant, vermilion-coloured, is suitable for an edging to a broad border and is less than 12 ins. in height. It is very hardy, but not very vigorous in growth, and produces clusters of flowers on the ends of its thin, wiry stems.

Gilia lutea, syn. *Leptosiphon aureus,* also has many varieties varying in colour from purple to lilac, red and white. Sow in the open during September to flower the following summer or during April or May to flower the same year. The Portuguese Violet Cress (*Ionopsidium acaule,* syn. *Cochlearia acaulis*) one of the hardiest annuals, has a spreading habit and is smothered with tiny pale lilac flowers. Sow in the open any time between the beginning of April and the middle of June.

Lobel's Catchfly (*Silene Armeria*) has glaucous-green foliage and dense clusters of deep rose-pink flowers attractive in the rock garden, and *S. pendula* is an invaluable plant for spring and summer bedding, its varieties, Double Salmon Pink and Dwarf Single Pink, being very showy and coming true from seed.

The Chinese Aster (*Callistephus*), one of the finest annuals for the garden or to cut for house decoration, should be sown out of doors early in May and the seedlings thinned out to 12 ins. apart.

Native Lowland Plants

Native lowland plants, many of which are creepers and have a long flowering season, are very useful in the garden, some for planting in the herbaceous border, and others in the rock garden, the moraine and wild garden and all are excellent as edgings or in colonies as a groundwork to taller plants.

The native wood anemone (*Anemone nemorosa*) is a graceful woodland plant, with fresh green leaves and snow-white flowers, and an ideal companion for primroses. Its beauty cannot be superseded even by the three good blue-flowered varieties of garden origin *Allenii*, Blue Bonnet and *Robertsoniana*. As soon as the leaves have died down, lift some of the black roots from a woodland area and dry them ready for replanting in the garden during autumn.

Thrift (*Armeria maritima*), also known as sea pink and cushion pink, is a dwarf, tufted perennial plant, with grass-like evergreen foliage, found growing abundantly on the tops of some of our mountains and in coastal areas. The flowering stems are simple and leafless, each bearing a globular head of deep pink to white flowers. Liking a sunny, open position and dry, deep gritty loam, it is propagated by division in March and all plants should be divided at least every third or fourth year.

Many native species of campanulas have long been favourites for their beauty in the herbaceous border and rock garden. The clustered Bell-flower (*C. glomerata*) is a creeping plant with erect flower stems, often more than a foot in height, and although the lower leaves are stalked the remainder are sessile and clasp the flower stems. The stalkless half-inch-long flowers are formed in small clusters in the axils of the upper leaves, making compact leafy heads, but the terminal bunches are always the largest. These plants thrive in dry soil, especially on a bank, and are often found near the sea where they become very dwarfed. The Ivy-leaved Bell-flower (*C. hederacea*, syn. *Wahlenbergia hederacea*), a graceful, delicate prostrate plant, is usually found in moist shady dells or on pasture land. Its stems are thread-like, creeping along the damp ground, and produce tiny ivy-shaped leaves and occasional light blue bell-shaped flowers. It thrives in lime-free, peaty soil which is slightly damp, but is difficult to grow unless cultivated with other creeping plants to provide partial shade —the back of the herbaceous border is excellent. The giant bell-flower (*C. latifolia*, syn. *C. macrantha*), a beautiful, tall-growing species with nearly simple stems, and pointed, toothed leaves, often 6 ins. long and 2 ins. across, has large, rich blue, bell-shaped flowers in

146

July, which may vary to white much more than any other species. Liking moist soil, it flowers profusely at the back of the herbaceous border.

The common bluebell of Scotland or harebell of England (*C. rotundifolia*) found abundantly in Britain is a handsome perennial plant under cultivation and dainty when grown under poor conditions. Its radical leaves are heart-shaped, often dying at flowering time, and its flowering stems, varying from 6-18 ins. long according to soil treatment, bear blue blooms, or sometimes white, either singly, or two or three together. The true *C. rotundifolia* should be propagated by division and never by seed as crosses frequently occur.

The sea-heath (*Frankenia laevis*) and sea milkwort (*Glaux maritima*) are low, decumbent, branching perennials, both spreading 6-8 ins., with creeping rootstocks. The latter is somewhat succulent, with very small leaves and covered with masses of small pale pink flowers, whereas the former has only a few, small, pale pink, stalkless flowers. Both are sea shore plants, thriving in a gritty garden loam containing a little peat and are useful for the paved garden or moraine.

A rare plant in Britain, *Gentiana verna* is now confined to a few areas in northern England, and produces numerous bright blue flowers in May, on such short stalks that they appear to be sessile on the tufts of leaves. It is difficult to establish and has only a short life, but may be cultivated successfully if cow dung is mixed with the soil before planting and the plants top-dressed with gravel chips to keep their bases dry during the winter months but plenty of moisture must be given during the growing season. Sow in March, or in the autumn if seed can be obtained and sown immediately, and keep moist until germination takes place, which may not be for a year or two.

The twin flower (*Linnaea borealis*), belonging to the honeysuckle family (Caprifoliaceae), is a slender evergreen, creeping along the ground for a foot or more. It thrives in warm soil and, in Britain, is found only in the woods of some of the eastern counties of Scotland and in Yorkshire and Northumberland. The small, obovate, slightly toothed leaves, grow in pairs and the graceful, thimble-shaped, drooping flowers of pale pink or white, are borne on short erect branches. It can be propagated by division of roots in March and by cuttings in the autumn.

Bird's-foot trefoil (*Lotus corniculatus*), produces pea-like yellow flowers throughout the summer. Either this, or the 3-in.-high double-flowered form *L. c. flore pleno*, is ideally suited for ornamenting a dry bank or a sunny ledge in the rock garden. Sow in April where the plants are required to flower as they have long tap roots and are difficult to transplant.

The oyster plant (*Mertensia maritima*) trails its glaucous blue leaves over the sand of its natural habitat, the sea shore, and is ideal for the moraine. It has rather small, brilliantly purplish blue flowers with protruding stamens.

The grass of Parnassus (*Parnassia palustris*), displays a wealth of bloom from the latter part of August and early September, and has single, white flowers borne on solitary stems, which stand out among short grass in marshy places on the slopes of our Scottish hills, though it is seldom seen in the plains or on the hill tops. It will, however, grow successfully in the garden in deep peaty soil, if given partial shade and plenty of water during the summer months, and can be propagated freely by seed. It produces a neat rosette of heart-shaped leaves and the pure white petals with delicate green veins are rather like those of snowdrop but are erect, not drooping.

An attractive primula (*Primula farinosa*), found on dry banks near the edge of mountain marshes, has mealy white lower leaves, leaf stems and flower stalks and small, compact, pale-lilac umbels of flowers. The stocky dwarf form *P. f.*, var. *scotica*, from Sutherland, has slightly larger purple flowers. For the rock garden, choose *P. vulgaris*, syn. *P. acaulis*, which has numerous graceful widely expanded fragrant flowers of a delicate sulphur yellow with a rich spot of clear yellow at the base of each petal, and thrives in partial shade in a rich loam.

Pyrola (winter-green) is the generic name of two very beautiful, native, dwarf perennials of the heath family. They are *P. rotundifolia* and *P. uniflora*, syn. *Moneses uniflora*, which grow in woods and moist, shady places in Scotland. The former grows 6-8 ins. high and has large white flowers resembling lily-of-the-valley, and the latter produces small, flat, glossy rosettes of leaves from which a single-stemmed, fragrant flower arises, rather like that of the nodding Grass of Parnassus.

Fragrant Plants

One of the most pleasant features of gardening is the sequence of varied fragrance throughout the year. One of the best sweet-scented February-flowering deciduous shrubs is *Chimonanthus fragrans*. The only species of the genus, its rich and powerful fragrance can scarcely be matched. The stalkless flowers are half-transparent, yellowish-red, borne on naked-looking shoots, and if a few are floated in a bowl of water, they perfume the room for many days. This shrub does best against a wall and, if pruned fairly hard back after it has bloomed, this encourages young wood to flower the following year.

Many Irises are sweet scented, especially the early kinds such as *Iris unguicularis* (syn. *stylosa*), which flowers from January to May when planted in a sheltered, dry and sunny spot. Very tender and susceptible to frost damage, the blooms are faintly violet-like and delicately scented, and a single flower is sufficient to scent a room for a couple of days. Rather more strongly scented, *Iris reticulata* does well in pots, though it should not be forced in heat or the plants will produce leaves at the expense of flowers. This species likes partial shade, in the open, with plenty of leaf-mould as a compost. The slaty-purple *Krelagei* variety of *I. reticulata*, of which some forms have broad-petalled flowers of a shade approaching crimson, is unscented. The exquisite *I. histrioides* produces sweet-scented flowers, with blotches and splashes of deep blue on a pale blue ground, in March at the same time as the grey-green foliage appears. The close-growing tufts of grass-like leaves almost hide the numerous lilac-purple flowers of *Iris graminea*, the sweetest smelling of the later blooming irises. The rich 'ripe-plum' fragrance compensates for the plant's lack of beauty. It is easily raised from seed.

If a semi-sheltered corner is devoted to primroses, polyanthus, cowslips, auriculas and primulas, the scent is intensely powerful. The cowslip may be the least handsome but is the most strikingly perfumed, and though auriculas or 'Dusty Millers' are rather pungent, they are regaining a degree of their one-time popularity now that they have been taken up by rock garden enthusiasts.

Together with the sweetness of wallflowers and daffodils of April and May, one can count on the daphnes and deciduous magnolias among the shrubs.

The peat and bog gardens can be rich in fragrant plants. The North American Wax Myrtle, *Myrica cerifera*, has very sweet per-fumed leaves and waxy exudations from the fruits. It is a suitable shrub for peaty, wet land and can be grown at a considerable ele-vation. Azaleas are also highly fragrant, and the charming little *Ledum buxifolia*, bears delightfully aromatic white flowers on its neat bush. In addition, the small evergreen leaves, often covered with a dense mass of felty hairs on the undersurface, are rather pungent when bruised.

An attractive evergreen shrub introduced from China, is *Osman-thus Delavayi*, which is spreading but bushy. The slender, stiffish shoots grow about 1 ft. in length during the summer and are smothered the following April with small white fragrant flowers, in clusters of four to eight from the leaf axils. The species is perfectly hardy, and the farther north the better it flowers, provided it is protected from cold winds in the spring.

The most delicately haunting of flower scents comes in May with apple-blossom, which is followed by honeysuckle, wild roses and sweet briar. A dwarf hedge of the last-named, *Rosa rubiginosa*, gives off an unforgettable fragrance after even a gentle shower, since the scent glands on the under surface of the leaves are slightly bruised.

All roses are expected to be sweet-scented but the new varieties have practically no fragrance despite their perfection in shape, size and colour. Perhaps the strongest and sweetest scent comes from three very old varieties—Climbing Gloire de Dijon, La France and Mrs. John Laing. Delicacy of form, colour, and scent are also certainly attributes of many Tea and Hybrid Tea roses, some having the refreshing aroma of ripe fruit. The old Maréchal Niel and William Allan Richardson (both climbing) are the most powerfully scented of all the noisettes. These varieties are well worth planting in the greenhouse for their sweet perfume, although being unfashionable they may be difficult to procure.

The numerous carnations, picotees, pinks and sweet williams of the Dianthus genus give both fragrance and brilliant colour during the summer and autumn. The picotees and pinks are valuable for the rock garden, and succeed in a gritty soil in the sunny chinks between the stones or on walls. The border pinks, which need sunshine and a well-drained soil, are sweetest of all early summer flowers. They are easily raised from seed sown in April out-of-doors, the seedlings being planted out later in the season.

Among the herbaceous plants that sleep during the day and waken as the sun sets are the tobacco plant, *Nicotiana affinis*, various kinds of stocks—*Matthiola*, Rocket, *Hesperis matronalis* and the *Oenotheras* (Evening Primrose). A general favourite, especially in old fashioned gardens is the Double Rocket, the flowers being especially fragrant in the evening. It is easily propagated from cuttings taken in the autumn and the single-flowered varieties are readily raised from seed. The small annual night-scented stock, *Matthiola bicornis* is almost unsightly in the day time, since the leaves are dull-grey and the flowers small and closed, but in the evening the flowers stand up and open out showing faint pink and lilac petals and are lavishly fragrant.

The fragrant annual Mignonette, *Reseda odorata*, will thrive in ordinary garden soil out-of-doors provided it is supplied with lime or lime rubble. Seed should be sown in firm soil during April and the seedlings thinned to form bushy plants. The perfume of the Mock Oranges, *Philadelphus* species and varieties, in the months of June and July is also delightful: *P. coronarius* may be too powerful to be pleasant when cut for house decoration, but the *Lemoinei* hybrids have the fragrance of ripe apples.

The sweet blooming lavender, *Lavendula*, is ornamental all the year round, makes a good dwarf hedge and should be clipped after the fragrant flower spikes are cut in summer. Bowls of crushed and dry lavender bloom should be kept in every bedroom. Everyone also appreciates the varied scents of rosemary, balm, thyme, mint and hyssop. A few twigs of each arranged in a vase in a sunny window will sweeten the atmosphere of any room and will help to keep insects away.

African Violets

The African Violet (*Saintpaulia*) is a native of tropical Africa, and grows in moist soil in rocky crevices, usually in the shade of other vegetation. One of the most useful and easily grown half-hardy perennials, it is dwarf and has very attractive flowers and foliage, which make it ideal for the greenhouse and the living room. It needs soil well drained and containing a fair amount of leaf mould.

Of the six species of Saintpaulia, three are under cultivation. The most popular (*Saintpaulia ionantha*)—known as the violet flowered—is stemless, with hairy pubescent leaves and is rather like the hardy alpine, *Ramondia pyrenaica*, in general habit and appearance. The profusion of violet blue, bilabiate flowers 1½ ins. across are borne in twos and threes on stout stalks several inches long. The flowers are almost like those of the cultivated sweet violet in size, shape and colour, although the golden stamens in the centre are an additional attraction, but the oval leaves are much more fleshy and wrinkled, and are 1½ ins. to 2 ins. long. Among the numerous varieties of the species are *S. i.*, var. *grandiflora violacea* which has single blue flowers larger than the type; *S. i.*, var. *albescens* with white flowers, delicately tinted in a light flush pink, and the dark purple *S. i.*, var. *purpurea*.

A native of Tanganyika, *S. longwensis* has elliptic or ovate-elliptic leaves, reddish purple below and rather hairy. Very similar to *S. ionantha* is *S. diplotricha*, but the latter has leaves entire and carrying long white hairs of varying length. A native of tropical Africa it needs a constant temperature of 70° F./21° C.

Many hybrids have been derived from crosses between *S. ionantha* and *S. longwensis*. Among the double blue-flowered varieties worth cultivating are Beatrice, Neptune and Pandora and the double-flowered bicolours Hermione, Rainbow Rose and Snow Line.

Propagation is by leaf cuttings, division of the old plants and by seed. Always use clean pans and boxes, and place a layer of sphagnum moss or partly decayed hardwood tree leaves between the crocks and the upper soil. The actual rooting media may include silver sand, vermiculite and a compost such as a mixture of sand, granulated peat and loam. Cuttings will also root in water.

Medium sized leaves from plants that are not fully grown may be taken at any season, but if taken in June and placed in a warm close moist atmosphere until rooted, the plants will produce flowers throughout the next spring and summer.

Cut the leaf stalks, leaving about $1\frac{1}{2}$ ins. attached to each leaf, and dip the ends in a rooting hormone, inserting the cuttings in the rooting medium about 2 ins. apart each way. The pans or boxes should then be placed in a propagation case, and the temperature maintained at about 60° F./16° C., care being taken to shade them from bright sunlight and to prevent damping off. Roots will form in three to six weeks, and in another six weeks young plantlets will appear from the base of the leaf stalks. When the latter are large enough to handle, they can be divided and either put separately into small pots or pricked off into boxes, using a compost consisting of two parts light loam, one part granulated peat or ground-down sphagnum moss and one part sharp sand. Pot lightly and keep the plantlets well shaded for a few days.

As soon as the small pots are full of roots, the plants can be transferred to $3\frac{1}{2}$-in. pots or else four or five plants can be grown in 6 in. pans, so that the effect is of a cushion of dark velvety green foliage covered with violet or rose coloured flowers. Well decayed farmyard manure should be added to the compost before the final planting, and good drainage and shade must be ensured. The plants benefit by a very light syringing of water on the staging and between the pots. It is also possible to root leaves in polythene bags, or in boxes covered with polythene, as moisture is retained round the leaves by this method. Old and unsightly plants are suitable for division. They should be taken from their pots and the crowns separated, those with roots being set into small pots and the healthy leaves prepared as leaf cuttings.

To root African Violets in water, cover the stems of the leaf cuttings to a depth of about 1 in., then place the container in a good light and cover with polythene until roots and plantlets form. These should be potted up in the same way as cuttings rooted in compost.

When sowing seed use a compost of granulated peat moss or ground-down sphagnum moss and silver sand. Press this mixture lightly down in the pans, then water thoroughly and allow to stand for a few hours before sowing. The seed should be sown thinly, mixed with sand, and should be pressed into the compost, shade being given with glass and newspaper. Germination will take place within 30 days. Seedlings grow very slowly, but when large enough to handle should be pricked out into other pans or boxes by dibbling them in 1 in. apart each way, then placed in a close frame for a few days and kept shaded. When three or four leaves have been produced, they are ready for potting up into 2-in. pots with the same compost as for plants raised from rooted leaf cuttings. As soon as they are growing freely, they need a combination of air and shade, since strong sunlight hardens the leaf tissue and retards growth. Before they become pot bound, they should be transferred into 3½-in. pots, with the same compost as used for plants grown by other methods. Six months from sowing, flower buds will appear and blooms should be produced for many months, provided that a complete liquid fertiliser is applied every 10 or 14 days. Always pick off all dead flowers and keep the roots moist.

Over-watering, however, sometimes brings trouble from damping-off, of which a first indication is a slight distortion of the flowers and rotting of the lower leaves. Greenfly often cause flower distortion and discoloration, but these and other pests can be controlled by clean cultivation, careful watering and airing, and under greenhouse cultivation routine fumigation with nicotine vapour or dusting with nicotine dust. When the plants are grown in the living-room, dusting with derris powder, which is non-poisonous, is safer.

Alpines

The cultivation of alpine plants under glass as a hobby has increased enormously in recent years. They need little attention and many only need repotting every second or third year after flowering. As a rule they produce a mass of bloom without artificial heat and the neat cushioned growth of many, e.g. the sedums and saxifrages, provides an interesting feature in the off-season. A great variety can be grown in little space, since they flourish in quite small pots.

These high altitude plants are completely hardy, therefore the main purpose of growing them under glass is to shelter the early flowering kinds from severe weather. In addition, many are so small that if they were planted in the rock garden they might be smothered or hidden by larger plants. Although the alpine house needs no artificial heat, it should run north and south to obtain maximum sun and the temperature should approximate to outside conditions within 5-10° F./2-5° C. It should be of the span-roof type with a low pitch and a double set of ventilators (one set on top near the ridge and the other flush with the staging on both sides) geared and worked by sectional levers to admit a constant current of fresh air, so keeping the atmosphere fresh and dry without undue draught. The aim should be, not to reduce the temperature by ventilation, but to prevent it from rising. The roof ventilators should never be closed except during severe frost, and the same applies to those at the side unless the wind is very strong.

Solidly constructed—preferably with a brick base—the house should be on an open site free from the shadow of trees or high buildings. It is useful to have under-stage ventilation through the brickwork, but small mesh wire netting must be used to protect against birds and rodents.

Staging should be set on both sides, near the glass and just below waist level, i.e. about 2½ ft. above the greenhouse floor. It should not be too wide, or the far row of plants will be difficult to reach. Pots and pans may rest directly on the wooden slates of the staging, or the latter may be covered by slates or corrugated iron topped with shingle. The floor should be of cement or brick, except under the staging, where soil may be left uncovered. Although the majority of greenhouse alpine enthusiasts grow their plants in pots and pans, there is no reason why they should not be planted out, for this has proved very successful.

Water these tiny cushion plants from beneath, never overhead. To ensure that not merely the surface, but all the soil, as well as the matted roots, are thoroughly watered, place the pots and pans in shallow water. It is useful to have a 3-in.-deep zinc tank at each end of the house, a method which also enables a large number of plants to be dealt with at once. Less watering is needed if the plant containers are plunged in sand or peat. The floor, as well as the sand or shingle should be damped down in mild weather, and when it is warm the foliage should be given a fine mist spray in the cool of the evening. Generally speaking, water in early morning during spring and autumn, and in the evening in high summer.

In the heat of the day, alpines need shading from the direct rays of the sun, and, if constant attention is possible, wooded slatted roll-up blinds are ideal, since they allow regulation of light and can be left up on dull days. Otherwise, wash the glass over with a mixture of whiting and milk, or using what the trade call 'summer cloud', which can easily be washed off early in September. Light butter muslin blinds inside the house will also prevent the flowers fading or foliage scorching, and are easy to handle.

Most alpines thrive in a gritty, fibrous compost, such as two parts fibrous loam (broken up with the hands, but not sifted), one part granulated peat, and one part coarse sand, but encrusted saxifrages like a little limestone or some lime rubble added. Prepare the compost some time in advance.

Pans 6-9 ins. in diameter and 5 ins. deep are usually the best for alpines, but tap-rooting varieties succeed better in ordinary deep flower pots. The necessary good drainage can be ensured by placing a piece of zinc gauze over the drainage hole, covering it with a good-sized convex crock, and then 2 ins. of finely broken crocks. Rough peat, chopped sphagnum moss or a layer of similar material should come next, in order to prevent the compost from drifting into the drainage material. Work some soil among the roots of the plants, tapping the pot gently on the bench, then add a further layer without pressing it down too hard, and repeat until the plant is firm and the collar half-an-inch below the rim of the pot. It may be necessary to wedge some small stones or limestone chips near the stem to prevent too much water getting on the collar and topdress with small chips to protect the roots from sunburn.

Scrupulous cleanliness must be observed; the windows should be clean, inside and out, and all pots and pans cleaned before use. Label the plants correctly and cut off all withered leaves and flowers (unless seed is required). The house should be periodically fumigated. It is advisable to have one or two cold frames to shelter plants from excessive moisture in winter and to provide protection when they are not wanted in the alpine house. In one place a thick layer of peat or sand into which pots can be plunged, but in the other leave a hard surface at the bottom on which the pots may stand.

Most alpine plants are propagated by division of the roots or by cuttings, taken preferably almost immediately after flowering. These should be plunged in a frame, so that they are shaded from the sun until roots are established.

Nearly all dwarf alpines are suitable for growing in the alpine house. The most beautiful are many of the typical, low-growing androsaces, which need ample drainage and a gritty, sandy loam.

155

Among the saxifrages, the Kabschia section and garden hybrids are suitable, and other excellent plants include some of the smaller lilies, e.g. *Lilium formosanum*; the hardy *Cyclamen europaeum*; many of the primulas; *Shortia uniflora* and *Shortia galacifolia*; lewisias and ramondias; dwarf daphne; *Dianthus alpinus* and *D. neglectus*; and the Mediterranean cress (*Morisia hypogaea*), which has deep yellow flowers in March and April. Dwarf rhododendrons, brought in from the cold frame when in bud, and some of the dwarf conifers, help to give a variety of level.

Many of the dwarf growing bulbous plants are among the most charming subjects—chionodoxas; many crocus species; fritillarias; *Iris persica*, *I. histrioides* and *I. reticulata*; the 'Heavenly Blue' muscari (*Muscari botryoides*); *Narcissus bulbocodium*, *N. cyclameneus*, *N. minimus*, and *N. triandus*; and many species of tulip. The bulbs should be potted in the autumn and the crowns placed so that they appear just above the surface of the soil. Soak the compost and place the pots in the cold frame on boards or slates, covering them with a 5-in. layer of peat, sand or old furnace ashes, and leave for 8–10 weeks. When the bulbs have made good roots, place them in the alpine house to flower.

Anemones

Anemones or windflowers belong to the Ranunculaceae family and are valued both in the garden and as cut flowers, especially as they bloom from earliest spring to late autumn. They are divided into three main groups, the woodland, the open space, and the high meadow types.

Among the woodlanders *A. nemorosa* is very common throughout Britain and very valuable for growing in the wild garden, where it makes a suitable companion for the purple hyacinth, primroses, wild violets and the golden flowered celandine, which all also flower in March and April. The flowers of the parent species are white with a reddish external tinge, but the many varieties vary from pure white to dark blue.

For a shady, cool, moist rich soil, the snow windflower (*A. sylvestris*) or the stronger and freer flowering variety *major* are excellent. If allowed to ramble, they will send up large white single flowers on wiry stems a foot high from May till October.

Sometimes thought to be a native of England, but probably a garden escape is *A. apennina*, which grows about 6 ins. high and flowers freely in April and May. Its blue flowers show to best advantage if planted in short grass at the foot of a tree, and it dies down immediately after flowering. Not unlike *Apennina*, but with larger and deeper blue flowers, *A. blanda* is a dainty rock garden plant which will flower profusely without forming too large a mass. Imported bulbils give a variety of beautiful colours.

A charming, early flowering dwarf with a compact turfy habit is *A. Hepatica*, syn. *Hepatica triloba*, which carries its flowers well above the dense mass of three-lobed leaves. All varieties succeed in rich soil, but since they dislike disturbance at the roots during the growing period, they should be increased by division while dormant. The double forms are beautiful, but shy in flowering.

The pasque flower (*A. pulsatilla*) is typical of the open space type. It does not creep as so many anemones do, but has short erect perennial root stocks and the leaves are produced on long stalks covered with silky hairs. The slender, slightly drooping violet-coloured flowers, with hair-covered surfaces, are about 1 ft. high, and the seed has a long feathery tail for wind distribution. It needs rich soil and loves lime and full exposure to the sun. A rare introduction from the Swiss Alps and useful in the rock garden is *A. Halleri*, which grows to about 6 ins. and has deep blue flowers in May. Valuable for a cool part of the bog garden is the 2-ft.-high *A. rivularis*, which has small white flowers in August. It goes well with bog-lilies and *Gentiana asclepiadea*, but wetness at the roots is essential.

In the high meadow group is the typical *A. sulphurea*, which needs a flow of pure air and thrives in any cool deep loam to which granite chips have been added. It does not like disturbance at the root. The flowers are a soft sulphur colour and appear in July and August, the seed being sown as soon as it is ripe.

Provided it has plenty of root room *A. alpina* will succeed anywhere, but particularly likes a damp peaty soil. The big white starry flowers are pale blue on the outer petals, and it produces masses of fern-like foliage.

The Japanese anemone (*A. japonica*) is an excellent cut flower, grows 2 or more feet high and has flowers—often semi-double—during August and September. The flowers are pink on the parent, but the variety *alba* has pure white flowers with a mass of yellow stamens. Both are easily propagated by division of roots.

The commercial anemones, grown for cut flowers, are chiefly hybrids of the Mediterranean poppy anemone (*A. coronaria*) and the scarlet windflower (*A. fulgens*), and their varieties and types: *A. fulgens* has a double-flowered form.

The De Caen (giant French) type has large single flowers ranging from white to purple and scarlet. Mixed colours are widely grown in southern England and France, but only a few are named, such as His Excellency, a deep scarlet with white base; Mr. Fokker, blue; Hollandia, scarlet; and Sylphide, delicate mauve.

Originating in Ireland and more delicate, and therefore less commercially grown than the giant French, is the St. Brigid type, which is semi-double, bearing a large number of narrow petals. Selected strains include Lord Lieutenant, mauve; The Admiral, deep pink ; and The Governor, scarlet.

Commercial growers choose a good fertile medium loam which is well drained, sheltered from strong winds and not in a frost pocket. The ground must be deeply dug and enriched well in advance of planting with a reasonable amount of well-decayed farmyard manure, followed by a fairly rich fertiliser worked into the surface. The raised beds are about 5 ft. wide and 6 ins. high—the higher level allowing improved drainage and easier warming of the soil by the sun. Weeding is done from paths running in between the beds. Plant the tubers in June or July in four rows 15 ins. apart along the length of each bed. Don't plant too deeply—roughly 1 in. deep on heavy soils and 2 ins. on porous—and set them in clumps of two to four, with the clumps 1 ft. apart in the rows. It is important that the tubers should be from 2 to 4 cm. in circumference. Hoe carefully during the summer to keep down weeds and preserve the moisture content in the soil, but avoid injury to the roots.

To obtain long-stemmed flowers, nitrogenous fertilisers are given as a top dressing when the foliage turns light green. Sulphate of ammonia or nitro-chalk can be used, but great care must be taken to avoid damaging the foliage, and the application should be made by hand when the leaves are dry. It is also usually necessary to give an application of sulphate of potash. Dutch lights are used in Devon and Cornwall, raised and supported above the beds, to stimulate length of stem.

Seed should be sown in March and April, having been stored for two or three weeks before in damp sand. Should the seeds be dry, they can be mixed with gritty sand and the mixture rubbed to facilitate the separation of the woolly-coated seeds from each other. Sow sparingly to avoid thinning and keep the beds weed free. Water freely in dry weather and sprinkle a little soil among the seedlings to encourage strong growth. Many of the plants will flower the following year.

During warm weather cut the flowers when the buds are tight and unopened, but in the winter only cut when the buds are almost open, as very small ones will not expand in water. Use a long knife, either at ground level or just a little below the soil surface, and place the stems in water for at least 12 hours before grading and packing them for market.

Antirrhinums

The true common snapdragon *Antirrhinum majus* is a low-growing shrubby plant of the Mediterranean region. Now naturalised in Britain, it will flourish many years in sheltered gardens, but far better results are achieved with its offspring, the decorative or florists' varieties, which are treated as annuals or biennials. Free-flowering and easily grown, antirrhinums are popular as bedding plants in public parks, as well as in private gardens, but despite frequent recommendation they are quite unsuitable for indoor decoration since once they are cut the blooms drop very quickly. Trials by the Royal Horticultural Society at Wisley have developed various admirable strains.

Classification is by height—tall, intermediate, dwarf or Tom Thumb, but the heights vary with soil and treatment, the tall being 30-36 ins., the intermediate 18-24 ins. and the dwarf 9-12 ins., measured from soil level to the top of the flower spike when in full bloom. Seed for all these types is sold either in separate colours or as a mixture. The intermediate section is the most popular, since it has the largest number of named varieties and the widest range of colour, as well as some varieties resistant to antirrhinum rust.

When treating antirrhinums as annuals avoid the common error of sowing too early. The correct time is about the end of February. Little heat is needed and they can be grown in a cold greenhouse, if protected from frost. Formerly, choice varieties were propagated by autumn cuttings rooted in an unheated frame, but seeds are nowadays plentiful, and produce plants which are true to colour. Amateurs should not save their own seed, unless the plants have been specially bred in isolation, otherwise the colour will not be true.

As the seeds are so tiny, sow them in small pans and cover lightly with fine soil, pricking the seedlings off into boxes or a cold frame as soon as they can be handled. Ensure that they grow in cool conditions, for antirrhinums dislike being coddled, and will not otherwise make a good hard growth. The finest flower spikes come from sturdy plants with medium-sized leaves.

When preparing the flower beds dig in partly decayed organic matter and soot, and, for particularly good results, rake a little bone

159

meal and hoof and horn meal into the surface before planting. Plants set out in May or early June begin flowering in July and continue well into October, and are most effective when each bed is planted with one colour, those nearby being chosen to harmonise.

When growing antirrhinums as biennials, which is not common in Scotland, sow in a cold frame in July, and transplant the seedlings to another frame as soon as they are large enough. By the following April they will be ready to be planted out-of-doors, but in sheltered districts, where the soil is light, they may be set straight out into their flowering quarters in the early autumn (all potential flower spikes having been removed) and wintered in the open. Such plants will come into flower in early June, and if the spent flower spikes are removed to prevent seeding, will produce a second crop of bloom in the autumn from lateral shoots.

Spring flowering plants for the greenhouse are raised from seed sown in boxes during July, using a moderately rich but fine compost. The seedlings are transferred to fresh boxes, using the same compost, as soon as they are large enough to handle, and at the end of October are placed in 4-5-in. pots containing a compost of rich fibrous loam, a little rotted manure, leaf mould and a sufficiency of sand to keep the mixture open. Placed on a bed of ashes in a cold frame, the pots are transferred in January to the greenhouse. The plants should be kept cool and well ventilated to prevent mildew, and, when the lower flower spikes begin to show, should be given weak liquid manure, to be applied after watering. Greenhouse culture will elongate the stems, but the clear pure colour of the flowers—produced from April to June—will compensate for this. Specimen spikes of bloom may be produced by pinching out the side growths allowing only a single stem to develop.

Antirrhinums can be used to fill up spaces in the herbaceous border, or to make bold groups where a wood or shrubbery joins the flower garden. There are also a number of beautiful species suitable for growing in the rock garden and the most interesting for this purpose is *A. glutinosum*, a native of the Spanish mountains, which flowers from late June until the end of August. A low growing, trailing plant, it has smallish yellow-white flowers, with a deeper yellow lip and a trace of purple above. The Italian snapdragon, *A. asarinum* is also useful, and has light, sulphur-coloured flowers 6 ins. high which last from May until the end of September. Its trailing habit makes it very attractive in a hanging basket in the greenhouse. These two, and the evergreen snapdragon *A. sempervirens*, which has white flowers throughout the summer, look their best on a dry wall

A hybrid tea, Super Star.

ROSES

The beds pruned and mulched in spring.

The Regal pelargonium.

PELARGONIUMS

King of Denmark.

or steep rock face, which shows their bushy, trailing growth and finely poised spikes of bloom to advantage. Each of these root readily from cuttings taken during August, and inserted in a sandy compost in a cold frame; and autumn-sown seed produces plants true to type which begin flowering the following summer.

Begonias

Begonias form a large genus in the family Begoniaceae, and compete in popularity with the dahlias as a summer bedding plant and with geraniums for greenhouse decoration. They are divided into five groups: species, fibrous-rooted, foliage, winter-flowering and tuberous-rooted.

The majority of the species are shallow-rooted and should be grown in broad pans, although the rather large *B. Haageana*, with its rose-coloured flowers on long stems and handsome foliage, requires ample root-room in rich soil. Contrasting with the pendulous species, suitable for hanging baskets, is the tall scarlet-flowered *B. fuchsioides* which is best trained against a pillar or over a pergola.

The fibrous-rooted begonias are hybrids of the Brazilian *B. semperflorens*. They are perennial, but can be treated as annuals if sown in early spring, and form bushy plants 1 ft. high, which flower profusely over a long period.

In the foliage group *Begonia rex* is a magnificent species with many descendants which have leaves of various colours—silver grey leaves with dark green margins; dark olive-green banded with a broad zone of bronze-red and silver-grey; grey-green veined with silver and tinted with bronze-red; metallic lustre with silver margins. But remember that they dislike frequent repotting.

Winter-flowering begonias are splendid for house-decoration, when they are best grown in 4-in. pots. The many varieties derive from a cross between *B. socotrana* and the tuberous-rooted types, which has produced strong-growing plants with large, brighter flowers. Their slender, graceful growth and wealth of bloom make them invaluable, one of the best being *B. Gloire de Lorraine*, which has given rise to several colour sports.

The majority of the modern varieties of the tuberous-rooted forms have been produced by British hybridists, the flowers being three times the size of the early ones and having an enormously greater colour range, and the stiff upright stems now developed needing very little support. They are good summer bedding plants and grow quite well in shady corners which are unfavourable to other plants. As greenhouse plants they are ideal for their flowering period lasts from early spring to late autumn. The quality of bloom and foliage among the double-flowered varieties (now highly hybridised) depends upon the strain, which needs careful selection, and much of the interest in growing this group comes from cross-pollinating one's own plants to produce fertilised seed and then selecting those with the best coloured flowers. An immense number of plants can be raised from seed, the finest being kept for greenhouse cultivation in pots, and the rest used for planting out in the open, but to ensure flowers in the first year, sowing must be done in January or early February. The compost should be specially fine, consisting of a good loam, with a little fibrous peat and coarse sand, and a pinch of charcoal. Shallow pans should be used, and since the seeds are so small they must not be covered with soil.

Germination should be encouraged by covering the seed pans with brown paper and panes of glass. To water, immerse the pans to within $\frac{1}{2}$ in. of the rim in tepid water until the moisture rises to the surface of the compost, then place them in a temperature of 70-75° F./ 21-24° C. To ensure that they do not dry out or become scorched by the sun, keep them covered until the seed leaves appear, when the tiny plants can be pricked off with a matchstick into other pans. When the seedlings have leaves the size of a halfpenny, the plants can be transferred to very small pots, using the same compost as before but with the addition of a little well-rotted farmyard manure. Keep the atmosphere slightly moist and the temperature fairly high to encourage vigorous growth.

Seedlings intended for flowering in the greenhouse should be potted into 3-in. pots, containing the same kind of compost as used for the initial planting, and later into 5 in. pots containing three parts fibrous loam, two parts leaf mould or peat, a little decayed cow manure and sharp sand. During flowering the temperature of the house should be reduced to 50° F./10° C. and the plants fed weekly with complete fertiliser in diluted liquid form. For outdoor planting, they should be very carefully hardened off, being first transferred to a cool house, then to a cold frame in which they are later fully exposed to air. In early June they should be set out in rich moist soil until tubers are lifted in late autumn, slightly dried and cleaned of soil, and then stored in dry sand or peat moss for the winter.

Next spring place the tubers in shallow trays, embedding them in leaf mould just level with the surface but not covering them. To start them growing spray daily overhead, and when roots and tiny shoots have formed transfer them into suitable pots or, if they are to

162

be planted out, to boxes. Careful watering is essential and they should be fed with a little complete fertiliser when the pots are full of roots to ensure good exhibition blooms. A small quantity of soot may be given, simply by tying it up in a bag and stirring it in the water.

Begonias may be propagated by cuttings which must be taken when the shoots are 2 to 3 ins. long. The cut bases must be dried for an hour or two by placing them on the greenhouse staging, so that a callus forms before they are potted. Use a sandy compost and insert the shoots round the sides of the pots, which are then placed under a bell glass in a temperature of 65° F./18° C. Keep a moist atmosphere and transfer the cuttings to small pots when roots begin to form, and they will then steadily develop well-formed tubers by the autumn.

Young plants can also be obtained from fully developed leaves, which should be cut off and the main veins nicked here and there, then pegged down with the underside placed on a sandy compost in a pan or box. A plantlet with roots will eventually form at each cut.

Begonias in pots should be supported by two or three thin stakes, i.e. split bamboo canes, linked by raffia passed round them a little above the tubers, and concealed beneath the foliage. When the plants have very large blooms curved wire in the form of a hoop may be used to keep them in position. Unless seed is needed for new stock, single flowers carrying seed pods should be cut off to allow the nutrient material to pass to the double flowers.

Bulbous Plants

Many so-called bulbous plants are not true bulbs. The latter, which may be formed either at soil level or beneath, consist of fleshy scales containing plant food, surrounding an internal stem, from the base of which roots develop. During the growing season the leaves play an important part in the production of the plant's food, a proportion travelling down to the bulb for storage, so that is is unwise to disturb them before the foliage has died down naturally.

True bulbs are divided into two sections, the scaly—in which the bulb scales are imbricated or overlapping, as in the lily; and the tunicated—in which the scales form a continuous coating, one within the other, as in the hyacinth, tulip, daffodil, snowdrop, muscari and scilla.

The bulb-like growths below ground produced by crocus, colchicum, gladioli and other plants, are corms—solid bits of stem with a thin, netted skin. Corms die at the end of the year, the daughter corms being produced on top of the withered parent, whereas bulbs live on, their offspring generally increasing annually alongside them. The more or less round, swollen, underground stems of cyclamen, tuberous-rooted begonia, and other plants are also sometimes referred to as bulbs. They are, however, tubers and new plants arise from the buds or 'eyes' with which they are covered. Corms and tubers fulfil the same function as bulbs, as stores from which the next season's initial growth is made, and in their case also the foliage should never be cut off but allowed to wither naturally.

The common daffodil (*Narcissus pseudo-narcissus*) is a native of Britain and most parts of Europe, but it is customary in this country to include under this name a great number of plants of the genus. It is common to hear all white *poeticus* forms and the bunched-flowered varieties generally referred to as narcissi, and the trumpet-flowered as daffodils. They need deep, rich soil, sufficiently open to allow proper drainage, and the addition of spent hops or decayed vegetable refuse dug in well in advance of planting, wood ashes and a little bone meal or basic slag will be beneficial. Lime is also necessary, especially in heavy soils.

Plant in September or October in holes 4 ins. deep, or slightly deeper if the bulbs have long necks. Set them in clumps of about half a dozen, or if the whole bed or border is filled with one variety, carpet the ground with forget-me-nots (dwarf myosotis) or arabis, which gives a pretty effect. When planting in grass, place the bulbs 4-5 ins. apart in irregular shaped masses of one variety. Remove a piece of turf and place some fine soil under each bulb, then replace the turf, or else merely loosen the soil beneath on raising the turf and having set the bulb in, cover once more with the turf.

Popular large yellow-trumpet varieties are Golden Harvest, and King Alfred, very large, golden yellow—an early forcer and one of the best for cutting. One of the largest trumpet daffodils in cultivation is Unsurpassable. Others of beauty in the large-cupped section are Carlton, Scarlet Elegance, John Evelyn, and in the small-cupped division, Amateur.

The tulip is native to the warmer parts of Asia and *Tulipa gesneriana*, introduced in 1577, is the parent of the garden varieties. Extensively cultivated in Holland, especially round Haarlem, the bulbs are exported in enormous quantities, and the flowers are also grown for market in some parts of Scotland. Tulips are classified into groups—Breeder, Cottage, Darwin, Triumph, Mendel, Double, Parrot and Rembrandt. The striping or variegation in the last group is caused by a virus, but the result is purely decorative. It is best to plant in October or November, setting the bulbs about 4 in. deep, and lifting them the following year after the foliage dies down, when they are dried, cleaned and stored. Among the best garden species are the wild yellow *Tulipa sylvestris,* the Lady Tulip *(clusiana),* and the very late-flowering *Sprengeri,* a brilliant scarlet which can be raised from seed and flowered in three years. Although tulips do not flourish in shade or among grass they give good results in a fairly stiff soil, but it should not be over-rich or the stems may fasciate. A fasciated stem may be broad and flat, sometimes giving the impression that two adjacent stems have joined together. For beds or borders such early single varieties as Fred Moore, orange, or Prince of Austria, a sweet-scented orange-red, combined with a carpet of forget-me-nots are very effective. If grown in a bed, tulips must be lifted and replanted annually, preferably in another place.

Many hardy bulbous plants are suitable for growing indoors. By using a mixture of peat fibre, shell grit and a little charcoal any ornamental bowls with or without drainage will serve as containers. The mixture is light, clean and not unpleasant to handle, and a slightly dampened layer should be placed in the bowl, the bulbs being set so that their tops are a little below the rim. They should then be almost covered with the fibre, which should not be too firm or the bulbs will force themselves out when they begin to grow. Either plunge the bowls in a cold frame, or place in a dark cupboard or cellar, and water occasionally. As soon as there is some top growth, transfer the bowls to a window or cool greenhouse. If earthenware pots are used, rather than bowls, a good compost can be made of soil with some granulated peat or leaf mould, gritty sand and a little bone meal, well mixed together. In this case the bulbs should be potted early in October, then plunged outside under peat moss or old furnace ashes, until they are well rooted. Later they can be removed to a cold frame and gradually exposed to light until they are ready to be brought into the house. They should be carefully watered as soon as growth is fairly well advanced and the flower buds can be seen. Hyacinths, tulips, and daffodils are most commonly used for pot and bowl culture, but it is well worth trying crocus, snowdrop, *Iris reticulata,* and *Scilla siberica* and *chinadoxa.*

Cacti and Other Succulents

The first to cultivate many cacti and other succulents were the Spaniards, who brought them from Africa and the New World to their own country. Originally all fleshy-stemmed, spiny plants were known as cacti, but the true members of the Cactaceae family are, with few exceptions, leafless and produce their flowers direct from the stems. The majority have blooms magnificent in size and colour, though some are charmingly modest, but they vary enormously in height, from a few inches to more than 20 ft.

In some species the fleshy fruit receptacles are edible, and both the strawberry pear (*Cereus triangularis*, now known as *Hylocereus undatus*) and the prickly pear (*Opuntia ficus indica*) have a very pleasant flavour. Some of the smaller varieties have a particular beauty in the symmetrical formation of their spines which vary in shape, colour and number.

Cacti and other succulents are easy to grow and the dwarf species do well in a small greenhouse with a moderate to cool temperature, although tall varieties are beyond the scope of the amateur. All types can be seen in the Royal Botanic Gardens at Edinburgh and Kew, but the dry atmosphere of the ordinary living room suits them so well that everyone can grow a few.

A large collection can be cheaply obtained because all these plants germinate readily from seed which can be obtained at a nominal price from most seedsmen. Although they can be sown at any time, the beginning of April is probably best, since this allows a whole season's growth before the onset of the dull days of winter. The temperature should be uniformly maintained at 50° F./10° C. and 6-in. porous seed pans are suitable as containers. Give thorough drainage at the bottom by using pieces of broken pot mixed with gravel, which should be covered first with a layer of leaf mould, and then a mixture of equal parts of good porous loam, well rotted leaf mould and coarse sand. Make the compost moderately firm to within ½ in. from the top, and then sow the fine seeds broadcast but press the larger ones lightly into the soil. Although the former should not be covered with soil, all seeds benefit from a light covering of rough sand which will prevent too rapid evaporation of moisture and help support the seedlings after germination.

Water by immersing the pans in shallow tanks, so that the moisture always rises through the compost, since watering from above may cause the tiny seeds to float. The first watering after sowing will be sufficient for about a week, according to the temperature, which is best kept steady by placing a sheet of glass covered with a piece of paper over the top of each pan: this also prevents the soil drying out too rapidly, but the glass and paper should be removed for an hour or so each day. Most cacti germinate in ten to fourteen days, but some may take a month or even longer. Unless there is overcrowding, early transplanting is unnecessary, but if the tiny seedlings are removed to other pans or placed in small pots, great care must be taken not to injure the rootlets. To help prevent infection by fungi withhold water for a few days after potting, and also keep the seedlings shaded.

Nearly all cacti can be propagated by cuttings, which are made by taking slips from the parent plant with a sharp clean knife. The cut surfaces should be exposed to the air so that the wounds may heal by forming a callus before the cuttings are inserted in sand or sandy soil to root. Some need only a few hours, and others a week or more, to form this protective layer, but it is essential to prevent the danger of bacterial rot. Many cacti cuttings root very readily in pure sand, but others need a mixture of soil and sand in equal proportions and may be potted into small flower-pots where they can be grown for some time after rooting. Until the roots have formed they should not be watered, although a fine spray overhead occasionally will keep them fresh and they should be shaded from bright sun to prevent excessive wilting. Prepared cuttings may also be placed on top of the sand or soil, but small sticks should be inserted by the side of each to keep them in position until they take root.

A very interesting way of propagating succulents is to use the fleshy leaves of such plants as sedums and crassulas. If a leaf is placed on the top of sand, very tiny sprouts and rootlets will appear at the base and margins. When rooted, the plantlets may be severed from the leaf and transferred to small pots.

The majority of cacti flourish in a fairly dry compost consisting of 3 parts fibrous loam, 1 part leaf-mould, and 2 parts sand, broken brick, old lime rubble and a little charcoal. It is best to pot them in March, using clean pots the lower third filled with clean crocks, covered with leaves or moss and the rest with compost. No watering should be done after potting for a week or more, according to the house temperature, but spray the plants lightly overhead every morning with tepid water.

In the growing season, up till September, cacti and succulents should be given plenty of water so that they may build up a stock of food and moisture, but from then onwards until March do not water and keep the house atmosphere dry. This will make them flower freely.

Genera worth cultivation are: the torch thistles (*Cereus*) which form three groups, globose, semi-trailing and night-flowering; the hedgehog thistles (*Echinocactus*) with very showy stems and spines; the Nipple-bearers (*Mammillaria*) mostly one-stemmed plants with spirally-arranged tubercles; *Melocactus*, so called because the stems are melon-shaped, which have small flowers followed by bright red cherry-like berries; the prickly pears (*Opuntia*) with either yellow or orange flowers, followed by edible ornamental fruits; the *Phyllocactus*, of which some species have flattened leaf-like stems and others three-angled stems with deeply notched margins; the old man cactus (*Cephalocereus senilis*), with shaggy locks of white wiry hair; and the fine-looking carrion plants (*Stapelia*) which have thick fleshy leafless stems producing starfish-like flowers covered with hairs.

Campanulas

The majority of campanulas (family Campanulaceae) are perennial, although a few are biennial and annual. Some are tall, pyramidal and imposing, well-suited to the herbaceous border, provided there is not too much shade; others are dwarf, fit for the rock and wall garden, or as path edgings; and yet others are tender and best grown for greenhouse decoration in pots.

The soil should be deeply dug rather than heavily manured, and occasional watering and a mulch of partly decayed leaves in early spring will ensure essential moisture at the roots during flowering.

Propagate by division, cuttings or seed in spring under glass, using a compost of loam, leaf mould and sharp sand, but no lime. Cover the seed with finely sifted sand, and shade from bright sun.

Three remarkably showy species which do well in the greenhouse are *Campanula isophylla*, *C. medium*, and *C. pyramidalis*. The light blue *C. isophylla*, and the white variety *alba*, are propagated by division after flowering in the autumn, or in spring by cutting of the young growing shoots which will readily root in gentle heat. These can be flowered in 4-in. pots, and tipping the young shoots as they grow will help to make bushy plants. Seed may be sown in a little heat, in April, and the seedlings, after germination, placed singly in thumb pots using a light loamy soil. The seedlings should eventually be moved into 4-in. pots to flower the following season. A pretty edging for greenhouse staging or arranged in groups of plants of contrasting colours, *alba* is also frequently met with in country cottages, as a window plant.

The old Canterbury Bell *C. Media* and its *calycanthema* variety, the cup-and-saucer flowered form, is of three distinct shades of colour—blue, white and rose, and grows in tall, spreading pyramidal stems 2-3 ft. high in May and June. There is also a tendency to doubling of flowers but these are not so handsome as the single ones. It is a biennial of the easiest possible culture. Propagation is by seed sown thinly in a pan or box, during April. Cover the seed very lightly with fine sand and place it in a cold frame to germinate. The seedlings should be pricked out into other boxes, and from there transplanted at 9-in. intervals in nursery rows 12 ins. apart. The plants are lifted in the autumn with a good ball of soil adhering to the roots and placed in 7- or 8-in. pots for flowering. A fairly rich soil and firm potting is essential and the roots must be kept constantly moist. After wintering in a cold frame, they can be brought into the greenhouse in March to flower during May and June, and should be liberally fed with liquid manure when the flower spikes begin to grow. Canterbury bells do exceedingly well when planted out in the open border in a rich soil. They last a long time in flower but in a dry, hot situation copious supplies of water are essential. The seed pods should be picked off as they form, thus prolonging the flowering period.

The chimney bell-flower, *C. pyramidalis*, light-blue, and the white form *alba* grow to a height of between 6 to 7 ft. They are sometimes propagated by cuttings of firm basal growths, but are usually raised from seed as advised for *C. medium*, although for best results, sowings should be made early in March. The seedlings are potted up into 4-in. pots, then into 9-in., and placed in a cold frame until the pots are full of roots. Strong plants may be placed out in the open during summer, wintered in a cold frame and then placed in the greenhouse in the spring to flower during summer. They must be well watered, more especially when in flower.

Some of the best campanulas for the herbaceous border are the light blue *C. glomerata* and its varieties *alba* (white), *pallida* (pale blue) and *dahurica* (pale purple). They grow about 18 ins. high and have heads of rather tubular-looking flowers. Another fine bell-flower is *C. lactiflora*, which bears soft electric-blue flowers in profusion, grows about 4 ft. tall, and by October produces great quantities of seed which germinates freely in the spring. By August the seedlings will be in flower. It is an excellent perennial plant for the wild garden where seedlings can be allowed to grow freely.

A native, giant bell-flower is *C. latifolia*, suitable for a fairly damp, shady situation. Two to three feet high it is a handsome plant with stout stems bearing very large pale blue flowers in July. There are many varieties of which *macrantha*—large, purplish blue—is probably one of the best. *Alba* is also a handsome variety.

The peach-leaved bell-flower *C. persicifolia*, grows 2-3 ft. high and is probably one of the best all-round campanulas for the herbaceous border and as a cut flower it is superb. The true species has large, graceful blue flowers. It seeds itself freely and soon grows into large clumps. There are numerous varieties—both single and double flowered—*grandiflora*, Blue; *grandiflora alba*, white; Moerheimi, double white; Telham Beauty, pale china blue in abundance; Daisy Hill, a semi-double in a delightful shade of lavender-blue; all easily increased by division in spring.

The nettle-leaved bell-flower *C. Trachelium*, with purple-blue flowers, is a very useful border plant. There are many varieties with double flowers that are easy to grow and give several shades of blue and white.

Many of the smaller companulas are brilliant in colour, easy to grow, and useful for open positions in the rock garden, wall crevices and the scree of the moraine. Generally the flowers of the dwarfer species are borne on single stems, but a few have several flowers on a stalk. The compost should be of a light loamy nature with ample grit and leaf mould, but no lime.

A few representative species are *C. alpina*, a plant that makes small, dense tufts of narrow, hairy, greyish leaves and sends out short stems with pendant steel-blue flower bells from May till July. Generally it grows quite well, but it is apt to die off after flowering. Propagation is by seed as it forms a taproot and a rosette of leaves on the ground. Valuable and easy to grow is *C. carpatica* which usually produces abundant light-violet coloured flowers in the rock garden. Some of its varieties have blue or white flowers, such as White Star, a very good variety with beautiful, wide open, saucer-like white flowers with blue centre. Another blue variety is China Cup, while Riverslea has large, deep violet bells and *multiflora* has compact, rather flat, medium blue flowers.

A trailing plant with pendant branches, *C. garganica* has wide, flat blue starry flowers. The variety *hirsuta* has pale blue flowers and is a good plant for a wall. It requires glass protection during winter. *C. muralis* (Portenschlagiana) is an evergreen and one of the most useful, all-round rock campanulas, propagated by cuttings taken in September. The bells are violet in colour and appear from June till August. Fairies' Thimbles, *C. pusilla*, often called *C. cochlearifolia*, has bell-shaped blue flowers and can be seen in many cottage gardens. This and the variety *alba* produce pendant bells in great masses during the summer. They are excellent for the rock garden, the paved walk and for carpeting. A very fine, late flowering variety called Profusion has deep blue bells and does best in the moraine.

A charming little hybrid of unknown origins is *C.* × *Stansfieldi* with reddish violet bells in June and July; *C. Waldsteiniana* has bright blue-mauve bells with white eye, star-shaped and erect, with wiry stems, and does well in the moraine and paved walk; *C.* × *G. F. Wilson* has lovely deep violet-blue bells with a white eye, flowers all summer, is semi-pendant, vigorously growing, rapidly spreading and distinctly bell-shaped, and is propagated by cuttings taken in the autumn.

Carnations

Border carnations bloom once during July and August, in contrast to the perpetual flowering, or tree carnation, which blooms throughout the year. Borne on stalks 1½ to 2 ft. long, the flowers are perfect in form and ideal both for garden decoration and cutting. All classes are reasonably bushy and hardy enough to winter out of doors. They are grouped as follows: the 'bizarres', with white, pink, crimson or lilac ground petals having irregular longitudinal markings or stripes of other colours; 'flakes' with a ground colour striped with another shade, similar to the bizarres; 'fancies', with a wide range of colour, and including those varieties which do not come into the other classes; 'selfs' which exhibit one colour only, being pink, rose, salmon, crimson or various shades of yellow; and 'picotees', having white or yellow petals edged with another colour, which should be marginal only; any markings throughout the petals are defects.

Carnations enjoy a good fibrous loam, and if the soil is light and sandy it should be improved by the addition of well-rotted farmyard manure, well in advance of planting, and good loam. On the other hand, heavy clayey soils should have gritty material worked in and be drained if necessary. If the ground is low lying, it may be an advantage to raise the beds a little above the surrounding level. Cultivation should be thorough and a final dusting of ground limestone forked into the soil surface will both improve the texture and aid growth. Once the plants are established, top dress with calcareous loam to keep the roots cool and moist during flowering.

Propagation is chiefly by layering and is done towards the end of July or early August, or when the flowers are at their best. First loosen the soil and place a 2-in. layer of compost (a mixture of leaf mould and sharp sand) round the plants. Remove all the lower leaves from the young shoots to be layered, but retain those on the part which will be left above ground. Short shoots with about six fully developed leaves are best for this purpose. Two joints below the

171

point where the leaves have been stripped off, make a tongue by cutting first half way through the stem and then upwards for 1½ ins. The prepared shoots or layers should then be fastened into the compost with wire pegs or bracken fronds, taking care not to damage the tongue, then mound a little soil over and around the tongue, and afterwards water well to prevent the cut surface of the layered stem drying out. Since the roots take five or six weeks to form, layering should be done as early as possible, so that well-rooted plants are ready to be set out in September and can become established before winter. To plant in the open or in small pots cut layers from the parent plant some days before lifting.

An alternative method of layering is to sink small pots filled with a good fibrous loam in the ground besides the plants. Layers are prepared in the usual way, then pegged into the pots, and when rooted, severed from the parent and planted out. See that the pots do not dry out while the layers are rooting.

If reliable seed is obtained, it is easy to raise plants by this method. Sow indoors during March or early April in a temperature of about 55° F./13° C. The resultant seedlings will be strong and robust, providing a wealth of flowers for cutting, and although they may not be of first rate quality, there is interest in growing them and watching their development. Prick the tiny seedlings off into boxes and place them in a cold frame until the weather allows them to be planted out, then select those which meet your requirements during the flowering period. Sometimes two or three years are needed to decide which are worth keeping.

Carnations planted in beds are usually set in four rows, the first 6 ins. from the edge and the others 15 ins. apart with the plants set at intervals of 15 ins. The rooted layers should be very firmly set in the soil, but do not bury the lower leaves or decay will be caused which will spread to all parts of the plant. They will need firming again during the spring, since winter frosts tend to loosen the young plants in the soil, and with exposed beds it is advisable to stake them.

In spring place a thin bamboo cane close to the flowering shoots of each carnation, securing each one separately by wire rings—a quicker method than tying with raffia or string, and better in that the rings hold the growth loosely. After staking, hoe between the plants to break up the crust caused by treading, to allow air to reach the roots. Lightly dress with a complete fertiliser once a month, and hoe it in afterwards. For exhibition blooms, disbud by removing all but the main flower bud at the apex of each stem, but for garden decoration this is unnecessary.

172

Chrysanthemums

The chrysanthemum is most popular, especially in Great Britain, Belgium, France, and the United States of America. Commercial supplies last from July until the end of January, a flowering period which few other plants can rival.

Although the several thousand varieties raised has made it necessary for the floral Committee of the National Chrysanthemum Society to classify them in eleven sections for exhibition and award purposes, the amateur divides his chrysanthemums according to season, as early or late flowering.

The early-flowering chrysanthemum blooms in the open ground with very little protection, except in exposed situations, from July until October, and the late-flowering varieties provide a wealth of bloom under glass from October until the end of January. Plants in both groups can be disbudded to produce a single flower on each stem, or grown as sprays.

When choosing varieties remember that dull or pastel shades are less attractive under artificial light than they are when seen blooming in garden or greenhouse, and that long stiff stems are essential if the heavy heads are not to droop, though modern varieties are less liable to stem weakness than some older ones.

To produce larger blooms, it is usual to pinch out the growing point of early flowering August and September varieties grown out-of-doors either just before or just after planting, in the second or third week of April, so that about six side shoots will form. Three or four flower buds will be produced at the tip of each of the side stems, but only the larger central one should be left, the others being removed a few each day. This disbudding helps the production of large flowers. Side shoots appearing lower down each stem where the leaves join it must also be removed. When sending out new varieties nurserymen often enclose cultural information, including pinching dates, which is very useful.

The early-flowering varieties of chrysanthemums may be used effectively for bedding out, either alone, when the beds should not be too large and each bed should contain one variety, or associated with gladioli and lilies. They may also be grown in the herbaceous border, where they are not generally disbudded because natural sprays of flowers are required. Good varieties are Chatsworth, bronze; Rosespray, bright rose; and Theta, apricot.

During the flowering period select healthy plants for stock purposes and mark any showing signs of eelworm infection, so that they

173

can eventually be uprooted and destroyed. In the autumn spray the selected plants with nicotine and soft soap to destroy any aphis at their bases, lift them carefully, and place in a cool house or frame to produce cuttings. Heat is unnecessary except during periods of very severe frost and water should only be given sparingly, but they do need plenty of air.

The young shoots which are used for cuttings appear through the soil near the base of each plant, and should ideally be about $2\frac{1}{2}$ ins. long, and of medium thickness. These can be rooted or 'struck' in pots, boxes or on the greenhouse bench in a good rooting compost comprising two parts loam, one part peat, one part sharp sand and a sprinkling of superphosphate. Set out the young rooted cuttings into 3-in. pots or in boxes, allowing plenty of space between the plants, as it is important that they should not receive a check in their early growth. Plant out in the open in May. A cold frame may be used for rooting early flowering varieties. If the young shoots are taken as soon as they develop in the autumn and inserted in a good rooting medium in the frame, they will produce well developed plants in spring and good blooms between July and October. Parent plants which do not produce cuttings outdoors in autumn, should be cut down, lifted and placed in a cold frame where they will produce basal growths.

Chrysanthemums grown in pots, usually for late flowering under glass, require a great deal of attention. They are propagated as described for early-flowering varieties to be planted out-of-doors, but after they are rooted they should be placed in 3-in. pots containing John Innes potting compost No. 1, which should be pressed firm, and later transferred to a cool greenhouse or garden frame. Just before they become pot-bound they should be transferred into 5-6-in. pots, containing John Innes potting compost No. 2, which must be made very firm to prevent the plants suffering from lack of moisture. The final potting, using 9-10-in. pots containing John Innes potting compost No. 3, is generally done at the end of May or early June, and the plants staked, tied and stood out of doors in rows on a bed of old furnace ashes.

Never allow the plants to suffer from drought and when they begin to make rapid growth water daily and feed with one of the specially prepared manures for chrysanthemums, as soon as flower buds appear.

Syringe the foliage regularly with an insecticide such as derris or nicotine to control leaf-miner and greenfly. During August and September disbud the plants gradually as with the early-flowering

174

varieties. At the end of September transfer them to an unheated greenhouse, and although a little fire heat may be given if there is a possibility of severe frost, the temperature must be kept moderately low and the atmosphere well ventilated if mildew is to be avoided.

A few early-flowering varieties worth trying are: Alfreton Yeoman, early September, maroon with silver reverse; Bronze George McLeod, September; bronze sport from the yellow George McLeod, a variety of easy culture and a great favourite; Apricot Sylvia Riley, early September; an apricot form of Sylvia Riley, a delightful pink; Evelyn Bush, September, and Ermine, August, both incurved white varieties and good for exhibition; Peter Shoesmith, September, with attractive orange flowers; Brenda Talbot, September, carnation-pink blooms; Westfield Flame, September, good sized red reflexing blooms; Sunavon, September, a lovely variety with clear yellow flowers.

Late-flowering chrysanthemums are: Ada Stevens, golden yellow; Aristocrat, deep pink, reflexed; Balcombe Perfection, amber bronze; Red Balcombe Perfection, a red sport from Balcombe Perfection; Loveliness, large silvery-lilac flowers of good colour and excellent habit; Pioneer, a reflexing orange-bronze variety; Princess Anne, light pink-tinted salmon; Madonna, incurved large creamy-white; Mayford Perfection, salmon-apricot; Tangerine, a lovely variety with tangerine-yellow flowers.

The flowers of incurved varieties are ball-like and have incurving petals, whose outer portions are exposed. Reflexed flowers are not so symmetrical in outline. Their petals grow outwards from the flower centres and hang downwards, so that their upper parts are seen.

Clematis

Among the most beautiful of plants, clematis are easily cultivated hardy climbers, varying in height from 2 to more than 50 ft. They are ideal for the decoration of walls, verandahs, arches and trellis work, and the *montana* group are very attractive when trained over old tree trunks or pillars on a lawn: there are also suitable types for the herbaceous border.

An ordinary light calcareous soil, enriched with well-decayed manure and leaf mould, suits the majority and an annual top-dressing of rotted leaves both keeps the roots cool in summer and protects them from frost. Dig in some builders' rubble, such as old lime mortar, and set the plants on a little mound: good drainage is essential, for the roots decay in an acid water-logged soil. Many will thrive in a westward position near a tree, when they will climb among the branches and their roots will be shaded, but if facing due south they will need to have their roots shaded, either by shrubs or tall herbaceous plants. Planting should be done either in autumn or spring, and until the plants become established in a year or two, they should be supported by twigs. Nurseries usually supply clematis in small pots, so that they become more easily established in their permanent quarters.

Propagation by seed is easy, but slow, since germination usually follows only after an interval of some months from sowing. However, some varieties have been known to flower the first year. Cuttings should be taken internodally from half-ripened wood, rather than in the usual way below a node, since by this method clematis produce roots more readily. For layering, the stems should be bent or twisted, then pegged down and covered with light, sandy loam. Commercial growers usually propagate by grafting scions onto pieces of rootlets from old specimens of *C. vitalba* or *C. montana*. These are potted and placed in a propagating case until union takes place. If grafted plants are objected to, they should be planted in a sloping position, so that roots will form from the stems above the union of scion and stock.

Among the best for the garden of the more than two hundred known species of clematis are the following: The deciduous climber *C. macropetala*, sometimes called the 'Downy Clematis', has slender stems, downy when young, especially near the nodes. The leaves are 3-6 ins. long, dividing into six or nine leaflets, and the pale lilac flowers, 2-3 ins. across, are produced singly in May and June on slender stalks. Conspicuous tufts of feathered seed vessels remain on the plants throughout the winter. A rampant grower in Scottish gardens is the Himalayan *C. montana* pure white and useful for covering arbours, summer houses and even tall buildings. In 1900 Wilson introduced from China *C. montana*, var. *rubens*, which produces an abundance of deep rose blooms in May: the flowers are slightly larger and the foliage darker than in the case of the Himalayan species. Another introduction by Wilson was a summer flowering form *C. Wilsonii*, which has pearly white flowers in June and early July. Mainly summer flowering, but sometimes blooming in November, is *C. tangutica* from Central Asia, which has golden yellow flowers followed by globular fluffy white clusters of feathered styles. The only British species is Traveller's Joy or Old Man's Beard (*C. vitalba*), found where the soil contains a quantity of chalk or limestone. A

A reflexed specimen in perfection.

CHRYSANTHEMUMS

Tricolor, Dobie's Rainbow
Mixture.

The lower leaves are removed

SHRUB CUTTINGS
Preparation for rooting.

A cut is made immediately belo_
a leaf joint.

very rampant grower, climbing through other shrubs by its twisting leaf stalks, it produces numerous greenish white flowers in summer and carries conspicuous tufts of feathered seed vessels in autumn and winter. All the foregoing blossom from the nodes of the previous year's growth, so that pruning should follow immediately on flowering in order that new growth may be made for the next year.

Useful varieties for the herbaceous border are the Chinese *C. heracleaefolia,* var. *Davidiana,* an erect grower about 3 ft. high, producing fragrant lavender-blue flowers in August; and *C. integrifolia* with drooping blue flowers and *C. recta,* 4 ft. high with very fragrant white flowers—both from south Europe. All these should be pruned close to the ground in autumn and then mulched with decayed manure. They are propagated by division of roots in autumn or cuttings in summer.

Florists' varieties produce a succession of blooms 4-9 ins. across, which are usually single, but as a result of cross-fertilisation some may be double or rosette. These are hardy and may be grown outdoors in well-chosen positions. Double white rosettes with a sweet scent are produced on the ripened wood of *C. florida* or *Fortunei,* so that it should be pruned by removing unripened shoots after flowering in July. Good varieties are Belle of Woking, silvery grey; Duchess of Edinburgh, pure white, double, and Lucie Lemoine, white.

The violet-purple, *C. Jackmanii,* the result of a cross between *C. lanuginosa* and *C. Hendersonii,* is still popular for the garden. Others in this section are: Comtesse de Bouchard, soft rose, tinted mauve, flowering from June till October; Madame Edouard André, deep rose with yellow stamens, flowering well from July to August; President, deep violet with darker centre; and Star of India, flowering from July to August, reddish-plum with red bar.

Varieties of *C. lanuginosa* are some of the largest and best flowering clematis, for example, *Henryii* has large creamy white flowers with dark stamens; *Hybrida Sieboldii* has mauve flowers with dark anthers and flowers in May, June and July; Lady Northcliffe, dark lavender tinted bright blue with purple bar and white stamens, is a very strong grower and free flowerer; Nellie Moser is mauve with red bar.

The bluish-lilac *C. patens* flowers in May and June on ripe wood of the previous years' growth. Good varieties are Lady Landesborough, silvery grey, Mrs. George Jackman, satiny white with cream bar; and The Queen, lavender.

Virgin's Bower, *C. Viticella,* an important species introduced in 1569, is loaded with purple blue starry blossoms. From it Ville de Lyon, small, bright carmine red flowers with a deeper red colour round the edges of the sepals, and *Viticella alba lucuriens*, pure white, semi-double, have been raised.

Crocus

Coming mainly from southern Europe and western Asia, there are an immense number of crocus species, not always easy to identify, but too much neglected by the amateur, for the majority grow easily without protection and give a fine display over a long period. Some bloom February-March, others April-May, and some in autumn. Hardy though most of them are, it is worth growing a few of the earlier flowering species in the cold alpine house or a cold frame, where the temperature should be only a few degrees higher than outside, since protection rather than warmth is the main consideration.

For greenhouse or indoor display, place a dozen corms of each of a number of varieties in 5-in. pans in September, and plunge into old furnace ashes or peat out-of-doors for a few weeks, to allow roots to develop and to bring the flowering shoots ahead of the leaves. Do not bring the pans into the house until the flower buds appear, and never try to force flowering with artificial heat as this produces plenty of 'grass' i.e. leaves, but few flowers. Each corm produces two or more blooms, so that the display from each pan lasts a considerable time.

The corm consists of two round solid bodies one on top of the other. The lower is usually wrinkled and brown, but the upper section, which stores food for the plants' growth is composed of starch and cellular tissue. It later enlarges and in some species several new corms, also known as spawn or offsets, will be formed at its apex. These are planted out after the foliage has died down and will bloom the second year.

Crocuses grown from seed take about four years to flower, but this is a most exciting method of propagation. Seed capsules are found during May and June on or just below the surface of the soil. Dry the seed and sow in small pans, not later than the beginning of September, placing them out of doors, sunk in the soil to the rims. After two years the small corms produced may be planted out where they are to flower.

A deep, well-drained soil, rich in humus is suitable for most species when grown out-doors. They should be planted 4 ins. deep in an inch layer of coarse sand to prevent rotting during the winter and to help show their position when they need to be lifted, cleaned and sorted into sizes every third or fourth years. The old tunics and withered portions of the previous year's growth should be removed before replanting, and a little bone meal mixed with the soil before the bulbs are covered.

Although the florists' forms, such as the Dutch yellows, may be planted in grass, other species are apt to be smothered by its fibrous roots and matted growth.

In the country pheasants will dig up and eat the corms, and in town and country sparrows pull the blossom to pieces in dry weather for the sake of the pollen and the drop of nectar in the throat of the flower: strands of black cotton stretched about 3 ins. above the plants will deter such attacks. Watch out also for mice and, if necessary, use a break-back trap baited with a couple of peas.

Among the species best worth growing are the many varieties of the Scotch crocus (*Crocus biflorus*), which may have originated as a seedling, for no crocus resembling it has been found growing wild. Easily increased by division, it has flowers larger than the species— white, with yellow throat and blue-purple stripes on the outside of the outer segments. From Asia Minor comes *C. candidus*, with pretty creamy flowers, yellow at the base and having the backs of the outer segments stippled with purplish blue. Very late flowering and seeding freely, it is attractive in both rock-garden and border. Some varieties of the early-flowering *C. chrysanthus* have orange-yellow flowers, and there are also sulphur-yellow and pure white forms.

From the mountains of Naples comes *C. imperati*, one of the finest of the crocus family. In bud it has a buff ground and darkly feathered segments, and when it is fully open the brilliant orange anthers are striking. The many forms of it all flourish in sunny positions in the rock garden. Varying in colour from lilac to white is *C. reticulatus*, in which the outer segments are sometimes striped and banded with purple. The small flowers are star-shaped when open in full sun and the forms are reticulated or netted. The old-world saffron crocus *S. sativus* has always been cultivated for the sake of the scented stigmas, which, after drying, provides the drug saffron. It has many forms, but is of uncertain origin, and the flowers appear in October after the grey-green narrow leaves. The corms should be lifted and replanted annually in a sheltered sunny position.

Highly recommended is *C. Sieberi*, which has received an R.H.S. Award of Garden Merit. Its lilac-blue flowers are among the first to appear, and are very attractive among heaths. Very showy are the violet-blue autumn blooms of *C. speciosus*, also available in mauve and other colours. It spreads freely under shrubs by means of small corms,

179

and will provide a carpet of flowers from September to November if left undisturbed. The Cloth of Gold crocus *C. Susianus* has lovely star-shaped golden flowers in February. A native of Dalmatia is *C. Tomasinianus*, varying from pure white to deep lavender and seeding freely. The large and showy *C. vernus* is a free-seeding species from which most of the Dutch varieties derive. They are useful for bold planting, border edges and naturalisation in grass.

One of the prettiest and easiest to grow, Cloth of Silver crocus (*C. versicolor picturatus*) has white flowers with the outer petals feathered in deep purple. It is often wrongly referred to as the 'Scotch Crocus' since it resembles *C. biflorus*.

Dahlias

Like many other popular flowers, the dahlia has been much improved during recent years, but although the new varieties introduced annually are very valuable many of the old favourites are indispensable. A large collection can be obtained cheaply as they are easily propagated by division of roots and by cuttings.

Take the tubers from store in the spring, and put them in the greenhouse in boxes containing light potting compost, or amongst compost on the greenhouse staging. Some of the thick fleshy roots may be rather long and should be cut to leave about 2-3 ins. of each, the cut surface being dried by exposure to the air for a few days. When growth has begun reduce the shoots to one or two per plant and set out intact, when all danger of frost is past, having thoroughly hardened them off first. With a little heat in the greenhouse, cuttings are also easily raised. Place the old tubers in boxes with a little soil, discard the first flush of shoots which are not usually ideal as cuttings, and select the shorter ones of the second crop. Take them off close to the old stems just above the tubers, ensuring that the base of each cutting is cut straight across beneath a 'node', i.e. below the point where a leaf stalk joins the stem of the cutting. Dibble them into pots or boxes containing a light potting compost and put them on the staging of a warm greenhouse, potting them up singly after rooting into 3-in. pots. containing a light potting compost. They are later moved to a cold frame to harden them off before planting out. If there are no special facilities for propagating cuttings in the greenhouse, then simply divide the tubers after growth has begun when they have been placed in boxes of soil. See that a fresh growth has been made after the division, then transfer them to other boxes of compost, and in due course harden them off for planting out.

Large quantities of farmyard manure are both unnecessary and undesirable for the preparation of dahlia beds and borders. A moderate dressing of manure or garden compost—according to the condition of the soil—should be given during the winter, and a sprinkling of slaked lime in the spring, with a little superphosphate and sulphate of potash worked into the surface ten days before planting, benefits the root system and aids the early stages of growth. A little liquid manure during the growing season will help the development of flowers.

Spacing of the plants depends on the type, but crowding is unwise, and sufficient room should be left to admit air and light, and allow development of side shoots. Firm planting is not essential but, since the somewhat soft growth is liable to injury from high winds, the vigorous growing cactus and decorative kinds should be tied to strong canes or sticks as soon as they are planted. It is a good idea to place the canes in position before planting. Stakes should be two feet high initially, and when growth has reached their tops, new ones should be placed in position according to the ultimate height of the variety. When tying allow the side shoots a little play, to avoid injury by the ties as the stems increase in size: soft garden twine looped up to the stakes is the best method.

Disbudding is unnecessary for garden decoration, where the number of blooms is more important than size. For exhibition purposes thinning of the shoots is especially important, since excessive growth hinders development of the flowers, but some varieties tend to produce coarse blooms and too severe thinning may accentuate this.

Dahlias of dwarf and medium habit are best, both for the garden and public park, for they come into flower early and bloom continuously. The Coltness types are considered by some as the dahlias of dahlias. They are dwarf, compact, need no stakes, and have single flowers. If old flower-heads are removed as the petals fall they will continue to bloom in sunshine and rain until cut down by frost. Good varieties are Coltness Gem, crimson-scarlet on stiff erect stems; Princess Marie José, satin pink; Paisley Gem, semi-double, orange-scarlet; and Shirley Yellow, bright yellow.

Immense advances have been made in the development of beautiful Cactus dahlias with erect stems standing well above the foliage, such as Doris Day, cardinal red; Golden Apricot; Elizabeth Sawyer, bright lilac rose and Doreen Wallace, brilliant orange.

The Pompon dahlias have small, compact, neat, ball-like blooms which are suitable for garden decoration and as cut flowers. Varieties

181

include Little Beeswing, yellow with red margin; Ideal, yellow; Glow, salmon-cerise and Queen of the Whites, one of the best whites.

Decorative dahlias are of all shades and carry their flower-heads well above the foliage. A small selection might include: Gerrie Hoek, pink, fine for cutting; House of Orange, soft orange, a good variety; Glorie of Heemstede, yellow, free flowering and good for cutting; and Edinburgh, a rich maroon bloom with a white tip to each petal.

Delphiniums

Delphiniums, or hybrid larkspurs, are the aristocrats of hardy herbaceous plants. Though intolerant of shade, they establish themselves quickly in any sunny position, but must have a soil enriched well in advance of planting by decomposed farmyard manure, supplemented by a mulch of the same when spring growth begins. Their extensive fibrous roots quickly absorb supplies of plant food, especially in light, gravelly soils, and this makes liberal feeding essential. A deficiency in phosphates should be remedied by a spring dressing of superphosphate at 2 oz. per sq. yard, worked in with a Dutch hoe. Horticultural peat may be substituted for farmyard manure, for though it has no value as fertiliser, it increases the water-holding capacity of the soil and delphiniums need plenty of moisture.

Seed will not always come true, but if freshly gathered and kept in a cool temperature (vitality is otherwise quickly lost) ninety per cent germination can be expected when sown in a cold frame, using a light porous compost. During the winter the seedlings should be kept fairly dry with plenty of ventilation on all suitable occasions, and should be transplanted in spring 15 ins. apart in their flowering quarters. Good plants will bloom the first year, but their real quality cannot be judged till the second or third.

Named varieties are best propagated by cuttings two to three inches long taken in February or March from clumps in the open, as soon as the leaves begin to unfold. The shoots are severed from the crown with a sharp knife, ensuring that part of the crown root is also taken to form a 'heel cutting'. These are then inserted about an inch deep in a bed or on a propagation bench. A cold frame can be used but a temperature of 50° F./10° C. is best. Roots appear in 3-5 weeks and when they are about 1 in. long, the plants should either be transferred to nursery rows outdoors or potted into small pots for later planting out, after being hardened off in each case.

Three-year-old plants can be lifted and divided, but if they are older hollow areas often develop at the heart making them less suitable for propagating purposes. The clumps should be split into sections in spring so that the individual crowns can be seen, these can then be divided and replanted, when they should be carefully shaded and watered. Do not let the shoots get too long before attempting division, since growth will be checked, due to excessive transpiration before an adequate rooting system can be established.

Layering can be done in May or June. Make a neat cut at the base of the stem, cover it with soil and stake the stem to keep it upright. Roots will develop from the callus formed in the next few days on the cut tissue. Layers should be left attached to the mother plant till next spring, then removed and planted out. Shoots should be thinned on established plants when they are 2-3 ins. high, leaving three to five shoots per plant, since good flowering spikes will not otherwise be obtained.

Staking is done early in the season, one being sufficient (behind and near the crown) for the first year, but three or four being needed for larger clumps—preferably one for each spike. Painted green, so as to be unconspicuous, they should be long and slender at the top, allowing a certain amount of play while the base remains firmly rigid in the soil. Cut off the main spikes above the foliage when they finish blooming, to induce lateral shoots to continue the flowering period, and when the leaves have matured, cut the stems to ground level. Cut flowering spikes for house decoration in the early morning when the tissue is most turgid, and select those on which only half the blooms are open and place them immediately in a deep bucket of water in a cool place.

Despite the many new delphinium varieties annually introduced, many older ones are still worth growing, and, before making a choice, it is worth while visiting a few nursery gardens to see them in bloom. So much is a matter of individual preference that it is hard to recommend varieties certain to please everyone.

Slugs are the worst enemy of delphiniums. They hide in the crown of the plant and often eat young shoots before they break through the soil. Control can be exercised by a poison bait of Metaldehyde Slug Control—often called Meta tablets—in February and March. Oatmeal should be added to the crushed tablets and the mixture protected from the rain by a piece of slate or an inverted flowerpot. Stunt disease sometimes attacks perennial delphiniums, dwarfing the plants and leading to a multiplication of weak, slender shoots; black necrotic areas appear on the leaf-blade and stems, and the shoots and foliage yellow prematurely and die soon after flowering. The plants should be uprooted and destroyed.

Ferns

Although the number of British fern species is not large, the many varieties make it interesting to grow them. Ferns belong to the class of flowerless plants, their vegetative organs comprising almost the whole of the plant. The so-called leaves (fronds) are peculiar in that they vary greatly in size and complexity, the much divided and crinkly varieties being most prized.

The roots are always fibrous, and both these and the fronds are produced—in most British ferns—from a creeping stem or rhizome. This makes propagation easy, for a portion with roots and fronds will readily form an independent plant if separated and planted out under favourable conditions.

The royal fern and many exotic species have a caudex, or upright stem, the fronds arising in a kind of crowded whorl from the termination of the axis of growth, and new ones springing from the inner side of those previously formed. Very fine exotic specimens some over 30 ft. high, grow in the palm house of the Royal Botanic Garden, Edinburgh.

Naturally, ferns are propagated by means of spores (analogous to the seeds of flowering plants) which are shed as soon as they are ripe and will germinate freely on damp soil, damp brickwork, or the sides of the pot in which the mother-plant grows, so long as they are undisturbed. Spores, although very small and often dust-like, may most conveniently be sown on the surface of pans of moist loam, a close, moist atmosphere being retained by a piece of flat glass laid across the top and the pans placed in water-filled saucers.

Generally speaking garden ferns need a certain amount of shade and shelter, as well as abundant moisture during the growing season, though this is not essential for all species. Useful sites are the rock garden, the north side of a house, under trees, and in the shade of shrubs where flowering plants would not succeed. A fernery need not, however, be quite flowerless, and one of my friends had an excellent collection of spring-flowering plants (polyanthus and primulas, Lenten roses, wood hyacinths, scillas, dog-tooth violets and anemones) growing among ferns in a shady border.

The parsley fern (*Allosorus crispus*) likes a rocky situation, growing among loose, half-rotten stone, and I have found it over a thousand feet up in the Cheviots. Planted in partial shade in a rock garden with a northern aspect, using a mixture of peat and loam freely intermixed with sand, and half buried with stone fragments, it grows easily. Free growth will even be stimulated if small stones are placed on the crown of the plant, but it resents disturbance once established.

Other interesting rock garden ferns are the beech fern (*Polypodium phegopteris*) and the oak fern (*P. dryopteris*), which do best in dry, shady pockets among stones, although they also make good pot plants. The common polypody (*Polypodium vulgare*) is evergreen, and one of the best cool-wall plants. It requires a light, porous soil and the rhizomes must be kept on the surface, since if it is planted unnaturally deep or in a clay soil, it loses vigour and eventually dies. On the other hand, placed on an old wall, the root-stock creeps along the joints and a glorious show of fronds—all the more valuable from being at its best in early winter when few ferns are seen—is produced. The rue-leaved spleenwort or wall rue (*Asplenium rutamuraria*) grows on rocks and ancient ruins, but is sometimes difficult to establish on ordinary garden walls unless kept fairly dry and given very porous soil with a large proportion of old mortar rubble. Since the roots cling fast to the stones on which they grow, this fern is not easy to propagate. The common spleenwort (*A. trichomanes*) should be treated in a similar way, but the green spleenwort (*A. viride*) requires a good deal of moisture at the roots to flourish. Easiest of the native ferns to cultivate is the lady fern (*Athyrium filix-foemina*) which is very attractive when planted among shady, moist rockwork, the soil being rather boggy but not stagnant.

The hard fern (*Blechnum spicant*) has many exceedingly curious and interesting varieties, and some of the crested forms make very beautiful greenhouse plants. An elegant evergreen, its fronds have a rigid harshness of texture and continue quite fresh through the winter. It needs plenty of peat or leaf mould and is very suitable for the damp, shady or wild garden. Very robust and easy to cultivate is the deciduous broad prickly-toothed buckler fern (*Nephrodium dilatatum* or *Lastrea dilatata*) which has dark green fronds some 2-3 ft. long with pale undersides, and will flourish in any good, moderately moist soil provided it gets a fair amount of shade. The smaller *cristata* variety of this species is an outstandingly beautiful fern.

The common male fern (*Lastrea filix-mas*) is a vigorous grower, producing leathery and durable fronds in a striking tuft round a central crown, and magnificent specimens will develop in a shady part of the garden.

Most stately and dignified of our indigenous ferns is the royal fern (*Osmunda regalis*) which does best in boggy or marshy situations, and is specially suited to occupy a prominent position on the shady side on the bank of a stream or pond where the roots can reach the water. The average height is 3-4 ft., but it may reach 8 ft., and old stems may bear their leathery green fronds on 'trunks' 1-2 ft. high. It is sometimes called the 'flowering fern' on account of the prominent spore cases, formed in terminal brown panicles above the fronds, which add considerably to its majestic appearance. *Cristata,* the beautiful crested form, produces large spreading fronds.

The soft prickly fern (*Aspidium* or *Polystichum angulare cristatum*) and the hard or prickly shield fern (*Polystichum aculeatum*, formerly known as *Aspidium aculeanum*) are evergreens and both have a host of varieties, ranging from dwarf forms measured in inches to tall, erect or spreading types with very sharply differentiated fronds. Planted in the shady part of a woody bank in loamy soil, they are the easiest of all large ferns to grow, and are equally suitable for pot culture, making admirable house plants.

Botanically distinct from all other native ferns is the hart's-tongue (*Scolopendrium vulgare*) of which there are at least 155 varieties, all having curious and distinct differences in the formation of their fronds. A most beautiful variety is *S. crispum*, with markedly undulating frond margins which give it a very elegant, curled or crisped appearance. Also curiously crested, but with broader fronds, is *S. marginatum*, and *S. multifidum* has forked fronds developing at their tips into irregular fan-shaped expansions. All are extremely decorative evergreens and if planted in well-drained light sandy loam with peat and leaf mould will succeed in any part of the garden.

Gladioli

Belonging to the iris family (*Iridaceae*) the gladiolus—diminutive of the *gladius*, or short sword, which its young shoot and leaves resemble—has some 200 species and a myriad brilliantly coloured varieties. Africa is the home of the genus, especially South Africa, but species are also indigenous to Central Europe and Western Asia—one even growing wild in rare instances in England.

The oldest cultivated species is the Mediterranean *G. byrantinus*, and in the eighteenth century *G. tristis*, with greenish-yellow petals and blotched throat, was introduced from Natal. These original species have long been superseded, however, by the efforts of the hybridisers, first in France by the introduction of *G. Lemoinei* and in the late eighteenth century by William Colville of Argyll who crossed *G. tristis* and *G. cardinalis* to produce the modern *G. Colvillei.* Other famed Scots breeders include the late George Mair of Prestwick and Gavin McKelvie.

Its beauty and length of life as a cut flower make the gladiolus increasingly popular, especially with the florist. The large flowers have plenty of substance in their segments and the long, symmetrical spikes generally have the blooms facing all one way and so spaced as just to hide the stem. Colours range from white through pale yellow, orange, pink and deep red to a lavender blue. Whether planted in beds, lines or groups, gladioli are equally effective and the cheapness of the corms means that they can be grown in large numbers.

Exhibition plants are best grown in a special part of the garden, so that damage by high wind and rain near the cutting stage can be minimised and scorching of the flowers be prevented by shading with some light protective material, such as tiffany.

Choose a sunny position and prepare the ground—preferably a good rich soil inclining to heaviness—by double-digging in early winter and applying a fairly heavy dressing of well-decayed farmyard manure to the top layer. Some weeks before planting fork into the top 6 ins. of soil 2 oz. of bone meal and 1 oz. of sulphate of potash per sq. yd., and a day or two beforehand hoe into the surface a sprinkling of lime.

Plant in April or early May, placing the corms 4 ins. deep about 9 ins. apart in clumps, or 12 ins. apart in rows, and surrounding each with a little sharp river sand as a protection against damp and to allow air circulation as the roots form. In light sandy soils, mulch with well decayed farmyard manure or leaf mould to a depth of 2 ins. as soon as the shoots are about 1 ft. high, when they should also be staked with bamboo and given some weak liquid manure. In cold, late districts try starting the corms into growth in boxes of potting soil under glass, and when the spikes are a few inches high, harden them off and plant them out, being careful not to break the brittle roots. Aphides may need to be controlled on the growing plants by an occasional dusting with derris dust.

Spikes grown for house decoration should be cut in the cool of the evening when the lowest two or three florets show colour, placing them immediately in water so that they can take up as much moisture as possible. Never allow the cut end of a spike to dry off or the flowers will not open, and always leave at least four leaves on the plant so that the new corm, which forms above the old one can be nourished and develop for another year. Gladioli grown for garden display should have the faded flower spikes cut off just below the lowest flower immediately the last flower has faded to prevent seed from forming.

In autumn dig up the corms on a dry day and leave them on the ground until quite dry, making sure that different varieties are kept separate and correctly labelled. Place in the greenhouse or shed. Quick drying is important. In about two to three weeks the roots and stalks can be removed, and the cleaned corms are then placed in small boxes or open-mouthed paper bags, a little derris dust being shaken into each bag to prevent an attack by aphides, and stored in a cool, yet frost-free, place for the winter.

It is interesting to raise gladioli from seed. When selecting a variety for intercrossing, remove the lower flower as it is not always typical, then select three others as they open, removing the stamens from each with a pair of scissors. When the lobes of each three-cleft stigma open out, lightly apply, with a camel hair brush, pollen from the other variety selected for intercrossing, then cut off the remainder of the flower spike. Place a muslin bag over the pollinated flowers to prevent foreign pollen reaching the stigmas. If you have been successful, the seed pods will begin to show in about ten days time and when they show signs of ripening should be cut off, labelled, and placed in a wide-mouthed jar to finish ripening and to allow the seed to become quite dry.

Sowing should be done in pots, under glass, the following April, and germination should follow in five to six weeks, although it is sometimes slower. Grow the seedlings on steadily in heat, never allowing them to become dry, and plant out in June. Lift and store in the autumn. Many seedlings will flower the second year, but they will not be at their best until the fourth.

Propagation can also be done vegetatively by the very small cormlets or 'spawn' produced around the large old corms, often, but incorrectly, called the "fruit" of the parent plant. Some varieties produce a large number of cormlets while others produce very few, if any. The flower colour and habit of growth will be exactly the same as that of the parent. Cormlets, which are the size of a sweet pea seed or a little larger, should be stored in a frost-free place in dry sand or peat during winter and planted the following spring, but they will not produce flowers the first year. Some may bloom the second year, but, others take three to four. It is best to prevent cormlets from flowering by removing the flower spikes until good sized corms have been built up.

The beginner should not buy too many varieties before finding out those that suit his soil, but the following are a useful selection:

188

early flowering—Abu Hassan, deep violet; Allard Pierson, salmon red; *Dr. Fleming, salmon-pink; Belle Jaune, golden yellow; Blue Sky, true blue; Circe, russet-orange; mid-season flowering—*Firebrand, deep scarlet; Harry Hopkins, claret; *Bloemfontein, salmon pink; Ravel, bright blue with reddish throat; Snow Princess, pure white; Picardy, apricot pink; late flowering—New Europe, geranium red; Marshal Montgomery, velvety red; *Evangeline, soft silvery-salmon pink. Those with an asterisk before the name are good for exhibition; others include Karen, which has a salmon-pink flower with white throat; Kosmos, salmon-pink with yellowish throat, and Life Flame, a scarlet flowered variety.

There is also the *Primulinus* type which, although producing tall spikes, does not have such large flowers as those in the large-flowered section mentioned above and the blooms are not so compact on the stem. They are, however, very beautiful and the following varieties should be tried: Scarletta, scarlet; L'Innocence, white; Bolinde, salmon; Souvenir, yellow.

Of the more recently introduced Butterfly Gladioli, with small, dainty flowers and colourings as beautiful as those of the butterfly, try the varieties Gipsy Love, salmon-orange with crimson-scarlet blotch; Melody, salmon-pink with cherry-red blotches; Elf, peach with scarlet markings.

Lilies

This large genus of most beautiful hardy and half-hardy bulbs is widely distributed throughout the world. Of those introduced to Scotland, the Indian species are the least hardy, since the young shoots are very susceptible to our late spring frosts which do more damage than a very severe winter.

Lilies are woodland plants, this being especially true of Japanese and American species, and grow in clearings or on wooded hillsides where they are shielded from cold winds and frost by undergrowth, and receive the partial shade they need. The fallen leaves of trees and shrubs provide a protective mulch in autumn which, as it decays, becomes plant food.

Good drainage is essential, and so the ground should be prepared by double digging, incorporating a fair proportion of leaf-mould or peat moss in the top spit. The majority of hardy lilies will thrive in the same type of soil that produces a good potato crop. The ideal site for a lily garden is in a thinly wooded coppice which will give them the combination of sun and shade they love, as well as protection from

189

drought, but they should be kept away from shrubs with strong deep roots which would starve them of food. For the herbaceous border the vigorous growing *candidum, chalcedonicum, testaceum* (syn. *excelsum*), *tigrinum* and most *umbellatum* kinds are suitable, while *tenuifolium,* and *umbellatum,* var. Vermilion Brilliant, grow well in the rock garden to a height of about 1½ ft.

Lilies make splendid pot plants for house and greenhouse decoration and, except the commoner varieties, almost all are acceptable and suitable for growing under glass, and some of the most popular are *auratum, Brownii, longiflorum, regale* and *speciosum.* Fill deep pots with a mixture of three parts fibrous loam to one part leaf-mould, with sufficient sand to keep the mixture open, and leave enough space for top dressing with a mixture of decayed farmyard manure and fibrous loam. Pot the bulbs in early autumn and place them in a cold frame, keeping them cool and slightly shaded at the roots. Ventilate well, but avoid draughts and syringe with tepid water to aid growth.

Propagation may be effected by offsets while the plant is at rest, scales being taken from the parent, with a portion of the base of the bulb, and placed in a cold frame in an upright position at a depth of one third their height, in a mixture of peat, leaf-mould and sand. Very little water should be given, and in the following May green shoots will appear with small bulbs eventually forming at the base. The plantlets are top-dressed with a good compost and left in the frame for another season. Many species, however, are propagated by bulbils produced on their stems, which should be removed and planted out near the surface in a cold frame, and with some it is possible to layer the flower stems in a preparation of peat and sand to stimulate the production of bulbils in the axils of the leaves.

Lilies raised from seed in pots or boxes vary in the time they take to germinate, some remain dormant for twelve months, while others germinate in only a few weeks, but they are usually ready to plant out into flowering quarters in two years, e.g. *Lilium regale.* Frost does not harm the seed and in fact it assists germination if the seed is allowed to become frozen in the boxes. To obtain a stock of some varieties it may be necessary to grow from seed each year, for example, *tenuifolium,* an attractive, little scarlet flowering gem from Siberia, which nearly always disappears after flowering.

When bulbs in the open become overcrowded and show signs of deteriorating they should be lifted and replanted, the larger-growing bulbs placed 6-10 ins. below the surface and the smaller 3-4 ins., measuring from the base of the bulb.

A number of lilies do well in most Scottish gardens, and *Lilium croceum* (often called the cottager's orange lily), a native of Corsica and southern France, thrives in any ordinary garden soil, being especially suitable in towns. It is a robust grower, bearing huge umbels of beautiful, orange-coloured blooms on stout stems. The 'Queen of Lilies' (*L. auratum*), a native of Japan, is a magnificent plant and there are many excellent varieties of which *platyphyllum* is one of the largest and best forms, producing stout stems with richly spotted flowers 12 ins. wide; it is sometimes difficult to establish out of doors, although it can be done by starting the bulbs in pots and planting them out in their pots when growth is fairly well advanced. 'The Madonna Lily' or 'The Annunciation Lily' (*L. candidum*), one of the oldest, will thrive in all kinds of soils, in full sun or partial shade, but should be planted early and not deeply, 2 ins. of soil on top of the bulbs being sufficient. It has two kinds of leaves, broad basal ones which appear early in autumn and are borne on the bulb scales, and narrow pointed stem leaves. 'The Scarlet Turk's Cap' (*L. chalcedonicum*), a lily of Greece, endures lime and should be planted in a sunny position, not more than 4 ins. deep. Stems are slender, bearing five to eight flowers. *L. elegans* or *thunbergianum* has been raised from garden sources, and its varieties are early-summer flowering, have a wide range of colour, and are suitable because of their dwarf size—12-15 ins. high—for the rock garden.

Tallest of all lilies is *L. giganteum*, of the Himalayan foothills, often 10 ft. tall with broad foliage and stately flower spikes. Pure white outside, the blooms have a tinge of purple inside, and the bulbs should be planted with the tops just above the level of a rich, deep loamy soil, but protected in winter by a mulch of leaves.

A splendid lily from central China, *L. Henryi,* is excellent for planting among shrubs. A stem rooting, lime-loving plant it thrives in the greenhouse provided a little shade is given to prevent the flowers bleaching and should be planted at a depth of 10 ins. Perhaps the most widely grown of all lilies, especially for commercial purposes, is (*L. longiflorum*) but this is essentially a greenhouse plant, and needs a rich compost with a generous quantity of decayed farmyard manure. The petals are pure white, and the thick, yellow, pollen carrying anthers are removed by the commercial grower before marketing to avoid spoiling the whiteness of the bloom. The 'Regal Lily' (*L. regale*) was introduced from China by E. H. Wilson in 1903 and first flowered two years later. One of the finest of all lilies, it has a wiry stem, freely clothed with dark green leaves, and the funnel shaped flowers **are** pink outside and white within, with a pale yellow throat. The bulbs should be planted 8 ins. deep in a sunny position and need no special soil. The 'Tiger Lily' (*L. tigrinum*) and its varieties are splendid garden plants. The giant of the group is the *Fortunei giganteum* variety, which has salmon-orange flowers, seldom opening before September. As it is a stem rooter, it should be planted at least 10 ins. deep, and propagated by bulbils taken from the leaf axils. Many varieties of *L. umbellatum* are regarded as hybrids from *L. davuricum*, an apricot coloured kind rarely seen today, and have been awarded the Royal Horticultural Society Award of Garden Merit. They are good plants for the herbaceous border, producing large umbellate heads of yellow, orange and crimson flowers.

Meadow Rues

The meadow rues (genus *Thalictrum*) are closely allied to the anemone and belong to the buttercup or Ranunculaceae family. There are about 130 species of these hardy perennials, which usually have fibrous roots, though a few are tuberous and others have yellow, creeping underground stems. The petal-less flowers (paniculate, or rarely racemose) have green, yellow, purple or white sepals—sometimes large and conspicuous and sometimes the opposite—the latter often dropping so quickly that the flowers seem to be all stamens.

Most rues come from north temperate and Arctic regions, though a few are natives of South America, and three valuable species— *T. Chelidonii*, *T. Delavayi* and *T. dipterocarpum*—come from China. There are also three native British species: *T. alpinum*, *T. flavum* and *T. minus*. Rues may be grown as much for their intricately divided foliage as for their flowers, which are in some species insignificant, and though some are well worth cultivation others are simply botanic garden specimens.

The crowns may ordinarily be divided in spring or autumn, but with double forms it is essential to choose spring. Seed may be sown in a cold frame in spring, but it is sometimes two years before germination takes place. The species vary in habitat some liking partial shade, others a sunny position in the herbaceous border or rock garden; some grow well near a pondside and some in open woodland. Most are very deep-rooting and like a soil enriched with turfy loam and decayed farmyard manure. On heavy soils the roots are liable to damp off during winter, and when replanting remember that the small crowns are apt to be loosened by frost, so plant them firmly.

To stimulate root growth the lower half inch may be treated with a hormone powder.

SHRUB CUTTINGS

The cuttings are inserted in a sandy mixture.

With hand forks.

Scabious plants.

DIVISION

Scabious cutting being prepare[d] for rooting.

Cultivated meadow rues fall into three groups—those with long ornamental sepals, usually mauve or purplish; those with conspicuous stamens; and those grown only for their foliage.

The alpine meadow rue (*T. alpinum*) is the smallest of the genus and rarely more than 6 ins. high. It has stoloniferous roots, leaf stems which split into three branches, each with three leaflets, and flowers borne in a single, nodding raceme, during July and August. The latter have no petals, but four small sepals and a conspicuous cluster of yellowish stamens. Found among short turf in the mountains of Scotland and Wales, it does well in a sunny position in the rock garden.

The rue anemone *T. anemonides* (syn. *Anemonella thalictroides*) is a native of North America which will thrive either in partial shade in the rock garden or in the unheated alpine house in a pan of gritty soil with a plentiful admixture of leafmould or peat. Rarely more than 6 ins. high, it has tuberous roots, fern-like, three-lobed leaflets and panicles of white flowers (resembling *Anemone nemorosa*) in April: *flore pleno* is a beautiful double-flowered variety.

The columbine-leaved rue (*T. aquilegifolium*) has long been cultivated in the herbaceous border. The fairly large glaucous leaves are moderately divided and, although the original plants had more or less yellow flowers, purple is now more usual. The stamens form a prominent foamy mass and the stems are hollow, purple and mealy. The many varieties average 3 ft., flower in June and July, and include *album*, white stamens; *atropurpureum*, rosy purple with dark stems; and *roseum*, pale lilac-rose. Any good garden soil suits them, but they prefer a strong loam with plenty of moisture at the roots.

The Chinese *T. Delavayi*, useful in both the herbaceous border and rock garden, has wiry thin 2-3 ft. high stems, and produces panicles of nodding mauve-tinted flowers among its finely divided foliage in July and August. A close relation is the 15 in. high Himalayan species. *T. Chelidonii* with foliage that is pale green above and downy below, and tiny bulbils in its leaf axils. Graceful sprays of silvery-lavender flowers appear in July and August. It is a somewhat difficult plant to establish. The lovely *T. dipterocarpum*, with smaller flowers than *Delavayi*, grows to 3-4 ft. in good conditions. It has small, smooth, slender leaves on wiry stems and the pendulous four-sepalled flowers are a delicate mauve.

Yellow meadow rue (*T. flavum*) grows to 1½ ft., and is useful both in the border and for bold grouping in the wild garden. It has yellow, stoloniferous roots, deep green foliage and feathery panicles of yellow flowers with prominent stamens, useful for cutting. The

N

lesser meadow rue (*T. minus*) is native to our rocky limestone regions and in favourable circumstances reaches a height of about 1 ft.: the flowers are insignificant, but the foliage elegant. Pretty cultivated types are the 1½-ft.-high dwarf *T. minus*, var. *adiantifolium*, a bushy plant with divided bluish green leaves and small greenish-yellow flowers; *T. elatum*, a 5-ft.-high bush with a cloud of greenish-yellow bloom; *majus* with 4-ft. stems, more leafy and with larger leaflets than the species; and *purpurascens*, purplish-flowered.

A native of Greece, *T. orientale*, is a sprawling plant never over 10 ins. and bears white flowers with yellow anthers in loose panicles in spring. The eastern North American *T. purpurascens* reaches 5 ft., and its glaucous stems and leaves, and dropping masses of purple, yellow-stamened flowers look well at the back of the herbaceous border. The border also needs a group of the 2-5-ft.-high *T. speciosum* (*T. glaucum*); the stamens are bright yellow, the sepals pale yellow, produced in feathery balls on branching stems. The tuberous-rooted meadow rue *T. tuberosum* is attractive in the rock garden, grows about 1 ft. high, and has much-divided leaves and clusters of small, pale-white flowers from July to September.

Phloxes

Phloxes or flame flowers, are natives of America, and the garden species are divided into three classes—annual, alpine and early and late flowering.

The half-hardy annual species *Phlox Drummondii* produces flowers of various colours all summer, and although both the type and the varieties are rather fragile in growth, they will stand summer storms reasonably well. Some varieties which come true from seed are *cuspidata* (pointed petals), *fimbricata* (fringed petals), *flore pleno* (double-flowered), *grandiflora* (large-flowered), and *nana* (dwarf).

Seed is sown during March in a heated frame, germinates, rapidly, and when the seedlings are large enough to handle they should be pricked out into other boxes and eventually hardened off for planting out at the end of May. When they are about 3 ins. high the buds should be nipped out to make the plants bushy.

Useful both in beds by themselves, and as edgings to other plants, *P. Drummondii* and its varieties should be planted about 6 ins. apart in fairly rich soil and full sun. If the shoots are pegged down, a close mat of colour will be formed.

The best dwarf varieties for the rock garden are forms of *P. divaricata*, *P. Douglasii* and *P. subulata* (syn. *setacea*).

Of a spreading habit *P. divaricata* produces stems 6-15 ins. long with pale blue flowers: *P. d. alba* is a good white and *P. d. Lapham* a plumbago blue. Growing prostrate, *P. d. Douglasii* is lavender blue with a yellow eye, but the variety *P. d.* Snow Queen has very attractive pure white flowers. The mossy pink *P. subulata* tends to be a prostrate in habit and grows to about 6 ins. high, forming a compact evergreen mass up to 3 ft. across, although in May and June the rose-coloured flowers completely hide the foliage. Among the numerous varieties are B. E. Chalmers, a soft heliotrope blue, which flowers freely from May to July; G. F. Wilson also free flowering and having delicious lavender-blue flowers; *Nelsonii*, which is moss-habited and has white flowers with a pink eye: *Nivalis*, a trailing plant with small pure white flowers; Sprite, rosy pink with a crimson eye; The Bride, another white variety with a pink eye; and Vivid, perhaps the best of the *subulata* varieties, which though not so robust as many others, has warm salmon-rose or flesh-pink flowers, and is ideal for the moraine.

All these plants grow easily in ordinary soil, to which sharp sand and half decayed leaves should be added, and they will grow in any position except in dense shade.

Alpine phloxes are easily propagated by cuttings taken in July which should be placed in sandy soil in a cold frame, and shaded from strong sunlight until firmly rooted. Sturdy plants will then be available for transplanting to flower beds the next spring.

Herbaceous phloxes divide into two types, the *suffruticosa*, earlier to flower, smaller in growth, and well suited to cool moist Scottish conditions; and the *decussata*, later to flower, with taller stems more naked at the base, throwing out lateral flower stems towards the top, and much hardier.

Although these are not fastidious plants, they must have well cultivated ground, and since they are gross feeders, with shallow roots, need a rich moist loam fairly heavily dressed with farmyard manure. In height they range from $1\frac{1}{2}$ to $4\frac{1}{2}$ ft., according to soil and climate, and flower best when the clumps are periodically lifted, reduced in size and transplanted to a fresh position.

Propagation is also possible from stem and root cuttings, the former taken in spring when the shoots are about 3 ins. long and placed in a sandy compost in a cold frame, and the latter taken at the same time, but rooted in pure sand. Both these methods ensure that the new plant will be exactly like the original, and usually also that the young plants will be free from phlox eelworm. Plants with half a dozen stems usually give better flowering spikes than those with double the number.

195

Unless they are in an exposed position, the plants do not always need staking, but three or four canes to a clump, with a double strand of twine tied round them, will prevent the breaking of promising shoots. Indoors the flowers commonly shrivel in the warmth of the room and the petals drop, so that they are unsuitable as cut flowers.

Modern varieties range in colour from white to rosy-pink and from lilac to deep crimson, and shades of rich salmon and carmine. When setting out plants have some colour scheme in mind, and take into account the heights of the various varieties.

The following *decussata* varieties are all large-flowered—Border Gem, violet-blue; Daily Sketch, pink with a crimson centre; Eva Foerster, salmon coloured with a white centre; Leo Schlageter, crimson; Sir John Falstaff, salmon-pink; Titanic, carmine; Windsor, cerise.

Primulas

The primulas (family Primulaceae) are among the oldest of our cultivated plants, and the number of species and varieties grown has greatly increased during this century. They are not easy to naturalise and, when grown among other plants they need to be replaced by seedlings as they die off, although most of the Asiatic species may establish themselves in specially prepared beds by a stream or in sub-marshy ground, and others will make a permanent home in woodland vegetation—among rhododendrons, for example, which share their love of peat and moisture.

The majority of primulas can be raised from seed sown thinly in March in shallow pans, using a mixture of 2 parts loam, 1 part leaf-mould or peat and 1 part sharp sand—the whole finely sifted. Merely cover the seeds with fine soil, shade until germination takes place and water carefully to prevent damping off. Prick out the seedlings into boxes or frames and grow on until large enough to be planted out, allowing them to become established before winter. Division of the perennial varieties should be done in spring just as they appear above ground. All need an ample top dressing in spring or early summer with partly decayed leaves or granulated peat.

First of the Asiatic species to flower in the open is *Primula denticulata*, which grows wild from Tibet to Burma. A robust grower, it needs a rich manured soil, and sends up strong, erect stems, carrying crowded heads of sessile flowers, which are faintly fragrant and appear before the flat leaves have time to unfold. Easily raised from

196

seed, it ranges in colour from lilac to white, and when established is just as easy to propagate by division—as are its varieties. These include *P. denticulata,* var. *magnifica purpurea*; *P. denticulata,* var. *alba,* a lovely white form; and *cashmeriana,* with longer, more convex, paler green leaves than the species, and the whole plant covered with a white, mealy powder which adds to its attractions.

Suitable for an attempt at naturalisation is the robust though short-lived perennial *P. pulverulenta,* which has large healthy leaves and brilliant rose-pink to maroon-crimson flowers produced in whorls on stout stems 2-3 ft. high—the latter are covered with farina, thus distinguishing it from *P. japonica.* It seeds freely in the open and seedlings are easily raised in a cold frame. Cockburn's primrose (*P. Cockburniana*) is almost a biennial, so that seed should be sown annually, and has bright orange scarlet flowers borne in whorls on slender stems. Quite hardy, it cannot stand damp and drainage must be perfected by adding plenty of gritty material to the soil. Seedlings are best wintered in a cold frame and planted out in spring. By crossing *P. pulverulenta* and *P. Cockburniana*—either way makes little difference to the seedlings—*P. unique,* a pretty shade of reddish crimson, is produced.

The queen of primulas is *P. japonica,* which flowers May to September and is a semi-bog species ideal for the side of a stream or a moist corner of the wild garden, though moisture should be within reach of the roots rather than submerging or partially submerging them. Sometimes a white form appears, but shades from dark purple to pale rose are more usual. Poorly coloured specimens should be annually rogued out to prevent seeding, for self-sown seedlings often appear in a shady position and only the best type should be preserved. Another gem is *P. rosea* which will increase annually by self-sown seed if grown among short grass in a boggy part of the wild garden. The flowers are a brilliant rose, and the variety *superba* is especially worthwhile. The Himalayan Cowslip *P. Sikkimensis* thrives luxuriantly in wet, boggy compost. Although growing at a height of 12,000 to 17,000 ft. in its native land, it also grows well in Scotland. The leaves disappear in winter and propagation is by means of seed sown as soon as ripe or by division of the crowns in autumn. Closely related is *P. pseudo-Sikkimensis,* and *P. Florindae* is another yellow flowered species which appreciates a similar setting, but it has larger flowers and the leaves are glossy with a cordate base. Much wider in the corolla than *P. Florindae* is *P. alpicola* (syn. *P. microdonta*), which has matt leaves and succeeds in a moist loamy soil, although it appreciates drier conditions during the resting period. The variety *violacea* has purple flowers with a cordate leaf base.

Suited to Scotland's climate, *P. Littoniana* thrives in partial shade in a deep peaty compost, although it doesn't like its roots in water. Dying down to a hard bud in autumn, it is one of the latest to start growing in the spring, but once begun it springs up rapidly and soon comes into flower. The tall stems terminate in a bright red spike, and the pendant flowers are arranged in cylindrical form and vary in colour from lilac to deep purple. Its roots spread more or less horizontally, having little hold on the soil, and care must be taken that it is not lifted out of the ground during frosty weather. Somewhat resembling *P. denticulata* in appearance is *P. capitata*, which comes into bloom when nearly all the other primulas are over, but it prefers a drier situation than the former liking loam, peat and sand with a quantity of broken brick and limestone to keep the soil open. The rich purple flowers vary in depth with different plants. After flowering it dies off, but grows readily from seed and sometimes flowers the same year. More of a perennial than *P. Littoniana*, is *P. chionantha*, which flowers and seeds freely and likes the same dry soil conditions which suit *P. capitata*. The leaves are long and narrow, of a dull green, and the undersides as well as the flower spike are heavily coated with golden meal. The flowers are large, white, deliciously fragrant and freely produced in whorls. Similar to the grape hyacinth, *P. nutans* has oval leaves covered with short hairs and deep violet flowers. It needs partial shade and a soil containing loam, leaf mould and sharp sand. A very free flowering variety of *P. Juliae*, known as The Jewel, is a fine hybrid with bright ruby purple flowers and distinct small golden yellow eye. Robust, easily grown, it requires occasional division after flowering, and makes a good edging plant, since it has crinkled green leaves of dark olive shade and grows only 4 ins. high.

Roses

Although clayey soil is not favourable for most plants, it is ideal for roses, provided it is reasonably fertile and not too wet. Roses occupy the same site for a number of years, so the ground should be well prepared, and if there is a 'pan', a hard impervious layer between the top soil and the subsoil, it should be broken up by double digging well in advance of planting. Work a good application of decayed farmyard manure, well decayed vegetable compost, or a combination of both, into the top foot of soil, not only to enrich it, but to improve its physical condition. The more decayed the manure, the more suitable it is for light, sandy soils. As a measure of practical economy, never add farmyard manure to the subsoil when double digging, although rough vegetable refuse from the compost heap is useful to improve its texture.

Give the ground time to settle down before planting, and a few days beforehand add 5 lb. of bone meal or steamed bone flour and 2 lb. sulphate of potash per 30 sq. yds. of rose bed, hoeing or forking it into the top few inches. Do not apply lime too freely as roses like a slightly acid soil.

Planting may be done at any time between late October and the end of March when the weather is favourable, unless the soil is wet and sticky. Rather than plant in insufficiently prepared ground, it is best to prepare the site in autumn or early winter and to plant in February or March the next year, in order to give the soil time to settle.

Plants should be ordered early in October and November, and if permanent planting cannot be done immediately on their arrival, dig a shallow trench elsewhere in the garden, and set the roses in it, covering their roots with sufficient friable soil to protect them against sun, wind and frost.

The distance between rose bushes should be from 18 ins. to 2 ft., according to the vigour of the variety, although 21 ins. is suitable for most. The hole should be dug wide enough to allow the roots to be spread out to their fullest extent, and deep enough for the union between the rose variety and the briar stock on which it is budded to be just below soil level. Too deep planting must be avoided. Any damaged pieces of root should be removed before setting the bush firmly in the hole, then cover the roots carefully with soil to avoid further damage when the earth is tramped down to ensure the firm planting that roses need. When finally refilling the hole with the soil previously removed, however, leave the top inch or two relatively loose, and always ensure that no farmyard manure comes in direct contact with the roots.

In the case of standard roses, remember that these will have been budded high up on the briar rose stock, so that the hole only needs to be sufficiently deep to permit all the roots to be covered with a reasonable amount of soil. It is also wise to avoid possible injury to the roots by first driving the supporting stake into the centre of the hole and then planting the roses close to it. The main stem should be tied to the stake as soon as planting is finished.

Climbing or rambler roses are planted in the same way, except that they should be placed about 6 ins. away from the structure they are to decorate, so that they lean back naturally against it. Poor soil or wide overhanging eaves, which tend to make the soil beneath too dry, are factors which sometimes prevent climbing roses from developing properly, and also render them susceptible to other troubles.

The various kinds of bush rose, whether planted in autumn or spring should be fairly severely pruned on the first occasion, and this should be done before young growths develop. All the shoots should be cut down so that only 2 or 3 buds on each are left showing above soil level, and the cuts should be made with a pair of sharp secateurs just above and clear of the bud, but not too far away from it. With climbing roses the first pruning involves no more than shortening the main shoots, leaving 3 to 4 ft. above soil level, the weaker shoots being cut shortest.

For ramblers the initial pruning consists of reducing each shoot to an average of 2 ft. Both climbers and ramblers should be fastened to the wall or trellis, and should be spread out at an angle to give an over all fan-like appearance.

Older bush roses of the H.P., H.T. and T. sections are also best pruned before the new season's growth begins. Start by cutting out all the dead wood and short, spindly growths, especially those in the centre. To obtain a good display, prune the remaining shoots according to length, i.e. the long ones should be reduced to about a foot with 7 or 8 buds, the medium to 5 ins., with 5 or 6 buds, and the short to 2 ins., with 3 to 4 buds. For exhibition blooms pruning must be more severe, only 2 to 3 buds being left on each stem.

Older floribunda roses are purely for decoration purposes, so that the only pruning needed is the removal of dead wood and last year's flower trusses, together with 2 or 3 ins. of the stem beneath, the cut being made above and just clear of a plump growth bud.

Climbing roses need little pruning after the first season's growth. Cut off dead growth; tie in the long, young shoots produced during the summer, and remove one or more of the older ones if there is overcrowding. Lateral shoots springing from the long main growths, many of which will have flowered last year, should be shortened to 2 or 3 buds.

Since rambler roses of the Dorothy Perkins type produce flowers on the long, lighter green, new shoots developed during the previous summer, the long and darker green shoots which have already borne flowers should be cut near to their bases. Avoid overcrowding but if the new growths are not sufficient to cover the trellis or other support, leave one or two older growths and simply shorten their laterals.

The long new shoots of climbers and ramblers should always be tied at an angle since, if they are trained perpendicularly, growth and flowers tend to be produced only at the top, leaving the lower portion bare.

It is useless or even harmful to top dress rose beds in late autumn or winter with farmyard manure, since it keeps the earth moist and therefore colder. Moreover, the nutritious elements are washed out by the autumn and winter rains while the roses are dormant, and so lost. Farmyard manure, or a substitute such as Growmore Fertiliser and horticultural peat, should be applied in spring after pruning, and hoed into the soil and then an inch or two of peat applied to the surface. Never dig deeply amongst rose bushes for fear of damaging the surface roots. Instead, use a digging fork to turn over the top few inches of soil, or better still use a Dutch hoe frequently during the growing season.

Occasionally suckers appear at the base of rose bushes, at some distance from them, having developed from the briar rootstock on which it has been budded, and if left undisturbed they will undermine its growth and vigour. They are easily identified since their much lighter green leaves are usually divided into 7 leaflets, whereas the cultivated rose leaf has only 3 to 5, often of a reddish tint. If the sucker is simply cut off, others will probably develop from the portion left beneath the soil, and it is far better to take a trowel and expose the point of origin, then simply to pull it away from the bush.

Greenfly are often troublesome, but insecticides, of which the non-poisonous liquid derris is most useful, provide an easy method of control. Mildew may be controlled by spraying with lime sulphur, or one of the special preparations for this purpose. When using a sulphur spray add a cupful of milk or a proprietary 'spreader' to every 2 gallons.

It is almost impossible to recommend rose varieties to please everyone but the following are very popular:

In the hybrid tea section, there is Comtesse Vandal, copper coloured with a yellowish bronze shading; Ena Harkness, red; Glory of Rome, and a good red variety for cutting; Grandmere Jenny, golden yellow edged with a rosy tinge of colour; McGredy's Yellow, a buttercup yellow; Peace, lemon yellow with a rosy edge; The Doctor, rose pink; Frau Karl Druschki (a hybrid perpetual), an old but still popular variety, which is a strong grower with white flowers.

Among the floribunda roses are: Frensham, a good grower with semi-double crimson flowers; Masquerade, produces big clusters of flowers of many colours, pinkish, red, yellow, orange, flame etc., Korona, is a beautiful free-flowering orange-scarlet; All Gold, is well named; Else Poulsen, semi-double rosy-pink flowers; Dickson's Flame, scarlet flowers.

In the climbing rose section, the old and still popular Gloire de Dijon is one of the first to flower; it has light buff orange-centred blooms. Madame Edouard Herriot, often called the Daily Mail rose, also flowers fairly early and is another widely-grown old favourite; its flowers are more of a coral red shaded with a tinge of yellow and rosy scarlet; Climbing Peace is a climbing type of Peace mentioned in the bush rose section. Climbing Madame Butterfly has pinkish flowers with an apricot tinge near the base.

The ramblers include another old favourite, Dorothy Perkins, with its beautiful pink flowers; Emily Gray, with yellow, almost golden-coloured flowers; Excelsa, scarlet; and a single-flowered variety which is a rather vigorous grower, called American Pillar, with pink-coloured flowers.

Roses : Species

Since old fashioned rose species do not produce such a glorious display as the modern hybrids, they sometimes suffer undeserved neglect. Their flowers, fruit and foliage place them among the most decorative hardy shrubs for planting in pleasure grounds, open woodland, as specimens on the lawn, as groups in the shrubbery and as ornamental hedges.

Plant them in an open position to ensure vigorous growth and well-ripened wood in the autumn, the essential prerequisites for abundant flowers and fruit. Roses respond to good cultivation and a well enriched clayey-loam soil suits them best, for the majority are strong and gross feeders. Double dig to a depth of 18 ins. well in advance of planting and add farmyard manure.

The surest method of propagation is by layering. It is essential to use young shoots on which the flowers have faded, and these should be bent towards the ground. A slit is then made about 18 ins. from the tip, taking it from below one joint through to the next one above it. The slit portion will now form an open tongue which is fixed into the soil either with a piece of bent wire or a wooden peg. Cover the cut part with about 3 ins. of fine soil and make firm.

It is also possible to 'tip' layer, as with brambles. The growing points of the current season should be buried in the soil up to 4 ins. deep and pegged, as in ordinary layering. If left undisturbed till the following autumn, they will be well-rooted and have formed a fairly strong shoot.

The majority of species can also be increased by cuttings taken from partially ripened wood and rooted in a cold frame, or in a propagating case with a little bottom heat. A few species, especially those which tiller freely, can be increased by division of clumps. Like many other shrubs, they form masses of roots which trail near the surface and develop growth buds and stems. Surface mulching, which conserves moisture and provides plant food, is ideal for them.

Cuttings, layering, and division are all preferable to propagation by seedlings, which do not always come true. Roses cross-pollinate so freely that, unless the flowers are protected from insects or are grown in great isolation, seed will be inferior. If this method is used, however, seed should not be stored dry when taken from the hips, but placed in damp soil or sphagnum moss and sown in the spring.

Grafting and budding are also undesirable, since suckers often grow from the rootstock, and if allowed to develop may kill out the species budded or grafted on it.

After planting little pruning other than removal of dead wood should be done, although older stems may be thinned-out during the winter to allow light and air to penetrate to the bush centre and to regulate the arrangement of the branches. Bareness at the base may be countered by cutting down a few lateral growths near ground level. No thinning or pruning should be done in summer. A selection should include some of the following:

The moss rose, *Rosa centifolia*, var. *muscosa*, now rarely seen except in old cottage gardens, has a number of varieties with white, pink, and crimson flowers and prickly stems and sepals. These need close pruning in spring and a very rich soil.

Eight to ten feet high is *R. Davidii*, which follows its rose-pink blooms of early summer with clusters of pendulous, bottle-shaped, scarlet fruits ¾-1 in. long.

A native of western China and one of the earliest to bloom— May and early June—is *R. Hugonis*, a graceful arching shrub with elegant, feathery foliage reaching a height of some 7 ft. and carrying canary-yellow blooms 2 ins. across.

The many distinct varieties of the musk rose, *R. moschata*, are all sweetly scented, but vary in height from 3-8 ft. The flowers are white, yellow-white and pink, and the stem prickles are scattered, very stout and recurved. They are useful as shrubbery specimens and as hedge plants.

A valuable species introduced from China by Wilson is the vigorously-growing *R. Moyesii*, which has single, recurved flowers of a rich terracotta-red, succeeded by large, brilliant-scarlet hips, bottle-shaped, which remain on the bushes till December. True colour must be maintained by layering, since seed-raised plants vary. A hybrid between this and the Spanish variety La Girada is *R. Moyesii Nevada*, which bears attractive pinkish buds opening in May into large single white flowers splashed with carmine on the outside. Another form with white flowers has been named *R.M. alba*.

Among the varieties of sweet briar (*R. rubiginosa*) are a number of delightful simple roses with foliage and flowers both scented, which are all strong growers. After flowering in June and July they have an enormous quantity of scarlet hips. These hybrid sweet briars, which make impenetrable hedges requiring very little pruning, were raised many years ago by Lord Penzance, from crosses between the common briar (*R. eglanteria*) and the Austrian copper briar (*R. foetida bicolor*). Some of the many forms are Jeannie Deans, with scarlet crimson flowers produced in clusters and deep green foliage; Lady Penzance, copper colour flowers with bright yellow at the base of the petals; and Lord Penzance, considered the best, with flowers of a soft shade of unbleached fawn, passing to a lovely yellow in the centre. Meg Merrilies is a very free flowering crimson.

A remarkable species is *R. rubrifolia* or *ferruginea* with beautiful hoary foliage and red stems which are particularly fine during the autumn. The ramanas rose *R. rugosa* from China and Japan, and its numerous varieties, produce large single and semi-double flowers succeeded by roundish bright orange-red hips, some as large as plums, with long pointed sepals. The foliage turns to a rich golden colour in the autumn and all varieties are perfectly hardy, robust growers, forming sturdy bushes 4-6 ft. in height, invaluable for massing near water. A few of the best varieties are *alba* with large white single flowers, *atropurpurea* with deep crimson flowers and Blanc de Coubart with large pure white, semi-double flowers, opening flat, 4-5 ins. across, and deliciously scented. All the varieties flower freely during May and again in the autumn.

The coral-thorn rose, *R. sericea pteracantha*, has large flat-shaped pointed thorns of a brilliant red colour on its branches. The foliage is very graceful and fern-like and the flowers are white, single, produced in June. Bushes grow 9-10 ft. in height, making a most attractive shrub.

The Bourbon thornless rose *R. Zephyrine Drouhin* worthy of a place in every garden, has silvery-carmine flowers, deliciously scented and freely produced on vigorous, thornless shoots, early and late. It can be used as a hedge, pegged down, or trained as a climber against a wall. Thinning out the shoots, rather than pruning, should be the rule.

Saxifrages

The Saxifrages (family Saxifragaceae) comprise innumerable species, natural hybrids and garden varieties, and vary from two inches to two feet in height. They usually flower in spring and early summer and there are kinds to suit every conceivable position in the rock garden, but some of the early flowering types are best suited to the alpine house where—hardy though they are—the flowers will not be spoilt by bad weather.

The silvery or encrusted rockfoils (Euaizoonia) are the most important rock garden group. Appreciating full sun, they form bold masses of silver-edged rosettes among rocks, in any limey garden soil, and are easily increased by offsets in September. Most suitable, are *Saxifraga aizoon* and its widely differing varieties. Some form tiny rosettes, others dense hummocks with sprays of flowers 2 ins. high, ranging from pure white to yellow and pink. The broad-leaved *balcana* has sprays of beautiful white flowers with pink-spotted petals; *rosea* is a good pink; and *flavescens* and *lutea* yellow.

The most handsome of the encrusted species, the queen of saxifrages, is *S. longifolia*, whose rosettes may take many years to reach flowering size. The long pyramidal truss of white bloom usually appears in June and the plant dies after flowering. No offsets are produced, but it is easily raised from seed. A really magnificent hybrid is Tumbling Waters, which has arching sprays of white flowers and is propagated by offsets. Suited both for the garden and alpine house are *S. cotyledon* and the variety *pyramidalis* which form large rosettes of silvery-margined leaves and plume-like stems of white flowers, a foot or more in length. The stems of the latter branch upwards from the base and the blooms are slightly spotted with pink. According to Farrer, the species *S. lingulata* is rather a collection of hard-to-classify hybrids—*lantoscana*, Dr. Ramsay, *superba*, *albida*, etc.—all with beautiful sprays of white flowers in May and June. These hybrids should always have a gritty loam, with plenty of lime rubble, packed firmly round their roots.

The cushion rockfoils or tufted saxifrages (Kabschia) include

205

species and hybrids growing very freely in any open situation. Generally the first to bloom is *apiculata*—sulphur or deep yellow— and the white variety *alba*. They should be planted in rather large clumps. The leaves of the flattened rosettes are bright green, narrowing to a sharp point, and the tightly-packed flower clusters are carried on 3-in. stems. A rare beauty with yellow flowers is *Saxifraga L. G. Godseff* (*Godseffi*) and *Elizabethae* has smallish rosettes and large citron-yellow flowers on 2-in. stems. Vigorous growing and free-flowering is *S. burseriana* and its varieties *sulphurea* (pale sulphur yellow), *major, minor, crenata, gloria* and *superba*, which are easily increased by cuttings and division in autumn. The late James Boyd of *Faldonside* raised *Boydii* (deep yellow), and *Faldonside* (yellow); and *Cherrytrees* (citron yellow); *S. Irvingii* a pale lavender-rose; and *S. Haagii* (sancta × Ferdinandi—Coburgi) a free-flowering natural hybrid with slightly glaucous foliage and short-stemmed orange-yellow flowers, which stands up well to outdoor conditions.

The red-flowering saxifrages (*Englaria*) closely resemble each other in habit and flower form, though pink and purple flowers are not exclusive to this group. The Macedonian *S. Grisebachii* and the Wisley variety are very attractive in the rock garden. They have handsome rosettes of silvery leaves, and the purplish crimson flowers have bright yellow stamens and are borne on coloured stems 9 ins. high which have green-tipped bract-like leaves and are covered with white hairs. A similar but more branched species is *S. Stribrnyi* with flowers covered with reddish-white granular hairs. The Transylvanian *S. luteo-viridis* bears three to five partly-closed pale yellow flowers on 3-in. stems. All this group flourish in a gritty loam with plenty of lime rubble, although the gloriously coloured early-flowering kinds show to best advantage grown in pans in the cool frame or greenhouse.

The opposite-leaved or purple-flowered saxifrages (Porphyrion), of which *S. oppositifolia* is one of the main species, are found in the mountains of North America, the Arctic Circle, Yorkshire and Scotland. A fleshy-leaved form which does best with moraine culture is *biflora*; *splendens* has purplish crimson flowers; *Latina* fair-sized soft rosy-purple ones; and *alba* is pure white. They need a fairly moist and gritty soil with plenty of humus.

The mossy or finger-shape-leaved rockfoils (Dactyloides) are regarded as 'too common' by the alpine enthusiast, and give more pleasure in the flower garden than the rock garden. The coloured forms are most popular, making a bright display in May and early June, but the white form *S. Wallacei* (syn. *Composii*) has the added charm that its snow-white flowers are sweet scented and followed by a light green carpet of foliage. Another good variable white form is *caespitosa*, a quick grower closely related to *decipiens*. The latter is probably the ancestor of many of the brightly coloured large flowered 'mossy varieties', and when crossed with *S. muscoides* variety *atropurpurea* produced 'Guildford Seedling', one of the best varieties. Descended from the same parent are *crocea*, yellow; *pygmea*, one of the smallest; and *Allioni*, white. All the mossy types thrive in a fairly well drained but moderately damp soil in a cool northern aspect.

London Pride (Umbrosa or Robertsonia) is useful for edging paths and will succeed in shade. Most often seen are the true London Pride *S. umbrosa*, which with its varieties has pinkish flowers; the rather smaller *S. Geum* which, however, has rounded leaves on long stalks; and *S. cuneifolia*, which has obovate leaves and white flowers with yellow spot at the petal bases.

The giant-flowered rockfoils (Megasea) are easily recognised by their massive evergreen leaves. They do well in the herbaceous border or wild garden and have strikingly beautiful trusses of pink, purple or white flowers in the early spring. Closely related are *S. crassifolia* and *cordifolia*, the former having obovate leaves and the latter being cordate at the base; both have rosy red to purple flowers in April. A handsome species with very dark bronze foliage is *S. Delavayi* (syn. *Yunnanensis*) which has bright rosy red flower spikes in April and May, and like the rest of the species seeds freely.

The largest member of the saxifrage family is the umbrella-leaved *Saxifraga peltata*, with handsome foliage which grows quickly and will soon cover a large area when planted near water. Borne on two or three foot stems, the loose rounded clusters of showy pink flowers appear in April and are followed by the giant umbrella-like leaves, often 2 ft. across, which are elegantly lobed with toothed margins and turn to a beautiful bronze in autumn. This plant grows well in company with *Senecio pulcher* and *S. Clivorum*, Astilbes, Spiraeas, Rodgersias, giant reeds, bulrushes and many other marsh-loving plants.

Sweet Peas

The kaleidoscopic colouring and fragrance of sweet peas, together with their long-flowering period from early spring to late autumn, make them first favourites among annuals for house and garden decoration. Like the rose, they are improved from year to year, and the carefully selected new varieties must be free-flowering, each flower stem being at least 18 ins. long, and carrying four blooms of good colour and lasting quality.

Among the many varieties, the following are popular: cream—Cream Elegance, Cream Delight; lavender—Gertrude Fingay, Mrs. C. Kay; light blue—Stylish, Myosotes; maroon—Warrior; salmon-pink—Princess Elizabeth, Piccadilly; scarlet—Welcome; white—Swan Lake, Gigantic. Two outstanding favourites are Air Warden, bright, orange-scarlet and Mrs. R. Bolton deep rose pink on white ground.

Many growers fail because of their faith in heavily manured, elaborately mixed soils, whereas the real essentials are good drainage, frequent (but light) applications of soluble phosphatic and potassic fertilisers, and plenty of water in the growing season. The ground must be double dug in autumn, the second spit not being brought to the surface, and 1 barrowload of well-decomposed manure incorporated in the top layer for every 10 sq. yds. A light dressing of lime on the top after digging should be left for the rain to wash in, and the surface left rough until it is worked down with a rake and trodden moderately firm in spring.

Choose a sunny but wind-protected site—peas sometimes make a good divider between the flower and vegetable garden, or are placed near the house for the sake of their fragrance. For flowering at the beginning of June, sow seed 2-3 ins. apart and 1 in. deep in boxes early in October. Sometimes a portion of the black-seeded varieties sown will not germinate unless the hard seed coats are 'chipped' with a nail file or a very small piece removed with a pen knife, to allow moisture to penetrate. The thin seed coats of the white-seeded varieties, however, render them liable to rot unless they are placed on a thin layer of sharp sand before being covered with soil. Seedlings should remain in the cold frame until the end of January, then be potted singly in fresh soil. If a greenhouse or frame is not available sweet peas may be sown directly outdoors in April, in their flowering ground, with good results, but many commercial and amateur growers sow in boxes under glass during February, pinching the tops off the seedlings when there is 6 ins. of growth and after thorough hardening off planting them out without intermediate repotting.

Gradually harden off the plants and transplant them 6 ins. apart in early April, keeping the single row, which is usually enough for the amateur, well clear of other plants and giving initial support with small twigs. The latter can be the remains of a worn birch besom. As the plants increase in height, hazel branch stakes 8 ft.

The perfect touch for a period house: *Magnolia alba superba*, and (inset) a
single bloom of *Magnolia soulangiana*.

Mock orange *Philadelphus*.

Male catkins of *Garrya elliptica*.

SHRUBS

Lilac, Charles X.

Flowering currant, *Ribes*.

high, special wire trainers, or 6 ft. high wide-mesh wire netting may be used. Exhibition growers usually favour double rows about 1 ft. apart with the plants 6 ins. apart in the rows. In this case one 6 ft. bamboo cane to each plant is secured to wires stretched between posts 6-7 ft. high and the plants are then trained up and tied to the cane until they reach the top, when they are carefully removed, laid along the ground (all in one direction) and re-trained up the canes which are within a foot of their growing points.

Remove all laterals and tendrils as they develop, and also all flower buds until the plants are about 3 ft. high. Old flowers must be picked off to prevent the formation of seedpods since otherwise new blooms will not be produced so freely.

In dry weather give a weekly soaking with water and conserve moisture in the soil by a surface mulch of decayed manure or peat moss litter. Feed with soluble quick-acting stimulants, such as weak liquid cow manure made by immersing a small bag of it in a good-sized tank of water and diluting the resultant fluid at the rate of 1 part in four of water. Always ensure that the ground is reasonably moist before applying liquid manure, if necessary watering with clear water first.

Cut the flowers for decoration just before they come into full bloom—do not wait until each individual flower on the stem has fully opened out—for when cut at this stage they increase in size on being placed in water. Aim at harmony of colour rather than sharp contrast—softening the effect with white gypsophila. Asparagus fronds and bronze-tinted foliage also look well with sweet peas, especially in artificial light, but the best effect is often achieved by using only one sweet pea variety with its own foliage.

Sweet peas suffer little from insects and fungoid diseases, but slugs and snails do much damage just after planting before rapid growth begins. A metaldehyde killer bait should be heaped at the rate of 1 tablespoonful every 3 ft. along the rows and covered with inverted flower pots or slates in showery weather, although still allowing easy access.

A mosaic virus disease, known at one time as 'streak' disease, will sometimes stunt the plants, producing mottling of the leaves and 'broken' colours and short stems in the flowers. Apparently not carried in seed, it is sap-transmissible; the only control measure is to uproot the affected plants and burn them.

If flower buds drop off without expanding this may be due to a sudden change of temperature or to watering in hot weather with ice-cold water—use water which has been exposed to air and sun for

o   209

twenty-four hours, or else add a little hot water to take off the chill.

Black cotton threads stretched along the rows will fend off birds attacking young plants in spring and picking out the growing buds, but the only preventive against tits, who pull unopened flower buds to pieces in August and September, is to have the entire rows netted with fine mesh netting. However, difficulties and troubles are fewer than with most flowering plants and sweet peas are most rewarding to cultivate.

Tulips species

Tulips need a well-drained loamy soil containing plenty of sand and enriched with leafmould or peat, cow manure and bone meal. They are sun-loving and need plenty of moisture at the roots while growing. Plant in October and leave undisturbed for a number of years, but if the bulbs in each group become overcrowded or cease to bloom—when only one large leaf is produced—they should be lifted in July and dried off in a warm place until replanted in enriched soil the following October.

Propagation is by seed or offsets. Gather seedpods when the edges of the seeds show through the outer covering, and although sowing may be done either in the autumn or spring, September is the best time. Sow in the open one inch deep and apply a light topdressing of leaf-mould or peat moss. The seed will germinate during April, and for the first year the growth appears similar to young leeks. After two years, when the slender leaves have died, lift the bulbils and store in sand until replanting in September.

Most tulip species produce a number of offsets. These should be planted 2 ins. deep during August, and covered with a 1-in. layer of peat moss in November.

Certain species, e.g. *T. Kauffmanniana* and *T. sylvestris*, have a tendency to develop 'droppers' (bulbs developed from small stolons).

The Painted Lady tulip (*T. clusiana*), introduced from Persia or the North West Frontier of India in 1638 and now naturalised in northern Italy and in Spain, grows about 10 ins. high and is suitable for a sunny part of the rock garden. It has white flowers, purplish black at the base, and flushed with rose on the outside of the petals, and blooms during April and May.

A Georgian species, *T. Eichleri*, which flowers in May, has large deep scarlet flowers and light reserve markings above a glistening black base. The offsets should be planted 6-9 ins. deep.

One of the most shapely of all tulips species is *T. Creigii*, which has either scarlet or yellow (heavily marked with scarlet) flowers and purple blotched leaves.

The water-lily tulip (*T. Kaufmanniana*), a native of Turkestan, is a rare, dwarf species, slightly scented and like a water-lily when fully open. Unlike other forms, the flowers are coloured in their early stages and are white, yellow or red, with golden yellow centres and frequently striped externally with rich carmine. Blooming in March and April, they should be planted in a sunny sheltered corner, 3 ins. deep in good loam, with a little sharp sand under and around the bulbs to prevent rotting. The flowers stand about 6 ins. above the foliage and look attractive among chionodoxas and muscari in the rock garden.

Another native of Turkestan is *T. kolpakowskiana*, normally yellow but sometimes tinged with red or green externally, or occasionally entirely coppery-red. The segments of the flowers roll back and give the flowers an inverted appearance.

The Persian *T. linifolia*, forms an almost prostrate rosette of small leaves and produces brilliant sealing-wax red flowers, with glistening, well-defined bases, in April. It needs well-drained, light rich soil and does well in a rock garden, but should not be disturbed and is difficult to propagate.

The brilliant vermilion *T. praestans* produces several flowers on each stem in May, has light green, downy foliage and is about 10ins. high. Van Tubergen's variety is scarlet-orange with two to four flowers on a stalk.

A soft pink Cretan species is *T. saxatilis*, which has bright glossy green foliage, and drooping blooms in early March. The bulbs should be lifted annually, dried off and kept warm until replanting in October: it produces stolons at the root.

The Armenian *T. Sprengeri* is the latest of the species to bloom (about the end of May) and has narrow, sharp-pointed orange-scarlet petals, brassy buff on the outside with a tint of green, and golden anthers. Standing a little over a foot in height, its glossy deep grass green leaves are narrow and almost erect. It is thoroughly hardy and, although it cannot be increased by offsetting, it will flower within three years from seed, provided this is sown immediately it ripens. It is very useful for the front of the herbaceous border, but unfortunately sometimes dies off suddenly.

A slightly scented species, opening only in the afternoon, is *T. strangulata primulina*, with soft primrose yellow flowers and delicate glaucous green foliage. It grows 1 ft. high and if planted among saxifrages the flowers will be protected from soil-splashing.

Resembling *T. saxatilis* in its tendency to produce unexpected stolons, is *T. sylvestris*, a scented golden yellow flower 18 ins. high, blooming in April and May. One of the best species for growing in grass, it will also grow through the boxwood edging of a path. A dwarf which grows well in the rock garden, is *T. tarda* (syn. *T. dasystemon*) which has white flowers with large yellow centres, three to five on a stem and increases its bulbs rapidly.

Wallflowers

The common wallflower (*Cheiranthus cheiri*), the parent of all the cultivated varieties, is frequently found growing in Britain amongst the cracks and crevices of old masonry—hence its name. A sub-shrubby perennial of the Cruciferae family, it is usually treated as a biennial for bedding-out purposes, being lifted after flowering in late May, and replaced by summer flowering plants. This method produces bushy plants with large and numerous blooms.

Wallflowers are completely hardy and should be treated as such, from the seedling stage to maturity, but there are two common mistakes—sowing too late in the year and sowing too thickly. Sow very thinly in an open, sunny part of the garden, not later than the third week of May, in any well-drained, good, but not over-rich garden soil. Damp clayey soils encourage rampant, soft growth, not able to withstand severe winter conditions. Ordinary kitchen garden soil with a little powdered lime raked into the surface makes an ideal seed bed, but the ground should never be heavily manured. Sow the seed very thinly in flat drills, about 1 in. deep and 12 ins. apart and cover it lightly.

Transplant the seedlings in a sunny nursery bed when they are 2 ins. high, placing them 6 ins. apart with 12 ins. between the rows. During the summer if any plant does not show signs of becoming a sturdy bushy specimen, with six to eight branches, pinch out the growing point. In October lift the plants and transfer them to their flowering quarters, allowing about 1 ft. each way so that they may become established before the severe winter weather begins. Spring planted wallflowers usually lose much of their foliage and have a shorter flowering period. They may be grown alone in borders and beds, or with a groundwork of arabis, aubrietias, or forget-me-nots, or mixed with daffodils and tulips.

The original wallflower was pale yellow but numerous colours have now been developed and improvements are continually being made. The yellow varieties, whose names usually indicate their

212

shade, are Cloth of Gold, Golden Monarch, Primrose Monarch, Crawford Beauty (golden yellow) and Hamlet (golden amber). The crimson forms, with dark velvety petals, make a striking contrast with the yellow and include Blood Red, Giant Blood Red and Vulcan. A few of the varieties with ruby colours are Ruby Gem, Purple Queen, and Ellen Willmott (pure ruby). Orange Bedder, Fire King and Apricot are orange. Scarlet Emperor is a vivid scarlet and, although Eastern Queen opens as a light chamois, it changes with age to rosy pink. Cluseed Giant Pink is another rosy pink variety and White Dame, although creamy yellow at first, changes to white.

There are two strains of double flowering wallflowers—the old form bears tall single spikes of very fragrant flowers and the double dwarf branching form is bushy with many short flower spikes. These plants should be treated as perennials and be propagated by cuttings. After flowering trim the plants neatly, so that a number of basal shoots are produced and cut off the sturdiest with a heel, trimming them lightly. If only a few plants are required, fill 6-in. pots with equal portions of loam, leaf mould or peat, and sharp sand, and make the compost firm. Dibble the cuttings in round the edges, water thoroughly and place them in a frame shaded from bright sunshine. If a larger number of plants are required, the cuttings may be inserted directly into a cold frame. When roots are formed transfer the plants first into 3-in. and then 6-in. pots, arranging them in a closed cold frame for a week or two. As soon as they are established give plenty of air, but avoid over-watering. Most of these old double varieties will flower best in a light airy green-house and, if given an occasional feed with liquid manure, will produce many blooms on long spikes in early spring. The more modern double forms are grown from seed and flowered out-of-doors but, to some people, they are not so attractive as the single varieties.

The old-world Harpur Crewe is a neat but now rarely cultivated variety. Growing to about 15 ins. high, it produces attractive sweet-scented yellow double flowers, and although not difficult to grow is best propagated by cuttings.

The several very lovely relatives of the wallflower are unfortunately not widely grown. The well-known Siberian wallflower (*C. Allioni*) is remarkably free flowering, with orange blooms, and makes an attractive bedding plant. It should be sown later than the common wallflower, to prevent it flowering prematurely in the autumn, and will grow to 15 ins. and flower from May until July. The alpine wallflower (*C. alpinus*), a native of southern Europe, is a useful border plant, forming dense compact masses, and producing a great number of lemon-yellow flowers in May. Self sown seedlings will grow freely and form attractive natural groups if left, but it is essential to grow this plant on a light soil. A Spanish species easily grown from seed on old walls or in rock gardens is *C. linifolius*, sometimes called *Erysimum linifolius*, which produces lilac-coloured flowers. To establish it on a wall mix a pinch of seed in some moist soil and place it in the cracks or crevices and, if the weather is dry, sprinkle with water daily until germination is complete. Once established this plant will soon spread by self-sowing. *Erysimum Perfskianum*, var. Golden Gem (Hedge Mustard), a hardy biennial which can be treated as an annual, is a near relative of *Chieranthus*. Sow out-of-doors during August to obtain a good show the following spring, or in the spring for a bright summer display.

·5·

Shrubs

Propagation by Cuttings 216. Hedges 218. Dwarf shrubs 221. Wall shrubs 223. Peat-loving shrubs 226. Barberries 228. Conifers 230. Daphnes 233. Rock roses and sun roses 235. Magnolias 238. Rhododendrons 240.

· 5 ·

Shrubs

SHRUBS ARE A favourite resort of the gardener who wants to cut his labour problem to a minimum, but great care should be exercised in choosing those which will not outgrow their setting and which are adapted to the site.

Propagation by Cuttings

Shrubs may be propagated by seed, cuttings, layering, budding or grafting, the best method varying according to species. For example, seed from variegated, weeping and double-flowering varieties does not propagate them true to type and they should be budded or grafted on to the common variety or a closely allied species. Again, trees and shrubs with opposite branches, though difficult to raise from cuttings, produce symmetrical, handsome plants from seed. Generally speaking, however, many shrubs are propagated readily by summer cuttings and whenever possible this is the most satisfactory method.

Even experts suffer loss in the rooting of cuttings, even though circumstances may apparently be most favourable, so that the beginner should not be discouraged if some fail to root. Taken in summer, young shoots which are just beginning to become firm— according to the Edinburgh Royal Botanic Garden authorities 'half made wood strikes best'—will usually root in a matter of weeks, if given a fair amount of bottom heat. Ideally, select semi-ripened shoots which have developed after the plant has flowered and take cuttings 2-4 ins. long. With a sharp knife cut immediately below a node, i.e. where a leaf stalk joins a stem or, if the leaves have fallen, where a bud joins the stem. Leaves should be removed from the lower part of the stem, and quick rooting can be encouraged by dipping the cut end first into water and then in a hormone rooting powder. Shake off any excess, then dibble the cuttings into compost to a depth equal to $\frac{1}{3}$ their length, and water lightly. With varieties that are difficult to root, it should be borne in mind that cuttings inserted near the side of the pot root slightly quicker than those placed in the centre. Use 6-in. clean pots and place crocks in the bottom for drainage, then place a layer of some fibrous material such as sphagnum moss over the crocks and fill up with a compost made of three parts good fibrous loam, one part leaf mould or granulated peat and one part rough sharp sand. Many kinds of shrubs will root in three to four weeks if given bottom heat, by placing the pots in a propagating frame heated by electricity or hot water pipes, or even in an ordinary hot bed made of stable manure and leaves.

To keep the soil compost moist and save watering, plunge the pots up to their rims in sand, peat or manure, and keep the frame closed, ventilating for only a few minutes daily. As soon as they are rooted the young plants may be transferred to 3-in. flower-pots, using the same compost as for cuttings. Place them in a cold frame but keep it closed for a few days. Afterwards free ventilation should be given throughout the winter as much as possible and in spring they can be planted out of doors.

Among the many hardy ornamental flowering and evergreen shrubs from which cuttings should be taken in July are *Aucuba japonica, Cornus mas* and *C. Spaethii, Deutzia gracilia, Diervilla* (syn. *Weigela*), *Escallonia* in variety, *Forsythia* in variety, *Fuchsia, Garrya elliptica, Griselinia littoralis, Hypericums, Jasminum, Kerria japonica, Laurus nobilis, Lonicera, Olearias, Philadelphus* in variety, *Prunus* in variety, *Spiraeas* and many of the dwarf ornamental conifers.

In the absence of artificial heat, cuttings may be rooted in a cold-frame or under a bell-glass, but they will take longer to root. Cuttings used for this method of propagation are best taken at leaf fall in September or October. They are then dibbled into sand, a mixture of sand and peat, or vermiculite, and should be given a thorough watering after insertion, the frame being kept closed and shaded from bright sun for a few days. Although the compost should never be allowed to dry out, little water will be needed during the winter, and the cuttings need not be disturbed until they begin to grow the following April. Ventilate the frames in spring to harden off the young plants, then either place them in nursery rows or leave them in the frame until the following autumn. Many species and varieties that root readily in a cold frame are liable to fail in heat—

among them *Berberis, Buddleias, Ceanothus, Choisya ternata, Cistus, Cytisus,* double flowered Gorse and *Helianthemum.*

Heaths and heathers (Ericas and Callunas) and the small-leaved dwarf rhododendrons are all best propagated in August. Cuttings of two former should be short—from 1-$1\frac{1}{2}$ ins.—and must be trimmed very carefully, since injury to the bark diminishes the chance of rooting. Insert them to about $\frac{1}{3}$ their length in a mixture of granulated peat and silver sand, setting about 2 dozen in each 6-in. flower-pot. Place the pots in a cold frame, plunging them up to their rims in a peaty soil, and if possible cover with a bell-glass. Alternatively, the cuttings may be inserted directly into a cold frame containing the mixture of granulated sand and peat.

Hedges

Hedges act as shelter from wind and sun and are also used ornamentally, to separate one feature of a garden from another.

The soil should be well dug and cleared of weeds, and firm planting must be practised to assist the young plants to become established. The normal clipping of holly, yew and box hedges is done during July and August, but severe cutting back into older wood should be carried out in April and early May. Hedges which have been neglected for a few years and have got out of hand can be pruned into shape by cutting one side and the top back to the required height with a pair of long handled secateurs and pruning saw. All large cuts must be protected by a coating of white lead paint to prevent the attack of fungoid diseases. Dead stumps should be cleared out from the base and any young fresh shoots laced and tied in between the bare limbs. In spring, when buds begin to show signs of growth, the stumps should be frequently syringed, especially during dry weather and gradually they will produce green shoots and present a clothed appearance. During the second season the remaining side may be cut back to the desired distance when growth will make rapid headway. These growths may have their points clipped back to induce further lateral shoots. When an old hedge has been restored it is well to have it pruned frequently. With hard pruning, cultivation of the surface soil along the foot of the hedge is important and should be followed with a liberal mulching of farm-yard manure or a complete fertiliser.

In laying out hedges it is well to use moderate-sized plants, not more than two to three years old, in single rows in close formation. Large specimens may be shaken by wind before they are established.

Young hedges, of whitethorn and myrobalan plum should be cut hard back in the spring after planting, and for two or three years afterwards the sides clipped hard in so as to ensure the bottom of the hedge will be well furnished with shoots. For beech, holly and yew hedges, use a pair of hand shears or mechanical shears, cutting the sides well in but leaving the leading shoots unpruned until the required height has been reached. For ornamental shrubs and all large-leaved subjects, prune carefully with a pair of secateurs, hand shears must not be used. In autumn clear hedge bottoms of all weeds and, to hedges that are weakly, apply a mulch of partly decayed farmyard manure.

The quickest shelter hedge is secured by planting a row of Lombardy poplars (*Populus italica*) to be headed back when they reach the required height. In exposed situations it is even worth while planting poplars to provide a temporary shelter while a permanent hedge is growing.

Miniature hedges 6-12 ins. high are sometimes used as permanent subjects to flower beds in the garden. The dwarf spindle-tree (*Euonymus radicans variegatus*) and the common box (*Buxus sempervirens*) are suitable for the purpose.

Beech (*Fagus sylvatica*) is distinguished as a hedge by its vigorous growth, its tolerance of shade—greater than in the case of any other broad-leaved plant—beautiful autumn tints, and retention of its leaves well into spring. Young two- to three-year-old plants in a single row 6 ins. apart make a good hedge quickly. The common beech has sported into copper and purple leaved types but both are often regarded as having too metallic a hue to be pretty as hedges. The 200-year-old beech hedge at Meikleour, Perthshire, is a well-known landmark today, and is probably the oldest hedge in Britain. Another very tall hedge can be seen in the Royal Botanic Garden, Edinburgh.

The leather-leaved holly (*Ilex aquifolium crassifolium*) and other thick-leaved varieties, where they will grow successfully, are a pretty sight at all seasons of the year. Hollies can be used to form low, medium or tall hedges. Choose specimens which have been frequently transplanted in the nursery and plant during September or late spring. Trimming with the hand shears should be done in July, allowing the centre shoots to grow to their full height before stopping and make the hedge slightly broader at the base than the top.

The poisonous properties of the common yew (*Taxus baccata*) are well known. Numerous deaths have been caused by the seed, and the leaves and the young bark are poisonous to stock. For decorative work in gardens and pleasure grounds the foliage is too dark and melancholy. I prefer holly or Lawson's Cyprus (*Cupressus Lawsoniana*); both are equally patient of the shears. The golden yew (*Taxus baccata aurea*) is a more beautiful subject than the common yew for training as a hedge and has the advantage of not being so rampant a grower. The yew is a greedy plant and can be much encouraged in growth by occasional applications of manure.

The oval-leaved privet (*Ligustrum ovalifolium*) and the common privet (*Ligustrum vulgare*) make fast-growing hedges. For low hedges the Chinese species (*L. Delavayanum, L. Prattii,* and *L. ionandrum*) are more useful, the small glossy leaves of these varieties being beautiful. The golden privet (*L. O. aureum*), too, is frequently used. All the privets require frequent pruning after they are established.

For a boundary hedge there is no better subject than the myrobalan or cherry plum (*Prunus cerasifera*); properly trimmed it is practically impassable.

The evergreen honeysuckle (*Lonicera nitida*) with its small shiny leaves is a close growing all-year-round hedge plant. Pruning should be done three times a year—in May, mid-summer and late September —the sides being cut straight down to the soil, leaving a very narrow slightly rounded top. It is very easy to propagate by cuttings.

In mild and sheltered parts hedges can be formed with such shrubs as *Olearia Haastii, Garrya elliptica, Pittosporum, Elaeagnus reflexa* and the beautiful free flowering *Escallonia* Donard's Seedling. The evergreen berberises, particularly *B. Darwinii, B. stenophylla* and *Sargentiana,* to mention only a few of them, make charming effects with their foliage, flower and fruit.

The relatively dwarf-growing *Veronica Traversii* is a valuable evergreen, easy to grow in any good well drained loamy soil. Its slightly glaucous foliage and white flowers are produced in July, and it is always a pleasant looking plant until it gets too old.

Fuchsia macrostemma, var. *Riccartoni,* forms a beautiful flowering hedge and can be seen at its best in the north and west of Scotland. It is cut down by frost every winter but makes annual shoots 3 to 4 ft. long and flowers freely throughout the summer and autumn. Propagation is easy by means of cuttings from the annual shoots which root readily when put in during the autumn out-of-doors. The following autumn the plants can be planted out 2 ft. apart in rows when they will soon become established.

Roses of the briar and *Wichuraiana* group can be used for hedges, provided they can be given some support and the young shoots trained in annually. The Poulsen varieties, although of more dwarfish growth, are very floriferous and should prove efficient subjects in sheltered positions.

The American thorn (*Crataegus macrantha*) with spikes 4 ins. long should be tried; it has white flowers in May and red fruits in autumn. Laurels, especially the Portugal variety (*Prunus lusitanica*) spread too much and become very untidy.

The Monterey cypress (*Cupressus macrocarpa*) is also frequently recommended as a suitable hedge plant. It certainly stands clipping into any shape, but the stems are too elastic to withstand wind.

The native sea buckthorn (*Hippophae rhamnoides*) and the evergreen, glossy-leaved *Griselinia littoralis* from New Zealand are effective as shelter hedges near the sea.

A good hedge should be shaped like an inverted V. Unfortunately, many are clipped to produce a flat top, and in time the lower portion becomes devoid of growth and foliage, and therefore unsightly.

Dwarf Shrubs

Low growing shrubs make an attractive surrounding for the rock garden, as well as providing shelter from cold winds and bright sunlight, and most are easy to grow if they are positioned carefully and the soil conditions are right. Many of them are natives of Arctic and high mountain regions, but retain their alpine characteristics if planted amongst boulders and low-growing plants.

There are dwarf types of almost all species, both deciduous and evergreen, and varying in colour and form. They divide into two main groups—those that can be grown in ordinary garden soil and those which thrive in a peaty compost. Dig the ground deeply, adding well-rotted lawn mowings and leaf mould or plenty of peat moss and sand, and plant deciduous shrubs when the leaves begin to fall, from the middle of October onwards, and evergreens in September or the beginning of May.

By a careful choice, it is possible to have a continued sequence of bloom, ornamental foliage and berries practically all the year round, so that the shrubs should be chosen not only for the colour of their flowers, but also for the time of year at which they bloom. When planting them as a background, avoid too great regularity. Preferably form them into bays to shelter plants from high winds and to provide a certain amount of shade.

Pruning depends on the season of flowering and whether the bloom is borne on the old or new wood. Those that flower in spring and early summer should be pruned after flowering, unless berries are required, to allow the new growth to develop and mature during the autumn, and to obtain shapely bushes.

Prune the summer and autumn flowering shrubs during February and March to admit plenty of air and light, necessary to ripen the wood and therefore encourage bloom. The removal of seed pods and superfluous buds should also be looked on as pruning, since this increases the size, vigour and quantity of the subsequent flowers.

Farmyard manure is unnecessary for shrubs since they are not gross feeders and decaying vegetable material, such as leaves and lawn mowings, will provide the required nutrients.

The following are a few of the best dwarf shrubs:

Rock abelia (*Abelia chinensis*), a pretty shrub about 3 ft. high, blooms in August and September, the white pink-tinted flowers, grouped in a star-like calyx, hang from a long delicate stem. Prune by cutting off dead blooms and old wood after flowering, and trimming to keep the bush in shape.

A variety of the Japanese maple, *Acer palmatum,* var. *septemlobum,* is a hardy deciduous shrub but needs a sunny sheltered position, and is very decorative in early spring when the leaves are deep red; *atropurpureum* has dark red leaves tinted pale yellow, and yet other varieties have fern-like, bronzy, beautifully cut purple-tinted leaves. These varieties do not need pruning.

The best of the round, hummocky shrubs is *Alyssum spinosum,* with silvery leaves and white and pink flowers, produced in terminal clusters from June until August. It grows about 1 ft. high and 2 ft. across and once established will seed freely but never becomes a nuisance.

A small-leaved, deciduous, creeping shrub, *Arctostaphylos alpina,* has white flowers, succeeded by black berries in autumn. It is propagated by seed and requires a damp peaty soil. The bearberry (*A. uva-ursi*), found in high altitudes in this country and Europe, is an attractive evergreen, fairly thick-growing in habit, which trails along the ground, and produces rosy-pink or white, wax-like, urn-shaped flowers in spring and coral red berries in winter.

A very hardy legume introduced from Arctic regions, and now naturalised in Scotland, *Astragalus alpinus* is prostrate in habit and has drooping purple flowers.

Needing a sandy peaty soil and partial shade, *Bryanthus* or *Phyllodoce empetriformis,* is a bush with reddish-purple flowers clustered near the apex of vivid crimson branches and minute heath-like foliage.

Thriving under similar conditions to heaths, *Bruckenthalia spiculifolia* forms a carpet of growth about 6 ins. high, and produces pinkish flowers in terminal racemes during June.

Blue spiraea (*Caryopteris mastacanthus*), introduced from China by Robert Fortune in 1844, but lost to cultivation for some years until it was re-introduced in 1880, is a very distinct autumn-flowering dwarf shrub. It has silvery grey foliage and clear blue flowers, produced in great profusion during September and October on the young wood made during the summer. Plant in a sunny, sheltered position and cut back the flowered shoots in spring.

A prostrate shrub, *Cassiope lycopodioides,* has slender shoots covered with minute ovate leaves and white bell-shaped flowers arising from the leaf axis; *C. selaginoides* received an Award of Merit in 1952 and is a fine compact little bush of a bright green colour, bearing fairly large white bell-shaped flowers; and *C. tetragona* (syn. *Andromeda tetragona*), is an absolutely hardy arctic plant which needs an open situation, grows 7-8 ins. high and is usually smothered with white, lily-of-the-valley-like bells, but do not allow the roots to become dry.

The dwarf rocksprays (*Cotoneaster*) are among the easiest shrubs to grow as they will flower and seed under poor soil conditions. As many varieties do not grow true from seed, those of a distinct or graceful habit should be propagated by layering in summer or by cuttings in the autumn. Excellent for creeping over stones, *C. adpressa* is a neat little bush with leaves turning to a deep red in autumn; *C. microphylla* is one of the more robust species, with small glossy leaves and pinkish-white flowers followed by red berries attractive to birds; *C. congesta* resembles *C. adpressa* in neat bush-like form, but has slightly larger leaves and is sometimes sold as *C. microphylla,* var. *glacialis;* and *C. thymifolia,* also sometimes considered as a variety of *C. microphylla,* grows to a straggly $1\frac{1}{2}$ ft., produces pinkish flowers in April and has scarlet berries.

The dwarf lavender (*Lavendula vera nana compacta*) is ideal for growing in poor, gritty, dry soils and has deep blue spikes of flowers larger than those of common lavender, and the leaves are fragrant when crushed. Autumn cuttings will root in a cold frame.

Wall Shrubs

Very few hardy plants will support themselves against a wall by aerial roots, like ivy, or by viscal discs on the tips of tendrils, like the *Vitis* (*Ampelopsis*), *Hydrangea petiolaris* and *Tecoma radicans*. Most shrubs used as climbing plants need support to enable them to clothe a wall effectively and many choice specimens that would not survive without shelter in the open may be grown in this way.

The California lilac (*Ceanothus*), of which there are over 40 species, mostly natives of North America, especially California, are most beautiful when grown against a wall and produce mostly blue flowers, although there are some rose-pink and white forms. Unfortunately, some of the species are not hardy enough for the Scottish climate, but a number of varieties are more robust.

The genus is divided into two groups, according to growth and season of flowering, which must be pruned at different times and by different methods. The spring and early summer flowering kinds should have the flowered shoots shortened immediately after the bloom falls, to encourage the growth of new wood. The summer and autumn flowering group produce blossom on the current season's growth and should be pruned in March, cutting back the previous year's flowering shoots to within 6 or 7 ins. of the base, but pruning weak shoots back to two buds, and removing all weak branches entirely. Attach the main branches to the wall, allowing the young flowering shoots to hang gracefully, and protect the spring flowering kinds with spruce branches during severe weather. They need a light soil and sunny position, doing especially well in seaside districts, and are propagated by cuttings of young side shoots taken in July and August and placed in a heated frame.

American Red-root (*C. Americanus*), a hardy type, although perhaps not the most beautiful, bears clusters of minute white flowers during summer and autumn and has 2-3-in. long leaves. This deciduous species has often been used in producing hybrids, all of which are even hardier and more useful for garden decoration than the parent. The blue ceanothus (*C. azureus*), another deciduous species, produces spikes densely covered with minute blue flowers during spring and early summer and is one of the parents of a group of fine varieties.

The best blue-flowered variety is *C. Gloire de Versailles*, a free-flowering shrub producing fine lavender-blue flowers, which is hardier than is generally thought, but for deep indigo blue flowers, darker in colour than any other form, and borne in numerous trusses, choose *C. Henri Defosse*.

A natural hybrid, with *C. thyrsiflorus* as one of its parents, is *C. Veitchianus* with rounded clusters of blue flowers during May and small shiny dark green leaves about 1½ ins. long.

A cross between *E. Philippiana* and *E. macrantha*, is *Escallonia langleyensis*, an elegant evergreen shrub sometimes reaching 15 ft.

The Butterfly Flower (*Buddleia variabilis*)   The double cherry (*Prunus Blireiana*)

Shrubs and herbaceous plants, a delightful combination.

A rock plant is placed in a dry stone wall.
THE WALL GARDEN
The stone is replaced.

when supported against a wall. It is gracefully pendulous, and has bright carmine flowers on the upperside of its branches.

A hybrid from *E. Philippiana* and *E. punctata, E. Edinensis,* has small but brilliant rose-pink flowers in dense profusion, covering the young branches from July until September. Both hybrids are easily propagated from cuttings of young firm shoots taken in August and rooted in a cold frame.

A fine trailing climber, producing a cloud of golden blossom in February and March, is *Forsythia suspensa,* invaluable for covering walls.

A unique evergreen shrub with ovate, wavy-margined leaves, which are thick, glossy and very resistant to smog is *Garrya elliptica,* which has long pendulous catkins of greenish-white flowers, often hanging on the tree from mid-winter to March. The plants are of two sexes, the male producing the finest catkins. Cuttings should be inserted in a cold frame in September.

The climbing hydrangea (*Hydrangea petiolaris*), also known as the tassel bush, is an attractive, sweet-scented climber, with heart-shaped leaves almost hidden by a wealth of clusters of creamy-white flowers: six or eight sterile florets, each with four creamy-white sepals, surround numerous small flowers with many projecting stamens. It is fairly hardy and creeps and clings like ivy to walls. There are many named varieties of which Parsival, a deep carmine with frilled edges, is one of the best.

A native of Japan, *Schizophragma hydrangeoides,* is a deciduous shrub allied to the Hydrangea family which it resembles. It is not well known, but is useful in milder districts of Scotland as a self-clinging climber for covering high walls and tree stumps and will grow to over 20 ft. The flowers are small and cream-coloured and the leaves broad. Perfect drainage is essential, for like all hydrangeas it needs plenty of water in the growing season. It is propagated by cuttings inserted in sand in a frame with a little bottom heat.

A very strong twining shrub, requiring ample room in height and breadth, *Polygonum baldschuanicum* produces a profusion of rosy-pink flowering panicles from June until September. Later, when the leaves have fallen, the seed capsules are very ornamental. This is an ideal climber for covering old buildings or tree stumps quickly.

The potato tree (*Solanum crispum*) produces clusters of pale blue, sweetly-scented, flowers, which resemble potato blossom. It is hardy and suitable for a west wall, but must be severely pruned to prevent it from spreading too far.

The evergreen *Stranvaesia Davidiana,* has clusters of white flowers

P

during May, like the hawthorn, but not scented, which are followed by orange-red berries, sometimes lasting throughout the winter. In early spring the leaves turn a brilliant bronze.

The climbing Chinese kidney-bean tree (*Wistaria sinensis*) is a favourite climber, with its long drooping racemes of mauve-blue flowers in early summer, and grows best in a fibrous loam, enriched with decayed farmyard manure. During August, to increase the quantity and quality of the bloom, prune back the young shoots made during the summer to two buds to form spurs, but leave the leading shoots unpruned and tie them to their supports.

Peat-loving Shrubs

Many of the rarer shrubs need acid conditions and do not thrive in heavily limed garden soil, especially in coastal areas where there are rich deposits of shell sand, as shells are very rich in lime. The natural habitat of these plants is in peaty and boggy land, where melting snow in spring supplies sufficient moisture during the growing season and the snow in winter protects them from excessive damp, and these conditions should be reproduced as closely as possible. If space allows plant three or four species of one genus together, rather than single specimens, to give a large mass of colour, in a specially prepared shrubbery or part of the rock garden. Transplanting is best done in early autumn, although specimens in pots may be planted out at any season, if the soil is not too dry and the ball of soil around the roots is allowed to remain intact. Always water thoroughly after planting.

Although peat-loving plants must all have well-drained soil, like other plants they have varying characteristics and habits.

The strawberry tree (*Arbutus unedo*), a native of South Ireland and Europe, has long been in cultivation and is a most attractive shrub found growing luxuriantly in England and Wales, but although hardy, needs a little protection from cold winds in Scotland. It belongs to the Ericaceae family and although most of these are shrubby the strawberry tree sometimes develops into a fine dwarf tree. The branchlets bear racemes of small pinky-white flowers and in the autumn produce edible strawberry-like fruits, scarlet in colour, globose and granular. By the time the fruits have become scarlet the secondary side branches should be in flower.

The deciduous Japanese azaleas (*Rhododendron mollis*) bloom from the end of May until early June, and in the autumn the foliage turns bright yellow and orange before falling.

The Ghent or honeysuckle azaleas (*Rhododendron pontica*) are easy

226

to grow, but should never be planted in full sun unless standard trees are planted amongst them to form shade. Plant the white flowered varieties near the edge of the path and the more shady end of the group, next the pale yellows and pale pinks and lastly the orange, scarlet and crimson types. Top-dress the beds annually with decayed leaves and granulated peat.

Marsh or wild rosemary (*Andromeda polifolia*), an attractive little evergreen about 2 ft. high, is a hardy native and thrives in full sun in a peaty moist soil. Its flowers are pinkish-white, heath-like, borne in sprays at the end at the end of the branches, like lily-of-the-valley. The North American fetterbush (*Andromeda* or *Pieris floribunda*) and the Japanese andromeda (*P. japonica*) are valuable garden plants, but the latter is less hardy and needs a little protection in winter. The former produces clusters of 20-30 white flowers at the ends of its branches on erect spikes in April and is a compact shrub about 4 ft. high, while the latter grows to about 8 ft. and has white, pendulous flowers.

A North American ericaceous plant which may eventually become a small tree, the evergreen *Arctostaphylos manzanita*, produces small panicles of white bottle-shaped pendulous flowers tipped with pink in February to March. The outer bark flakes off annually showing the reddish-brown stems underneath. The bearberry (*A. uva-ursi*), a small trailing evergreen shrub, has small round yellow leather-like leaves and rose, shaded with white, flowers during April and May. It is indigenous to certain moorland districts and is excellent for the front of a border.

The Irish heath (*Daboecia cantabrica*, formerly called *D. polifolia*) is a native of Ireland and thrives in dryish peat in partial shade. It is a dwarf, straggly-growing evergreen with white, purple-white and mauve-crimson flowers.

A native of China and Japan, *Enkianthus campanulatus* is a beautiful shrub which likes a sheltered sunny position in a non-calcareous moist peaty soil. Its creamy bell-shaped flowers are borne on short stems radiating horizontally from the main branches in May. In autumn the foliage turns red. Disappointing in its white flowers, which appear in March, *E. perulatus* compensates by foliage which turns bright yellow in autumn.

A handsome evergreen with leather-like leaves, the Chinese *Eucryphia cordifolia* has tapering heads of sweet-scented white flowers of the rose type with five sepals and five petals: the stamens, with red filaments and brown anthers, give a touch of colour. Another Chinese introduction, deciduous and rather hardier, is *E. pinnatifolia*, with dissected leaves and flowers with large white petals and yellow stamens. Their close connection with the rose family makes both of special interest to botanists.

The winter-green (*Gaultheria*) are a genus of dwarf, slow-growing evergreen shrubs excellent for a shady slope fringing azaleas. The heathlike flowers are followed by brilliant berries which remain on the plants all winter. A rare Chinese species, *G. cuneata,* has small lily-of-the-valley like flowers followed by large pure white berries and is 6-7 ins. high; *G. nummularioides* has white bell-shaped flowers in August-September; *G. tetramera,* seldom over 2 ft., has racemes of delicate heath-like flowers.

The Kalmias, named after Peter Kalmia, a Swede who studied botany in Canada, New York and Pennsylvania, are all North American dwarf shrubs. The sheep laurel (*K. angustifolia*) grows to 3 ft. and has clusters of purple-red or white flowers in June, and the mountain laurel or calico bush (*K. latifolia*) is a beautiful 6-ft. shrub with a mass of rose-pink flowers, flourishing in a sunny position.

Prickly heath (*Pernettya mucronata*), a hardy shrub 3-4 ft. high, has plain tiny white flowers in July but produces an abundance of semi-translucent, globular berries, white and rich-rose pink on stems covered with small sharp-pointed glossy-green leaves.

The bilberry or whortleberry (*Vaccinium myrtillus*) is a pretty, heath-like shrub with drooping pink flowers during May and showy blue-black globular fruits during August. The blaeberry (*V. corymbosum*) is particularly suitable for the bog garden and has pale pink or white flowers and blue fruits, produced in great profusion.

Barberries

The Berberis family (*Berberidaceae*) have ornamental foliage, flowers and fruit, and since some of the deciduous species and varieties have wonderful autumn tints and others are evergreen, a border planted with both kinds will provide interest throughout the year. They are also excellent for ornamental hedges or as single specimens.

Barberries are amongst the easiest of hardy shrubs to cultivate, transplant easily because of their fibrous roots, and will withstand drought better than most. Deciduous species are best planted in late autumn and evergreens in late spring, leaving a good ball of soil attached to the roots. They are not gross feeders—a poor, gravelly soil, produces the best autumn leaf-tints—but need an open, sunny, position, although the Oregon grape is useful to grow as a carpet under deciduous trees. As they are likely to occupy the same position for many years, give an annual top dressing of decayed leaves to protect the roots.

A number of species planted together will produce a large quantity of seed and the resultant new hybrids can be reproduced by cuttings taken with a 'heel' in October and rooted in a cold frame, or by layering young shoots in the summer. Among the many Wisley hybrids raised this way are Autumn Cheer, Coral, Fireflame, *rubrostilla* and its variety Autumn Beauty and Sparkler, the majority being the offspring of chance pollinations among such Chinese species as *B. aggregata, B. polyantha, B. Wilsonae* and *B. Yunnanensis*.

Pruning is very important and should be done during winter, or soon after the fruits have fallen, by thinning out the older wood and weak shoots so that new shoots will be produced and form shapely bushes. The following are a selection of species and varieties differing widely in habit of growth and fruiting:

The attractive evergreen *Berberis acuminata*, has large handsome metallic-like leaves which turn brilliant crimson in winter, and produces lemon-yellow flowers in clusters on arching shoots. Valuable for cutting, the Oregon grape (*Berberis aquifolium*, syn. *B. Mahonia*) has large, shiny holly-like leaves that turn bronze-red in winter, or dark red, if the stems are placed in a red aniline dye, and mix well with jasmine or forsythia flowers; it freely produces fragrant golden yellow flowers in spring and the attractive blue berries can be made into jelly. The Himalayan *B. aristata* is almost evergreen and grows into a large, spreading shrub with brilliantly-coloured foliage, attractive yellow flowers and red fruit.

Sometimes classified as a variety of *B. japonica*, *B. Bealei* (syn. *Mahonia Bealei*) has immense green pinnate leaves—some over 2 ft. long—clusters of pale yellow flowers with a fragrance like lily-of-the-valley, and large glaucous fruits which remain until August. Reaching 4-5 ft., it does best in partial shade and fine specimens are often seen in Scottish gardens. Its upright habit makes the 3-ft. *B. Gagnepainii* useful for the rock garden and as a hedge plant, and the clusters of large bright yellow flowers borne on slender stalks during May are followed by long glaucous-blue fruits: the leaves are fairly long and spiny and a metallic-green, shaded to purple.

One of the best evergreen species, *B. Darwinii* has dark shining small leaves with clusters of rich orange flowers in April and May, followed by blue berries. Unfortunately, when it is planted in a large group it tends to lose its foliage near the ground. Unsurpassed by any other deciduous species, the Chinese *B. polyantha*, grows 6-8 ft. high, and produces arched branches laden with drooping racemes of yellow blossoms in June followed in autumn by masses of brilliant coral-red berries. There are frequently over one hundred blooms in a raceme followed by the same number of fruits. The evergreen *B. replicata,* with small leaves, grey below, produces yellow flowers along the branches early in the year, and deep crimson fruits, and often reaches five feet high.

The queen of barberries (*B. stenophylla*), a beautiful evergreen hybrid of weeping habit, which is useful for planting near water, although it must not be grown in water-logged soil, is wreathed with lemon-yellow flowers during April and May. It may be grown as a hedge plant, in bold masses, or as a wall shrub, if it is not over-pruned. Propagation is by cuttings or the freely produced suckers. The many fine varieties include Brilliant, a very showy specimen with brilliant scarlet leaves in winter; *corollina,* with vivid scarlet buds; *Irvinii,* a very compact rock garden subject, both blooming prolifically and having ornamental foliage; and *nana compacta,* a close-growing version of its parent.

One of the best deciduous Japanese species is *B. Thunbergii,* a very popular low-growing spreading plant, with glowing red foliage in the autumn, suitable either as a dense hedge or for lawn grouping. It has small, pale yellow flowers with reddish sepals and bright red, handsome, fruits, produced singly or in pairs. A smaller variety of this species, *minor* is useful for planting in the rock garden; and *atropurpurea,* retains its rich red foliage throughout the winter. Two members of the family which are very effective in autumn are *B. virescens,* with its orange to crimson leaves, and, after leaf fall, red-barked young shoots, and *B. Wilsonae,* a fine dense-growing ornamental dwarf never exceeding 2 ft. with stems and leaves armed with long spines, and golden yellow flowers which are followed by brilliant scarlet, glaucous tinted fruits in autumn.

Conifers

Conifers were, at one time cultivated on a grand scale for ornamental purposes in Scotland, and the tree forms are ideal for planting alongside avenues and as specimens in a park, but the kinds to be grown will depend on the soil. Many species have juvenile foliage which can be retained permanently by propagating from cuttings, producing dwarf and bushy plants suitable for the shrubbery, rock garden and window boxes.

Typical examples of conifers, or 'cone-bearers', are the arbor-vitae, cedars, pines and firs. The few cone-scales of the juniper are fleshy, forming a fruit called a galbulus, and those of the cypress are dry but similar. The yew has only one seed, surrounded by a fleshy mass with bracts at the base, and although it is sometimes classed in a separate family, it and the cupressus and juniper are closely related to the conifers. All conifers, except larch (*Larix*), *Metasequoia* and swamp cypress (*Taxodium*) are evergreen, but vary considerably in appearance.

The adult leaves are mostly ovate, needle-like, flat and linear, or assume the form of closely pressed scales. The male and female flowers are produced separately, either on the same tree, or on different trees, and are wind pollinated. The male flowers are usually yellow, violet or deep crimson, and hang in catkin-like clusters. The female flowers are borne in cones, each consisting of a bract and a scale, the lower bract being sterile and the upper fertile.

Seedlings commonly form the best trees, but various varieties which do not come true from seed can be rooted from cuttings, or by layering, but the trees may be misshapen. Sow thinly in the autumn or spring in the open in a light well-drained soil and cover lightly, or in pots placed in a cold frame to germinate. Insert cuttings in a frame in a sandy soil during August. Graft in spring, under glass, onto rootstocks which have been established in pots the previous autumn.

The ground should have been well worked over before planting in April. Do not set the trees deeply and leave the upper roots covered by only an inch or two of soil. Little pruning is needed, but small trees that make duplicate leading shoots should be pruned as early as possible, in about August, and hedges of yew or cypress should be clipped towards the end of July so that they produce a flush of fresh growth before winter.

The noble fir (*Abies procera,* syn. *Abies nobilis*), an ideal avenue tree, often reaching 250 ft. has a smooth greenish brown bark when young which becomes deeply divided by flat ridges and reddish brown when old. It is very attractive, bearing large erect purple cones 10-12 ins. long and 3-4 ins. in diameter and has been extensively grown for ornamental purposes.

A distinct and beautiful fir with bright rusty-red corrugated young shoots contrasting with its dark shining green foliage, *Abies Forrestii* has bright purple cones when quite young, which are conspicuous even at a distance.

The monkey puzzle (*Araucaria imbricata*), is a remarkable introduction, but it is a garden tree and if planted in parks should be grouped and not planted among deciduous trees.

Cedars, easily distinguished from larch by their evergreen leaves and large cones with deciduous scales, are hardy but need plenty of space and are not suitable for small gardens.

The Mount Atlas cedar (*Cedrus atlantica*), is pyrimidal in habit when young and has an erect leading shoot. The variety *aurea* has attractive golden leaves, but is difficult to cultivate. The deodar (*Cedrus deodara*), from which a fragrant oil is distilled, is pendulous and has long needles. The cedar of Lebanon (*Cedrus Libani*), an imposing avenue tree, neads well drained, deep, rich sandy soil.

The Lawson cypress (*Chamaecyparis* or *Cupressus Lawsoniana*), with its many cultivated forms, is one of the trees which is useful when there is little space for lateral development. When conifers are planted to form avenues they should be set well back, or they may need much lopping in later years to keep them within bounds, and where possible grow a double line, angled on each side. To obtain uniform growth it is important that all the trees should be the same age, and they must be protected from cattle and ground game. The variety *Allumi* or *Fraserii* is an attractive little tree of a narrow compact habit, with glaucous foliage; *argentea* varies in habit and colour, the foliage being either silvery or glaucous and two of the best forms of this are Triomphe de Boskoop and Silver Queen; *conica,* a slow growing pyramidal form, has minute fern-like foliage, glaucous blue-grey in colour, but unfortunately the branchlets often twist and become fasciated; *erecta-viridis* is narrow in growth and has a dense mass of erect green branches; *Fletcherii* has juvenile glaucous green foliage and is the finest cultivated dwarf Lawson cypress; and *Stewartii,* has fine yellow leaves which eventually become green.

The Sawara cypress (*Chamaecyparis* or *Cupressus pisifera*) has attractive juvenile forms—*plumos alba picta* has small leaves arranged in pairs, green on top and whitish underneath and *squarrosa* forms a dense pyramidal bush with awl-shaped foliage which can be clipped into any shape.

There are various forms of the Japanese Cedar (*Cryptomeria japonica*), introduced from Japan in 1844. The juvenile variety, *elegans,* is often found in gardens and has bright green foliage in summer which changes to reddish-brown in autumn. The very dwarf *nana* is suitable for growing in a sheltered corner of the rock garden, and *albo-variegata,* another dwarf, has shoots which are nearly white when young but change to a pale green with age.

Junipers will strike readily from cuttings and are easy to grow. There are four species, the Chinese (*Juniperus chinensis*), which bears juvenile and adult foliage on the same plant, and of which fine

232

specimens can be seen at Spottiswoode, Berwickshire; the Savin (*J. sabina*); the pencil (*J. virginiana*) and the common juniper (*J. communis*), of which the variety *compressa*, with many synonyms, is the daintiest of all dwarf junipers, never growing more than an inch a year and rarely reaching 3 ft. in twenty years: it needs a sheltered position, as cold winds 'brown the tips', and looks best in groups.

A procumbent shrub with spreading branchlets is *Juniperus sabina* and the very prostrate variety *tamariscifolia* will give a glaucous green covering to rocks and steep banks. A species with numerous dwarf varieties is *J. virginiana* the most important being *argentea*, silvery-leaved; *aereo spica*, golden; and *glauca*, a handsome plant with glaucous foliage.

Daphnes

Daphnes, of which there are some fifty species from Southern Europe, Asia and Japan, flower in early spring and summer and are mostly hardy. The taller forms are suitable for grouping in shrubberies and woodlands and the dwarf, trailing kinds for rock gardens and scree. Daphnes are either evergreen or deciduous shrubs with alternate leaves and short petioles. The flowers are apetalous, four in number, cross-shaped with thick tubes and eight stamens. Beneath the tubes are bright-green, urn-shaped ovaries surrounded by spreading pale-purple discs, each containing one seed.

There are four main methods of propagation—cuttings, layering, grafting and seed. Select well-ripened wood for cuttings in July and insert them in boxes or pots, containing a mixture of loam, peat and sand or crushed pumice, under bell-glasses in a cool greenhouse until spring. When rooted, they should be transferred to pots, being kept in an unheated frame until they are ready to be planted in their final quarters. Some species do not root readily from cuttings, and layering during April or May is the best method. In the case of prostrate kinds, the making of cuts beneath the layered branches is optional, but they should be kept in position with small stones or pegs and covered with one inch of peat and sand. The following spring, when they are rooted, pot them and place in a frame for a month or two for hardening off, and plant out in the autumn. Grafting is simple, but it should be done under glass in spring, using healthy scions and, as rootstocks, two-year-old seedlings of *D. Mezereum* for deciduous kinds or *D. laureola* for evergreens. The seedling rootstocks of these have a comparatively large rooting system and grow more rapidly than cuttings. The most common way is to wedge-graft the scions on to potted-up seedlings and to place them in a propagating case until the union has taken place, although some kinds may be saddle-grafted on to fleshy pieces of roots then plunged in sand and given gentle bottom heat.

Most daphnes ripen seed freely, but unfortunately birds are very fond of these fruits and black thread must be wound round the trees, when the fruit is still green, to scare them away.

Seed sown in pans, immediately after harvesting, may germinate the following spring or may remain dormant for up to fifteen months. Transfer the seedlings to small pots, when they are large enough to handle, first plunging them in sand, then planting them out in their permanent quarters before they become pot-bound.

Although daphnes usually grow wild in limestone regions, under garden conditions they seem to grow quite well in the slightly acid soil which suits calcifuge plants such as heather, rhododendrons and many lilies, but all forms dislike root disturbance and rarely reach a great age.

Among recommended garden species *D. alpina,* from the Spanish Pyrenees, is a rare deciduous, upright shrub in the Alpinae section. Its racemes of fragrant white flowers in June are followed by orange-red fruits in autumn.

In the Cneorum section Garland Flower (*D. Cneorum*), a native of central and southern Europe, is a favourite for the rock garden and produces fragrant rich rosy-pink flowers in May and June. It is an attractive hardy evergreen dwarf, growing to about 9 ins. high, and will root readily from cuttings taken during July and August and placed in a cold frame. The following spring plant out the rooted cuttings a few inches apart so that they will merge and form a clump. There are two or three good varieties of which *grandiflora* is the best.

A native of the southern Tyrol, *D. petraea* (syn. *D. rupestris*), produces bright rose-pink scented flowers in late spring, and thrives best when the compost, containing a small quantity of old lime rubble, is rammed hard into a crevice in a rock face exposed to the sun, but may also be grown in a pan in the cool alpine house. The hard and glossy leaves are about $\frac{1}{2}$ in. long, and the plant takes several years to grow to its full height and diameter—both 6 ins.

In the Collinae section, *D. Blagayana* is a native of Eastern Europe, and produces sweetly scented, creamy-white flowers, in clusters of ten to twelve blooms on the ends of the previous year's growth. The plants are trailing in habit and suitable among scree in the rock garden if shaded from the midday sun. As soon as new shoots are large enough they should be pegged down, and top

234

dressed with a good compost and small stones so that roots eventually form, and the plant gains renewed vigour. The evergreen *D. sericea* (*D. collina*), a compact rounded bush, produces pale rosy-pink fragrant flowers in April and May, and has narrow, leathery irregularly-shaped leaves.

Mezerion (*D. Mezereum*), the type-plant of its section—also known as Dwarf Bay, Flowering Spurge, Lady Laurel, Spurge Flax and Spurge Olive—was so named from the old Persian name Madzaryon, meaning 'destroyer of life' because all parts of this shrub are poisonous, and especially, the bark, roots, seeds and seed cases. Robins and sparrows, however, pick the seeds out of the unripe fruits but reject the pulp and so are not harmed. This shrub has been growing in this country for several centuries and is often to be seen in cottage gardens. It produces strongly scented pink flowers, in spring before the leaves appear, which last for more than a fortnight. Seeds set freely and by the end of May the green berries are full size and in July they ripen to scarlet, containing a single black seed. Mezereum may reach five feet in height but in some strains the lower parts are bare of shoots. There are forms which grow into attractively shaped bushes, and it is these which should be propagated. *D. Mezereum album* and Bowles's white form are two white varieties, the best being the latter, but there are unfortunately a number of very washed-out shades.

The Laureola section contains two well-known species—*D. Laureola* and *D. pontica*. The spurge laurel (*D. Laureola*) and its variety *Philippii* are evergreen and succeed well under the shade of trees in almost any soil. They flower from December until March, producing yellowish-green blooms, beneath the leaves, which emit a faint perfume during a mild evening. Resembling the spurge laurel in appearance is *D. pontica*, but it carries only two flowers on each stalk, which are above instead of beneath the leaves, and the plants grow more rapidly, are taller and more upright.

A deciduous Japanese species, *D. Genkwa*, is one of the most attractive, but it is not quite hardy in Scotland and should be grown in a greenhouse. It has large, sweet-scented rich lilac-coloured flowers which appear before the leaves in spring.

Rock Roses and Sun Roses

Rock roses (genus *Cistus*) are confined to the Mediterranean area and there are some twenty species, natural hybrids and varieties. They differ from the closely allied sun roses (*Helianthemum*) in having five to ten-celled seed vessels instead of three-celled. Although most flourish outdoors a few species are not fully hardy so that they were, at one time, confined to the cool greenhouse.

Rock roses vary in height from 1-8 ft., and have single white or pink flowers superficially resembling the dog rose and lasting about eight hours in bright sun, though some natural hybrids keep their petals longer. A bundle of bright yellow stamens surrounds the ovary.

Sown in spring in gentle heat, they germinate in seven to ten days and are best quickly pricked off into small pots, since the seedlings do not readily transplant. They can then be hardened off and planted out to flower in June. The potting compost should consist of fibrous loam, leaf mould and coarse sand, but no lime.

Cuttings taken in August will readily root in a warm frame and flower in the second year, but they are liable to damp-off and must be kept fairly dry in winter. Over-rich soil encourages soft succulent growth susceptible to early spring frosts, so plant in a well-drained, stony, poor soil on a bank facing due south, giving winter protection if the site is exposed. Damp is fatal.

A shrubby moderately hardy species which needs winter protection is *C. crispus* which grows to 2-3 ft., has easily recognised greyish, stalkless leaves with wavy margins and purplish-red flowers about $1\frac{1}{2}$ ins. across. The variety Sunset flowers later than the parent and has rosy-carmine blooms.

Source of Ladanum gum, used in perfumery, is *C. ladaniferus* which attains 7 ft., and has long fragrant leaves which are dark and shiny above and woolly beneath. The fine solitary white flowers have brownish-red blotches at the petal bases and are 4 ins. across: an unblotched white variety is *albiflorus*. Since *ladaniferus* is not very hardy, cuttings should be taken annually for replacements, and some protection given in severe winters by tying spruce branches in among the shoots.

Largest and hardiest of the genus is the laurel-leaved rock rose *C. laurifolius* which attains 8 ft. The dark green leaves are glaucous, and downy beneath, and the numerous pure white flowers are $2\frac{1}{2}$ ins. across. It is difficult to strike from cuttings and should be grown from seed.

Useful for the shrubbery is the similar *C. cyprius*, a natural cross between *C. ladaniferus* and *C. laurifolius*. About 6 ft. high, it has fragrant shoots; greyish green, glutinous leaves; and 3-in. white flowers, with crimson blotches at the petal bases, which are borne on long stalks.

A cross between *C. ladaniferus* and *C. villosus* has produced *C.*

purpureus, 4 ft. high, with downy shoots and lanceolate, greyish green leaves, downy beneath. Although perhaps the handsomest of the dark-flowered hybrids, with reddish-purple flowers, blotched with dark red at the base, it is not very hardy.

Resembling *C. villosus*, of which it may be a seedling, is *C. Silver Pink*, raised in Winchester in 1916, which grows to 2½ ft. The leaves are 3 ins. long and grey-green on the underside, and the flowers are 3 ins. across and silvery pink with golden stamens. It is not very hardy, but planted en masse makes an effective dwarf shrub for the rock garden. Cuttings grow easily and flower the second year.

The hairy rock rose (*C. hirsutus*) was introduced long ago from Spain and is free-flowering and fairly hardy. It forms a spreading shrub, has ovate leaves 2½ ins. long, and has white flowers touched with yellow at the base and 1½ ins. across. Crossing readily with other species, it is best propagated by cuttings. A natural hybrid between *C. hirsutus* and *C. salvifolius*, is *C. obtusifolius*, a shapely 2-ft.-high bush, both hardy and easy to grow, which is useful for a sunny position in the rock garden. The foliage is dark green and glossy, and the white flowers are touched with yellow in the centre of the petals.

An elegant 4-ft. shrub when well grown, *C. monspeliensis* produces clusters of small white flowers and has sticky, stalkless, lanceolate leaves.

Sun roses (*Helianthemum*) include about one hundred species of evergreen shrubs, sub-shrubs, herbaceous plants, and annuals from Europe, Africa and North America. Disliking damp and shade, they are mostly hardy and flourish in free open soil and, unlike the rock roses with which they tend to be confused, the shrubby and sub-shrubby kinds need no winter protection. The latter are more or less trailing in habit and make excellent rock garden plants, but should be cut back annually after flowering: propagation is by softwood cuttings taken in August and September and rooted in a cold frame.

A tufted shrubby plant, very attractive in the rock garden, is *H. alpestre*, with its green leaves, slightly hairy on both sides, and downy stems.

Introduced from the Mediterranean two hundred years ago *H. umbellatum* resembles a miniature rosemary in having small, narrow, stalkless leaves, but is still a rare plant, seen only in botanic gardens and private collections. An evergreen, with foliage bright green above and downy beneath, it grows to about 18 ins. and has a wealth of white flowers with patches of yellow at the petal bases. The blooms open in the sun in the early morning and droop by early afternoon, but it makes a brave show and is easily propagated by cuttings.

A flourishing native both of Britain and Europe is the spreading but semi-erect shrub *H. nummularium* (syn. *H. vulgare*), which has wide-oblong leaves, green above and a downy grey-green beneath. Many of the garden varieties come from cross between this species and *H. glaucum,* and include *alba plena,* double white; The Bride, white; Fireball, double bright red; *luteum,* yellow, rose queen, single bright pink; *sulphurea,* single sulphur yellow; *venustum plenum,* double scarlet.

Magnolias

The very large magnolia genus includes some of the most beautiful deciduous and evergreen trees and shrubs, some hardy and some half-hardy. As many of the deciduous kinds bloom very early in spring, even before the leaves appear, and others very much later it is possible, by careful selection, to have a good show for much of the year.

The majority are perfectly hardy and fairly easy to grow, but all do best in a heavy soil if they are occasionally mulched with well-rotted farmyard manure and decayed leaves or peat moss. They may be used in the shrubbery, as single specimens on the edge of the lawn, or can be trained against walls—the early flowering kinds which need protection from spring frosts are especially suited to the last method since they could otherwise only be grown in a greenhouse. Magnolias grown in this way form a perfect decorative screen of blossom and foliage, but they should not be nailed flat against the wall. Only the main branches should be fixed and the other shoots merely spurred back, where necessary, after flowering. Some of the finest specimens are to be seen against the boundary walls of the Royal Botanic Gardens at Kew and Edinburgh.

Planting is best done at the end of March, since they dislike root disturbance when dormant, and if mulched with farmyard manure or decayed forest tree leaves and watered occasionally, they will soon become established.

Growing from seed, which is sown in a little heat in spring, is a slow process since magnolias take a long time to germinate and to reach flowering size. Most of the deciduous species and varieties can be grafted in spring or budded in autumn, *Magnolia acuminata* seedlings being the usual rootstocks used for both methods, but layering is becoming increasingly popular and is easy with shoots near the ground. Make a sloping cut about half-way through the stem near a node to arrest the flow of sap and fix each layer into the

238

ground using either a piece of wood, with a long wire nail affixed in the form of a hook, or a flat stone. Cover with a fibrous compost, made very firm and kept moist to assist root formation. Root formation may also be encouraged if the stems are twisted to split the bark, then bent upwards, or tied to a stake to check the flow of sap. When branches are not low enough to reach the ground, layer into large flower pots on a platform. After about two years, when the layers are well rooted, sever the branches from the parent plant and water well for some months until lifting during March, taking care not to damage the brittle roots.

The most beautiful magnolia for a small garden is *M. stellata* (sometimes called *M. Halleana*), which produces in March and April a profusion of narrow-petalled, pure waxy white blooms, about six inches across, and star-shaped. It flowers when quite small, even when growing in a six inch pot, but takes many years to form a dense twiggy bush and attain its full height of 6 ft. Planted in a group they look like a bank of snow from a distance, especially if backed by evergreen shrubs, and may also be planted in the rock garden. Since the blooms do not all open at once it has quite a long flowering period, but it should be sheltered from spring winds and frosts. A rare variety which has delicate pink blooms is *M. s. rosea*.

A species with flowers of about the same size as *M. stellata*, but purple and white outside and white within, is *M. obovata*, which is also loose in habit of growth.

The Lily tree or yulan (*M. conspicua*), will often reach 20-30 ft. in its native China but in Scotland attains a height and breadth of only about 8 ft. It is deciduous and its flower buds, large and conspicuous during the winter, develop into large, fleshy, sweet-scented, creamy white flowers, 6-8 ins. across, in late March or April. This species is excellent for growing against a wall, but may also be grown as a bush and flowers when quite small. It is usually grafted on to *M. Soulangeana*, making it a slow grower in its early stages. At one time *M. conspicua* was used for forcing, and it can be easily grown and flowered in a cool greenhouse. Of the several good varieties, *M. C. alba superba*, which grows more quickly than its parent and produces numerous pure white flowers, is best and should be pruned only lightly after flowering to keep it in shape.

A cross between *M. conspicua* and *M. obovata*, *M. Soulangeana*, produces many rosy-purple tinted, large white flowers during April and May and from its fertile seed many further varying forms have been produced. Although *M. Lennei*, which flowers in July, has the same parentage as *M. Soulangeana* it differs considerably, having

239

more handsome foliage, and large flowers with broad petals, dark purplish-rose outside and glistening white within.

A native of Northern India, *M. Campbellii* is a magnificent species for training against a wall but it is advisable to hang a double fold of herring net in front of the bush to protect the rosy-pink 9-in. blooms from the March frosts. This species is not often seen in gardens but there are fine specimens in Kew Gardens and at Inverewe, Wester Ross.

Swamp Bay (*M. glauca*) is an almost evergreen native of North America with bright velvety glaucous colouring on the leaf undersides and creamy white blooms in late summer. A number of named forms of this species are in cultivation, but the variety *Thompsoniana* is an improvement, with its larger leaves and freely produced sweet scented, white flowers. Another North American species is the evergreen *M. grandiflora*, flowering from July until September, which has large, creamy white blooms, sweetly-scented, and is suitable for growing against a high wall. It has several beautiful forms.

From China comes *M. fuscata* (syn. *Michelia fuscata*), a bushy evergreen shrub which thrives best in the greenhouse, either trained against the wall or grown in pots. It produces very fragrant purple flowers in April and does not need frequent repotting if top-dressed annually with a mixture of loam and well-decayed farmyard manure and occasionally watered with weak liquid manure to keep the foliage healthy and form plump flower buds. Propagation is by cuttings of semi-matured wood taken in autumn and rooted under a bell glass in the greenhouse.

Rhododendrons

For screening and to cover a large area with evergreen foliage, rhododendrons (which include the azaleas) are unequalled, and even the more delicate-looking deciduous kinds stand up well to smog. Their main requirements are good drainage, moisture during the growing season, and partial shading from the midday sun. If possible plant the shrubs in a wood which has been thinned, so that the tree-tops will provide shade and protection from the wind, and on a slight slope, in porous well-drained soil, free from lime and chalk. If the topsoil is heavy add some peat moss and leaf mould.

Since rhododendrons are surface rooters do not plant too deeply— the top of the ball must just be covered. On a slope conserve moisture at the roots by scooping out a little soil to form a saucer around the plants and filling it in with horticultural peat, fresh leaves, lawn

A well established corner.
THE WALL GARDEN
A superb show of aubrietia at Pollok House, Glasgow.

Primula marginata being taken from pots for planting during April/May in an ideal crevice.

Being placed in position.

THE ROCK GARDEN

Well-established.

mowings, etc. It is then only necessary to water during times of severe drought.

At the end of February or in early March, mulch with horticultural peat and grass mowings, adding hardwood leaves to keep the mixture open and avoiding the formation of a sodden mass which may harm the roots.

Unlike other shrubs, rhododendrons do not need ordinary pruning, and are best pruned as little as possible to preserve a natural appearance. It may be necessary, however, to remove one or two branches to develop a particular shape or to prevent them becoming too high. This is best done in February, the cut surface being afterwards painted with white lead paint as protection against the entrance of fungus spores. After flowering, remove the old flower heads, unless seed is required.

Propagation is by seed, cuttings, layering and grafting. Rhododendrons are easily raised from seed which, if kept dry, retains its viability for a number of years, according to variety, but the plants may not be true to colour. Fill small pans firmly with rough sand intermixed with soil and peat, placing them in saucers of water until they are thoroughly soaked, and then drain. In spring sow on the surface and do not cover with compost, but lightly with fine sand and shade the pans with newspaper placed over a sheet of glass to provide the subdued light which assists germination, then place in a cool greenhouse. Spray the pans at intervals to keep the compost moist. After germination, which follows in about fourteen days, prick the seedlings off when large enough to be handled into boxes or pans, containing the same compost and keep them shaded in sunny weather. After about two months, remove to a cold frame and allow them to remain there until spring the following year. Then plant out in a sheltered, lime-free nursery bed, and leave until they are large enough to be removed to their permanent quarters.

The smaller species and hybrids and azaleas nowadays included in the rhododendron group, will root from cuttings, but not the large-leaved kind. Remove lateral shoots in February and March, insert them in a sandy-peat compost, then place them under bell glasses or frames heated to 65-70° F./18-21° C. and keep moist. In about four weeks, when they have rooted, transfer singly to 3-in. pots and place in a cold frame until planting out in nursery rows the following spring.

Almost all professional growers graft in spring onto *R. ponticum* rootstocks, using the wedge or saddle method, to raise large numbers of the hardy evergreen types.

Layering is both reliable and easy. The simplest way is to give a shoot which is near the soil surface a single twist and peg it into the ground, covering it with peat moss or leaf-mould. After about two years when the branch is well rooted it can be separated from its parent, and planted in its permanent quarters.

The following are suitable for growing in reasonably textured, well-drained soil containing sufficient humus and free from chalk and lime, and are adaptable to all Scottish conditions.

One of the many species of the triflorum group, belonging to a series of the genus which has become established in our gardens, is *Rhododendron Augustinii,* which was introduced over fifty years ago and named after Professor Augustine Henry, who found it in Yunnan. This somewhat twiggy plant often reaches 7 ft. and produces flowers of various colours—the best being light lilac.

Introduced from Western China, *R. calophytum* is free flowering, like its many hybrids, producing bell-shaped, pure white blooms, with a dark blotch inside the uppermost petal, and a big yellow stigma.

An old evergreen species is *R. campanulatum* of which there are several varieties. It grows to over 30 ft. and has bell-shaped lilac-purple or white, flowers and leaves that are dark green above and covered with felty rusty hairs below.

One of the loveliest of Sikkim's species, is *R. campylocarpum,* which forms a neat bush, 6-10 ft. high and has loose trusses containing six to eight sulphur yellow, fragrant blooms in May and June. Seedlings are easily raised but not always true to colour.

One of the best of all flowering shrubs is the Chinese evergreen *R. Fortunei,* which has loose racemose saucer-shaped white flowers tinged with pink and very fragrant. A cross between *R. Fortunei* and *R. Griffithianum, R. Loderi* produces large, delightfully fragrant flowers, and is a vigorous grower and very hardy. Other hybrids which have received awards are the Duke of York and Duchess of York.

Growing abundantly all over Scotland, and seeding freely, *R. ponticum* has bell-shaped purple flowers, distinctly lobed and produces dense bushes. There are numerous varieties.

The fairly hardy *R. praecox,* a cross between *R. ciliatum* and *R. dauricum,* sometimes has its rosy purple flowers, produced in February and March, damaged by frost, but *R. Yunnanense,* another of the triflorum group, has a great number of pale pink flowers, with crimson spots in May.

In addition to the numerous species, the most popular varieties of easy culture to give a gorgeous display include: Alice, rose pink; Ascot Brilliant, red-crimson; Brittania, scarlet; Christmas Cheer, pale rose; Corona, deep pink; Cunningham's Sulphur, pale yellow; Cynthia, carmine; Doncaster, bright scarlet; Harmsworth Early, white; Loder's White, pure white; Mother of Pearl, soft pearly white; Pink Pearl, pink; Purple Splendour, dark purple; and Royal Purple, vinous purple.

Dwarf rhododendrons are ideal for the rock garden and have attractive flowers and foliage: *R. calostrotum* has clear rose blooms in April and grey-green foliage; *R. ciliatum,* produces pale pink flowers, which are deeper pink in bud, in April; *R. fastigiatum,* has deep-lilac-blue flowers in April and May, and grey-tinted foliage; *R. ferrugineum,* a European Alpine rose, has rose-coloured flowers in May; *R. hippophaeoides,* a slightly taller dwarf, produces lavender blue flowers April-May and dark green foliage: *R. racemosum,* a very floriferous species, with short ovate leaves and bright pink flowers will grow to 5 ft. and is, therefore, suitable as a background for a rock garden but needs pruning to prevent it becoming thin and weak-looking.

·6·

The Rock Garden

Construction 246. Alpines 248. Arctic plants 250. Heaths 253.

·6·

The Rock Garden

Construction

THE ROCK GARDEN should be sited where it appears most natural and presents as little sudden contrast with the formal garden as possible, the approach preferably being made by paths passing through an increasingly natural setting. The decision whether to introduce water, in the form of a stream or pool, should be made at the outset, since it involves substantial modification of the design through the removal of earth and gravel, or its subsequent utilisation in forming abrupt sun-trap banks to give shelter from wind. It need hardly be said that, from the point of view of appearance, water is one of the greatest advantages the rock garden can have.

Opinions differ as to the best stone to use, but if there is abundant porous rock in the district, this is the ideal solution as to choice of material, otherwise there are three types in general use. Very common are the various grades of sandstone, some hardening under exposure to weather and others disintegrating into sand particles and so constantly increasing the porosity of the planting area they enclose. The regular character of the stratification common to them all renders it difficult to use these sandstones without monotony, and they are best arranged in bold outcrops.

Limestone is the favourite with the owner of the small garden and with exhibitors at the Chelsea Flower Show. It weathers beautifully and, when carefully placed in its original strata with the unquarried edges to the front, looks long-established from the start. Large random fragments set in a lawn give the impression of an outcrop or may be left haphazardly to suggest they have rolled down from a cliff. The slight weathering which occurs in soft limestones provides the lime chippings amongst which many alpines revel.

The conglomerates of parts of Perthshire and the granites of Aberdeenshire and Dumfriesshire can be used to give bold, massive effects, but they take a long time to weather into harmony with their setting. Whatever happens, never use the dreadful mass of shiny, glazed lumps of concrete and brickbats which so often appears in the amateur's garden—an eyesore in which half-starved plants struggle for existence.

When arranging the stone, remember not only to follow any distinct lines of stratification, but also ensure that there is a sufficient quantity of soil; both under and between the stones. Alpines send their roots down through the cracks and crevices in search of moisture and food, as well as coolness, and the stones should slant slightly back, so that rain water will be directed where they can reach it. Avoid having stones in perpendicular positions where they neither protect nor conserve moisture, and look extremely unpleasant. Make your mounds of soil look as natural as possible rather than too artificially steep, embed the stones firmly so that they do not move when you rest your weight on them, and vary the soil pockets between them from a few inches in diameter to as many feet. The pockets of soil should be amply drained to prevent their becoming too wet and sour. If there is a tendency to wetness, remove the original soil to a depth of about 2 ft., and place a 6-in. layer of clinkers or broken brickbats in the bottom, before replacing it.

Always use the same kind of stone for paths as that used in the general construction and not, for example, seashore pebbles among limestone. Keep any stepping stones—very useful in marshy ground —irregular in outline though smooth-topped enough for easy walking.

A compost of fibrous loam, leaf mould or peat (or both), and some sharp river sand suits 50 to 60 per cent of rock garden plants, the quantity of one or more of the constituents merely needing to be varied according to their respective requirements. For heaths—60 per cent granulated peat, some leaf mould, sharp sand and a little fibrous loam; and for encrusted saxifrages and sedums, a fibrous loam with limestone chips. As to position, they all have individual preferences, sun or shade, dry ledge or moist crevice.

The only trees to be included in the rock garden should be the dwarf pines, abies, and cypresses, and these—like suitable shrubs— should be associated with the bolder rock masses and set back sufficiently far to avoid overshadowing the smaller inhabitants or depriving them of food.

Alpines

Rock garden alpines may be propagated by seed or, in the case of many garden forms and varieties, such as those with cut leaves and variegated foliage which do not come true, by various artificial methods.

Early flowering kinds, such as anemones, crocuses, many campanulas and the mossy saxifrages, should be sown in May and June as soon as the seed is ripe. By the autumn quite strong plants should be ready for lining out in a cold frame—except in the case of the bulbs, corms and tubers—and no coddling is needed. The colder the winter, the better the plants will be in spring for planting outdoors in nursery rows, where they will grow for a year before being set out in their permanent positions—in drifts or colonies rather than as single specimens.

Later flowering kinds which ripen seed in August and September should be sown during September in pans or boxes, and plunged outdoors in old furnace ashes, so that the seed and soil may be frozen and germination hastened, but protection from birds should be given.

Collect seed before it has a chance to be shed, dry it in the sun on sheets of paper for a few days, and see that the pans or boxes for sowing are well drained by a layer of large crocks with smaller pieces above, topped by a layer of moss or partly-decayed leaves. The actual compost should be sandy, with a sprinkling of silver sand on the surface and the filled pans or boxes should be set in water to soil level before sowing, rather than risk washing out the seed by watering afterwards.

Among species easily grown from seed are: alliums, aubrietias, androsaces, aethionemas, *Aster alpinus,* many campanulas, dianthus, gentians, geraniums, linums, poppies and primulas.

Methods of vegetative propagation are by division, cuttings, layering, root severance, twisting and ringing.

Division is easiest and is best done in spring or autumn. Lift the plants by inserting two hand-forks vertically downwards, then levering gently upwards, so that a good ball of soil keeps the roots entire. Then, carefully divide the plants into pieces, either by using a sharp knife, or by pulling them apart. Each piece should have a healthy quota of roots, and the older, central portions should be discarded. The young, strong, outer pieces should either be replanted straight away, or potted up in a compost of turfy loam, leaf mould and sharp sand. Plants of the *Achillea, Armeria, Aster, Saxifraga* and *Veronica* genera may be increased by this method.

Cuttings are taken when shoots begin to ripen, since wood about to mature produces a callus and roots more readily. Strong, sturdy side shoots 1½-10 ins. long, and near the ground, should be removed with a very sharp knife. Prepare them by cuttings straight across just below a leaf stalk, joint or bud, leaving the joint itself intact. If the buds or joints are close together on the shoot, cuttings may be 1½-3 ins. long, and should be inserted in the rooting medium to half their length; but if buds or joints are more than 2 ins. apart, as with many hard wood cuttings, then they should be inserted to a depth of 4-5 ins.

'Soft' cuttings, such as those from various species of dianthus and mossy saxifrages, strike best under a hand-light or frame. Never make the cuttings longer than necessary and strip off the lower leaves before inserting them in a light compost of fine silver sand, or a mixture of peat and sand, which allows air to pass freely. The less hardy and vigorous should be placed at the side of the pan or box. Semi-hard-wood cuttings are more difficult to strike than the soft-wooded, and are best taken with a 'heel' of the previous year's wood.

All cuttings need shade from bright sunlight and shelter from wind until well rooted, when ventilation must be given whenever possible and all decaying leaves removed to avoid 'damping off'. Especial care must be taken, if pots are used, to ensure that they are clean and well-drained: about seven cuttings can be placed around the edge of a 4-in. pot.

Soft-wood cuttings form roots in about a month and can be potted on into small pots or wintered in a cold frame; hardwood cuttings may need 12-18 months and should be placed in a sheltered position outdoors at 6-in. intervals in rows 12 ins. apart.

Layering is useful for propagating evergreens, which resemble border carnations in being difficult to root as cuttings. An upward cut should be made just below a joint in a lower shoot, taking it from the underside through to the centre and then on for 2-3 ins. towards the growing point. The latter is turned upward to check the flow of sap and encourage root formation, and the open 'tongue' pegged down, and covered with a 6-in.-deep layer of loamy compost which is firmly pressed down. Semi-hard-wood cuttings will root in about three months, and hard-wood, e.g. rhododendrons, may take a year or more.

Root severance is an especially easy method of propagation for fleshy-rooted plants and is done in late autumn or winter. Place the root cuttings vertically, right way up, in fairly deep pots or pans so that the part of the root once nearest the stem is just level with the soil surface. Then winter in a cold frame and give heat in spring to assist growth. A good example of a plant which can be rapidly increased by this method is Mediterranean cress (*Morisia hypogaea*), a charming and rare cruciferous plant about 3 ins. high, with golden-yellow flowers in April and May, and roots a foot or more long.

When plants have very fleshy roots, such as *Ourisia elegans* and *Sanguinaria canadensis*, the crowns can be cut off and new ones will form in their place.

Dwarf shrubs difficult to root from cuttings can be induced to form roots by twisting the lateral shoots, and tying them securely to stakes until they form a callus. The callused shoots are then layered so that roots form, and later the rooted shoots may be removed from the parent plants and set out in the open.

Another method to induce roots on hard-wooded plants is by 'ringing', which involves the removal of a narrow band of bark around the stem in the place where roots are desired. A callus will form on the upper bark which in time will emit roots. Branches treated in this way should be firmly pegged down with soil on top, and kept well watered.

Arctic Plants

Many arctic wild flowers are worth cultivation in the rock garden. Some are small creeping or succulent plants, and others form cushions, or mats, but they have large flowers—varying greatly in depth and range of colour. Any high summit may yield a few varieties of dwarf willow (*Salix*), whitlow grass (*Draba*), star-wort (*Cerastium*) or stone-crop (*Sedum*), such as occur more abundantly in Scandinavia, the Alps and Pyrenees and to a less extent in England and western Ireland. In Scotland the really rich hills are limited to Ben Lawers and the Cairngorms, but although most alpines occur at these heights, they will also grow at lower altitudes. The yellow saxifrage (*Saxifraga aizoides*), for example, can be found on the shores of Loch Tay and in the Tweed valley, and the sea pink (*Armeria maritima*) and rose root (*Sedum roseum*) at sea level, though both are drought resisters and need perfect drainage. However, never rob the hills, but buy from your alpine plant nurseryman.

Few of these high altitude plants are found growing fully exposed to the sun, and they should, therefore, be shaded by large stones or given a northern exposure. The mica-schist rock of the hills easily splits and accumulates as a fine soil in chinks and fissures, being held in place by larger stones and plant roots as the pockets enlarge. Snow collects in the corries and crevices from October to April, sheltering the plants from sun, wind and frost, then melts to supply the roots with moisture just before flowering. Some alpines are shy growers, difficult to propagate, but others are so easy to cultivate that they almost become 'weeds'.

The mountain avens (*Dryas octopetala*), a pretty white flowering trailing evergreen, thrives in a cool, gritty soil and, like numerous other alpine plants, grows naturally on ledges in pockets of soil where water drips from above throughout the growing season, so that rock garden conditions should resemble this as closely as possible.

Mountain cudweed (*Antennaria dioica*), makes a good carpet plant in a sunny position if set in gritty loam. Of creeping habit, it forms tufts of silvery foliage and bears masses of tiny pink flowers in summer.

The black or Alpine bearberry (*Arctostaphylos alpina*), is a little shrub, rarely exceeding 10 ins. in height, which bears red or white flowers in September. The common bearberry (*A. uva-ursi*), a pretty trailing evergreen shrub, is found in dry places and can be cultivated quite easily from seed if given similar conditions, but it dislikes lime. It has glossy dark green leaves, rose to white flowers and bright red, smooth berries.

Cuckoo flower or lady's smock (*Cardamine pratensis*), of which there is now a very attractive double variety (*C. pratensis fl. pl.*), grows 6-12 ins. high and produces pretty, lilac-coloured flowers during May and June.

The dwarf growing fleabane (*Erigeron alpinus*) is excellent for a sunny position and produces purple flowers on 10-in. spikes. It is propagated by division of roots during March.

A handsome dwarf juniper for permanent planting is *Juniperus communis* and the trailing azalea (*Loiseleuria procumbens*), a little shrubby plant with purple-pink flowers, is excellent for a moist situation, thriving in peat, sand and leaf mould. Propagate by cuttings in a cold frame in September.

The bog violet (*Pinguicula vulgaris*), a perennial bog plant easily cultivated either in the cool alpine house or in moist, peaty loam, in a shady position, has yellow-green leaves with a glutinous surface, and tiny gloxinia-like purple flowers about 3 ins. high in April and May. The Alpine pearlwort (*Sagina nivalis*), an arctic plant found in the courses of tiny streams near the summit of Ben Lawers, has a tuft of moss-like foliage and tiny white flowers during summer, and as it is a creeper should be planted in the paved garden. Dwarf willow (*Salix herbacea*), is very ornamental when planted to creep over a stone and given a northern aspect. It is too slow growing to need pruning and should be planted in October in moist soil.

The saxifrages or rockfoils are among the most beautiful of our alpine plants, and the 3-5-in.-high *Saxifraga aizoides* may be found abundantly near water trickling down from a corrie spring, producing yellow flowers during May and June. On the schist rock near the top of Ben Lawers, *S. cernua*, may still be found, but it is not so plentiful as it once was. About 6 ins. high, it has erect stems with palm-shaped lobed leaves and scarlet bulbils in the axils of the leaf stalks, and it thrives in a moist but well drained soil. It is often thought to be an alpine form of *S. granulata*, but they are both distinct species. Dovedale Moss (*S. hypnoides*), is a mossy saxifrage which forms a dense emerald green carpet profusely decked with large white flowers during the spring. There are many varieties of this, some of the best known being *S. h. Kingii*, *S. h. affinis* and *S. h. Whitlavii*. A rare little plant, found either singly or in tiny clusters when growing wild, *S. nivalis* flourishes in a moist but well drained soil. Its solid leathery leaves lie flat on the ground and the pretty white flowers are produced in clusters on stems 3 ins. high in June and July. The purple saxifrage (*S. oppositifolia*), found growing all over the whole of the northern arctic region, is a prostrate, creeping plant with fairly long wiry, evergreen leaves and deep roots. The purplish-crimson flowers are produced in March and April and there are many forms under cultivation. The best results are obtained by growing the plants in a partially shaded position facing west, and cuttings taken in early summer will root freely in a sandy soil. All forms are suitable for growing in pans in the cool alpine house. Short-lived in cultivation, *S. stellaris*, so named from the starry appearance of its flowers, which are white, spotted with purple at the base, must be frequently renewed from seed. The rose root (*Sedum roseum*), growing to 12 ins., has reddish-purple flowers in summer and succulent foliage which enables it to withstand long periods of drought and to be successful in a dry light soil or where little soil is available.

Moss campion or cushion pink (*Silene acaulis*), has pink flowers on stems about 2 ins. high, and the crowns need protection under glass in winter. The common bilberry (*Vaccinium myrtillus*), a pretty heath-like shrub 15-18 ins. high, has pale pink flowers in May and June followed by showy dark-blue globular fruits. It can be propagated by cuttings under glass in spring and by root-suckers in the autumn.

Heaths

Heaths and heathers are very popular dwarf shrubs for the rock garden and in front of the shrub border, since they give a wealth of bloom from January till December and are very adaptable, provided the situation is open and sunny. A gentle slope to the south or south-west is best-suited to the heath garden, and any tendency to monotony can be relieved by varying the level with well-placed boulders, or by interspersing groups of taller varieties among the dwarf kinds. Any Scottish heather moor will supply the gardener with useful hints, and it is a good idea to have a few dwarf alpine rhododendrons here and there, and a few larger shrubs to form a background where space permits. Well suited for the latter purpose are the brooms *Cytisus scoparius,* with the varieties *sulphureus* and *Andreanus,* though a few are ample, *C. praecox* and *C. albus* are also delightful shrubs. For a glorious display of golden yellow flowers in May and June the Spanish Gorse (*Genista hispanica*) will blend with the smaller heaths, especially when planted near an out-crop of rock. Plants of the same family as the heaths may be used with good effect, for example, the *Andromedas*. The *Pieris floribunda* and *Pernettya mucronata* hybrids, with their beautiful many coloured fruits, and even *Berberis Darwinii, B. stenophylla* and *B. Thunbergii,* with its beautiful bronze autumn foliage, should also be considered.

Prepare a sketch-plan before planting, showing where each group is to be established, and bear in mind that the upright growing kinds, such as *Calluna vulgaris,* var. *Alportii,* and *C. v. Hammondii* take up less room than the more spreading kinds and varieties of *Erica carnea* and *E. cinerea.* Make the groups irregular, each running into the other, narrowing at the back, and ensure that the essential paths have a natural appearance, winding gently so as to avoid a boulder or out-crop of rock.

Heaths will grow and thrive in any lime-free and *not* over rich soil, but are so decidedly calcifuge that most of them will sicken and die if lime is present in any quantity, though one or two natives may grow in it if plenty of acid peat is put around the roots at planting time. Any loamy soil may be rendered suitable for heaths by mixing with it plenty of decayed hardwood leaves, sphagnum moss when partly decayed, or horticultural peat. The humus is necessary as a reservoir of food and moisture and helps to make cool soil warm in summer so that the fine roots enjoy freedom of growth. Drainage they must have; drought they can endure. The soil may be 'soggy'and become hard and dry, but the fibrous material will improve its physical condition and even a few stones about the roots assist drainage and encourage root action.

The majority of heaths should be planted by November, although those from pots may be planted in the spring provided the holes are 'puddled' to withstand undue evaporation before the plants become established.

Now a selection of species and varieties to grow :

At the beginning of the year *Erica mediterranea* will make a brave show with its pale rose-purple flowers. A little later the *E. carnea* varieties, of which at least twenty can be bought, including Winter Beauty, King George, Springwood white and Vivelli, which give a large range of colours. They are all dwarf growing plants, making dense spreading mats of growth and flower from December to April. Others which flower between December and April are *E. arborea* and *E. lusitanica*. The Dorset heath *E. ciliaris* and its fine variety Maweana are found in boggy places, but that does not mean they will not do better in well-drained soil, and *E. c. alba* has pure white flowers which should be given a place in every collection. Flowering a little later in the season is the cross-leaved heath, *E. tetralix,* this spreading though compact shrub well known in Sweden and North Germany, produces clusters of six to eight drooping bell-like flowers at the ends of the young twigs from June till October. *E. Lawsoniana* is also a compact grower and its silvery-grey foliage is very attractive.

The Cornish heath, *E. vagans,* is a strong upright growing plant: *grandiflora* is larger with a more straggling habit than its parent, and *rubra* is a deeper coloured variety. Most nursery firms list more than a dozen varieties and give the range of colours. The flowering season extends from late summer well into autumn, and after the blooms fade the masses of brown heads are still decorative.

The common ling or heather, *Calluna vulgaris* and its many varieties flower in late summer and autumn. The varieties *aurea* and *cuprea* have yellowish coloured foliage throughout the year; *pygmaea* is a very distinct dwarf form; the white flowered *Serlei* is exceptionally beautiful; and *Alportii* has crimson flowers and almost black foliage.

Heaths and heathers can be propagated from seed, or by layers, division and cuttings. Nearly all species can be obtained by sowing seed in the spring, in pans or boxes filled with a mixture of two parts finely sifted leaf-mould or peat and one part sharp sand. Cover the seeds lightly, place in a cold frame, shade from bright sun and always keep the compost damp. When the seedlings are large enough to handle, prick them out into boxes using a similar compost, and watering carefully. When the boxes are full of roots, the plants may be planted out into nursery rows where the soil contains some peat or leaf-mould. This encourages good root formation and makes final transplantation easier.

Layering can also be used for almost all varieties of heaths and heathers, being best done in spring. A compost of leaf-mould and sand is placed round the plants to be propagated and the branches near the ground are pegged down with bent wire, or held in position by small stones, which will also help to conserve moisture. It is best to let the layers remain on the plants for two years so as to encourage a better root formation.

For division, a large plant is dug up and pulled to pieces. The lanky parts are discarded, and the best retained and planted out to establish themselves in a specially prepared bed.

Good-sized plants may also be lifted and replanted very deeply using plenty of leaf-mould and sand round the upper portions of the branches. After two years branches which have rooted can be removed as rooted plants. Many heaths form low mats of dense growth which cover the ground and root readily into any peaty soil, or even into humus formed by their own leaf-fall, and such naturally rooted branches are treated in the same way as layers.

Perhaps the most general method of propagation, however, is by cuttings taken in July and early August. Unflowered shoots, about half to one inch in length, are best as they are not too hard. Pull the tiny shoots off with a 'heel' if possible, trim with a sharp knife, and insert in a cold frame in silver sand and peat, watering afterwards to settle the sand round them. If a slight bottom heat is given they will often root in four or five weeks, but otherwise require much longer. Ventilate as soon as there are indications that the cuttings are rooted, a little at first, then increase the amount gradually until the plants are given full exposure.

The young plants must not lack water, and daily syringing is beneficial. Once rooted, the cuttings may be left in the frame, without heat, all through the winter, provided they are well ventilated. During the following spring the plants can be 'lined out' in nursery rows and when well rooted planted out in the heath garden.

Monthly Calendar

Vegetables	**JANUARY**
Carrots	Make very small sowing of Early Short Horn or Amsterdam Forcing in heated frame. Examine roots in store.
Chives	Plant a few roots in pots and place in greenhouse.
Frames	When weather conditions are favourable, carefully ventilate crops in frames but protect from frost, and only water when necessary.
Lettuce	Transplant into heated frame and tomato house.
Mustard & Cress	Sow thickly and cover with paper, sowing the cress 3 days before the mustard, and place in a heated frame or greenhouse.
Onions	Sow in boxes in heat.
Parsnips	If there is a risk of frost lift a few roots for immediate use.
Potatoes	Select seed tubers, especially of early varieties and place in a frost-free place in trays, to sprout, keeping them near the light to prevent 'drawing'.
Seed list	Select and order vegetable and flower seeds. Have seed order dispatched at once.
Rhubarb	Force by placing barrels over the established crowns and packing stable manure around them on the outside.
Fruits	
Planting	Planting may be done when weather and soil conditions permit.

A gem among suburban rock gardens.

Planting out heaths.

Primula Rosea Marcia de Cret in a sunny corner.

THE ROCK GARDEN

An attractive show in July.

Pruning	Complete the pruning of all spur-bearing trees and bushes, burning the woody material, but saving the ashes for use as a potash fertiliser.
Spraying	Tar-oil spray trees and bushes during mild, dry weather.
Tomato border	Sterilise soil borders with steam or chemicals.

Flowers

Bulbs	Continue to remove bulbous plants from under ashes or peat, protecting them from frost.
Chrysanthemums	Propagate the late flowering varieties using cuttings of shoots about 3 ins. long, and give them bottom heat.
Fuchsias	Prune plants which have been resting, repot in rich soil and place in gentle heat.
Greenhouse	As light is limited at this season, make the most of it by ensuring that the glass is washed and the house cleaned. Force azaleas, gardenias, lilac, lily-of-the-valley, and dwarf rhododendrons, into flower, syringing the plants daily until they show flowers.

Vegetables

FEBRUARY

Broad beans	Make a drill 3 ins. deep and 6 ins. wide towards the end of month, and place the seeds in a double row, 5 ins. apart.
Cabbage	Stir the soil and draw a little towards stems of spring cabbage.
Cauliflower	Make a small sowing of an early variety in a cold frame, pricking off the seedlings when large enough to handle.
Horse-radish	Short pieces of roots may be taken from established plants and set out about 1 ft. apart.
Lettuce	Sow a pinch of All the Year Round in a sunny position and protect with cloches.
Onions	Prick out into boxes seedlings raised last month, if large enough to handle.
The cold frame	Give plenty of ventilation and remove fading leaves from plants wintered in cold frames.

R

Fruits

Apple store   Examine stored apples, removing any that are decayed.

Fruit trees   Plant when the soil is reasonably dry.

Strawberries   Place cloches over a few plants for early picking.

Tomatoes   Sow in heat using John Innes compost.

Vines   Commence forcing vine rods by giving a little heat and maintaining a moist atmosphere.

Winter spraying Complete winter spraying of all fruit trees and bushes as soon as possible.

Flowers

Annuals   Sow small pinches of various annuals in pots for early flowering.

Dahlias and   Cuttings about 3 ins. long may be taken and
  fuchsias   placed in bottom heat.

Flower garden   Transplant shrubs and herbaceous plants where necessary, when the weather is favourable, and sweep lawns to scatter worm casts.

Greenhouse   Place heaths and flowering plants in a cool and airy part of the house and geraniums in a warmer part to encourage growth.

Vegetables   MARCH

Broad beans   Sow main crop varieties, such as Broad Windsor or Longpod, towards end of month.

Brussels sprouts Sow main crop in seed bed when soil is workable.

Cabbage   Transplant autumn-sown varieties and red cabbage and sow Paragon and Winningstadt in seed bed.

Carrots   Sow small bed of Early Horn type about end of month.

Cauliflower   Continue to make small sowings in cold frame for transplanting later.

Celery   Make principal sowing in gentle heat early in month.

Leeks   Sow main crop early in the month in frames, or towards the end outdoors, for transplanting later in the season.

258

Lettuce	Transplant seedlings from frames to a warm border and protect with cloches.
Mint	Lift and divide roots. Plant out new bed.
Onions	Transplant autumn-sown onions in rows one foot apart. Sow, out of doors, large quantity for pulling green during summer and, if not already done, prick the January-sown seedlings into boxes.
Parsnips	Sow main crop as early in the month as weather permits.
Peas	Sow an early variety at intervals for a succession.
Potatoes	Plant an early variety towards end of month.
Shallots	Plant shallots, when soil and weather conditions are favourable.

Fruits

Blackcurrants	Give each bush 2-3 graipefuls of rotted dung. Examine bushes for big bud, picking off the affected buds burning them, or in severe cases uproot and burn the bushes.
Hardy fruits	Complete planting and pruning of all trees and bushes.
Strawberries	Plant a new bed, placing the crowns at 18-24-in. intervals, in rows 2 ft. 6 ins. apart.
Tomatoes	Transfer seedlings to small pots.
Vines and peaches	Spray vine rods and peach trees daily until flowering.

Flowers

Chrysanthemums	Repot rooted cuttings, and take cuttings from early flowering varieties.
Dahlias and fuchsias	Continue to take cuttings as in February.
Greenhouse plants	Repot plants which are most active and topdress those that may not require shifting.
Sweet peas	Sow early in month for planting out later. Harden off autumn-sown seedlings and prepare ground for planting out.
Half-hardy annuals	Sow about the middle of the month in a warm greenhouse for summer bedding, pricking out seedlings in due course.
Roses	Prune and then apply farmyard manure, or fertilisers plus peat or vegetable refuse, between the bushes.

259

Vegetables   APRIL

Broccoli	Sow one or two varieties to provide a succession.
Brussels sprouts	Plant out autumn-sown plants into their permanent quarters, spacing them 2½-3 ft. apart each way.
Cabbage	Continue to transplant autumn-sown plants.
Carrots	Sow early and main-crop varieties at the beginning of month, using a seed dressing to prevent carrot fly.
Cauliflower	Plant out early raised cauliflowers for a succession, and protect with cloches.
Celery	Prick plants raised in heat into boxes or frames and prepare trenches 2 ft. wide and 6 ins. deep, for early planting.
Lettuce	Sow small quantities of Favourite or Trocadero Improved for a succession.
Leeks	Sow outdoors early for transplanting later.
Onions	Begin to harden-off young plants ready for planting out early next month.
Peas	Make two sowings of a second early variety and stake early sowings as soon as necessary.
Potatoes	Finish planting all varieties early this month.
Salads	Sow mustard, cress and radishes out of doors at intervals for a succession.
Seeds beds	Sow main crop Brussels sprouts, cabbage, cauliflower, kale and savoy in outdoor seed bed for planting in June.
Spinach	Make small sowings for a succession.
Turnips	Make sowing of Early Milan or Snowball on rich but firm soil.
General	Surface cultivate between rows of growing crops throughout the summer when soil and weather conditions permit to keep weeds under control and to produce a fine tilth on the soil surface.

Fruits

Blackcurrants	Spray bushes with lime-sulphur when the first leaves are about the size of a florin, to control big bud mite.

260

Fruit trees	Top-dress lightly with dung or compost to provide food and conserve moisture, and spray with lime-sulphur to control apple and pear scab.
Grafting	Graft early in the month.
Peach trees	Disbud peach shoots where necessary. Thin fruits partially at an early stage of their growth.
Cucumber	Towards the end of the month, sow ridge varieties in greenhouse, for planting outdoors later under cloches.

Flowers

Chrysanthemums	Place young early flowering plants in cold frame and keep closed for a few days, gradually hardening them off.
Flower garden	Prick off seedlings of bedding plants reared under glass and estimate the quantity of each for planting later. Sow hardy annuals where they are to flower.
Gladioli	Plant all classes of gladioli out of doors.
Herbaceous	Finish planting herbaceous plants in their permanent quarters.
Sweet Peas	Transplant autumn-raised seedlings 6 ins. apart and give support.
Lawns	Give spring dressing.

Vegetables MAY

Asparagus	Begin to cut 2-3 in. shoots.
Beet	Sow maincrop beet such as Detroit Globe towards middle of month.
Brassica family	Plant out spring-sown cabbage, savoy, curly greens and Brussels sprouts when ready to handle, dusting the dibbled holes with 4% calomel dust as a club root control measure.
Broccoli	Early in the month sow St. George, Royal Oak and other suitable varieties in prepared seed bed. When present season's crop is finished, clear the ground and manure in readiness for leeks.
French and runner beans	Make sowings of both about middle of month.

Herbs	Plant out those raised from autumn cuttings.
Onions and leeks	Plant out those raised under glass during the first week.
Peas	Continue to make sowings for a succession.
Potatoes	Break up soil between rows and earth up early varieties when haulm is about 6 ins. high.
Salads	Continue to make sowings of lettuce, mustard, cress and radishes for a succession.
Turnips and swedes	Sow swedes and a few more turnips early in the month allowing 22 ins. between rows and thin early sown turnips 3 ins. apart.

Fruits

Apple trees	Apply lime-sulphur spray to control apple scab before flowers open. Dilute as recommended on container.
Peach trees	Continue to thin fruits where necessary. Tie in young shoots and syringe trees daily to check red spider mite.
Tomatoes	Transfer plants to cool house.
Vines	In fine weather late vines require little or no fire heat.

Flowers

Bedding plants	Harden off and plant out towards end of month.
Chrysanthemum	Early in the month plant out of doors early flowering varieties.
Greenhouse	If weather is warm and sunny, lightly shade glass and ventilate freely.
Herbaceous border	Thin out, stake and neatly tie up plants where necessary.
Rose garden	Keep look out for greenfly and spray with derris or nicotine if necessary.
Wallflower	Sow in open about the third week in the month for transplanting later.

Vegetables

JUNE

| Broccoli | Plant out heading-type broccoli in their permanent quarters towards end of month. |

Cabbage	Continue to plant late varieties for winter supply.
Endive	Sow green curled summer endive, and thin out to 9 ins. apart.
Peas	Make final sowing of peas early in month and continue to stake earlier sowings.
Green vegetables	Continue to plant out Brussels sprouts, kale, savoys and leeks.
Leeks	Commence to plant outdoor sown leeks when large enough.
Parsley	Make small sowing Myatt's Garnishing for spring supply.
Potatoes	Fork between rows, and earth up main crop varieties.
Root crops	Thin beet to 8 ins., carrot to 3 ins., parsnip to 9 ins., early turnips to 6 ins. and swedes to 9 ins. apart.
Marrow	Plant out hardened-off plants and water freely.

Fruits

Apples	Spray trees with lime-sulphur solution against scab.
Peaches	Thin out fruits to 9 ins. apart each way.
Strawberries	Straw down beds to keep fruit clean.
Vines	Thin berries, taking care not to damage those intended to remain. Tie up shoulders and remove tendrils.

Flowers

Bedding plants	Continue to plant these out in the flower garden.
Biennials	Sow canterbury bells, aquilegia, hollyhock and polyanthus in a prepared seed bed.
Carnations	Disbud border carnations, and carefully stake plants.
Chrysanthemums	Pinch out terminal bud of each main shoot to encourage strong lateral shoots for flower production.
Greenhouse	Dry off cyclamen. Plunge heaths and azaleas for summer. Feed flowering plants with liquid manure.
Sweet Peas	Remove weathered blooms and tendrils and give weak liquid manure.

Vegetables # JULY

Broccoli	Continue to plant out heading broccoli into firm soil, placing them in rows 2½ ft. apart with 2 ft. between each plant.
Carrots	Lift early-sown carrots for use as required when ready.
Cabbage	Sow McEwan's Early at the end of month for planting out in autumn, ready for spring cutting.
Cauliflower	Plant out late crops 2 ft. apart each way.
Celery	Finish planting late supplies early in the month, and loosely tie the leaves of early crops, keeping them all well watered.
Endive	Sow in cold frame.
Leeks	Finish planting late crop, and keep early plants watered and fed with liquid manure.
Onions	Make two sowings of Silver-skinned Bunching, a fortnight apart, for pulling in spring.
Parsley	Make final sowing in frame for spring use.
Potatoes	Lift early varieties as and when ready for use. Earth up and spray late crops with Bordeaux Mixture to prevent blight.
Salads	Sow lettuce, radishes, mustard and cress frequently.
Shallots	Lift and thoroughly dry off plants when foliage dies down.
Spring cabbage	Sow McEwan's Early about the third week of the month for autumn transplanting and cutting in spring.
Tomatoes	Keep side shoots pinched out, tie in growing points and top dress with complete fertiliser at end of month.
Turnips and swedes	Thin out early sowings and make a final sowing. Thin swedes to 9 ins. apart.

Fruits

Apples & pears	Shorten the lateral shoots of trees growing against walls to 6 leaves.
Vines	Syringe vines on which fruit is growing frequently to keep foliage healthy.
Strawberries	After fruiting, weed all beds and remove runners not required for propagation.

Flowers

Biennials and perennials	Transplant seedlings of aquilegia, polyanthus, and wallflower 4 ins. apart each way.
Carnations	Propagate border varieties by layering.
Cinerarias and calceolarias	Transfer seedlings to 6-in. pots, placing them in a cold frame and shade from bright sun.
Herbaceous border	Cut out withered flower shoots to prevent seeding, and stake and tie flower stems that require support.
Rock garden	Many trailing plants, such as sun roses, will require to be kept within bounds by cutting out underneath over-grown shoots.

Vegetables AUGUST

Beans, runner	Give light dressing of manure. Pull pods at frequent intervals when young and tender.
Brussels sprouts	Sow small quantities thinly on about 12th August to provide plants for early cropping next year.
Cabbage	If a sowing of McEwan's Early was not made in July, sow early this month for autumn planting to be used in spring.
Celery	Loosely tie leaves of late variety and earth up plants.
Cauliflower	Sow an early variety in a cold frame for spring planting.
Endive	Prick out seedlings into cold frame.
Onions	Make a sowing of Ailsa Craig, early in month for use next year.
Potatoes	Continue to spray main crops with Bordeaux or Burgundy Mixture to prevent blight, if the weather is showery.
Shallots	If not already done, lift and dry off bulbs when the foliage has died down.

Fruits

Apples	Keep woolly aphis under control by painting infested areas on shoots with methylated spirits.
Blackcurrants	Dig up and burn bushes affected by reversion.

Peaches and nectarines	Tie in new shoots and expose to sun. Net fruits becoming ripe and water borders when necessary.
Plums	Prop the branches of trees carrying heavy crops.
Strawberries	Make and plant out new beds as runners become available.

Flowers

Annuals	Sow hardy annuals, such as cornflower, candytuft, Shirley poppies, to flower early next summer.
Bulbs	Prepare beds and plant daffodils. Pot up early batches of Roman hyacinths and Paper White narcissi.
Carnations	Finish layering border carnations.
Chrysanthemums	Disbud when necessary and feed with weak liquid manure.
Lavender	Cut flower spikes to dry and insert cuttings in cold frame.
Primulas	Pot up *Primula obconica* into 6-in. pots, keeping plants cool and shaded.
Propagation	Take cuttings of bedding plants and insert in cold frame.
Roses	Disbud bedding roses and control greenfly by spraying with nicotine, liquid derris or other suitable insecticides.
Shrubs	Clip yew hedges. Many kinds of shrubs should be propagated this month by inserting cuttings of half-ripened wood in a sandy compost.

Vegetables

SEPTEMBER

Beet and carrots	Lift and store early varieties in sand or peat. Use damaged roots at once.
Brussels sprouts	Prick out August-raised seedlings 4 ins. apart into a cold frame, or in a very sheltered area outdoors. They may also be left in the seed drills, if not overcrowded.
Cabbage	Plant out when ready July-sown seedlings of early varieties 15 in. × 12 in. apart.
Cauliflower	Continue to cover heads of maturing curds. Prick out August-raised seedlings 4 ins. apart into a cold frame.

Celery	Continue to earth up plants when soil is fairly dry.
Endive	To blanch, tie up maturing heads, or cover plants with inverted flower pots. Prick late-sown seedlings into cold frame.
Herbs	Cut and tie into bunches and dry off balm, rosemary, sage, tarragon, and thyme for winter use. Place a few cuttings of each in cold frame.
Leeks	Regularly hoe between rows to keep down weeds.
Lettuce	Sow either Arctic King or Iceberg for next spring's supply.
Onions	Early in month loosen roots with digging fork and later pull up bulbs and hang over trellis to dry.
Potatoes	Lift and store crops as they mature.
Marrow	Store mature fruits in cool, dry frost-proof place for winter use.

Fruits

Apples and pears	Pull early varieties and store in cool, clean frost-proof store.
Blackcurrants	Prune bushes by cutting away old wood, retaining young shoots for next year's fruit.
Raspberries	Cut out old fruited canes to allow young ones to mature.
Strawberries	If not already done, prepare ground for new plantation and plant out runners during dull weather. Keep beds already planted free from weeds.
Vines	Give plenty of air during day and remove superfluous laterals.

Flowers

Carnations	Plant border varieties in their flowering quarters, or pot up and winter in cold frames.
Chrysanthemums	Lift and place in greenhouse mid-season and late-flowering varieties which have been grown outdoors and ventilate freely.
Hardy annuals	Sow clarkia, godetia, etc., in light compost and prick out when ready into 4-in. pots for spring display in greenhouse.
Rambler roses	Prune old flowered wood when plants have finished flowering.

267

Shrubs — Transplant evergreen shrubs, watering them after planting. Many types of cuttings can be set out in frames.

Sweet Peas — Sow thinly in pots about middle of month and place in cold frame, keeping a watch for mice and slugs.

Vegetables

OCTOBER

Cabbage — Hoe between rows of early planted seedlings.

Cauliflower — Protect maturing heads of late varieties from frost by tying the leaves over curds.

Celery — Towards end of month finish earthing up main crop.

Chives — Lift and divide crowns: plant patches 6 ins. apart.

Endive — Continue to blanch heads as they are required.

Lettuce — Examine plants in frames, removing all decayed leaves, and slightly stir up the soil between the plants.

Onions — Store ripened bulbs in a cool, dry frost-proof shed.

Potatoes — Lift and store late varieties in pits, covering them with straw or turf and later with plenty of soil to exclude frost.

Rhubarb — Lift a few roots and expose to frost, before forcing crowns.

Root crops — Lift and store all carrot and beet roots in sand or peat.

Runner beans — Collect mature pods for drying.

Turnips and swedes — Draw some soil towards roots to protect them from severe frost.

Fruits

Apples and pears — Continue to pull and store late varieties. Apples keep best in an underground chamber which should be cool and slightly moist. Pears mature better in a warm, dry room.

Gooseberries — Propagtae bushes by cuttings of 12-in.-long shoots, removing buds from lower part and leaving only four on top. Insert them 4-6 ins. apart in rows 1 ft. asunder.

Vines	Maintain a buoyant atmosphere in vinery to prevent berries damping off.
Raspberries	Tie young canes to wire supports.
Tomatoes	Gather ripe fruit and store in warm dark place.

Flowers

Anemones	Plant tuberous-rooted anemones in open 4-5 ins. apart and at a uniform depth of 3 ins.
Crocuses	Plant corms in groups amongst shrubs and along edges of flower beds.
Chrysanthemums	Lift any late varieties still growing outdoors and place in greenhouse, supporting the plants with stout stakes. Ventilate freely but water with care.
Flower garden	When summer bedding plants are removed, fill the beds with wallflowers, narcissus and tulip bulbs.
Roses	May be planted any time between the end of the month and the end of March, when soil and weather conditions are favourable, in ground prepared well in advance of planting. Never plant in insufficiently prepared soil. It is better to prepare the site in autumn and defer planting till February or March.

NOVEMBER

Vegetables

Artichokes (Jerusalem)	Cut down stems to within one foot of ground, placing them around crowns to protect tubers from frost.
Brussels sprouts	These are winter and spring vegetables and should be left over, especially where supplies of cabbage are available.
Cauliflower	Keep seedlings in frames hardy by exposing them to the air at all times except during frost.
Celery	If not already done, finish earthing-up of plants, and protect heads from frost by placing a layer of straw or bracken fronds over them.
Digging	When soil and weather conditions permit, commence manuring and digging all vacant ground for next years' vegetable and flower crops.

Endive	Place a few plants in a frame for blanching.
Horse-radish	Lift crowns and make new bed.
Lettuce	Protect September-raised seedlings with cloches or Dutch lights.
Onions and shallots	Examine stored bulbs, removing any showing signs of decay.

Fruits

Blackcurrants	Prune out old wood, cutting to a fork, and retain young shoots to carry next year's crop. Using young shoots, take 9-12-in.-long cuttings, severing them beneath the lowest bud and removing the tip just above a bud, but not removing the buds. Insert them outdoors at 4-6-in. intervals in rows a foot apart.
Fruit store	Remove any fruit showing signs of decay.
Hardy fruit	Plant all kinds of fruit trees and bushes, if weather and soil conditions are favourable.
Peaches	Ventilate freely.
Pruning	Begin pruning fruit trees, though not in frosty weather.
Strawberries	Hoe to keep the ground weed-free between rows.
Gooseberry and red currant bushes	Late in the month protect buds from birds by placing strands of black cotton thread around and over the bushes, or use a net supported with stakes, etc.

Flowers

Bulbs	Towards the end of the end of the month, place early bulbous plants which have been under ashes or peat, in heat, as required—the temperature not to exceed 50° F./16° C.
Cinerarias	Give plenty of air, and control greenfly by fumigating the house frequently.
Chrysanthemums	Water sparingly and keep temperature relatively low but several degrees above freezing point. Disbud where necessary.
Dahlias	Early in the month lift and dry roots, afterwards placing them in a cool dry place, free from frost.
Greenhouse	November is usually a month of little sunshine, therefore, keep the temperature reasonably low to correspond with the limited amount of light.

Herbaceous border	Make new borders and plant when the soil and weather conditions are favourable.
Rock garden	Fix a piece of glass over hairy-leaved plants to protect from excessive water.

Vegetables

DECEMBER

Artichokes	Normally tubers are lifted as required, but if frosty weather is anticipated lift and store some in a dark shed as a precautionary measure.
Chicory	Take up a few roots and place in frame to blanch.
Digging	When soil and weather conditions are favourable, continue to dig and manure ground for next years' vegetable and flower crops.
Endive	Continue to blanch a few plants in frame.
Lettuce	Keep glass clean, in order to give the plants plenty of light.
Liming	Have soil tested for lime and, if required, apply it evenly over surface after digging.
Parsley	As a precaution against frosty weather diminishing the supply place a few plants in a frame or cover with cloches.
Rhubarb	Crowns which have been lifted and exposed to air should be placed in greenhouse for forcing.

Fruits

Hardy fruits	When soil and weather permit, plant all kinds of trees and bushes. In planting them against a wall, place base of stem about 6 ins. away from its foot.
Pruning	Continue pruning except in frosty weather.
Vines and peaches	Prune vine and peach trees. Wash down glass and woodwork, and limewash walls. Remove a few inches of top soil from borders, and replace with fresh loam plus a little bone meal and potash.

Flowers

Christmas roses	Place frame or cloches over plants just before blooms open.

271

Chrysanthemums	Keep plants which have finished flowering in a cold frame as 'stock plants' for propagation purposes.
Rock garden	Protect choice alpine plants from excess moisture by a sheet of glass supported on stiff wire.
Shrubs	Prune deciduous shrubs and trees to develop well-balanced specimens, but not in frosty weather.
Sweet Peas	Transfer autumn-raised plants to small pots and avoid using rich soil.

INDEX

Abies, dwarf, 247
Abies Forrestii, 231; *procera* (syn. *A. nobilis*), 231
Acer palmatum atropurpureum, 222; *p. septem-lobum*, 222
Achillea millifolium, 141; *roseum*, 141
Achilleas, 140; in rock gardens, 249
Aethionemas in rock gardens, 248
African Violets, 151-3
Agaricus campestris, 57
Agriotes, 32
Agrostis tenuis, 22, 23
Aldrin, 33, 35
Alkanets, 141; Dropmore, 141; Opal, 141
Allium sativum, 70; *schoenoprasum*, 69
Alliums in rock gardens, 248
Allosorus crispus, 184-5
Alpine houses, 154, 205; fumigation of, 155
Alpine rose, 243
Alpines, 153-6, 248-50; dwarf, 155-6; potting, 153; propagation, 155, 248-50; shading, 154-5; soil for, 155; under glass, 153-6; watering, 154
Alstroemeria chilensis, 141
Alyssum spinosum, 222
American Red-root, 224
Amphorophora cosmopolitana, 86
Anchusa italica, 141
Anchusas, 141; Dropmore, 141; Opal, 141
Andromeda floribunda, 227; *polifolia*, 227
Andromedas, 227, 253; Japanese, 227
Androsaces, 155; in rock gardens, 248
Anemone Allenii, 146; *alpina*, 157; *apennina*, 156; *blanda*, 157; *coronaria*, 157; *fulgens*, 157; *Halleri*, 157; *Hepatica* (syn. *H. triloba*), 157; *japonica*, 157; *j. alba*, 157; *nemorosa*, 146, 156, 193; *pulsatilla*, 157; *rivularis*, 157; *Robertsoniana*, 146; *sulphurea*, 157; *sylvestris*, 156
Anemones, 156-8, 184, 192, 269; fertilisers for, 158; harvesting, 158-9; in rock gardens, 248; propagation, 157; soil for, 158
Blue Bonnet, 146
commercial, 157-9
De Caen, 157-90. *Varieties:* His Excellency, 158; Mr. Fokker, 158; Hollandia, 158; Sylphide, 158

Japanese, 157
Mediterranean poppy, 157
rue, 193
St. Brigid, 158-9. *Varieties:* Lord Lieutenant, 158; The Admiral, 158; The Governor, 158
wood, 146
Antennaria doica, 251
Anthriscus cerefolium, 51
Antirrhinum asarinum, 160; *glutinosum*, 160; *majus*, 159; *sempervirens*, 160-1
Antirrhinums, 159-61; as biennials, 160; classification of, 159; fertilisers for, 159-60; from cuttings, 161; propagation, 159, 160; treated as annuals, 159
Amuraphis roseus, 85-6
Aphides, 85-7, 128, 174, 187, 188; as virus-carriers, 128; control of, 86
Aphis, blackcurrant, 86; gooseberry, 86; green apple, 85; leaf-curling currant, 86; leaf-curling plum, 86; peach, 128; root, 35; rosy apple, 85-6; strawberry, 87; woolly, 86-7
Aphis grossulariae, 86; *pomi*, 85; *pruni*, 86
Apples, 35, 85-6, 87, 88, 97, 100-4, 258, 262, 263; bark-ringing, 104; blossom wilt, 94; brown rot, 94; budding, 101-2, bush, 103-4; canker disease, 94-5; checking exuberant growth, 104; cooking, 104; cordons, 100-3; crab rootstocks, 89; cracking of, 92-3; dessert, 90, 99, 103, 104; dwarf bush, 84; English Paradise rootstocks, 89, 90; fertilisers for, 103-4; greenfly damage to, 85-6; half-standard, 104; harvesting, 98-9, 267, 268; Jaune de Metz Paradise rootstocks, 90; mildew, 93-4; mulching, 103; pests, 87; pruning, 97-8, 102, 103, 264; pruning bush, 103-4; pruning cordons, 102-3; rootstocks, 89, 90, 101-2; scab, 92-3, 104; self-fertile, 88-9; self-spurrers, 97-8; self-sterile, 88; spraying, 93, 94, 262, 263; standard, 104; storing, 99-100, 268; sulphur-shy, 93, 104; tip-bearers, 97; woolly aphis, 265. *Varieties:* Allington Pippin, 94, 97; Beauty of Bath, 93, 99, 103; Bismarck,

Apples—*cont.*
94; Bramley's Seedling, 88, 89, 104; Christmas Pearmain, 103; Charles Ross, 104; Cox's Orange Pippin, 93, 104; Egremont Russet, 103; Early Victoria, 88, 94, 104; Ecklinville Seedling, 94; Ellison's Orange, 88, 103, 104; Gladstone, 99; Golden Spire, 94; Grenadier, 104; James Grieve, 90, 97, 100, 103, 104; Lane's Prince Albert, 88, 93, 97, 99, 104; Laxton's Advance, 99, 103; Laxton's Fortune, 103, 104; Laxton's Superb, 102, 103; Lord Grosvenor, 94; Lord Lambourne, 103; Merton Prolific, 103; Irish Peach, 97; Newton Wonder, 93; Rival, 93; Stirling Castle, 93, 99, 102; Sunset, 103; Worcester Permain, 97
Aquilegias, 141, 263, 265
Arabis, 164
Arabis albida flore pleno, 140
Araucaria imbricata, 231
Arbor Vitae, 230
Arbutus unedo, 226
Arctic plants, 250-2; propagation, 251-2
Arctostaphylos alpina, 222, 251; *manzanita,* 227; *uva-ursi,* 222, 227, 251
Armeria maritima, 146, 250
Armerias in rock gardens, 249
Artemesia dracunculus, 52
Artichokes, Chinese, 69
Jerusalem, 268; harvesting, 271
Ashes, use of on clay, 15
Asparagus, 17, 35-7, 261; fertilisers for, 36; for decoration, 209. *Varieties:* Argenteuil, 37; Connover's Colossal, 37; Mary Washington, 37
Asparagus officinalis, 35-7
Aspidium aculeanum, 186; *angulare crustatum,* 186
Asplenium nitamuraria, 185; *trichomanes,* 185; *viride,* 185
Aster alpinus in rock gardens, 248
Asters, 139, 140, 141; Chinese, 145; in rock gardens, 249
Astilbe Davidii, 141; *Moerheimii,* 141
Astilbes, 207; Vesuvius, 141
Astragalus alpinus, 222
Athyrium filix-foemina, 185
Aubretias, 140; in rock gardens, 248
Aucuba japonica, cuttings, 217
Auriculas, 35, 149
Avens, mountain, 251
Azaleas, 149, 228, 263; deciduous, 226; Ghent, 226; honeysuckle, 226-7; Japanese, 226; trailing, 251. *See also* Rhododendrons

Balm, 51, 151; harvesting, 267
Barberries, 228-30; evergreen, as hedge, 220; Chinese, 229; common, 251; cuttings, 218; for heath gardens, 253;

Japanese, 230; propagation, 230; pruning, 229. *Varieties:* Autumn Beauty, 229; Autumn Cheer, 229; Brilliant, 230; Coral, 229; Fireflame, 229; Oregon Grape, 228, 229; Sparkler, 229; Wisley hybrids, 229
Bark-ringing, 104
Basic slag, 20, 36. *See also* Fertilisers
Basil, Bush, 51; Sweet, 51
Bay, dwarf, 235
Beans, 18, 26, 27, 38-40, 41, 42, 43; fertilisers for, 39; sowing, 28
broad, 28, 38, 39-40, 258; attacks by weevils, 39; black-fly on, 39. *Varieties:* Champion, 40; Exhibition, 40; Broad Windsor, 258; Green Windsor, 40; Longpod, 40, 258; Prolific, 40; White Windsor, 40
dwarf. *See* Beans, French
French, 29, 31, 38, 40, 70, 261. *Varieties:* Canadian Wonder, 40; The Prince, 40
runner, 29, 31, 38, 40, 261, 268; harvesting, 265. *Varieties:* Exhibition, 40; Prizewinner, 40; Scarlet Emperor, 40
Bearberry, 222, 227; Alpine, 251
Beech as hedge, 219; clipping, 219
Beet, 18, 27, 31, 261, 263; fertilisers for, 71; globe, 71; sowing, 29; storing, 71, 266, 268; tap-rooted, 71. *Varieties:* Bell's Non-bleeding, 71; Detroit Globe, 71, 261; Dobie's Purple, 71; Egyptian, 71
Begonia fuchsioides, 161; *Gloire de Lorraine,* 161; *Haageana,* 161; *rex,* 161; *semperflorens,* 161; *socotrana,* 161
Begonias, 161-2; as greenhouse plants, 162; fertilisers for, 162; fibrous-rooted, 161; foliage group, 161; from cuttings, 163; pendulous, 161; potting, 161, 162; propagation, 162-3; soil for, 161, 162, 163; species, staking, 163; tuberous-rooted, 161-3, 164; winter-flowering, 161
Bell-flowers, 146; Chimney, 168, 169; giant, 146; ivy-leafed, 146; nettle-leaved, 170; peach-leaved, 169-70
Berberis. *See* Barberries
Berberis acuminata, 229; *aggregata,* 229; *aquifolium* (syn. *B. Mahonia*), 229; *aristata,* 229; *Bealei* (syn. *Mahonia Bealei*), 229; *Darwinni,* 220, 229, 253; *Gagnepainii,* 229; *japonica,* 229; *polyantha,* 229-30; *replicata,* 230; *rubrostilla,* 229; *Sargentiana,* 220; *stenophylla,* 220, 230, 253; *s. corollina,* 230; *s. Irvinii,* 230; *s. nana compacta,* 230; *Thunbergii,* 230, 253; *T. atropurpurea,* 230; *T. minor,* 230; *virescens,* 230; *Wilsonae,* 229, 230; *Yunnanensis,* 229
Big bud mites, 109, 258, 260
Bilberries, 228, 252; propagation, 253
Bird's-foot trefoil, 147
Blackberries, 110-12; fertilisers for, 111;

Blackberries—*cont.*
propagation, 110-11; pruning, 111;
training, 111. *Varieties:* Ashton Cross,
111; Himalayan Giant, 110, 111;
John Innes, 111; Merton Thornless,
111; parsley-leaved, 111
Blackcurrants, 86, 89, 113-18, 259; big bud,
113-14, 259; classification of, 116-17;
fertilisers for, 116; propagation, 113,
114-16, 270; pruning, 116, 267, 270;
reversion, 113-14, 265; spraying, 114,
260. *Varieties:* Amos Black, 117;
Baldwin, 116, 117; Bangup, 117;
Black Bunch, 117; Black Champion,
117; Black Naples, 116; Blacksmith,
117; Boskoop Giant, 116, 117; Carter's Champion, 117; Cotswood Cross,
117; Coronation, 117; Daniel's September Black, 117; Davidson's Eight,
117; Dutch Black, 117; Edina, 117;
French Black, 116; Goliath, 117;
Hill-top Baldwin, 117; Hoogendyke's
Seedling, 117; Invincible Giant Prolific, 117; Laxton's Giant, 117;
Laxton's Grape, 117; Lee's Prolific,
116; Mammoth, 116; Mendip Cross,
117; Mite Free, 116; Monarch, 117;
Nigger, 117; Ogden's Black Grape,
116; Prince of Wales, 117; Raven,
117; Seabrook's Black, 117; Silver-
gieter's Black, 117; Tinker, 117;
Tony Black, 117; Victoria, 117;
Wellington XXX, 117, 118; West-
wick Choice, 117, 118
Blackfly, 39
Blaeberries, 228
Blechnum spicant, 185
Blood, dried, 20
Bluebells of Scotland, 147
Bocconia cordata, 141
Bog gardens, 149, 157
Bog lilies, 157
Bog plants, 251-2
Bog violet, 251
Bone-meal, 18, 20, 43, 104, 107; steamed,
20, 21. *See also* Fertilisers
Bordeaux Mixture, 93, 114, 265
Borecole. *See* Kales
Box, as hedge, 218, 219; clipping, 218
Boysenberries, 112
Brambles. *See* Blackberries
Brassica oleracea Caulo-rapa, 70
Briar, Austrian copper, 204; common, 204;
Sweet, 204
Broccoli, 27, 44-6, 260, 261, 262, 264;
fertilisers for, 47; purple sprouting, 47;
results of overfeeding, 47; sowing, 29;
sprouting, 47; white sprouting, 47.
Varieties: Clucas's June, 46; Leaming-
ton, 46; Royal Oak, 46, 261; St.
George, 46, 261; Snow's Winter
White, 46
Brooms for heath gardens, 253

Bruckenthalia spiculifolia, 223
Brussels sprouts, 26, 27, 40-1, 47, 258, 260,
261, 263, 265, 266, 269; fertilisers
for, 41; sowing, 29. *Varieties:* Dalkeith,
41; Rous Lench, 41
Bryanthus empetriformis, 222
Buckthorn, sea, as hedge, 221
Budding, 89-92
Bulbous plants, 163-5
Bulbs, 140, 156, 163-5, 210-12, 257, 266,
269, 270; defined, 164; grown indoors,
165; potting, 156
Bullaces, 107
Bulrushes, 207
Burgundy Mixture, 265
Buttercups, 192
Butterfly flower. *See* Schizanthuses
Buxus sempervirens, 219

Cabbage-root fly, 44
Cabbages, 17, 18, 26, 27, 39, 40, 41-4, 47,
54-5, 257, 258, 260, 261, 263, 265,
266, 268; fertilisers for, 43-4; maincrop, 43; red, 43; sowing, 29; spring,
42. *Varieties:* Flower of Spring, 42;
Golden Acre, 43; January King, 43;
McEwan's Early, 42, 264, 265;
Paragon, 258; Winningstadt, 43, 258
Cacti, 165-8; edible fruits, 166; from
cuttings, 167; potting, 167; propa-
gation, 166, 167; soil for, 166, 167;
temperatures for, 166; watering, 167.
Varieties: Carrion Plants, 168; Hedge-
hog Thistles, 167; Nipple-bearers,
167; Old Man, 168; Torch Thistles,
167
Calceolaria Banksii, 138; *Clibranii*, 138
Calceolarias, 137-8, 265; greenhouse,
137-8; outdoors, 137-8; propagation,
138
Calendula officinalis, 144
Calico bush, 228
California lilacs, 224
Californian Poppy, 143
Calliopsis, 143
Callistephus, 145
Calluna vulgaris, 254; *v. Alportii*, 253, 254;
v. aurea, 254; *v. cupra*, 254; *v. Hammondii*, 253; *v. pygmaea*, 254; *v. Serlei*,
254
Callunas, 214, 254; propagation, 218
Calomel dust, 40, 41, 43, 44, 47, 261
Campanula alpina, 170; *carpatica*, 170;
cochlearifolia, 170; *c. alba*, 170;
garganica, 170; *g. hirsuta*, 170; *Campanula × G. F. Wilson*, 171; *glomerata*,
146, 169; *g. alba*, 169; *g. dahurica*, 169;
g. pallida, 169; *hederacea* (syn. *Wahlenbergia hederacea*), 146; *isophylla*, 168;
i. alba, 168; *lactiflora*, 169; *lactifolia*
(syn. *C. macrantha*), 146; *latifolia*, 169;
l. alba, 169; *l. macrantha*, 169; *Medium*,
168, 169; *muralis*, 170; *persicifolia*,

Campanula—contd.
169-70; *p. grandiflora*, 170; *p. g. alba*,
170; *p. Moorheimi*, 170; *pusilla*, 170;
pyramidalis, 168, 169; *p. alba*, 169;
rotundifolia, 147; *rotundifolia*, propagation, 147; *Campanula* × *Stansfieldi*,
171; *Trachelium*, 170; *Waldsteiniana*,
171
Campanulas, 140, 146, 168-71; for rock
gardens, 170, 248; hybrids, 171; in
pots; 168; propagation, 147, 168, 169,
170; potting, 169; rock, 170-1; soil for,
168. *Varieties:* China Cup, 170; Daisy
Hill, 170; Fairies' Thimbles, 170;
Moorheimi, 170; Profusion, 170;
Riverslea, 170; Telham Beauty, 170;
White Star, 170
Campion, moss, 252. See also Lychnis
Canary Creeper, 145
Candytuft, 265
Canker disease, 94-5
Canterbury Bells, 168-9, 263; in pots, 169;
watering, 169
Capitophorus fragariae, 87, 128; *ribes*, 86
Carabid beetle, 33
Caraway, 51
Cardamine pratensis, 251; *p. flore plenum*, 251
Carnations, 18, 32, 150, 171-2, 265;
'bizarres', 171; border, 249, 263, 267;
'fancies', 171; fertilisers for, 171;
'flakes', 171; for exhibition, 172;
layering, 265, 266; 'picotees', 171;
propagation, 171-2; 'self', 171; soil
for, 171; staking, 172
Carrot-fly maggot, 72
Carrots, 18, 27, 32, 71-2, 256, 258, 260,
263, 264, 266; soil for, 71; sowing, 29,
71; storing, 72, 266, 268; thinning
out, 72. *Varieties:* Amsterdam Forcing,
31, 71; Early Horn, 71, 258; Early
Market, 71; Early Nantes, 31, 71;
James's Scarlet Intermediate, 71;
St. Valery, 71
Carum carui, 51; *petroselinum*, 52
Caryopteris mastacanthus, 223
Cassiope lycopodiodes, 223; *selaginoides*, 223
Caterpillars, 41, 44; control of, 41;
spraying against, 44
Catmint, 140
Cauliflowers, 18, 26, 27, 31, 44-6, 257, 258,
260, 264, 265, 266, 269; fertilisers for,
45, 46; greenhouse, 46; protecting
curds, 46, 268; sowing, 29. *Varieties:*
All the Year Round, 45, 46; Early
Autumn Giant, 46; Early London, 31,
45, 46; Cambridge Early No. 5, 45;
Snowball, 31, 45; Veitch's Autumn
Giant, 46; Walcheren, 46
Caustic soda wash, 94
Ceanothus, 218, 224; cuttings, 224
Ceanothus Americanus, 224; *azureus*, 224;
Gloire de Versailles, 224; *Henri Defosse*,
224; *thyrsiflorus*, 224; *Veitchianus*, 224

Cedars, 230, 232; dwarf, 232; Japanese,
232; Lebanon, 232; Mount Atlas, 232
Cedrus atlantica, 232; *a. aurea*, 232; *deodara*,
232; *Libanii*, 232
Celandines, 156
Celeriac, 71, 73
Celery, 17-18, 27, 31, 55-6, 73, 75, 258,
260, 264, 265, 267, 268; blanching,
55-6; fertilisers for, 55; protecting
from frost, 269; self-blanching, 31, 55,
56; sowing, 29. *Varieties:* Dobie's
Invincible White, 55; Giant White,
55; Golden Self-blanching, 55; Major
Clark's Red, 55; Paris Golden Self-
blanching, 55; Superb Pink, 55
Centaurea Cyanus, 143; *imperialis*, 143
Centipedes, 34
Cephalocereus senilis, 168
Cerastium, 250
Cereus, 167; *triangularis*, 166
Chalk, 63; plants, 141
Chamaecyparis pisifera. See Cupressus pisifera
Chamaecyparis Lawsoniana. See Cupressus
Lawsoniana
Cheiranthus Allioni, 213; *alpinus*, 213-14;
cheiri, 212; *linifolius*, 214
Cherries, blossom wilt, 94; brown rot, 94
Chervil, 51
Chicory, 69; blanching, 270
Chimonanthus fragrans, 148
Chinese kidney-bean tree, 226
Chinese Pinks, Gaiety, 143
Chionodoxas, 156
Chives, 69, 256, 268
Choisya ternata, cuttings, 218
Christmas Roses, 270
Chrysanthemums, 21, 173-5, 257, 259, 261,
262, 263, 266, 267, 269, 270; cuttings,
174; disbudding, 173; fertilisers for,
174; incurves, 175; pests, 173-4;
pinching out, 173; propagation, 257,
259; reflexes, 175; soil for, 174;
spraying, 174; under glass, 174-5
early flowering, 173, 175. *Varieties:*
Alfreton Yeoman, 175; Apricot Sylvia
Riley, 175; Brenda Talbot, 175;
Bronze George McLeod, 175; Chats-
worth, 173; Ermine, 175; Evelyn
Bush, 175; George McLeod, 175;
Peter Shoesmith, 175; Rosespray, 173;
Sunavon, 175; Sylvia Riley, 175;
Theta, 173; Westfield Flame, 175
late-flowering, 174-5. *Varieties:* Ada
Stevens, 175; Aristocrat, 175; Bal-
combe Perfection, 175; Loveliness, 175;
Madonna, 175; Mayford Perfection,
175; Pioneer, 175; Princess Anne, 175;
Tangerine, 175
Cichorium endivia, 69; *intybus*, 69
Cineraria grandiflora, 139; *intermedia*, 139;
stellata, 139
Cinerarias 139, 265, 270
Cistus, 235-7; *crispus*, 236; cuttings, 218;

Cistus—cont.
  cyprius, 236; *hirsutus*, 237; *ladaniferus*,
    236; *l. albiflorus*, 236; *laurifolius*, 236;
    monspeliensis, 237; *obtusifolius*, 237; *pur-
    pureus*, 237; *salvifolius*, 237; *Silver Pink*,
    237; *villosus*, 236, 237
Cladosporium fulvum, 79
Clarkia elegans, 143. *Varieties:* Glorious, 143;
    May Blossom, 143; Orange King, 143;
    Purple King, 143; Salmon Queen, 143
Clarkias, 143, 267
Clematis, 175-8; cuttings, 176; Downy,
    176; fertilisers for, 175; layering, 176;
    montana group, 175; propagation, 176;
    soil for, 175-6. *Varieties:* Belle of
    Woking, 177; Comtesse de Bouchard,
    177; Duchess of Edinburgh, 177;
    Lady Landesborough, 177; Lady
    Northcliffe, 177; Lucie Lemoine, 177;
    Madame Edouard André, 177; Mrs.
    George Jackman, 177; Nellie Moser,
    177; President, 177; Star of India,
    177; The Queen, 177; Ville de Lyon,
    177; Virgin's Bower, 177
Clematis florida, 177; *Fortunei*, 177; *Hender-
    sonii*, 177; *heracleaefolia Davidiana*, 177;
    integrifolia, 177; *Jackmanii*, 177; *lanugi-
    nosa*, 177; *l. Henryii*, 177; *l. hybrida
    Sieboldii*, 177; *macropetala*, 176; *montana*,
    176; *m. rubens*, 176; *patens*, 177; *recta*,
    177; *tangutica*, 176; *vitalba*, 176;
    Viticella, 177; *V. alba lucuriens*, 178;
    Wilsonii, 176
Click beetle, 32-3
Cloches, 31, 45, 258
Clover, 23
Clubroot, 26, 40, 42, 43; precautions
    against, 40, 42
Cockchafer grubs, 34-5
Colchicum, 163
Columbines. *See* Aquilegias
Compost, 13, 14, 16, 18, 19, 21, 43, 54, 107
Cone Flower. *See* Rudbeckias
Conifers, 156, 230-3; propagating, 230,
    231; pruning, 231
Coreopsis, 142, 144-5. *Varieties:* Crimson
    King, 145; Yellow Beauty, 145
Coreopsis bicolor, 144-5; *grandiflora*, 145;
    tinctoria, 145
Corms, 163-5, 178; defined, 164
Corn cob. *See* Sweet Corn
Cornflowers, 143, 265
Cornus mas, cuttings, 217
Cornus Spaethii, cuttings, 217
Cotoneaster adpressa, 223; *congesta*, 223;
    microphylla glacialis, 223; *thymifolia*, 223
Cotoneasters, 223
Couch grass, eradicating, 21
Cowslips, 149; Himalayan, 197
Crambe maritima, 37
Crane-fly, 33-4
Cranes-bill, 141
Crassulas, 167

Crataegus macrantha as hedge, 221
Cress, 73, 75; Mediterranean, 156, 250
Crinkle, 128-9
Crocus biflorus, 179, 180; *candidus*, 179;
    chrysanthus, 179; *imperati*, 179; *reticula-
    tus*, 179; *sativus*, 179; *Sieberi*, 179; *speci-
    osus*, 179-80; *Susianus*, 180; *Tomasianus*,
    180; *vernus*, 180; *versicolor picturatus*, 180
Crocuses, 156, 163, 178-80, 268; avoiding
    bird-damage, 179; Dutch, 179, 180; in
    greenhouses, 178; in rock gardens,
    248; indoors, 165, 178; propagation,
    178; saffron, 179; Scotch, 179; traps
    for mice, 179. *Varieties:* Cloth of Gold,
    180; Cloth of Silver, 180
Crop-rotation, 26-9, 39, 40, 41, 42, 43, 53,
    124; scheme for 27-8
Cross-pollination, 87-9
Cryptomeria japonica, 232; *j. albo-variegata*,
    232; *j. elegans*, 232; *j. nana*, 232
Cuckoo flower, 251
Cucumbers, 47-50, 261; fertilisers for, 49;
    in frames, 49-50; in greenhouses, 47-9;
    ridge, 50; temperature required, 48-9.
    Varieties: Conqueror, 50; King of the
    Ridge, 50; Ridge King, 50; Telegraph,
    50
Cudweed, mountain, 251
Cupressus Lawsoniana, 220, 232; *L. Allumi*,
    232; *L. argentea*, 232; *L. conica*, 232;
    L. erecta-viridis, 232; *L. Fletcherii*, 232;
    L. Fraserii, 232; *L. Stewartii*, 232;
    macrocarpa as hedge, 221; *pisifera*, 232;
    p. plumos alba picta, 232; *p. squarosa*, 232
Currants, 86, 88; aphis, 86. *See also* Black-
    currants and Red currants
Cushion pink, 252
Cuttings, 249; 'soft', 249
Cyclamen europaeum, 156
Cyclamens, 156, 164, 263
Cypresses, 220, 221, 231, 232, 247;
    as hedges, 220, 221, 231; dwarf, 247;
    Lawson's, 220, 232; Monterey, 221;
    Sawara, 232; swamp, 231. *Varieties:*
    Silver Queen, 232; Triomphe de
    Boskoop, 232
Cytisus, cuttings, 218; *albus*, 253; *praecox*,
    253; *scoparius*, 253; *s. Andreanus*, 253;
    s. sulphureus, 253

Daboecia cantabrica, 227; *polifolia*, 227
Daddy-long-legs, 33-4
Daffodils, 140, 149, 163, 164, 265; com-
    mon, 164; fertilisers for, 164; grown
    indoors, 165; naturalising, 164; soils
    for, 164. *Varieties:* Amateur, 164;
    Carlton, 164; Golden Harvest, 164;
    John Evelyn, 164; King Alfred, 164;
    Scarlet Elegance, 164; Unsurpassable,
    164
Dahlias, 161, 180-2, 258, 259; cuttings,
    180; disbudding, 181; fertilisers for,
    181; for exhibiting, 181; propagation,

Dahlias—*cont.*
180; soil for, 181, spacing of plants, 181; staking, 181; storing tubers, 270
Cactus, 181. *Varieties:* Doreen Wallace, 181; Doris May, 181; Elizabeth Sawyer, 181; Golden Apricot, 181
Coltness, 181. *Varieties:* Coltness Gem, 181; Paisley Gem, 181; Princess Marie José, 181; Shirley Yellow, 181
Pompon, 181-2. *Varieties:* Glow, 182; Ideal, 182; Little Beeswing, 182; Queen of the Whites, 182
Daisies on lawns, 23
Damping-off, 249
Dandelions on lawns, 21, 23
Daphne alpina, 234; *Blagayana,* 234-5; *Cneorum,* 234; *C. grandiflora,* 234; *collina,* 235; *Genkwa,* 235; *Laureola,* 233, 235; *L. Philippi,* 235; *Mezereum,* 233, 235; *M. album,* 235; *petraea* (syn. *D. rupestris*), 234; *pontica,* 235; *sericea,* 235
Daphnes, 149, 233-5; Cneorum, 234; Collinae, 234; dwarf, 156; from cuttings, 233; from seed, 234; Garland Flower, 234; grafting, 233-4; Japanese, 235; Laureola, 235; Mezereon, 235; poisonous, 235; propagation, 233-4; soil for, 234
Dard, 96
D.D.T., 33, 35, 64. *See also* Insecticides
Delphinium Belladona, 141
Delphiniums, 139, 140, 141, 182-4; cuttings, 182; diseases, 183-4; division of, 183; fertilisers for, 182; layering, 183; pests, 183; propagation, 182, 183; soil for, 182; staking, 183. *Varieties:* Blue Gown, 141; D. B. Crane, 141; Hudson Dell, 141; Lady Eleanor, 141; Wendy, 141
Deodar, 232
Derris, 39, 41, 44, 65, 86, 87, 115, 174, 201, 266
Destructive Insect and Pests Act, 65
Deutzia gracilia, cuttings, 217
Dianthus alpinus, 156; *Heddewigii,* 143; *neglectus,* 156
Dianthus, 150; in rock gardens, 248, 249
Dicentra spectabilis, 140
Diervilla (syn. *Weigela*), cuttings, 217
Digging, 14-17, 27, 269, 271; double-, 14-17, 27, 83
Diploids, 88
Docks, 21
Dovedale Moss, 252
Draba, 250
Drainage, 14
Drought, effects of, 18
Dryas octopetala, 251
Dutch lights, 45, 46, 55, 126, 127, 158; heating, 30; protection from frost, 31
'Dusty Millers.' *See* Auriculas
Dwarf Bay, 235

Echinocactus, 167
Eelworm, chrysanthemum, 173-4; phlox, 195; potato, 68; strawberry, 129
Eleagnus reflexa as hedge, 220
Emilia flammea (syn. *Cacalia coccinea*), 145
Endives, 69-70, 73, 74, 263, 264, 265; blanching, 74, 267, 268, 270, 271. *Varieties:* Green Batavian, 69; Green Curled, 69, 74; Round-leaved Batavian, 74
Enkianthus campanulatus, 227; *perulatus,* 227
Erica arborea, 254; *carnea,* 253, 254; *ciliaris,* 254; *c. alba,* 254; *cinerea,* 253; *Lawsoniana,* 254; *lusitanica,* 254; *mediterranea,* 254; *tetralix,* 254; *vagans,* 254; *v. grandiflora,* 254; *v. rubris,* 254
Ericas, 218, 251, 253, 254; propagation, 218
Erigeron alpinus, 251
Eriosoma lanigerum, 86-7
Erysimum linifolius, 214; *Perfskianum* Golden Gem, 214
Escallonia Edinensis, 225; *langleyensis,* 224-5; *macrantha,* 224; *Philippiana,* 224, 225; *punctata,* 225
Escallonias, cuttings, 217; Donard's Seedling as hedge, 220
Eschscholtzia californica, 143
Eucryphia cordifolia, 227; *pinnatifolia,* 227-8
Euonymus radicans variegatus, 219
Evening Primrose, 150

Fagus sylvatica, 219
Fennel, 51
Fennel-flower. *See* Love-in-a-mist
Ferns, 184-6; as house plants, 186; beech, 185; buckler, 185; common male, 185; common polypody, 185; 'flowering', 186; for greenhouses, 185; hard, 185; hart's-tongue, 186; lady, 185; oak, 185; on walls, 185; parsley, 184-5; prickly, 186; prickly shield, 186; propagation, 184; royal, 184, 185-6; sites for, 184; soil for, 185
Fertilisation. *See* Pollination
Fertilisers, 13, 14, 16, 17-20, 21, 22, 27, 28, 36, 39, 41, 43, 46, 47, 48, 49, 54, 55, 56, 58-9, 60, 63, 67, 70, 71, 78, 79, 84, 103, 104, 107, 111, 116, 120, 122, 158, 159-60, 164, 171, 182, 198-9, 201; compound, 20-1; containing aldrin, 35; lawn, 22; phosphatic, 20
Festuca fallax, 22, 23
Fetterbush, North American, 227
Filberts, 88
Finger-and-toe disease, 26, 40, 42; precautions against, 40, 42
Firs, 230, 231
Flame flowers. *See* Phloxes
Fleabane, 251
Fleshy-rooted plants, propagation, 250
Flowering Spurge, 235
Flowers, 136-214, 257, 258, 259, 261, 262,

Flowers—*cont.*
   263, 265, 266, 267, 269, 270, 271;
   cultivation, *see* individual flowers;
   fertilisers for, 142; for greenhouses,
   151; hardy annuals, 142-5; perennials,
   141-2; propagation, 142-3, 266
Foeniculum vulgare, 51
Forget-me-nots, 164, 165
Fork, digging, 12, 15
Forsythia suspensa, 225
Forsythias, cuttings, 217
Fragrant plants, 148-51
Frames, 30-1, 45, 55, 126-8, 256, 257;
   crops for, 31; fertilisers for, 30; making
   beds for, 30-1
Frankenia laevis, 147
French gardening, 29-31; fertilisers for,
   30; use of cloches, 31
Fritillarias, 156
Frost, protection from, 31
Fruits, 82-133, 256, 258, 259, 260-1, 262,
   263, 264, 265-6, 267, 268-9, 270, 271;
   budding, 89; cordons, 84; cross-
   pollination, 87-9; cultivation, *see*
   individual fruits; dwarf pyramidal,
   83; effects of frost on, 83; fan-trained
   trees, 84; fungoid diseases, 92-5;
   greenfly damage to trees, 85-7; harvesting, 98-9; pests, 85-7; planting,
   84; preparation of soil, 83; pruning,
   84, 94-8, 257, 259, 264, 267, 270, 271;
   scab, 92-3; soils for, 83; spraying, 257,
   258, 260; storing, 98-100; winter-
   pruning, 94-8
Fumigation, 153
Fungicides, 92-5, 104
Fungoid diseases, 26, 92-5
Funkias, 140
Fusarium, 59
Fuchsia macrostemma Riccartoni as hedge, 220
Fuchsias, 258, 259; cuttings, 217

Garden chafer, 35
Garlic, 70
Garrya elliptica, 217, 220, 225; as hedge,
   220; cuttings, 217
Gaultheria, 228; *cuneata,* 228; *nummularioides,*
   228; *tetramera,* 228
Genista hispanica, 253
Gentiana asclepiadea, 157; *verna,* 147
Gentians, 157; in rock gardens, 248
Geophilus, 34
Geranium armenum, 141
Geraniums, 141; in rock gardens, 248
Germination, 28
Gilia lutea (syn. *Leptosiphon aureas*), 145
Gladioli, 163, 173, 186-9, 261; fertilisers
   for, 187; for exhibition, 187, 189; pests,
   187; propagation, 188; soil for, 187;
   storing corms, 188. *Varieties:* Abu
   Hassan, 189; Allard Pierson, 189;
   Belle Jaune, 189; Bloemfontein, 189;
   Blue Sky, 189; Circe, 189; Dr.

Fleming, 189; Evangeline, 189; Fire-
   brand, 189; Harry Hopkins, 189;
   Karen, 189; Kosmos, 189; Life
   Flame, 189; Marshal Montgomery,
   189; New Europe, 189; Picardy, 189;
   Ravel, 189; Snow Princess, 189
Butterfly, 189. *Varieties:* Elf, 189; Gipsy
   Love, 189; Melody, 189
Primulinus type, 189. *Varieties:* Bolinde,
   189; L'Innocence, 189; Scarletta,
   189; Souvenir, 189
Gladiolus byrantinus, 186; *cardinalis,* 187;
   Colvillei, 187; *Lemoinei,* 186; *tristis,*
   186, 187
Glaux maritima, 147
Goat's Beard, 141
Godetia amoena rubicunda (syn. *Oenothera
   amoena*), 144
Godetias, 144, 267
Gooseberry sawfly, 115
Gooseberries, 86, 88, 89, 113, 118-21;
   fertilisers for, 120; pests, 120-1;
   preventing bird-damage, 120, 270;
   propagation, 119-20, 268; pruning,
   120; spraying, 121
green skin, 118. *Varieties:* Howard's
   Lancer, 118; Keepsake, 118; Lancer,
   118
red skin, 118-19. *Varieties:* Dan's Mistake, 118; Lancashire Lad, 118; May
   Duke, 119; Warrington, 119; Whinham's Industry, 119
white skin, 118. *Varieties:* Careless, 119;
   White Lion, 118
yellow skin, 119. *Varieties:* Early Sulphur,
   119; Golden Ball, 119; Golden Bull,
   119; Langley Gage, 119; Leader, 119;
   Leveller, 119; Moss's Seedling, 119
Gorse, cuttings, 218; Spanish, for heath
   gardens, 253
Grafting, 89, 131-2, 261
Grape Hyacinths. *See* Muscaris
Grapes, 130-3, 258, 259, 262, 264, 267,
   269; fertilisers for, 132, 271; grafting,
   131-2; greenhouse temperatures, 133;
   harvesting, 133; layering, 131; propagation, 131; pruning, 132, 271; soil
   for, 132; spraying, 259; thinning-out,
   132; tying-up, 132. *Varieties:* Black
   Hamburgh, 130-1; Buckland Sweet-
   water, 131; Golden Chasselas, 131;
   Gros Colman, 130, 131; Gros Colmar,
   130, 131; Muscat of Alexandria, 131;
   Royal Muscadine, 131; Tynningham
   Muscat, 131
Grass of Parnassus, 148
Grasses, 22-3. *Varieties:* Brown-top Agrostis, 22, 23; Chewing's Fescue, 22, 23;
   evergreen rye-grass, 22
Greek Mallow. *See* Sidalceas
Green-petal virus, 129
Greenfly, 85-7, 128, 153, 174, 201, 262,
   270

Greenhouses, 46, 79, 125-8, 136-9, 257, 258, 259, 262, 270; fumigating, 153, 270; plants for decoration, 137-9
Griselinia littoralis as hedge, 221; cuttings, 217
Ground beetle, 33
Gypsophila elegans grandiflora, 144; *paniculata,* 141
Gypsophilas, 141, 144, 209. *Varieties:* Bristol Fairy, 141; Rosy Veil, 141

Harebell, 147
Hawthorn, 226
Hazel nuts, 88
Heath gardens, 253-4
Heathers. *See* Heaths
Heaths, 148, 223, 234, 253-5, 258, 263; layering, 255; planting, 254; prickly, 228; propagation, 218, 254-5; root division, 255; siting, 253; soil for, 253-4. *Varieties:* Cornish, 254; Dorset, 254; Irish, 227; King George, 254; Maweana, 254; Springwood, 254; Vivelli, 254; Winter Beauty, 254
Hedge-cutters, 13
Hedge Mustard, 214
Hedges, 150, 151, 204, 205, 218-21, 231, 266; clipping young, 219; cutting back, 219; fertilisers for, 218; flowering, 220-3; low, 220; miniature, 219; mulching, 218, 219; pruning, 218-19, 220; shape of, 221; soil for, 218
Hellebore, False. *See* Veratrum
Heleniums, 141. *Varieties:* Moerheim Beauty, 141; Riverton Beauty, 141; Riverton Gem, 141
Helianthemum alba plena, 238; *alpestre,* 237; *glaucum,* 238; *luteum,* 238; *nummularium* (syn. *H. vulgare*), 238; *sulphurea,* 238; *umbellatum,* 237; *venustum plenum,* 238
Helianthemums, 235, 237-8; cuttings, 218
Helianthuses, 144
Herbaceous borders, 139-42, 146, 160, 168, 169, 177, 194, 261, 262, 265, 271; area of, 139; management of, 140-1; siting of, 139
Herbs, 50-3, 262, 267; cuttings, 51
Hesperis matronalis, 150
Hexyl insecticide, 65
Hippophae rhamnoides as hedge, 221
Holly, clipping, 218, 219; for hedges, 218, 220; leather-leaved, as hedge, 219; trimming, 219
Hollyhocks, 262
Honeysuckle, 147, 150; evergreen, as hedge, 220; pruning, 220
Hoes, 13, 17
Hoof and horn meal. *See* Fertilisers
Horse-radish, 257, 269
Hot-beds, 49
Humus, 18-19

Hyacinths, 156, 163; grown indoors, 165; Roman, 266; wood, 184
Hydrangea petiolaris, 223, 225
Hydrangeas, 225; Parsival, 225
Hylocereus undatus, 166
Hypericums, cuttings, 217
Hyssop, 151

Iberis, 140
Ilex aquifolium crassifolium, 219
Indian maize. *See* Sweet Corn
Indian Pinks, Gaiety, 143
Insect pests, 26, 32-5
Insecticides, 39, 41, 44, 65, 201, 266
Ionopsidium acaule (syn. *Cochlearia acaulis*), 145
Iris graminea, 149; *histrioides,* 149, 156; *persica,* 156; *reticulata,* 149, 156; *r. Krelagei,* 149; *unguicularis* (syn. *stylosa*), 149
Irises, 149, 156, 165, 186; dwarf, 140, 156; grown indoors, 165
Ivy, 223

Japanese wineberry, 112
Jasminum cuttings, 217
John Innes composts, 76, 77
Julus (Blanjulus) Pulchellus, 34
Junipers, 230, 231, 232-3, 251; Chinese, 232-3; common, 233; dwarf, 233, 251; pencil, 233; procumbent, 233; propagation, 232; Savin, 233
Juniperus chinensis, 232-3; *communis,* 233; 251; *c. compressa,* 233; *sabina,* 233; *s. tamariscifolia,* 233; *virginiana,* 233; *v. aereo spica,* 233; *argentea,* 233; *v. glauca,* 233

Kainit, 20
Kales, 27, 260, 261, 26; sowing, 293
Kalmia angustifolia, 228; *latifolia,* 228
Kalmias, 228
Kerria japonica, cuttings, 217
Kohl Rabi, 70; Early Purple, 70; Early White, 70

Lady Laurel, 235
Lady's smock, 251
Larches, 231
Larix, 231
Larkspurs, 141, 182. *See also* Delphiniums
Lastrea dilatata, 185; *d. cristata,* 185; *filix-mas,* 185
Laurels as hedges, 221; Lady, 235; mountain, 228; sheep, 228; Spurge, 235; Portugal, as hedge, 221
Laurus nobilis, cuttings, 217
Lavatera, 144
Lavender, 151; dwarf, 223; harvesting, 266
Lavendula, 151; *vera nana compacta,* 223
Lawn-mowers, 13, 23
Lawns, 21-3, 258, 261; destroying leatherjackets in, 33-4; feeding, 23; grasses,

Lawns—cont.
22; moss on, 23; mowing, 23; sowing, 21-3; weed-eradicating preparations, 23; weeds in, 23; worm-casts on, 23
Layering, 171-2, 249
Leaf-curling aphis, 86
Leaf-miners, 174
Leather-jackets, 33-4; trapping, 34
Ledum buxifolia, 149
Leeks, 27, 39, 40, 53-5, 75, 258, 260, 261, 263, 264, 267; blanching, 54, 55; exhibiting, 54-5; fertilisers for, 54; sowing, 29. Varieties: Finney's Tynedale, 53; London Flag, 53; Musselburgh, 53; Northumberland Long Blanch, 55; Northumbrian, 53; Pot-, 53; Prizetaker, 53; The Lyon, 53; Walton Mammoth, 53, 55
Lenten roses, 184
Lettuces, 17, 31, 32, 73-4, 256, 257, 259, 260, 262, 264, 267, 271; fertilisers for, 74; sowing, 29. Varieties: All the Year Round, 74; Arctic King, 267; Continuity, 74; Favourite, 74, 260; Green Frame, 31; Gotté à Forcer, 31; Iceberg, 267; Trocadero Improved, 74, 260; Webb's Wonderful, 74
Lewisias, 156
Ligustrum ionandrum, 220; Delavayanum, 220; ovalifolium, 220; Prattii aureum, 220; vulgare, 220
Lilies, 156, 163, 173, 189-92, 234; as pot plants, 190; propagation, 190; sites for, 189-90; soil for, 189. Varieties: Annunciation, 191; Cottager's Orange, 191; Madonna, 191; Peruvian, 141; Queen of, 191; Regal, 191; Scarlet Turk's Cap, 191; Tiger, 192; Vermilion Brilliant, 190
Lilium auratum, 190, 191; a. platyphyllum, 191; Brownii, 190; candidum, 190, 191; chalcedonicum, 190, 191; croceum, 191; davuricum, 192; elegans, 191; formosanum, 156; giganteum, 191; Henryi, 191; longiflorum, 190, 191; regale, 190, 191; speciosum, 190; tenuifolium, 190; testaceum (syn. excelsum), 190; thunbergianum, 191; tigrinum, 190, 192; t. Fortunei giganteum, 192; umbellatum, 190, 192; u. Vermilion Brilliant, 190
Lily tree, 239
Lime, 18, 20, 34, 43-4, 45, 58, 270; effects of over-use, 21; garden, 21; ground, 63; hydrated, 21; testing soil for requirements, 21
Lime-sulphur, spraying, 65, 93, 94, 104, 109, 260, 262, 263
Limnanthes Douglasii, 145
Lings, 254; propagation, 254-5
Linnaea borealis, 147
Linums in rock gardens, 248
Lobel's Catchfly, 145
Loganberries, 112

Loiseleuria procumbens, 251
London Pride, 207
Lonicera, cuttings, 217; nitida, 220
Lotus corniculatus, 147; c. flore pleno, 147
Love-in-a-mist, 144
Lowberries, 112
Lowland plants, native, 146-8
Lupins, 139, 140, 141; Russell, 141
Lupinus polyphyllus, 141
Lychnis chalcedonica, 141
Lychnis, Jerusalem Cross, 141

Magnolia acuminata, 238; Campbellii, 240; conspicua, 239; c. alba superba, 239; fuscata (syn. Michelia fuscata), 240; glauca, 240; g. Thompsoniana, 240; grandiflora, 240; Halleana, 239; Lennei, 239; obovata, 239; Soulangeana, 239; stellata, 239; s. rosea, 239
Magnolias, 238-40; budding, 238-9; Chinese, 240; deciduous, 149; fertilisers for, 240; for the greenhouse, 240; grafting, 238-9; North American, 240; propagation, 238-9; protection from frost, 238, 240; rootstocks, 238; siting, 238; soil for, 238, 240; Swamp Bay, 240
Mallow, Rose, 144; Sutton's Loveliness, 144; Tree, 143
Mammillaria, 167
Mange-tout. See Sugar Peas
Manure, farmyard, 13, 14, 16, 18-20, see also Fertilisers; liquid, 18, see also Fertilisers; pigeon, 18, 19, see also Fertilisers; poultry, 18, 19, see also Fertilisers
Manuring for Fruit (Griffiths), quoted, 119
Maples, Japanese, 222
Marigolds, 144; Scotch, 144. Varieties: Lemon Queen, 144; Orange Queen, 144
Marjoram, 50; pot, 51-2; Sweet, 52
Marrows, 31, 47, 56-7, 262; bush, 56-7; fertilisers for, 56; storing, 266; trailing, 56-7. Varieties: Bush Green, 57; Bush White, 57; Long Green, 57; Long White, 57
Matthiola, 145, 150; bicornis, 145, 150
May-bug grubs, 34-5
Meadow Rue, 192-4; alpine, 192; cultivated, 193; fertilisers for, 192; habitat, 192; propagation, 192; lesser, 194; tuberous-rooted, 194; yellow, 193
Mediterranean cress, 156, 250
Melissa officinalis, 51
Melocactus, 167-8
Melolontha vulgaris, 34-5
Melons, 47
Mentha viridis, 52
Mertensia maritima, 148
Metaldehyde for slug-control, 183, 209
Metasequoia, 231
Mezerion. See Daphnes

Micháelmas Daisies, 139, 140, 141.
  Varieties: Gay Border Supreme, 141;
  Little Boy Blue, 141
Mignonettes, 150-1
Mildew, apple, 93-4; pea, 65
Milfoil, 141. *Varieties:* Cerise Queen, 141;
  Pearl, 141
Milkwort, sea, 147
Millipedes, 34; snake, 34; spotted, 34;
  trapping, 34
Mint, 50, 52, 151, 258; forcing, 52
Mock Orange, 151
Monkey Puzzle, 231
'Moorband', 14-15
Moraine, 146
Morisia hypogaea, 156, 250
Mosaic virus disease, 122
Moss Campion, 252
Moss, Dovedale, 252
Moss on lawns, 23
Mowrah Meal, 23, 34
Mulberries, 88
Mullein. *See* Verbascum
Muscari botryoides, 156
Muscaris, 156, 163, 198; 'Heavenly
  Blue', 156
Mushrooms, 57-9; medium for, 57-8;
  pests, 59; preparation of beds, 57-9;
  spawn, 58; temperature of house, 58
Mustard and cress, 73, 75, 256, 264
Mustard, Hedge, 214
Myrica cerifera, 149
Myrobalan plum, 83
Myrtle, North American Wax, 149
Myzus persicae, 128

Naphthalene, whizzed, as repellent, 33, 34
Narcissi, 156, 164, 269; Paper White, 266
Narcissus bulbocodium, 156; *cyclameneus,* 156;
  minimus, 156; *poeticus,* 164; *pseudo-
  narcissus,* 164; *triandus,* 156
Nasturtiums, 145; Tom Thumb, 145
National Growmore. *See* Fertilisers
Nectarines, 266
Nephrodium dilatatum, 185; *d. Cristata,* 185
Nettle-leaf disease. *See* Reversion
Nettles as breeding-places for aphides, 86
Newberries, 112
Nicotiana affinis, 150
Nicotine, 86, 174, 265. *See also* Insecticides
Nigella damascena, 144
Nitrate of soda. *See* Fertilisers
Nitro-chalk, 19-20, 122
Nitrogen, 17-21, 26, 27; atmospheric, 38.
  See also Fertilisers
Nutrients, plant, 17

Ocymum basilicum, 51; *officinalis,* 51
Oenotheras, 140, 150
Old Man's Beard, 176-7
Olearia Haastii as hedge, 220
Olearias, cuttings, 217
Onion-fly maggot, 61-2

Onions, 18, 27, 31, 39, 40, 59-63, 73, 256,
  257, 259, 260, 262, 264, 265, 267, 268,
  270; exhibiting, 61; fertilisers for,
  60, 61, 62; green, 75; harvesting, 62,
  267; pickling, 62; preparation of bed,
  60; raised under glass, 61; salad, 62;
  sets, 61-2; sowing, 29; storing, 62, 268;
  thinning-out, 60. *Varieties:* Ailsa Craig,
  62, 265; James's Long-keeping, 62;
  Kelsae, 63; Silver-skinned Bunching,
  62, 75, 264; Silver-skinned Pickling,
  62; Stuttgarter Riesen, 62; The
  Queen, 62; White Lisbon, 62, 75
Opuntia, 168; *ficus indica,* 166
Orchards, siting, 82-3
Oregon grape barbarry, 228, 229
Origanum majorana, 52; *onites,* 51
Osmanthus Delavavi, 149-50
Osmunda regalis, 184, 186; *r. Cristata,* 186
Ourisia elegans, 250
Oyster plant, 148

Paint-brush flower, 145
'Pan', soil, 14-15
Pansies, 140
Papaver Rhoeas, 144
Parnassia palustris, 148
Parsley, 50, 52, 263, 264, 271; Myatt's
  Garnishing, 263; sowing, 29
Parsnips, 27, 71, 72, 256, 259, 263; harvest-
  ing, 72; sowing, 29. *Varieties:* Hollow
  Crown, 72; Student, 72
Pasque flowers, 157
Peaches, 261, 262, 263, 266, 270; fertilisers
  for, 271; in greenhouses, 271; pruning,
  271; spraying, 259
Pearlwort, Alpine, 251-2
Pears, 88, 104-7; blossom wilt, 94; cordons,
  105-6, cracking, 92-3; cross-pollination, 106; dessert, 100; diploid, 106;
  espalier, 105-6; fertilisers for, 106-7;
  fungicide for, 93; harvesting, 98, 107,
  267, 268; pruning, 97, 264; rootstocks,
  90, 107; scab, 92-3, 105; self-fertile,
  88-9; self-sterile, 88, 89; soil for, 105;
  spraying, 93; storing, 99-100, 107, 268;
  test for ripeness, 100. *Varieties:* Beurre
  d'Amanlis, 89; Clapp's Favourite, 89,
  93, 105; Conference, 89, 93, 116;
  Dr. Jules Guyot, 105; Doyenne d'Eté,
  100; Doyenne du Comice, 93, 106;
  Fertility, 93; Glou Morceau, 106;
  Jargonelle, 89, 100; Joséphine de
  Malines 106; Laxton's Superb, 105;
  Louise Bonne d'Avranches, 105-6;
  Louise Bonne of Jersey, 105-6; Marguerite Marillat, 105; Pitmaston
  Duchess, 106; Souvenir de Congrès,
  105; William's Bon Chretien, 89
Peas, 18, 26, 27, 31, 38, 41, 42, 43, 63-5,
  259, 260, 262, 263; fertilisers for, 63;
  heights of varieties, 63; insecticides for,
  65; pests, 64-5; round-seeded, 63;

Peas—*cont.*
    sowing, 29, 64; staking, 64; sugar, *see*
      Sugar Peas; wrinkled, 63
    early dwarf, 29, 63. *Varieties:* Kelvedon
      Monarch, 63; Kelvedon Viscount,
      63; Kelvedon Wonder, 63; Laxton's
      Progress, 63; Little Marvel, 63;
      Meteor, 63; Peter Pan, 63
    late (main-crop), 63, 65. *Varieties:*
      Achievement, 65; Gladstone, 63;
      Lord Chancellor, 63
    second early, 63. *Varieties:* Admiral
      Beatty, 63; Onward, 63; Senator, 63
Peat, 13, 14-15; as substitute for farmyard
    manure, 182; gardens, 149. *See also*
    Fertilisers
Pemphigus auriculae, 35
Pernettya mucronata, 228, 253
Peruvian Lilies, 141
Phenomenal Berry, 112
Philadelphus, cuttings, 217
Philadelphus coronarius, 151; *Lemoinei*, 151
Phlox decussata, 196; *divaricata*, 194-5;
    d. alba, 194; *d. Lapham*, 194; *Douglassii*,
    194-5; *Drummondii*, 194; *D. cuspidata*,
    194; *D. fimbricata*, 194; *D. flore pleno*,
    194; *D. grandiflora*, 194; *D. nana*, 194;
    paniculata (syn. *decussata*), 142; *subulata*
    (syn. *setacea*), 194-5; *s. Nelsonii*, 195; *s.*
    Nivalis, 195; *suffruticosa*, 195
Phloxes, 140, 142, 194-6; eelworm, 195;
    large-flowered, 196; propagation, 194,
    195; soil for, 195; staking, 196
    Alpine, 195
    Annual, 194-5
    dwarf, 194-5. *Varieties:* B. E. Chalmers,
      195; G. F. Wilson, 195; Snow Queen,
      195; Sprite, 195; The Bride, 195;
      Vivid, 195
    herbaceous, 142, 195-6. *Varieties:* Border
      Gem, 196; Daily Sketch, 142, 196;
      Eva Foerster, 196; Karl Foerster,
      142; Leo Schlageter, 196; Zeppelin,
      142; Sir John Falstaff, 196; Titanic,
      196; Windsor, 196
Phorid fly, 59
Phosphate, 17. *See also* Fertilisers
Phyllodoce empetriformis, 222
Phyllocactus, 168
Picotees, 150
Pieris floribunda, 227, 253; *japonica*, 227
Pincushion Flower. *See* Scabious
Pines, 230; dwarf, 247
Pinguicula vulgaris, 251
Pinks, 18, 140, 150; border, 150; Chinese,
    143; cushion, 252; Indian, 143; sea,
    250
Pisum sativum saccharatum, 70
Pittosporum as hedge, 220
Plant labels, 13
Plantago, 86
Plaintains, 23, 86; as breeding-places for
    aphides, 86

Plums, 86, 88-9, 98, 107-10, 266; as hedges,
    219, 220; blossom wilt, 94; brown rot,
    94; cherry, 83; cross-pollination, 110;
    culinary, 109-10; dessert, 109-10; fan-
    trained, 108; fertilisers for, 109; frost-
    damage to, 108; myrobalan, 83, 219;
    propagation, 108; pruning, 98; root-
    pruning, 109; rootstocks, 90; self-
    fertile, 88-9; self-sterile, 88, 89; soil
    for, 108-9. *Varieties:* Coe's Golden
    Drop, 89, 109-10; Czar, 89, 109-10;
    Denniston's Superb Gage, 109; Early
    Laxton, 109; Gisborne's Prolific, 89,
    110; Golden Transparent Gage, 109;
    Jefferson's Gage, 89, 109; Kirke's
    Blue, 89, 109; Magnum Bonum, 110;
    Monarch, 110; Oullin's Golden Gage,
    89, 109; Pershore, 89; Pond's Seedling,
    89, 110; President, 109; River's Early
    Prolific, 110; Victoria, 89, 108, 110;
    Warwickshire Drooper, 110; Yellow
    Pershore, 108
Pollination, 87-9; by insects, 88; by wind,
    88; effects of wind on, 88
Polyanthuses, 184, 263, 265
Polydesmus complanatus, 34
Polygonum baldschuanicum, 225
Polypodium dryopteris, 185; *phegopteris*, 185;
    vulgare, 185
Polystichum aculeatum, 186; *angulare cris-*
    tatum, 186
Poor man's orchid. *See* Schizanthus
Poplars for shelter, 219; Lombardy, 219
Poppies, Alpine, 140; Californian, 143;
    in rock gardens, 248; Oriental, 140;
    Plume, 141; Shirley, 144, 266
Populus italica, 219
Portenschlagiana, 170
Portuguese Violet Cress, 145
Portulaca oleracea, 52
Pot plants, 21
Potash, 17, 18, 19-21. *See also* Fertilisers
Potash, muriate of, 20. *See also* Fertilisers
Potash, sulphate of, 17, 18-19. *See also*
    Fertilisers
Potato tree, 225
Potatoes, 18, 21, 27, 32, 41, 42, 43, 65-7,
    256, 260, 262, 263, 264, 265, 267, 268;
    blight-resistant, 66; diseases, 68; earth-
    ing-up, 67; eelworm, 68; fertilisers for,
    67; first early, 65; immune to wart, 65,
    66; lifting, 67; maincrop, 65; scab, 68;
    second early, 65; storing, 67-8; treat-
    ment of seed tubers, 66; virus diseases,
    65; wart disease, 65. *Varieties:* Arran
    Pilot, 66; Catriona, 66; Di Vernon, 65;
    Duke of York, 65-6; Dunbar Rover,
    66; Dunbar Standard, 66; Golden
    Wonder, 66; Home Guard, 66; Kerr's
    Pink, 66; Midlothian Early, 66;
    Redskin, 66
Potting, 136-9; soil for, 136-7
Pre-harvest hormone, 99

Prickly pears, 166, 168
Primroses, 149, 156
Primula alpicola (syn. *P. microdonta*), 197; *a. violacea*, 198; *capitata*, 198; *chionantha*, 198; *Cockburniana*, 197; *denticulata*, 196, 198; *d. alba*, 197; *d. magnifica purpurea*, 197; *farinosa*, 148; *f. scotica*, 148; *Florindae*, 197; *japonica*, 197; *Juliae*, 198; *Littoniana*, 198; *malacoides*, 137; *nutans*, 198; *obconica*, 137, 266; *o. gigantea*, 137; *pseudo-Sikkimensis*, 197; *pulverulenta*, 196; *rosea*, 197; *r. superba*, 197; *Sikkimensis*, 197; *sinensis*, 137; *unique*, 197; *vulgaris* (syn. *P. acaulis*), 148
Primulas, 35, 137, 148, 149, 156, 184, 196-8, 266; Chinese, 135; fertilisers for, 196; in rock gardens, 248; naturalising, 197; propagation, 137, 196-7; soil for, 137, 196. *Varieties:* Mauve Queen, 137; Pink Sensation, 137; Red Chief, 137; The Jewel, 198; Wyaston Wonder, 137
Privet as hedge, 220; Chinese species, 220; common, 220; cuttings, 217; golden, 220; oval-leafed, 220
Prunus cerasifera, 83, 220; *insititia*, 107; *lusitanica* as hedge, 221
Psalliota campestria, 57
Psila rosae, 72
Pulmonaria officinalis, 140
Purslane, 52
Pyrethrums, 142. *Varieties:* Dr. Borsch, 142; Eileen May Robinson, 142; James Kelway, 142; Mont Blanc, 142
Pyrola rotundifolia, 148; *uniflora* (syn. *Moneses uniflora*), 148

Quince rootstocks, 90

Radishes, 73, 74-5; 262, 264; sowing, 29. *Varieties:* Black Spanish, 75; French Breakfast, 75
Rakes, 12-13
Ramondia pyrenaica, 151
Ramondias, 156
Raspberries, 89, 112, 121-4, 269; fertilisers for, 121, 122; harvesting, 122; mosaic virus disease, 122, 123, 129; propagation, 121; pruning, 121-2, 123, 267; site for, 121; virus diseases, 129. *Varieties:* Antwerp, 122; Baumforth's 'A' and 'B', 122; Burnett Holm Seedling, 122; Hornet, 122; Lloyd George, 123; Malling Enterprise, 123; Malling Exploit, 123; Malling Jewel, 123; Malling Promise, 123; Norfolk Giant, 123; St. Walfried, 122-3; Seedling 'E', 123; Seedling, 'J', 123; Superlative, 106, 122
Red-core in strawberries, 129, 130
Red currants, 86; protection from bird-damage, 270
Red spider, 262

Reeds, giant, 207
Reseda odorata, 150-
Reversion, 109, 265
Rhododendron Augustinii, 242; *calophytum*, 242; *calostrotum*, 243; *campanulatum*, 242; *ciliatum*, 242, 243; *dauricum*, 242; *fastigiatum*, 243; *ferrugineum*, 243; *Fortunei*, 242; *Griffithianum*, 242; *hippophaeoides*, 243; *Loderi*, 242; *mollis*, 226; *pontica*, 226-7; *ponticum*, 241, 242; *praecox*, 242; *racemosum*, 243; *Yunnanense*, 242
Rhododendrons, 196, 234, 240-3; Chinese, 242; cuttings, 249; dwarf, 156, 243; dwarf alpine, 253; evergreen, 242; for rock gardens, 243; grafting, 241; layering, 242; propagation, 218, 241-2; pruning, 241, 243; rootstocks, 241; Sikkim, 242; siting of, 240; soil for, 240-1, 242; triflorum group, 242; use of peat for. *Varieties:* Alice, 243; Ascot Brilliant, 243; Britannic, 243; Christmas Cheer, 243; Corona, 243; Cunningham's Sulphur, 243; Cynthia, 243; Doncaster, 243; Duchess of York, 242; Duke of York, 242; Harmsworth Early, 243; Loder's White, 243; Mother of Pearl, 243; Pink Pearl, 243; Purple Splendour, 243; Royal Purple, 243
Rhubarb, 256, 268, 271; forcing, 268
Ribes grossularia, 118
Ringing, 250
Rock gardens, 146, 148, 149, 150, 160, 170, 184-5, 194, 205, 221, 230, 234, 237, 243, 246-55, 265, 271; alpines in, 248-50; construction, 246-8; shrubs in, 247-8; soil for, 247; suitable stone for, 246-7; trees in, 247-8
Rock roses, 235-7; hairy, 237; laurel-leaved, 236; propagation, 236, 237; Sunset, 236
Rockets, 150; double, 150
Rockfoils, 205-7; cushion, 205-6; encrusted, 205; finger-shape-leaved, 206-7; giant-flowered, 207; in rock gardens, 252; mossy, 206-7; propagation, 205; silvery, 205
Rocksprays, dwarf, 223
Rodgersias, 207
Root division, 248-9, 250
Rootstocks, 89-92, 101-2; Broad-leaved English Paradise, 102; Doucin, 102; English Paradise, 90; Jaune de Metz, 101, 102; Malling No. 1, 90; myrobalan B, 108; Paradise, 103; Paradise Type I, 102; Paradise Type II, 102; Paradise Type IX, 101, 102; quince, 90
Rosa centifolia muscosa, 203; *Davidii*, 203; *eglanteria*, 204; *ferruginea*, 204; *foetida bicolor*, 204; *Hugonis*, 203; *moschata*, 203-4; *Moyesii*, 204; *m. alba*, 204;

Rootstocks—*cont.*
m. *Nevada*, 204; *rubiginosa*, 150, 204; *rubrifolia*, 204; *rugosa*, 204; *r. alba*, 204; *r. atropurpurea*, 204; *servicea pteracantha*, 204; *Zephyrine Drouhin*, 204

Rose chafer, 35
Rose root, 250, 252
Rosemary, 151; harvesting, 266; marsh, 227; wild, 227
Roses, 21, 35, 139, 150, 198-205, 207, 262, 269; alpine, 243; as hedges, 204, 205, 220-1; Austrian copper briar, 204; Bourbon thornless, 204; briars, 204; budding, 203; bush, 199, 200; coral-thorn, 204; cross-pollination, 203; cuttings, 203; dog, 236; fertilisers for, 198-9, 201; grafting, 203; layering, 202-3; musk, 203-4; pests, 201; Poulsen as hedges, 220-1; preparation of beds, 198-9; pruning, 200, 259; ramanas, 204; rock, *see* Rock roses; scented, 150; soil for, 198-9, 202; spacing of bushes, 199; spraying, 201, 265; staking, 199; standard, 199; suckers, 201, 203; sun, *see* Sun roses; sweet briar, 204; *Wichuriana* group as hedges, 220; wild, 150. *Varieties:* La France, 150; Mrs. John Laing, 150
climbing, 150, 199-200; pruning, 200; tying-up, 201. *Varieties:* Climbing Madame Butterfly, 202; Climbing Peace, 202; Daily Mail, 202; Gloire de Dijon, 150, 202; Madame Edouard Heriot, 202; Maréchal Niel, 150; William Allan Richardson, 150
floribunda, 200; pruning, 200. *Varieties:* All Gold, 202; Dickson's Flame, 202; Else Poulsen, 202; Frensham, 202; Korona, 202; Masquerade, 202
hybrid perpetual, 200; pruning, 200. *Variety:* Frau Karl Druschki, 201
hybrid tea, 150, 200, 201; pruning, 200. *Varieties:* Ena Harkness, 201; Comtesse Vandal, 201; Glory of Rome, 201; Grandmere Jenny, 201; McGredy's Yellow, 201; Peace, 201, 202; The Doctor, 201
moss, 203; pruning, 203
rambler, 199-200, 202; pruning, 200-1, 267; tying-up, 201. *Varieties:* American Pillar, 202; Dorothy Perkins, 200, 202; Emily Gray, 202; Excelsa, 202
species, 202-4; as hedges, 204, 205; layering, 204; propagation, 202-3, 204; pruning, 203, 205; site for, 202. *Varieties:* Blanc de Coubart, 204; Jeannie Deans, 204; La Girada, 203; Lady Penzance, 204; Lord Penzance, 204; Meg Merrilees, 204
tea, 150, 200; pruning, 200

Rubus fruiticosus, 110; *laciniatus*, 111; *phoenicolasius*, 112
Rudbeckia speciosa, 142
Rudbeckias, 142
Rues, 52; columbine-leaved, 193; meadow, *see* Meadow rues; wall, 185
Ruta graveolens, 52

Sage, 50, 51, 52; harvesting, 267; *see also* Salvias
Sagina nivalis, 251
Saintpaulia diplotricha, 151, 152; *ionantha*, 151, 152; *i. grandiflora violacea*, 151; *i. albescens*, 151; *i. purpurea*, 151; *longwensis*, 151
Saintpaulias, 151-3; effects of overwatering, 153; fertilisers for, 153; pests, 153; potting, 153; propagation, 152-3; rooting in water, 152-3; *Varieties:* Beatrice, 152; Hermione, 152; Neptune, 152; Pandora, 152; Rainbow Rose, 152; Snow Line, 152
Salad crops, 68-71, 73-5
Salix herbacea, 250, 252
Salvia officinalis, 52; *superba*, 142; *virgata nemorosa*, 142
Salvias, 142
Salsify, 27, 71, 72
Sanguinaria canadensis, 250
Satureja hortensis, 52; *montana*, 52
Savory, 52; Summer, 52; Winter, 52
Savoys, 26, 27, 260, 261, 263
Saxifraga Allioni, 207; *aizoides*, 250, 252; *aizoon*, 205; *a. balcana*, 205; *a. flavescens*, 205; *a. lutea*, 205; *Boydii*, 206; *caespitosa*, 207; *cernua*, 252; *cordifolia*, 207; *cotyledon*, 205; *c. pyramidalis*, 205; *crassifolia*, 207; *crocea*, 207; *cuneifolia*, 207; *decipiens*, 207; *Delaveyi* (syn. *Yunnanensis*), 207; *Elizabethae*, 206; *Geum*, 207; *granulata*, 252; *Griesebachii*, 206; *Haagii*, 206; *hypnoides*, 252; *h. affinis*, 252; *h. Kingii*, 252; *h. Whitlavii*, 252; *Irvingii*, 206; *L. G. Godseff* (*Godseffi*), 206; *lingulata*, 205; *l. albida*, 205; *l. lantoscana*, 205; *l. superba*, 205; *longifolia*, 207; *luteo-viridis*, 206; *muscoides atropurpurea*, 207; *oppositifolia*, 206, 252; *O. alba*, 206; *O. biflora*, 206; *O. splendens*, 206; *O. Latina*, 206; *pygmea*, 207; *nivalis*, 252; *stellaris* 252; *Stribrnyi*, 206; *umbrosa*, 207; *Wallacei* (syn. *Composii*), 206-7
Saxifrages, 153, 156, 205-7; broad-leaved, 140; Dactyloides, 206-7; Englaria, 206; Euaizoonia, 205; in alpine houses, 205; in rock gardens, 248, 249, 252; Kabschia, 205-6; opposite-leaved, 206; Porphyrion, 206; purple-flowered, 206, 252; red-flowering, 206; Robertsonia, 207; sites for, 205; tufted, 205-6; Umbrosa, 207; yellow, 250. *Varieties:* Cherrytrees, 206; Dr. Ramsay, 205;

Saxifrages—*cont.*
Faldonside, 206; Guildford Seedling, 207; Tumbling Waters, 205
Scab, 68
Scabiosa caucasica, 142; *Goldingensis*, 142
Scabious, 142. *Varieties:* Clive Greaves, 142; Constancy, 142
Scarlet runners. *See* Beans, runner
Schizanthus, 138-9; Dr. Badger's hybrids, 139; danger of to tomatoes, 79; fertilisers for, 139
Schizophragma hydrangeoides, 225
Sciarid flies, 59
Scilla chinadoxa, indoors, 165
Scilla siberica, indoors, 165
Scillas, 163, 165, 184
Scolopendrium crispum, 186; *marginatum*, 186; *multifidum*, 186; *vulgare*, 186
Sea heaths, 147
Sea milkwort, 147
Sea pinks, 250
Seakale, 37-8; blanching, 38; fertilisers for, 38; forcing, 38; propagation, 37-8
Sedum roseum, 250, 252
Sedums, 153, 167, 250
Seed bed, preparation, 28; protection, 28
Seeds Act, 60
Seeds, sowing, 28-9
Senecio Clivorum, 207; *pulcher*, 207
Shallots, 27, 258, 269; harvesting, 263, 265
Shortia galacifolia, 156; *uniflora*, 156
Shrubs, 148-50, 216-43; as climbing plants, 223-6; creeping, 222; cuttings, 216-18, 229, 230; fertilisers for, 222; layering, 216, 229; peat-loving, 226-8; propagation, 216-18, 220, 223, 229, 230, 236, 266, 268; prostrate, 223; pruning, 218, 219, 221-2, 229, 241, 272; soils for, 221, 222, 226, 227; wall, 223-6; dwarf, 221-3, 253-5; dwarf, propagation of, 250
Sidalceas, Interlaken, 142; Sussex Beauty, 142
Silene acaulis, 252; *Armeria*, 145; *pendula*, 145
Silenes, Double Salmon Pink, 145; Dwarf Single Pink, 145
Silver leaf disease, 94, 110
Silver Leaf Order (1923), 94
Skip-jack, 32-3
Slipperworts. *See* Calceolarias
Slugs, 34; poison bait for, 183
Snails, 34, 209; poison bait for 183
Snapdragons, 159, 160-1; Italian, 160
Sneezewort. *See* Heleniums
Snowdrops, 163; indoors, 165
Soil, acid, 18; alkaline, 18; clay, 13-17, 19, 20; improvement of, 13-17; insects, 32-5; pests, 32-5; preparation of, 13-17, 27; sandy, 13, 19, 20; sterilising, 55, 59, 68; testing, 21
Solanum crispum, 225
Soot, 20

Sorrel, 73, 75; broad-leafed French, 75; propagation, 75; round-leafed French, 75
Sow thistle as breeding-place for aphides, 86
Spades, 12, 15
Spinach, 27, 52, 70, 260; sowing, 29
Spindle tree, dwarf, 219
Spiraeas, 207; blue, 223; cuttings, 217
Spleenworts, Green, 185; rue-leaved, 185
Sprayers, 92; bucket, 92; knapsack, 92
Sprays, 'spreaders' for, 93; 'wetters' for, 93
Spurge Flax, 235
Spurge laurels, 235
Spurge Olive, 235
Stachys tuberifera, 69
Stapelia, 168
Star-wort, 250
Stereum purpureum, 94
Stockholm tar, 94
Stocks, 150; night-scented, 145
Stone-crop, 250
Stranvaesia Davidiana, 225-6
Strawberry pears, 166
Strawberry tree, 226
Strawberries, 87, 88, 89, 124-30, 258, 259, 263, 264, 266, 270; eelworm, 129, 130; fertilisers for, 124, 125, 126, 127; green-petal virus, 129; infected by crinkle, 128; insect pests, 128; layering runners, 126; outdoor, 124-5; pests, 87, 128-30; planting out, 124; pollination, 127; propagation, 130; protection against birds, 125; red-core, 129, 130; runners, 125; soil for, 124; soil-borne virus attacks, 129; Special Stock-runner Certificate, 129; Stock-runner Certificate, 129-30; strawing, 125, 127; susceptible to yellow edge, 128; tarsonemid mite, 129, 130; under cloches, 126, 127-8; under Dutch lights, 126, 127-8; under glass, 125-8; virus diseases, 128-30. *Varieties:* Auchincruive Climax, 125; Cambridge Favourite, 125, 128; Cambridge Vigour, 124; Early Cambridge, 126; Huxley Giant, 125; Red Gauntlet, 125; Royal Sovereign, 125, 126; Scarlet Queen, 125; Sir Joseph Paxton, 125; Talisman, 124, 125; Tardive de Leopold, 88
Stunt disease, 183
Succulents, 165-8, 250; propagation, 167; soil for, 167; temperature for, 166; watering, 167
Sugar Peas, 70-1; fertilisers for, 70
Sulphate of ammonia, 19-20. *See also* Fertilisers
Sun roses, 235, 237-8; propagation, 237; soil for, 237
Sunflowers, 144
Superphosphate, 18. *See also* Fertilisers
Swedes, 27, 71, 73, 262, 263, 264; fertilisers

Swedes—*cont.*
for, 73; protection from frost, 268; sowing, 29
Sweet briar, 150, 204
Sweet Corn, 37; cooking, 37; fertilisers for, 37; harvesting, 37. *Varieties:* Golden Bantam, 37; Golden Market, 37; John Innes Hybrids, 37
Sweet peas, 207-10, 259, 261, 263, 272; bud-drop, 209-10; cutting flowers, 209; fertilisers for, 208; for exhibition, 209; mosaic virus disease, 209; pests, 209; propagation, 208, 268; protection against birds, 210; site for, 208; staking, 208-9; watering, 209. *Varieties:* Air Warden, 208; Cream Delight, 208; Cream Elegance, 208; Gertrude Fingay, 208; Gigantic, 208; Mrs. C. Kay, 208; Mrs. R. Bolton, 208; Myosotes, 208; Piccadilly, 208; Princess Elizabeth, 208; Stylish, 208; Swan Lake, 208; Warrior, 208; Welcome, 208
Sweet Sultans, Giant, 143
Sweet Williams, 18, 150
Syboes. *See* Onions, salad

Tar-oil washes, 86
Tarragon, 52; harvesting, 267
Tarsonemid mite, 129, 130
Taxodium, 231
Taxus baccata, 219, 220
Tecoma radicans, 223
Thalictrum alpinum, 192, 193; *anemonides* (syn. *Anemonella thalactroides*), 193; *a. flore pleno,* 193; *aquilegifolium,* 193; *a. atropurpureum,* 193; *a. roseum,* 193; *Chelidonii,* 192, 193; *Delevayi,* 192, 193; *dipterocarpum,* 192, 193; *d. flore pleno,* 142; *elatum,* 194; *flavum,* 192, 193; *glaucum,* 194; *majus,* 194; *minus,* 192, 194; *m. adiantifolium,* 194; *orientale,* 194; *purpurascens,* 194; *speciosum,* 194; *tuberosum,* 194
Thalictrums, Hewitt's Double, 142
Thinning-out, 28
Thorn, American, as hedge, 221
Thrift, 146
Thrips, pea, 64
Thyme, 50, 51, 151; common, 53; lemon, 53; harvesting, 267
Thymus citriodorus, 53; *coccineus,* 140; *vulgaris,* 53
Tickseed, 143
Tipula oleracea, 33-4
Tobacco plant, 150
Tomatoes, 21, 32, 75-9, 257, 258, 259, 264; attacks by *Cladosporium fulvum,* 79; blossom-end rot, 78-9; blotchy ripening, 78, 79; dry-set, 77, 78, 79; fertilisers for, 76, 78, 79; green-backs, 78, 79; greenhouse, 76-7; harvesting, 269; physiological disorders, 78-9;

ring-culture, 77; root-rots, 79; spotted wilt virus disease, 79; spraying, 77; toe-rots, 79; yellow varieties, 78. *Varieties:* Ailsa Craig, 78; Golden Perfection, 78; Golden Sunbeam, 78; Market King, 78; Moneymaker, 78; Potentate, 78
Tools, care of, 12-13
Trace elements, 17
Transplanting, 28
Traveller's Joy, 176-7
Triploids, 88-9
Trees, 230-3, 238-40; dwarf, 247-8
Tropaeolum canariense, 145; *majus,* 145; *peregrinum,* 145
Tubers defined, 164
Tulipa clusiana, 165, 210; *Eichleri,* 210; *gesneriana,* 164; *Greigii,* 210; *Kaufmanniana,* 210, 211; *kolpakowskiana,* 211; *linifolia,* 211; *praestans,* 211; *saxatilis,* 211; *Sprengeri,* 165, 211; *strangulata primulina,* 211; *sylvestris,* 165, 210, 211; *tarda* (syn. *T. dasystemon*), 211
Tulips, 140, 156, 163, 164-5, 210-12, 269; Breeder, 164; Cottage, 164; Darwin, 164; Double, 164; 'droppers', 210; fertilisers for, 210; indoors, 165; Lady, 165; Mendel, 164; offsets, 210; Painted Lady, 210; Parrot, 164; propagation, 210; Rembrandt, 164; soil for, 165, 210, 211; Triumph, 164; water-lily, 211; wild, 164. *Varieties:* Fred Moore, 165; Prince of Austria, 165; Van Tubergen, 211
Turnips, 18, 31, 71, 72-3, 260, 262, 263, 264; fertilisers for, 73; protection from frost, 268; sowing, 29. *Varieties:* Demi-longue à Forcer, 31; Early Milan, 72, 260; Golden Ball, 72; Orange Jelly, 73; Snowball, 72, 260
Twin flower, 147

Vaccinium corymbosum, 228; *myrtillus,* 228
Vegetables, 26-79, 256, 257, 258-9, 260, 261-2, 263, 264, 265, 266-7, 268, 269-70, 271; crop-rotation, 26-9; cultivation, *see* individual vegetables; fertiliser-requirements, 27; rarer, 68-71; root, 71-2; sowing, 28-9; thinning-out, 28; transplanting, 28
Veratrum nigrum, 142
Verbascums, Gainsborough, 142
Veronica rupestris, 140; *Traversii* as hedge, 220
Veronicas in rock gardens, 249
Violas, 140
Violets, dog-tooth, 184; bog, 251; wild, 156
Vines. *See* Grapes
Virgin's Bower, 177
Virus diseases, 65, 128-30
Vitis (Ampelopsis), 223

Wallflowers, 149, 212-14, 262, 265, 269; Alpine, 213-14; cuttings, 213; propagation, 212, 213; Siberian, 213; soils for, 212; Spanish, 214. *Varieties:* Apricot, 213; Blood Red, 213; Cloth of Gold, 213; Cluseed Giant Pink, 213; Crawford Beauty, 213; Ellen Willmott, 213; Fire King, 213; Giant Blood Red, 213; Golden Gem, 214; Golden Monarch, 213; Hamlet, 213; Harpur Crewe, 213; Orange Bedder, 213; Primrose Monarch, 213; Purple Queen, 213; Ruby Gem, 213; Scarlet Emperor, 213; Vulcan, 213; White Dame, 213
Walnuts, 88
Wart disease, 65
Weed-killers, 23
Weevils, pea and bean, 39, 64
Whitethorn as hedge, 219
Whitlow grass, 250
Whortleberries, 228

Wild gardens, 146, 156
Willow, dwarf, 250, 252
Wind-breaks, 82-3
Wind-flowers, 156-8; snow, 156
Wineberries, 106; Japanese, 106
Winter-green, 148, 228
Winter spraying, 86
Wireworms, 32-3; trapping, 33
Wisley, experiments at, 88
Wistaria sinensis, 226
Woolly aphis, 265
Worcesterberries, 107

Yarrow, 141; Cerise Queen, 141; Pearl, 141
Yellow edge in strawberries, 128
Yew, clipping, 218, 219, 265; common, poisonous properties of, 219; for hedges, 218, 231; golden as hedge, 220
Yulan, 239

Zea mais, 37